Fragments of history

Rethinking the Ruthwell and Bewcastle monuments

⌘

Fred Orton and Ian Wood
with Clare A. Lees

Manchester University Press

Manchester and New York

The right of Fred Orton, Ian Wood and Clare A. Lees to be identified as the authors of this work has been asserted by them in accordance with the Copyright, Designs and Patents Act 1988.

Published by Manchester University Press
Oxford Road, Manchester M13 9NR, UK
and Room 400, 175 Fifth Avenue, New York, NY 10010, USA
www.manchesteruniversitypress.co.uk

Distributed exclusively in the USA by
Palgrave, 175 Fifth Avenue, New York,
NY 10010, USA

Distributed exclusively in Canada by
UBC Press, University of British Columbia, 2029 West Mall,
Vancouver, BC, Canada V6T 1Z2

British Library Cataloguing-in-Publication Data
A catalogue record for this book is available from the British Library

Library of Congress Cataloging-in-Publication Data applied for

ISBN 978 0 7190 7256 7 *hardback*
ISBN 978 0 7190 7257 4 *paperback*

First published 2007

15 14 13 12 11 10 09 08 07   10 9 8 7 6 5 4 3 2 1

Typeset in Scala
by Koinonia, Manchester
Printed in Great Britain
by Biddles Ltd, King's Lynn, Norfolk

While digging in the grounds for the new foundations, the broken fragments of a marble statue were unearthed. They were submitted to various antiquaries, who said that, so far as the damaged pieces would allow them to form an opinion, the statue seemed to be that of a mutilated Roman satyr; or, if not, an allegorical figure of Death. Only one or two old inhabitants guessed whose statue those fragments had composed. (Thomas Hardy, *Barbara of the House of Grebe*)

Contents

⌘

Illustrations

⌘

Colour Plates

The plates can be found between pp. xvi and 1.

Figures

The figures can be found between pp. 120 and 121.

Acknowledgements

⌘

Many individuals contributed to the making of this book. We take this opportunity to acknowledge the following few for providing help, advice, guidance, references and research materials: Paul S. Austen; Richard N. Bailey; Paul Bidwell; Allan Biggins and David Taylor; George Hardin Brown; Celia Chazelle; J. R. R. Christie; Derek Craig; Rosemary Cramp; Carol Farr; Ian Fisher; Alex Hannay; Jane Hawkes; Andrew Hemingway; Yitzhak Hen; Martin Henig; John Higgitt; Joyce Hill; Mike Jackson; Catherine E. Karkov; Jo McIntosh; Andrew McMillan; Allan A. Mills; Éamonn Ó Carragáin; Gillian Overing; Tim Padley; Reverend Jim Williamson; A. O. Wood; Geoff Woodward; and Brian Young. We also acknowledge University College London for inviting Fred Orton to give the 2002 Tomás Harris Lectures, which gave the book its structure, and the Arts and Humanities Research Council for the award that facilitated his leave of absence from teaching and the matching leave provided by the School of Fine Art, History of Art & Cultural Studies, University of Leeds, 2005-2006, which helped him bring all the fragments together.

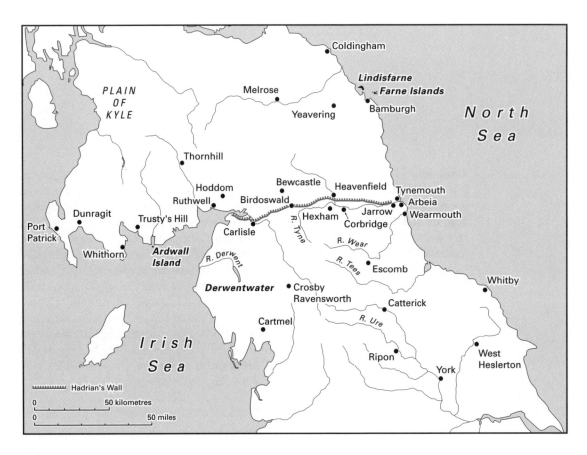

Map of southern Scotland and northern England in the eighth century, showing 'Northumbrian' places mentioned in the book.

I Ruthwell monument, east (now south) side, upper and lower stones

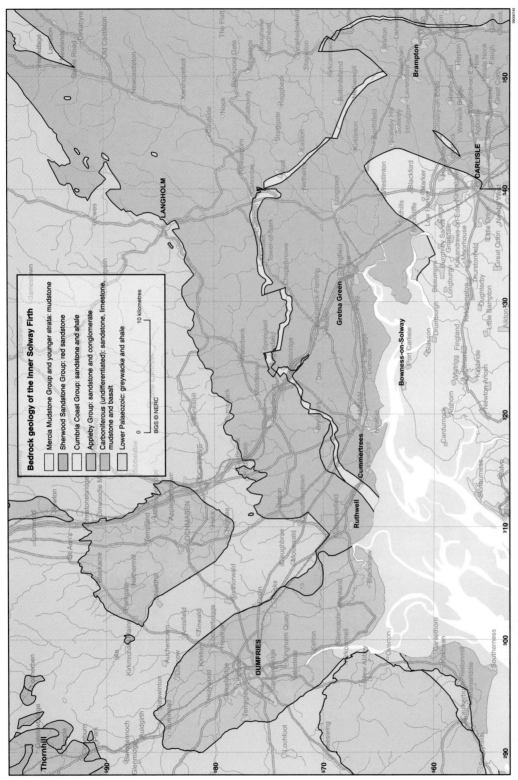

II Bedrock geology of the Inner Solway Firth

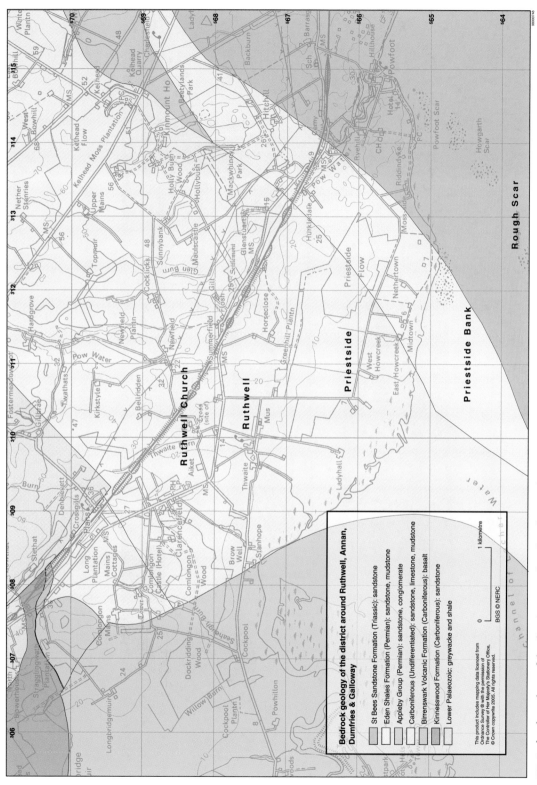

Bedrock geology of the district around Ruthwell, Annan, Dumfries & Galloway

St Bees Sandstone Formation (Triassic): sandstone

Eden Shales Formation (Permian): sandstone, mudstone

Appleby Group (Permian): sandstone, conglomerate

Carboniferous (Undifferentiated): sandstone, limestone, mudstone

Birrenswark Volcanic Formation (Carboniferous): basalt

Kinnesswood Formation (Carboniferous): sandstone

Lower Palaeozoic: greywacke and shale

0   1 kilometre

BGS © NERC

III Bedrock geology of the district around Ruthwell, Dumfries and Galloway

IV Bewcastle monument, west and south sides

Exordia

⌘

Every writer knows that the choice of a beginning for what he will write is crucial not only because it determines much of what follows but also because a work's beginning is, practically speaking, the main entrance to what it offers. Moreover, in retrospect, we can regard a beginning as the point at which, in a given work, the writer departs from all other works; a beginning immediately establishes relationships with works already existing, relationships of either continuity or antagonism or both. (Edward Said, *Beginnings: Intention and Method*)[1]

Two of us – Fred Orton and Ian Wood – met in the late 1970s but our book had its beginnings before then when, years apart, independently, we each discovered what for the moment we shall call the 'Ruthwell Cross' in the parish church (Col. Plate I, Fig. 42) a mile or so from Ruthwell, Dumfriesshire, Scotland, and the Bewcastle monument a few feet south of the west end of St Cuthbert's (Col. Plate IV, Fig. 15), Shopford, in the parish of Bewcastle, Cumbria, England. These monuments, which are decorated with high-quality relief sculptures set in panels and accompanied with various kinds of inscriptions, are arguably the finest surviving examples of pre-Viking Age stone sculpture in Britain. George Baldwin Brown surveyed the Ruthwell Cross for the Royal Commission on the Ancient and Historical Monuments of Scotland in 1920.[2] Rosemary Cramp surveyed the Bewcastle Cross for the British Academy *Corpus of Anglo-Saxon Stone Sculpture* in 1988.[3] A bronze plaque close by the Ruthwell Cross gives its history thus: 'Dates from Anglo-Saxon times: destroyed during the conflicts which followed the Reformation; lay in the earthen floor of the church 1642 to 1790: erected in the manse garden in 1823: erected here and declared a monument under the Ancient Monuments Act, in 1887.' Set in concrete, immovable under the roof of a specially constructed apse, it was, in fact, the first freestanding monument to be brought under the protection of the Act. A ruin of a reformed nation. No such plaque accompanies the monument at Bewcastle. Outside and unprotected, host to lichen and breaking gently, it inclines to the west on uncertain ground filled with the past. We are ignorant of how it became a fragment. Separated by thirty or so miles as the crow flies and unconnected by any direct modern road or ancient route, the two monuments have, at least since the publication of Reverend Daniel Henry Haigh's 'The Saxon Cross at Bewcastle', 1856, been seen as in some close relation of association.[4] Each monument is decorated with a panel representing Christ standing on the heads of two beasts (Figs 23 and 55) and another apparently representing John the Baptist with the Agnus Dei (Figs 24 and 54) that are taken to be similar; and both monuments are decorated with inhabited plant-scroll, which, in certain respects, is also seen as similar. When Baldwin Brown wrote his 'Report on the Ruthwell Cross' for the R.C.H.A.M., he felt it necessary to add some 'references to that at Bewcastle'. He saw the Bewcastle Cross as the Ruthwell Cross's 'sister monument' from which 'it cannot be properly separated'.[5]

Out of the way, one approaches Ruthwell parish church either from the modern A75 'high' road between Annan and Dumfries or from the B724 'low' road along the Solway Firth and across the southern edge of Lochar Moss. Neither route takes you there quickly. One approaches the church indirectly, as one must approach the Ruthwell Cross when one actually comes in front of it for, as it was re-erected in the church, it is misaligned and incorrectly oriented. At the moment it was produced and first used, the monument would have been aligned as the Bewcastle monument still is. The present north side (with the panel representing Christ over two beasts) originally faced west; the present south side (with the representation of Christ and Mary Magdalen) originally faced east (Fig. 63); the present narrow east and west sides originally faced north and south respectively (Figs 59 and 68). We shall refer to the monument in its original orientation thus: the west side (now north side); east side (now south side); north side (now east side); and south side (now west side).

Even more out of the way, you can approach Bewcastle parish church only from a high road. The most direct route takes one north from Brampton and Hadrian's Wall. It's the right and proper way in so far as it takes one through a special, always resonant historical geography that directly pertains to seeing and understanding the monument.

Once located, the monuments affect one with an insistent materiality that is eminently sculptural and, because of their fragmentary materiality and their complex interactions of figure work and text, bring about a profoundly hermeneutic response. As sculpture, each monument prompts a keen kinaesthetic effect: one needs to work one's way around it *as if* to confirm the unity of the shape of its form and the diversity of its sides. One then has to sum perception and observation: an emphatic and properly aesthetic affect that brings about an inquisitive mode of attention. Once seen, the two monuments can become endlessly absorbing.

Another beginning was established, after we'd met and were both teaching at the University of Leeds, the one in the Department of Fine Art, the other in the School of History. We found that we shared an interest in the Ruthwell and Bewcastle monuments and began a conversation about them that has lasted twenty-five years. We talked about how one might go about interpreting and explaining them, and how we might come together to teach them. Conversations we had back then with J. R. R. Christie in the Department of History and Philosophy of Science helped shape our thinking in fundamental ways. As did reading the two essays, both written and published in the 1940s, that were the first real attempts by art historians to come to terms with the meaning that the Ruthwell Cross might have had for the persons who produced and first used it: Fritz Saxl's 'The Ruthwell Cross', which was published in the *Journal of the Warburg and Courtauld Institutes*, 1943, and Meyer Schapiro's 'The Religious Meaning of the Ruthwell Cross', which was published in the *Art Bulletin*, 1944.[6] Thinking about it now, we realise that, all those years ago, these essays – by two persons who seem never to have seen the actual monument – set the trajectory for the conversations and collaboration that would eventually become this book. These same articles have also been central to a course that we taught on and off over the years to Leeds students of Fine Art, Art History and History at undergraduate and postgraduate level.

It seems that Saxl, in London, and Schapiro, in New York, were ignorant of each other's work on the Ruthwell Cross until they were ready for publication. Though they were different (but not antipathetic) kinds of art historian – Saxl, who had studied under Max Dvorak in Vienna and became Aby Warburg's librarian and assistant, was, after Warburg's death, Director of the Warburg Institute, first in Hamburg and then in London; Schapiro, who had arrived in the United States from Lithuania as an infant, and as a young man attended and then taught at Columbia University (he had, by 1944, been teaching there for some sixteen years) was one of the inaugurators of Marxist art history in capitalist countries – they shared an initial insight and, with it, reached compatible conclusions.

Saxl's was the first attempt to explain the programmatic theological significance of the figure panels on the west (now north) and east (now south) sides of the Ruthwell Cross – he realised that one had to move round the monument to understand it – and to situate them stylistically and iconographically in relation to the 'Mediterranean models' that might have been used to make them. Thereafter, on the basis of his understanding of the theological significance of the figure panels and situating it in relation to the panels' Mediterranean models, he tried to date the monument. Schapiro was also concerned to interpret the meaning of the monument but was less interested in what models might have been available in the visual culture of the Anglo-Saxons. He was more concerned with how the monument's religious meaning accorded with the conditions that prevailed around Ruthwell and in Northumbria at the moment the monument was produced and first used. Both Saxl and Schapiro, the one with regard to style and iconography, the other with regard to what for want of a better term we refer to as 'social history', had recourse to comparison with the Bewcastle Cross.

Saxl and Schapiro took the largest panel on the Ruthwell Cross containing the representation of Christ on the beasts as key to the monument's meaning. (Fig. 55) Until then, this sculpture had usually been taken to illustrate Psalm 90.13: 'Thou shalt tread upon the lion and the adder: the young lion and the dragon shalt thou trample under foot.' It was clear to Saxl and Schapiro that, in this case, Christ is not trampling on two wild, ferocious animals, vanquishing powers of evil. Rather, he is being supported by two docile creatures that are clearly as devoted to each other as they are adoring of him. Though the sculpture related to the Psalm in general terms, it more closely illustrated the inscription that accompanied it: +IHSXPSIVDEX:AEQVITATIS·BES TIAE·ET·DRACONES·COGNUERUNT·INDESERTO·SALVA?OREM· MVNDI (Jesus Christ: the judge of Justice: beasts and dragons recognised in the desert the saviour of the world).[7] Schapiro puzzled the complexity of this inscription – how it seemed to be made of several references to scripture: bits of various Psalms perhaps, and Mark 1.13 undoubtedly – and saw it, and the scene represented in the panel, as drawing on the old Messianic wish that for centuries had nourished the fantasy of hermit monks and religious reformers of wild beasts submitting to them and helping them.[8] This idea, he pointed out, was very much in accord with the kind of monasticism that characterised the early church with 'the hermit monks and the independent religious spirits, like St Francis, who were possessed by a more spontaneous and lyric Christianity and took as their model the Christ of the desert or the open country and the streets'.[9]

Saxl and Schapiro then went on to consider the other panels in relation to their way of seeing Christ on the Beasts. Above this largest panel there is a representation of what they understood to be John the Baptist (Fig. 54) who 'lived in the desert and preached in the wilderness'; and below there is a representation of Sts Paul and Anthony breaking bread in the desert (Fig. 56), as Saxl saw it, according to a rite of *cofractio* practised by the Irish Church.[10] Below Paul and Anthony there is a representation of the Flight into or, as some would have it, out of Egypt (Fig. 57), which Schapiro saw as having the same desert setting as Paul and Anthony, and which Saxl saw as relating to the story in Pseudo-Matthew that dragons, lions and panthers adored the Holy Family as it travelled across the desert.[11] Both Saxl and Schapiro saw this side of the monument as dominated by references to the desert and the idea of the eremitic life or monasticism. To which interpretation Schapiro added the scene on the opposite side of the monument that has Mary Magdalen anointing Christ's feet, washing them with her tears and drying them with her hair (Fig. 63). Schapiro noted a formal resemblance between this panel and Christ on the Beasts and saw it as signifying a monastic sense also, for Mary Magdalen

> is the traditional Christian figure of the contemplative life. In the Gospels it is not clear that the repentant sinner Mary, at the house of Simon, and Mary Magdalen from whom Christ expelled the seven devils (Luke VIII, 2), and Mary, the sister of Lazarus, are one person; but Western commentators identified them as the same individual, who became in time the model of female asceticism and penitence.[12]

Saxl was aware of this possibility but preferred to see the image as representing 'forgiveness'. Taking this as key, and going further than Schapiro, Saxl thought that the two sides were made of different but related programmes: there was the desert side, dominated by the image of Christ Victor, Judge and Saviour of the World; the other side was dominated by an image of Christ as Forgiveness.[13]

Notwithstanding local differences, Saxl and Schapiro were in agreement about the importance of the references to the desert and the way they connoted the idea of kind of monasticism. The programme on the monument's west side represented the kind of monasticism that prevailed in Northumbria until the Synod of Whitby in 664,[14] after which – this is Schapiro – it was eventually 'moulded into a more sociable, communal pattern, culminating in the Rule of Saint Benedict'.[15]

During King Oswiu's reign there was conflict in Northumbria between those who followed the traditions of Iona mediated through Lindisfarne, which had been founded by Aidan, and those who followed the traditions of the Church of Rome, espoused by Benedict Biscop and Wilfrid. As Schapiro understood it 'the conflict was finally between a particularist monastic church, shaped by the conditions of tribal society, and a church which aimed at universality and the integration of local peoples into the larger ambient of European and Mediterranean life'.[16] The two traditions were different in structure, organisation and discipline: they had different modes of baptism, of tonsuring monks and clerics, of ordaining bishops, and of calculating the date of Easter. The Synod of Whitby was convened to debate these differences and put an end to the conflict, with Oswiu, as king of Northumbria, deciding the matter. In the end, according to the surviving historical record, everything depended on the correct way of calculating the date of Easter.[17] Having listened to the arguments of both parties, Oswiu came down in favour of the Roman Easter and, in so doing, decided that Northumbria would withdraw from the orbit of Iona in favour of the Church of Rome. Saxl and Schapiro were agreed: the Ruthwell Cross must have been produced in the period immediately following the Synod of Whitby and its content was made of – as Schapiro put it – 'the native Churches' and the victorious – and, as Saxl interpreted it, forgiving – triumphalism of the Church of Rome.

Despite what were already clear chronological problems, Saxl's and Schapiro's work on the programmatic theological character of the monument's figure panels proved very suggestive – we had not yet read Éamonn Ó Carragáin's 'Liturgical Innovations Associated with Pope Sergius and the Iconography of the Ruthwell and Bewcastle Crosses', 1978, which was even more suggestive.[18] Most of the interesting work on this aspect of the monument over the last thirty years or so, in one way or another, has been indebted to it. What we found most stimulating, however, lay in what Saxl had to say and could not say about the style and iconography of the 'Mediterranean models' and what Schapiro had to say and could not say about the monument's 'place' and 'historical moment'.[19]

Saxl began his investigation of the Mediterranean models for the Ruthwell Cross by way of reference to the Bewcastle Cross, which, 'with its similar programme and figure types', was 'obviously so closely related to the Ruthwell Cross that the question of the relationship of the two monuments' had 'to precede any discussion of the Ruthwell sources'[20] (Figs 17, 18, 19, 20). Understanding that relation could help establish a priority that might help date them. Or so he thought.

Saxl noted that

> On three of its sides the [Bewcastle] Cross has only an ornamental decoration, but on the fourth there are four panels. In one is a runic inscription; each of the others contains a monumental figure. In the centre is Christ standing over the Beasts; at the top St John with the Lamb; and at the base the so-called falconer, most probably St John the Evangelist with the Eagle.
>   The programme is thus identical with that of parts of the Ruthwell scheme. But the role of the Evangelist differs on the two crosses.[21]

The iconographical programme on the monument at Bewcastle is simpler than that at Ruthwell.[22] It is also made of a different style. The figures at Ruthwell are characterised by 'round and even bulging forms'; those at Bewcastle are 'longer and square'.[23] There are also differences in the way the figures are clothed. The draperies are arranged in different ways. Some of those at Bewcastle have a 'more "classic" simplicity' and evidence a 'preference for symmetrical long folds' lacking at Ruthwell.[24] He summed his comparison in this way:

> The programmes of the two crosses have each their own logic; that of Bewcastle being narrow and severe, that of Ruthwell, as far as we understand it, less concise but richer. The Bewcastle style is mild and its forms less extravagant than those of Ruthwell ... The same tendency to remain within a more classical 'canon' is apparent in the Bewcastle transformation of the Mediterranean dress.[25]

Saxl took these differences to indicate that the Bewcastle Cross was made before the monument at Ruthwell, 'within a comparatively short time, perhaps one generation'.[26] It remained to be seen whether the different sculptors 'worked independently from the same model or whether Ruthwell followed the Bewcastle example'.[27]

We were intrigued by how quickly Saxl's analysis of similarity turned into the identification, description and discussion of difference. Perhaps difference becomes interesting only in the context of claimed similarities. We thought that it might prove more cognitively productive to puzzle the differences than try to establish on the basis of stylistic judgements, and iconography considered as an aspect of style, which monument was produced first.

Saxl then went in search of the Mediterranean models. He acknowledged that travellers returning from Rome might have brought back early Christian painted books containing all kinds of subjects but thought it more likely that sculptors would make reference to works in relief.[28] Saxl limited his search to images that might have provided models for the representation of Christ on the beasts. Several kinds of scenes carved on fourth- and fifth-century sarcophagi and others found on early Christian lamps from Rome, Naples, Arles, Athens and elsewhere were considered; as was a type of Christus Miles in one of the stuccoes in the Orthodox Baptistery and a mosaic in the Archbishop's Palace at Ravenna, which was repeated on a late Saxon ivory plaque from the church of St Martin, Genoels-Elderen, now in the Musées Royaux d'Art et d'Histoire, Brussels.[29] But no 'source' was found. As represented on the monuments at Ruthwell and Bewcastle, Christ standing over the beasts unaccompanied by angels, with either 'swine' or animals with the same bodily postures, was a 'Northumbrian type' or 'variant' that derived from 'a widely used Mediterranean formula'.[30] Though Saxl realised it was unlikely that 'one Mediterranean model contained the whole Bewcastle design', in the end he assumed that 'only one ivory showing Christ over the Beasts and narrative scenes reached the North, and provided the model for both Crosses'.[31]

This was a disappointing conclusion to an interesting discussion. The idea of an unknown or lost archetype to which, by virtue of precedent and unchanging being, everything can be referred to for explanation came in, as it usually does in discussions of style, as *deus ex machina* with no cognitive gain. What's more, Saxl had no need of it. When he had noted that it was unlikely that one model would have contained the whole Bewcastle programme he had added, 'single figures can be fitted together from two or three models'.[32] You could say that this was the insight to which his mode of interpretation was blind. We thought it made more sense to see each panel, and each programme, like this, as a representation that was made of several possibilities that the resources of the sculptors' culture had made available. These resources – different types of iconography and formal patterns, for example – would have been manipulated and brought together according to different interests, skills and competences, and perhaps different cultural and historical specificities also. This idea of representation informs all that follows.

Thus far Saxl had considered only the iconographical resources that were available in the early Christian art of Italy and the Mediterranean region. More enabling, and more in accord with the likelihood that the sculptors appropriated several models, was his discussion of the formal resources available in the kind of Mediterranean art that was indigenous in and native to Northumbria: Romano-British sculpture. With one eye on the sculpture from around Hadrian's Wall in the collection of Tullie House Museum, Carlisle – his examples were the 'Gravestone showing a Lady with a Fan' (Fig. 9) and the 'Seated Mother Goddess' (Fig. 10) – and the other on the Anonymous *Life of St Cuthbert*, which recorded that at Carlisle the saint was taken on a tour of the Roman remains of the town, Saxl saw it as not illogical to assume that the whoever made the Ruthwell and Bewcastle monuments must have been aware of the relation between what was imported and 'the old Roman stone work still everywhere visible, and probably in particular profusion in Northumbria'.[33] Saxl seems not to have known that the Bewcastle monument was sited in the remains of a Roman fort or that the 'Seated Mother Goddess' had been discovered there in 1765 and, very likely, was around the place, perhaps *in situ*, when the monument was produced (Fig. 11).[34] The area along Hadrian's Wall, especially its western section, became vivid for us: whatever of Ancient Rome survived in the area must have been very much part of the lived reality of the Anglo-Saxons who had their being-the-world there.

Schapiro's explanation of the 'religious meaning' of the Ruthwell Cross was very like Saxl's but he was at pains to interpret how that meaning related to the historically specific circumstances of material and spiritual life that pertained at Ruthwell in the latter half of the seventh century. And since nothing was then known about the early history of Ruthwell, he approached it by way of what he knew about the region as a whole.

Relying mainly on what he'd read in Baldwin Brown's *The Arts of Early England*, 1921, Schapiro thought that Ruthwell was located in the old British kingdom of Strathclyde, which extended from the River Clyde south to the Solway Firth and beyond to Liddle Water.[35] As he understood the history, which he acknowledged was based on insufficient information,[36] Strathclyde had been conquered by the Northumbrian Angles, first by King Oswald and then by Oswiu. He thought that the struggles between the native peoples and their Northumbrian rulers persisted until a combined force of Britons and Picts defeated Oswiu's son and successor, Ecgfrith, at the Battle of Nechtanesmere in 685. Whereafter, Northumbria's power in the region came to an end and Northumbria declined as a kingdom. Schapiro reasoned that, because the Ruthwell Cross is inscribed with a 'poem' in 'an early Northumbrian dialect' comprising some 'verses' of *The Dream of the Rood*, 'like Constantine's vision of the cross of victory', it must pre-date Northumbria's defeat at Nechtanesmere and subsequent decline.[37] This he saw confirmed by 'the similar cross at Bewcastle, which is in Anglian territory and commemorates by a vernacular inscription Ecgfrith's brother, Alcfrith, a local ruler around 663'.[38] Alcfrith was, with his friend Wilfrid, 'instrumental in calling the Synod of Whitby'.[39] Bewcastle was located securely in Anglian territory close to 'Wilfrid's centre at Hexham, the religious capital of the newly Romanised Northumbrian Church'.[40] Ruthwell was located elsewhere: in the once British kingdom of Strathclyde. Though he did not go so far as Baldwin Brown had done and claim that King Ecgfrith set up the Ruthwell Cross, Schapiro's conclusion was very much along the same lines. The Ruthwell Cross was probably 'a monument of the newly established Northumbrian power on the Scottish border and of the decision at Whitby'.[41] It was 'intrusive as a commanding silhouette, as a piece of carving, and as a complex of decorative forms' and, in so far as its 'vernacular poetic inscription' was 'in a language foreign to the region', even though 'the native clergy could recognise in the images the most impressive models of their own religious will', it was exclusive of the region's native peoples.[42]

Schapiro then went on the consider how the differences between the monument's form – classic, Mediterranean and Anglian – and content – eremitic, native and 'Celtic' – corresponded to the material and spiritual conflicts between Northumbria and Strathclyde. Did the eremitic content evidence the resistant strength of the defeated native Church? Or was it evidence for an asceticism that persisted within the newly established Church of Rome, which was more at home in the conquered 'Celtic provinces'?[43] Although Schapiro knew that 'we cannot draw a sharp line between Anglian and British asceticism nor distinguish nuances in their common devotions which will help to elucidate the origins of the Cross', he found it 'difficult to imagine that a work with the content of the Ruthwell Cross could have been created in Northumbria itself'.[44] He imagined instead that 'there existed in Ruthwell in the second half of the seventh century a religious community of Britons and Anglian settlers, ruled by Northumbrians who belonged to the older generation that owed its Christianity to the teachings of Aidan and Columba and its ecclesiastical privilege in hostile Strathclyde to the power of the Northumbrian king'.[45]

By the time we were thinking about contributing something to the scholarship of the Ruthwell and Bewcastle monuments, a great deal more was known about the material and spiritual history of Strathclyde and Northumbria in the early Middle Ages. The runic inscriptions on the monument at Ruthwell could no longer be taken as written in an early Northumbrian dialect no later than the seventh century nor could the inscription on the Bewcastle monument be taken unproblematically as commemorating King Alcfrith or as evidence that the monument had been erected shortly after his death. It seemed unlikely that either monument was erected around Ecgfrith's time. The *Corpus of Ango-Saxon Sculpture* dates the Bewcastle Cross to the first half of the eighth century.[46] Also, though the Picts, because of their victory at Nectanesmere, had been able to recover lands that were once occupied by Northumbria, and some Britons regained their freedom, there is nothing to suggest that the British tribes of Strathclyde were on the winning side or that Northumbrian control of the area around Ruthwell was affected by Ecgfrith's defeat. Moreover, despite the fact that the finest of Northumbria's military aristocracy had been killed in the battle and its hopes and strength as a kingdom began to 'ebb and fall away',[47] its spiritual culture experienced something of a renaissance. By the 1980s, it was relatively clear that the area around Ruthwell might not once have been part of the ancient kingdom of Strathclyde. Another kingdom was being brought into the published histories of Scotland, a British kingdom that, at one time, perhaps extended eastwards from around Dunragit in the Rhinns of Galloway, on the north side of the Solway Firth, and south, across the Carlisle plain and down the Eden Valley into Lancashire: Rheged.[48] Rheged, or some part of it, came under Northumbrian control during the course of the seventh century. Scholars had begun to think of Ruthwell as a place that was once in Rheged, not Strathclyde.[49]

Forty years on from its publication, it was relatively easy to dismiss Schapiro's essay out of hand, especially if one's idea of what constituted interpretation was focused or fixated on coming up with the date of the Ruthwell Cross *as if* that date would provide the monument's 'context'. To our way of thinking, to take Schapiro's account to task for being wrong on several points or for the way it misunderstood historical geography or the conflicts between Northumbria and the Celtic kingdoms, and especially the events around the Battle of Nectanesmere, rather missed the point. Schapiro's aim was, after all, to give the most complete explanation of the religious meaning of the Ruthwell Cross as could be given, at that time. That meant explaining how what he saw as the monument's Anglian form and Celtic content had been determined by conflicts in the religious sphere that were, themselves, aspects of conflicts in the social and political sphere: conflicts in the social and political sphere that were, themselves, determined by base conflicts between different ethnicities and territories, by the Northumbrian kings' imperative need to acquire more and more land and, once they had acquired it, to organise the occupied territories into a 'Northumbrian state'.[50] Schapiro perhaps exaggerated the differences between what he referred to as the 'Celtic and Anglian Churches' but he was surely not wrong to see ideological centralisation as a feature of the consolidation of Northumbrian hegemony across its different territories, and to see the Church as playing a key role. It was clear to us, reading Schapiro, that any account of the production and first use of the Ruthwell and Bewcastle monuments had to hold on to the idea that each monument was determined by historically and culturally specific social oppositions – differences of ethnicity, class, ideology and so on – that were represented and reworked, contested and made compatible, in and by its formal and iconographical content. The monuments were made of dynamic contradictions: material and spiritual, secular and religious, residual and emergent, and so on. Schapiro's materialist mode of interpretation suggested the best way forward to providing as thorough an account as possible of the concrete historical circumstances in which the monuments were made and the ways in which form and content could be seen as having been defined by those circumstances. Our book tries to give just such an account in the knowledge that it will not be a complete account, knowing how difficult it often is, in this area of inquiry, to establish even a simple 'fact' beyond question, including the fact of what *is* there to be seen and understood and the fact of how it *has* been seen and understood.

Another beginning: we remember how important were some remarks in Rosemary Cramp's 'The Anglian Sculptured Crosses of Dumfriesshire', published in the *Transactions and Journal of Proceedings of the Dumfriesshire and Galloway Natural History and Antiquarian Society* in 1961.[51] To recall only 'some remarks' is not to demean Cramp's essay or her remarkable Jarrow Lecture of 1965, *Early Northumbrian Sculpture*.[52] Both studies let loose so many hares that most have yet to be coursed and caught. Rather these remarks confirmed what we were thinking after reading Saxl and Schapiro and established an attitude or frame of mind with which we approached the task of rethinking our two objects of study. Cramp recognised that the Ruthwell Cross and the Bewcastle Cross were 'related' but emphasised that the former is 'a highly individual monument' and, most important, that 'the two monuments are different in intention and thus difficult to compare in their complete schemes'.[53] Intention presupposes a relation between an object and the circumstances of its production and use. When the monuments were produced and first used they were produced to different ends or purposes.

From the beginning, following Cramp's observation, we tried always to be attentive and sympathetic to the differences between the monuments and to keep them in mind as signifying different ends and purposes. The differences of form and iconography, place and historical moment, for example, suggested that the Ruthwell Cross and the Bewcastle Cross were two very different monuments that were built to meet different needs, to be used in conjunction with different activities according to different functions. The one thing we were sure of from the beginning, and we took it from, this, Cramp's first published essay on Anglo-Saxon stone sculpture, was that our objects of study, whatever their similarities of form and iconography, were different; they were made of *different intentions*, had *different functions* and would have had, at the moments they were produced and first used, *different meanings*. Related in some way, though they may be, we always saw and *see* the Ruthwell and Bewcastle monuments *as* different.

Of course, there were lots more beginnings some of which, permissible at the time, at a different time proved not permissible. Some, which can be traced, for example, to writing by Patrick Wormald and non-medievalists such as Marx and Engels, Wittgenstein, N. R. Hanson, Nelson Goodman, Roland Barthes, Michel Foucault, Thomas S. Kuhn and Barry Barnes, were already in place informing our individual research projects before we began to turn our combined attention to the monuments at Ruthwell and Bewcastle. In various ways, these historical and philosophical, semiological and epistemological writings gave that attention its created inclusiveness. Together, they account for the book's apparent slips between different levels of engagement with the matter in hand as well as its idiosyncratic view and communal concern.[54]

A beginning is always already under way before one recognises it as such. The last beginning in this list of recollected beginnings was not with a monument or a text but with another friendship and a commitment to a project that went well beyond what could have been expected. The book, already begun, would not be what it is if Clare Lees, Department of English, King's College London, had not provided it with its discussion of the vernacular runic inscriptions on the Ruthwell monument's narrow north and south sides and their relation of association with *The Dream of the Rood*. Some of the texts that were our beginnings were Clare's also but she brought to the project the different skills and competences of someone well-versed in the literary theory and history of Old English. To art history and history, then, were added ways of thinking about formal patterns of language, spoken and written, heard and seen, in various media (stone, parchment, metalwork) within the Anglo-Saxon period and after.

This book finds space for our differing disciplinary emphases and insights within a mutually agreed and capacious interdisciplinary framework. Fred Orton was responsible for the chapters on a sense of place, fragments and history, style and seeing ... as, different forms of difference, and reckoning time; to which Ian Wood added his chapters on Northumbria and the

Northumbrian cross; Clare Lees contributed the chapter on the vernacular runic inscriptions and poetry. Fred Orton was the lead scholar as well as editor. Our collective and cumulative conversations over the last couple of years are what gave the book its definitive focus and final shape. This, then, is who 'we' are – sometimes the dominant voice in the 'we' is Fred's, sometimes it is Ian's or Clare's – and it is a prose style and pronominal form apt for this collaborative project.

The few beginnings recalled here, personal and political, especially with regard to theory – which is nothing more nor less than a way of seeing and understanding and bringing that seeing and understanding to practical consciousness – suffice to give some idea of where our book began: of its intention and method: of its relations with works already existing, relations of continuity or antagonism or both: and of where it is going. Like the monuments that are its objects of study, it now lives beyond itself subject to the intentions of others. Much depends on which sets of discourses it encounters, which communities pay any attention to it and whether they are indifferent to theoretical problems or impatient of assumptions modified or abandoned. In other words, much depends on how much the circumstances of its use will differ from the circumstances of its production. It will prove recalcitrant if pulled into some discourses, but will fit into others comfortably. We hope its future will be one of understanding and usefulness or, at least, not too much misundersanding and misuse.

1

Place[1]

⌘

Place is the first of all beings, since everything that exists is in a place and cannot exist without a place. (Archytas, as cited by Simplicius, *Commentary on Aristotle's Categories*)[2]

What do people make of places? What gives them their identity and meaning? How when one's attention is focused on the Bewcastle monument with the intention of explaining its meaning, can we hang on to the idea of 'place' and our sense of 'place' in relation to it? The Bewcastle monument (Figs 17, 18, 19 and 20) has probably stood where it is since it was produced and first used, some time probably in the eighth century between 700 and 750.[3] Hand-built, rock-sure. A sandstone mass of stubborn resistance. A shape in the memory. A fragment of history. Catching sight of it, we are struck again by its grace and expressiveness, in contrast to its surroundings, effecting a charm and an element of paradox and uncertainty that stimulates inquiry.[4] With only a few exceptions, everyone who has inquired of it has concentrated not on its place but on its material form or its elaborate decoration. Indeed, until recently, most attention was paid to the decoration on its west side: John the Baptist with the Agnus Dei; Christ on the Beasts; a long runic inscription; and the representation of a man with a large bird of prey, probably the main man mentioned in the inscription above;[5] an inhabited plant-scroll on its east side; plant-scrolls and interlace patterns on its north side; plant-scrolls, interlace patterns and a sundial on its south side. If the place of this or any survival of Anglo-Saxon stone sculpture was considered at all it was by way of reference to regional geology and topography, historical background or context and, sometimes, to whatever was known about its circumstances of production. Each volume of the *Corpus of Anglo-Saxon Stone Sculpture*, for example, includes a useful discussion of geology and topography, which *must* figure in any discussion of place, but that discussion is there primarily to help identify, in as precise or general terms, the stone type and petrology of each individual survival. To some extent geology and topography determine place, but they are not place. We might want to move closer to understanding the monument by answering questions such as: For whom was it made? To do what kind of job? How was it made? What was the degree of possession or separation of those who made it and used it from ownership of the means of making it? How was it understood by those who made it and by those first used it? And so on. These are questions about the monument's circumstances of production and how they are answered can help explain how history came in place and was given a specific form.

'Place' is the area of one's being-in-the-world: of being-alongside things; of being-with others and being-one's-self; of feeling and understanding one's relations with other things and other individuals. It's a part of a region brought close to one's being-in-the-world. A 'region' is a large area of land, a more or less defined extent of the Earth's surface, especially as distinguished by climate, natural features, fauna and flora, by things that are within the world but not necessarily as the effects of human intervention. It's the general whereabouts of something. A human individual arrives in a region and gets to know the natural things or mere things there, the earth, rocks and soils, springs, rivers and lakes, plants, trees and animals that are present-to-hand there, and that individual opposes himself or herself to them. He or she recognises these mere things for what they are and realises that equipment or ready-to-hand things – a hammer or an axe or a plough, for example – can be assigned use there so that the mere things can be appropriated in forms adapted to the individual's own wants. By becoming involved in a region in this way, by intervening in the present-to-hand and modifying it with the ready-to-hand, the human individual recognises what is pre-given in the region, brings it close-to-hand, and uses it; comes to a general sense of things as a whole there, becomes changed by them and changes them; builds there and dwells there, cultivates crops and rears animals, puts up habitable and non-habitable structures; comes to understand what is there, to represent it in language and, every day, to be engaged in it; makes a place there.

Place is determined by the deep structure, composition and history of the earth, the lie of the land, and so on, but they alone do not determine it. They contribute to it. But place is constituted by human intention, intervention, agency, including how we make sense of what's there in terms of 'geology', 'topography', 'history', and so on. So, unlike a region, a place isn't something a human being just comes across: human beings make it, they constitute it by their activity, by their being-in-the-world.[6]

> Thus the first fact to be established is the physical organisation of these individuals and their consequent relation to the rest of nature ... the natural conditions in which man finds himself – geological, orohydrographical, climatic and so on. The writing of history must always set out from these natural bases and their modification in the course of history through the action of men. (Karl Marx and Frederick Engels, *The German Ideology*)[7]

In order to write the sense of place at Bewcastle and the monument's location in that place, it seems best to approach it from a physical and temporal distance. Proximity and distance pertain to place, what lies around about and what is nearby. Perhaps the intimacy of place can be brought into focus only by first establishing its separation from us, and then by keeping it in mind.

By way of delimiting it, we can take our region to comprise the northern tip of the county of Cumbria (Cumberland and Westmorland) a few miles west of where it meets Northumberland. It began in Carboniferous times when most of it was a shallow tranquil sea with rivers flowing into it from the north-east. This sea was bordered on the north by what is now the Southern Uplands of Scotland and on the south by the Cumbrian and Alston blocks. A process of cyclic sedimentation continued without a break throughout the Carboniferous and Triassic: the sea depositing marine limestones, shales and sandstones; the rivers invading it and depositing different kinds of sand; marine sedimentation giving way to river sedimentation; interdigitation; swamp; and so on, and so on. A moment of volcanic activity came up with a single outcrop of basalt lava – the Kershopefoot Basalt – and a few thin bands of tuf. Then, towards the end of the Carboniferous and subsequent Triassic period, the region was subjected to immense forces from within that caused widespread folding, faulting and uplifting – it is likely that the present drainage system was formed at this time. In the Ice Age, glaciers pushed and shoved the surface into shape and overlaid it with areas of disparate sands and gravels. And last in this brief survey of the region's beginnings in geological time and how it was readied for place by natural forces, after the melting of the ice, the post-glacial climate encouraged the growth of peat on the uplands and lower-lying plateaux.[8]

Today, the Scottish border crosses the region about seven miles north-west of Bewcastle. Within it, the ground rises from below 200 feet on the low-lying Carlisle Plain in the south-west to over 1700 feet in the north and north-east. In the north the high ground coincides with the county border between Cumbria (Cumberland and Westmorland) and Northumberland and locally forms the primary watershed between the River North Tyne, which flows eastwards to the North Sea, and the Cumbrian and Scottish border rivers, principally Liddel Water, the rivers Lyne and Irthing, which discharge south-westwards into the Solway Firth.[9]

The orohydrography, geology and topography of the region have ensured a predominantly agricultural subsistence. Arable crops are important on the lower ground bordering the Carlisle Plain, but most of the ground between the plain and the high fells forms rough pasture, much of it poorly drained. Some thin coals were once mined in the region. Limestone has been quarried there since it was occupied by the Romans, but its moment of industrial development, which also saw some coal mining, has long gone by and only a few commercial quarries are still working.[10]

Bewcastle, such a remote place to remove the distance between the region and us, transport and guide us into it, bring near the faraway, is in the River White Lyne Catchment, the surface area from which rainfall flows into the White Lyne directly or indirectly. Bewcastle sits on the north bank of Kirk Beck between Bride's Gill on its east and Hall Sike on its west. Much of the area around it, up to 800 feet or so, is covered with a grey or chocolate brown till or boulder clay.[11] In the north-east and east, sandstone outcrops form prominent crags such as the Long Bar and Christianbury Crags.[12] In some places in the valleys, the rivers have formed gravel beds and terraces.[13] Peat covers much of the high ground, particularly in the east and south-east above High Grains and on Spadeadam Waste, with thinner covers in the west on the Bailey and Arthurseat.[14] The lower beds of peat contain many old birch and pine stumps, evidence that the region once enjoyed a drier, warmer climate than it does now.[15] And below these superficial deposits there is the deep geology of a giant dome or anticline, the Bewcastle Anticline, which resulted from the several deformational episodes of folding, uplift and faulting that occurred during post-Carboniferous pre-Tertiary times.[16] The centre of this dome forms the lower ground of the White Lyne flowing through Nixonstown to the north-west of Bewcastle, which is where one finds the oldest rocks.[17] The youngest rocks lie under and to the east of Bewcastle, the sandstones, shales and limestones of the Bewcastle Beds. Further east and south-east, these rocks and later limestone groups rise and then dip or slope over the Bewcastle Fells into the Irthing Valley and on towards Hadrian's Wall, where they become the crags and wild country of Northumbria.[18]

Last in this incomplete description of the area's geology are the glacial deposits that are widely distributed throughout most of the southern half of the region, excepting the Spadeadam area.[19] We should note here a few small mounds or low hills of sand or sand and gravel, associated with drainage channels in the upper White Lyne valley. The hamlet of Shopford on the south side of Kirk Beck is flanked to the north by two such hills. The eastern hill, a relatively flat-topped low hill of sand, with a spring in its south-east scarp trickling into a bog or an area of quicksand, is of particular interest to us because it provided the site for the monument, a Roman fort, a church, a castle and various other buildings[20] (Figs 1, 2 and 3). Though the castle, Beuth's Castle or Bew Castle, gives its name to a parish, to the monument and to several geological and topographical features around about, such as the Bewcastle Anticline, the Bewcastle Beds and the Bewcastle Fells, our place has never been named by the Ordnance Survey. That is to say, in as much as Bewcastle is a place, it occupies the relatively flat-topped low hill of sand just across Kirk Beck from Shopford.

Rocks, streams, valleys and the rest: the 'natural conditions' or 'natural bases' in which people find themselves. Ur-conditions that cease to be natural as soon as people modify them and themselves by being there: build, dwell and think there. We can and should set out from these natural bases, to which history is so often indifferent, but only in so far as we recognise that our knowledge of them, and the knowledge that we will produce of them, is part of the historically and culturally specific process of intervening in and modifying them. This is to say that, although explanation of the Bewcastle monument might set out from a consideration of natural conditions, we should keep in mind that those natural conditions are never in essence more important than how they exist. They are, rather, essentially historical.

The sandstones and limestones of the White Lyne Catchment support a light, impoverished soil, producing grassland of indifferent quality. Though attempts were made to develop it under the various Acts of Enclosure in the nineteenth century, Bewcastle has never been turned over to large-scale arable farming. Sheep and some cattle could be raised there, of course. And surely there must have been game to be had. Pollen evidence brought to light by archaeological excavations at Birdoswald (*Banna*) suggests that in prehistoric times the area seems to have been heavily forested.[21] Birch and pine once grew here, but evidence has also been found for hazel, willow and some oak.[22] So far, there is no evidence for alder, which is so common in the area now. Alder can thrive in marshy conditions up to 1500 feet. We do not know when it arrived and established itself but it probably coincided with or accompanied the climate change to wetter and colder conditions in the Bronze Age. Alder was the predominant species of tree around Birdoswald, just over six miles south of Bewcastle, when the Romans began work there on the Turf Wall in the AD 120s.[23]

Though the present-to-hand of the region has never offered much that was useful for being-in-the world, the area around Bewcastle seems always, from prehistoric to present times, to have attracted human beings who have built and dwelled there and realised a surplus from it.

A scatter of prehistoric sites has been identified. We count sixteen in the parish of Bewcastle where the remains of buildings or tools and utensils have been found, all of them on the rising ground to the north-west, north, north-east, east and south-east – traces of the likely first persons to have moved into and across the region and made places around the low hill of sand on the north side of the beck, if not on it.[24] All the sites date from the moment of transition from late-Neolithic times to the Bronze Age.

Little remains of 'The Currick' (Fig. 6) on Bailey Hope Common, near Skelton Pike, a once great stone cairn that is the only characteristic Neolithic building to have been found in the area.[25] It seems to have been an outlier, one of three in Cumbria, of a group of long cairns related to those found in Galloway and Dumfriesshire.[26] From what remained of it in the nineteenth century, John Maughan, antiquarian and Rector of Bewcastle from 1836 to 1873, could describe it as having been 'rectangular, about 45 yards long, 20 broad, and about 10 feet high'.[27] At the moment it was built and first used the Currick must have been an impressive sight. It surely remained so until most of it was taken away to build dry-stone walls during the enclosures, around 1813. It was computed to contain ten thousand cartloads of stones.[28] Now almost entirely surrounded by thick, mature forest, it still stands to a height of 8 feet. Two indentations in what remains of it are probably the absent presences of two burial chambers.[29]

The other prehistoric sites are characteristically Bronze Age. Whoever the Bronze Age people were around Bewcastle, they lived in circular huts, single huts or sometimes in settlements of two or three, and they buried their dead in round barrows or cairns along with some of the tools and utensils that have come to be regarded as the material signature or characteristic artefact assemblage associated with the 'Beaker phenomenon'.[30] Two sites that were excavated in the 1930s brought to light typical Beaker things. A hut circle about half a mile east of Woodhead – one of several in the general area – produced finds that included a perforated jet button and a perforated jet ring of 'well-known Bronze Age types'.[31] 'Shield Knowe', a large tumulus on the edge of Black Lyne Common, yielded two burial cists and a cremation hollow.[32] The 'well and elaborately constructed' primary cist contained a pair of nearly perfect food vessels and evidence of both inhumation and cremation. The secondary, smaller and less elaborately constructed cist, about five feet away from the central cist, contained another food vessel.[33] Bone from the cremation hollow indicated that two corpses had been burned there.[34] To the north-west of Shield Knowe, between it and the Currick, the 'Camp Graves' (a circular cairn or heap of stones piled up without observing any regular order, about twelve yards in diameter and about six feet high) was 'opened' in the 1790s. This cairn was found to contain two chambers, each with bones and an urn holding black ashes. About thirty Roman coins, a sharp-pointed two-edged iron sword, 30 inches long, and a bronze 'pint jug' were also found.[35] Camp Graves seems to have been a Bronze Age burial that was reused during the Roman occupation of the district. Some three miles to the west, a 'similar cairn, but rather larger', was opened about 1814. It was found to contain two 'similar' graves, each held an urn as well as a quantity of bones and pieces of human skulls, but no coins.[36]

Around 1907, a large, much repaired, bronze cauldron of the second century, or probably earlier, was found while cutting peat on Black Moss.[37] The repairs – nineteen bronze patches to its inside and outside – suggest that it was a highly valued and long-cared-for possession. Though it is in certain respects different, it is taken to be 'similar in style' to a cauldron that was found at Stanton Darnham, Suffolk, in 1897.[38] Other 'similar' cauldrons, also much repaired, include one that was found in Carlingwark Loch, Dumfriesshire, and two that were found in Ireland. The 'Bewcastle Cauldron', as it is called, seems to be a stray that came into the district by trade or was left behind by someone passing through; it's one of those finds of tools or utensils that turn up but seem not to relate to the existence of any local society corresponding to it.

Though one might have expected them, as yet no traces have been found of continuity of settlement through the Iron Age. If there was an Iron Age culture in the region, it seems to have left the area around Bewcastle unaffected.[39] The lack of a resourceful present-to-hand would have discouraged the development of an Iron Age presence of any scale or complexity.[40]

Though the late Neolithic-cum-Bronze-Age character of the area likely remained undisturbed until the coming of the Romans, it is difficult to imagine what kind of character that presence around Bewcastle might have had. So much has been literally carted off. Just the same, the clusters of hut circles and the cairns, characteristically located on rising ground away from the river, marking a territory or preserve, and with good prospects of the valley, are particularly representative of the Bronze Age and suggest that the area was important in prehistoric times as a place of cultivation and construction, habitation and funerary activity, religion, ritual, prestige and cult.

We do not know why or whence the first inhabitants of the area around Bewcastle came. It seems to have been a back of beyond into which people drifted or wandered, some from Dumfriesshire in the west and probably more from the Eden Valley in the south, and some perhaps, via that route, from Yorkshire.[41] Peoples who came from outside the region, orienting themselves towards and within the given present-to-hand. But we do know whence the people who marked the region most indelibly came and why. The Romans, came from the frontier zone along the line of Hadrian's Wall (Fig. 5), some time between about AD 122 and AD 139/142, to build a fort (Fig. 4). This fort would be one of three outpost forts north of the Wall's western section; the others would be established at Netherby ([*Axeldunum?*]*Castra Exploratum*) and Birrens (*Blatobulgium*).[42]

Hadrian's Wall was built to establish the material and ideological boundary that divided the inhabitants of the Roman Empire from the Barbarians, the people of Britain from the peoples of what are now the Borders, the Scottish Lowlands and beyond.[43] It ran some 76 Roman miles (about 70 statute miles) along the topographical northern edge of the natural gap formed by the valleys of the rivers Tyne and Irthing and connected Newcastle-upon-Tyne (*Pons Aelius*) in the east with Bowness (*Maia*) on the Solway Firth in the west. It was conceived and initially constructed as a stone wall 10 Roman feet wide (about 9 feet 2 inches) that ran for 45 Roman miles (41 statute miles) from Newcastle to the Irthing at Willowford and, thereafter, for the remaining 31 Roman miles (28 statute miles), as a wall made of laid turves: the 'Broad Wall' and the 'Turf Wall'. Work on the Wall began in the early AD 120s after Hadrian's visit to Britain and was probably completed by around AD 138. Some time towards the end of the AD 130s, even before the Wall was completed, work began rebuilding the Turf Wall in stone.

As well as being a powerful sign of the presence and power of Rome, Hadrian's Wall would have hindered large-scale direct attacks on Britain and prevented petty raiding. It also allowed the army to supervise and control the small-scale movement of people across and along the frontier and encouraged the peaceful development of economic and social relations up to and beyond it. Moreover it could protect, if necessary, the vital east–west line of communication that pre-existed it, the road that connected Corbridge (*Coria*) and Carlisle (*Luguvalium*), the Stanegate, this name being a mix of Old English and Norse meaning 'stony road', which attests to its continued use in the early Middle Ages. Hadrian's Wall marked and controlled a more or less open frontier.[44] As for the outpost forts like Bewcastle, it seems that their primary purpose was not to give advance warning of any impending attack on the Wall – that could have been given by scouts – but, more likely, to keep secure a part of Britain that had become isolated from the province by the Wall.[45] Of course, in protecting Britain North-of-the-Wall, the outpost forts would also have protected the Wall itself.

Between the late AD 130s or early AD 140s and the late AD 150s or early AD 160s, Hadrian's Wall was partially abandoned while the Romans tried to establish a new frontier about a hundred miles north by building another turf wall, the Antonine Wall, across the Forth–Clyde isthmus. Netherby and Birrens were probably built at this time as hinterland forts on the western trunk road north through Annandale, Nidderdale and Clydesdale to this new frontier.[46] When the Romans gave up the Antonine Wall in the late AD 150s or early AD 160s and re-commissioned Hadrian's Wall as the frontier, the hinterland forts of Netherby and Birrens were reused and rebuilt to function as outpost forts. Bewcastle, it seems, was the only outpost fort in the frontier zone north of the western section of the Wall, and, of all the forts that might be regarded as outpost forts, probably the only one that was so purpose-built from scratch.[47] Indeed, it seems to have been an integral part of the original plan for the Wall.[48] We'll develop this point in a moment. Here we need only mention that at Milecastle 50 on the Turf Wall between the 'primary' forts Birdoswald and Castlesteads (*Camboglanna*) a special road was provided through the Wall that seems to have been set on a line over Gillalees Beacon towards Bewcastle.[49] Once Birdoswald, the primary fort closest to Milecastle 50, came in place on the Wall the decision was made that the road should start from there and it was relocated.[50]

The fort at Bewcastle, which encompasses an area of about six acres, covers the whole of the fairly level top of the hill[51] (Figs 3 and 4). It seems always to have had the shape of an irregular hexagon,[52] an unsual shape for a Roman fort that is generally explained by the need to maximise the hill's natural defensive position. A not necessarily incompatible explanation is that the fort was built to accommodate a *cohors milliaria peditata*, a cohort of some eight hundred infantry, or a *cohors milliaria equitata*, a mixed unit of infantry and cavalry with more than a thousand troops.[53] This would have required using the maximum area made available by the hilltop and thus breaking with a fort's usual four-sided playing-card shape. However, a certain measure of standardisation in some of the Wall forts has been discerned, and Bewcastle may conform to that standard but peculiarly because of its atypical shape. Several forts, for example, no matter what their area, have 580 feet as the length of either the main or the minor axis. At Chesters (*Cilurnum*), Birdoswald, Burgh-by-Sands (*Aballava*) and Bowness the main axis is 580 feet. So is the minor axis at Stanwix (*Petriana*).[54] It is probably no coincidence that this is the approximate measure of the fort at Bewcastle according to the most recent dead reckoning of its ground plan, curtain wall to curtain wall, east to west and north to south across lines projected from those bits of the *via decumana* (the street leading from the rear of the headquarters building to the rear gate) and the *via praetoria* (the street leading from the headquarters building to the front gate), and across the *via principalis* (the main street across the fort), that have been found by archaeology.[55] Bewcastle, with its internal area of about six acres, is a very large fort, close in acreage to Chesters (5.75 acres) and Bowness (5.88 acres). Of the forts on or connected with the Wall only Stanwix (9.32 acres), which was the military centre of the whole frontier and garrison to the largest cavalry unit or *ala milliaria* stationed in Britain, is bigger than these.[56] The *cohors I Dacorum*, which may well have been the first unit stationed at Bewcastle and had the fort as its primary garrison, was one of only two *cohors milliaria peditata* stationed in Britain.[57] The *cohors I Nervana Germanorum milliaria equitata*, which may well have been stationed at the fort in the third century, was one of only five such units stationed in Britain; several of these were, at one time or another, garrisoned in the outpost forts at either end of the Wall.[58] In so far as a fort's size, or the likely units that were stationed in it, might be taken as a indication of its strategic importance in the planned military order of things, the fort at Bewcastle must have been a very important fort from the first. Given that it seems to have been conceived as an integral part of the plan for the Wall from the beginning, and bearing in mind the size and strength of its garrison, we might be wrong to regard it as 'secondary' to the primary forts built on the line of the Wall.

The fort, which like all Roman forts was packed full of buildings and people, seems to have gone through four periods of structural change.[59] In the first period, the moment of its Hadrianic foundation, about AD 122–139/142, its defences consisted of a ditch and turf revetted rampart, possibly with stone gateways (without guard chambers), perhaps a stone headquarters building (*principia*) and certainly a stone bath-house (within the walls) (Fig. 8). The other buildings would have been fabricated in timber. In the second period, about AD 163–180/207, a stone wall replaced the primary turf revetment and the rampart's tail was cut away to make room for a new intervallum road. The south portal of the north-west gate (*porta decumana*) was blocked (and perhaps converted into a guardhouse). The commander's house (*praetorium*) was rebuilt in stone, and stone buildings replaced some of the original timber buildings. In the third period, about AD 180/207–273, the rampart was removed to increase the area of the fort, some levelling of the site was undertaken, some buildings were rebuilt and some new buildings were added to the *praetorium*. In the fourth period, about AD 273–310/312, when the garrison was perhaps reduced, the fort's defences were altered. The *porta decumana* was demolished and a new fort wall was built on top of the old south-west wall. It's possible that the north wall was also demolished at this time and brought forward and realigned, thus putting the demolished *porta decumana* and the north-west barrack blocks (*centuriae*) outside the fort. The interior seems to have been comprehensively replanned with some of the stone buildings being remodelled and perhaps given different functions. The fort was probably garrisoned until about AD 312 and possibly until about AD 370.[60]

In the nineteenth century, an altar was found by the side of the Roman road about three-quarters of a mile south of the fort to the west of Oakstock, and fragments of two altars were found to the south-east of the fort in Kirk Beck, about fifty yards upstream from the site of Byer Cottage. A cemetery and temples in this area, in sight from the fort, on well-drained land to the east where the road crossed the beck and then proceeded to the main gate (*porta praetoria*), would conform to the usual pattern.[61]

So much for the fort. If we take a closer look at its situation we can see that the low hill on which it is built projects as a small spur into the little valley of Kirk Beck. The hill is easily approached from the north up a slight slope that offers no natural protection. On the west and the east, however, it is flanked by Hall Sike and Bride's Gill respectively and its sides become progressively steeper as they approach Kirk Beck some forty feet below the crest of the abrupt south scarp.[62] It is sited in the middle of a natural basin whose north, east and south sides make a 'wide amphitheatre of bleak and lofty hills'[63] that affords only restricted views with distances of just over a mile to the north and south and perhaps two miles to the east and the watershed at Hazel Crag and Barron's Pike. The outlook is open only to the west where the view extends some five or so miles to the horizon-ridge at Roadhead, between the Black Lyne and the White Lyne. The fort's position is commanding but in a topographical cul-de-sac. Tactically, the low hill is strong but strategically it commands nothing more than the basin. There's now a route across from Bewcastle to Kershopefoot and from there into the Southern Uplands of Scotland. This route may have pre-dated the fort or it may have arrived when cross-border commerce in livestock began to establish its drove roads in the fourteenth century.[64]

Though many Roman forts were built on low ground, often with limited outlooks, the choice of Bewcastle as the site of an important outpost fort is puzzling at first. It's on a road that goes nowhere and goes there precisely. The fort is hidden away in the bottom of a natural basin and out of direct visual communication with the primary fort on the Wall to which it was connected. It may be that the site was a British fort reoccupied by the Romans. But, even if we discount this idea, we need not discount the possibility that the Romans occupied a British place, a natural feature – a low hill of sand with hazel and willow growing on it, and perhaps a little oak, with a spring issuing into a bog, in the bend of a river – with which the indigenous people of the region had already established a lived relation, invested with shared bodies of local knowledge and endowed with special significance; thought sentient; made numinous.[65] As a cult site, for example, or sanctuary that the Romans considered was best occupied, or otherwise appropriated. Devoted to Cocidius, perhaps.

Any place can be the site of gods who are fled, gods present still, and gods arriving. Indeed, one would expect it to be so. Cocidius was a Celtic deity who was appropriated by the Romans and honoured on a large scale along Hadrian's Wall between Housesteads (*Vercovicium*) and Stanwix.[66] At the last count, twenty-five dedications to him are known, six or possibly seven coming from Bewcastle, including those on two punched and pinched silver votive plaques (Fig. 7) that were found in the fort's strong-room (*sacellum*).[67] Cocidius was identified with Mars at Bewcastle and with Silvanus at Housesteads.[68] So, he seems to have had at least two sides to his character: he was a deity with warrior characteristics, and he was also a deity of woodlands and hunting. It has been suggested that 'Cocidius' means 'The Red One', which either by warfare or the chase or both, for they are related activities, would permit connotations of bloodedness.[69] It may well be that the fort at Bewcastle – where amongst the dedicants we find unit commanders[70]

– is *Fanum Cocidii*, the shrine or temple of Cocidius that was listed in the Ravenna Cosmography along with the names of most of the primary forts at the western end of the Wall.[71]

It is possible that the fort's shape and the strength of its garrison were determined as much by the hill's importance as a pre-existing cult site or sanctuary, and the need to occupy and appropriate it effectively, as by any more straightforwardly military reason. In other words, the fort's military importance may have been contingent on the importance that the low hill already possessed as a cult site. In this case, once the fort was in place, its military importance would have been enhanced by its appropriation of the cult site. And, once appropriated, the cult site's importance would have enhanced the importance of the fort. That possibility would explain why a temple or shrine was included in a list of primary forts on Hadrian's Wall. *Fanum Cocidii* may well have been an important fort because it was an important sanctuary.

If the hill and the area around it was not a cult site or sanctuary – devoted to Cocidius, perhaps – before the Romans arrived and recognised it as something close-to-hand that could be used, it became one when they arrived and built their fort there.[72]

As yet no traces of a township (*vicus*) have come to light. North of the Wall, and in a region with little that was useful for being-in-the-world, the fort may not have attracted the development of a *vicus* or a large *vicus*. But, if the fort was built partly with the intention of occupying or appropriating an important native cult site or sanctuary, the Romans may not have permitted the development of a *vicus*, limiting its size to better control the site and the immediate area as a place that was both a military installation and a temple or shrine. Notwithstanding that, it's worth noting that the topography restricts the possible location of any *vicus* to the narrow area of land on the west between the fort, the descent to Hall Sike and Kirk Beck, and to the northern approaches where the ground is relatively level.[73] The topography of the immediate area may not have been amenable to establishing a very large, fully developed *vicus*.

We mentioned a moment ago that Bewcastle (*Fanum Cocidii*) was probably an integral part of the original plan for Hadrian's Wall. It would seem that the original plan was that the Wall would have twelve primary forts spaced, with no special regard for whether they would be at strong or weak points, at intervals of 7⅓ Roman miles (6.8 statute miles).[74] Surely it is no coincidence that Bewcastle is about 7⅓ Roman miles from both Milecastle 50 on the Turf Wall and Birdoswald.

Let's follow the route taken by the road that was built to connect Birdoswald to the fort.[75] After leaving Birdoswald the road immediately crosses the natural drainage basin of Midgeholme Moss, deforested before the Romans arrived and perhaps already boggy ground, and then, rising slightly, crosses the boggy Whitehead Common, before climbing to the boggy plateau of Spadeadam Waste and yet more boggy ground until it arrives at the southern rim of the natural basin through which runs Kirk Beck. From the rim, looking at the land extending around them and down in the basin, it is clear why the

Roman surveyors built their fort where they did. About 6½ boggy Roman miles from Birdoswald, the two glacially deposited hills of sand on the north side of the beck, the only sand hills of any size in the area, and especially the low hill to the east, just over a mile away, offered a prime site. While more or less everything around the hill couldn't be excavated to any depth, ditches could be dug in it and turf ramparts could be raised on it; timber suitable for construction work must have been readily available there; it was well drained and a good water supply was close by; and the surveyors would have known that, if and when it was needed, sandstone, limestone and other stone suitable for building work were available a short distance away.[76] But, from the rim, around High House, it would also have been clear to them that, were they to continue their road on its line to the hill, they would have to cross White Beck at the point where the terrain was most ravine-like and then negotiate the scarp and the bog on the north side of Kirk Beck. That's probably why they redirected it to the east, over more favourable terrain, to cross Kirk Beck clear of the bog and thence up a gentle slope to the fort.[77] Down in the basin, the fort wouldn't be in visual contact with Birdoswald but, mathematically and topographically, it was where the surveyors wanted it to be, and visual communication could be achieved between it and Birdoswald by building two observation or relay posts: one on the ridge to the north-north-east at Barron's Pike; the other, back along the road, on the south side of Gillalees Beacon on Spadeadam Waste at the Butt.[78] Given the topography, geology and orohydrography of the region, the relatively flat-topped low hill above the beck presented the surveyors with an almost ideal site straight out of the manual: they built their fort on it and, if it were not one already, it became a place – a Roman place.

The Romans came, and the Roman army went. The question now is: What kind of place was Bewcastle (*Fanum Cocidii*) after the Roman forces had quit? Did it continue or did it cease being a place? And, if it continued, what kind of pre-given place was it when the Anglo-Saxons recognised what was there and brought it close-to-hand, including perhaps something residual of its cult-centredness, built and dwelt there, and erected the monument that provides us with whatever continuity we have with them, with their time and their place?

Those who have synthesised what archaeology has uncovered with the historical record to explain how and why Hadrian's Wall was abandoned have always had to make a little go a long way. Making do with the little we have, we should always push what we have to the limits of explanatory possibility, while avoiding illusion and make-believe. When new matter is brought to light it may take the explanation further along the usual way or it may take it in a different direction. Several almost paradigmatic explanations have been given for why the primary and outpost forts were abandoned. Some might have been abandoned as an effect of Constantine's visit to Britain in AD 312. Others may have been abandoned as an effect of the Barbarian Conspiracy of AD 367 or as part of the reorganisation of the frontier in AD 396. Others would not have been abandoned until the Romans withdrew from Britain in AD 410. It was once thought, as one authority teased, that 'the end of the northern frontier saw the Roman soldiers packing up their bags and heading south, leaving their forts and their wives' hearts empty, at the mercy of the northern equivalent of tumbleweed blowing down the streets of a ghost town of the American West'.[79] It may be that the accounts of problems posed by the Barbarian Picts and Scots and the victorious campaigns against them are best understood less as historical actualities and more as a *topos* with which to affect the folks back in Rome.[80] Given what has been excavated, analysed and synthesised over the last twenty years, it seems that at certain forts along the Wall, such as *Vindolanda*, Housesteads and Birdoswald, and at some related forts, such as South Shields (*Arbeia*) and Corbridge for example, or at Binchester (*Vinovia*) about thirty-five miles south from Corbridge along Dere Street, the theory of sudden and catastrophic withdrawal of the military and the collapse of the Roman administration will not exactly hold.[81] These forts remained occupied until the late fourth to fifth century, some of them through to the mid sixth century, some perhaps continuously or intermittently until their communities became Anglo-Saxon by a process of immigration and integration, cultural assimilation or redefinition.

At Birdoswald, only about $7\frac{1}{3}$ Roman miles by Roman road from Bewcastle, where the fort continued to be occupied during the late fourth century and into the fifth century, we know that building continued, at first in stone and then in timber, and that it followed on directly from the Roman buildings without a break. Traces of two large, well-constructed timber buildings have been found suggesting that, though the community lost the skills necessary for maintaining stone buildings in good repair, it was more than capable of erecting substantial, habitable wooden structures which could still have been in use in the sixth century, possibly in the early seventh century. It is not known whether the fort was continuously occupied during this period or was deserted and reoccupied, but the discovery, to the east of the fort, of an eighth-century Anglo-Saxon gilt-bronze disk-headed pin decorated with a cross and four simple *triquetras* (Fig. 12) is, to say the cautious least, 'intriguing'.[82]

We know what a Roman place was like. But what of a sub-Roman early Anglo-Saxon place? At South Shields, the courtyard house was maintained, if not to previous Mediterranean standards, and occupied until at least the early fifth century.[83] At Binchester, in the middle of the fourth century, the fort was replanned to accommodate a large house that was subsequently rebuilt, redecorated, generally maintained and used until some time in the middle of the sixth century.[84] In the fifth or sixth century, at Wroxeter (*Viroconium Cornoviorum*), a *civitas* capital far from the Wall, Roman stone buildings were replaced by timber buildings if not in a classical 'style' then with something of the 'Roman' about them.[85] There were sub-Roman people in a sub-Roman world living sub-Roman lives in sub-Roman places. Something more than groups of enslaved Britons survived from Roman Britain into Anglo-Saxon England.[86]

It may be that the area around Bewcastle persisted in a sub-Roman way, perhaps as part of the territory of the Carvetii (the 'deer folk'), the *civitatas*

Carvetiorum,[87] but one cannot talk about what kind of place it may have been if it persisted as a sub-Roman place. If one wants to get some idea of what a late-Antique place was like in seventh- to eighth-century Northumbria then Carlisle, 23 miles (25 Roman miles) from Bewcastle via Birdoswald, perhaps the *civitas* capital of the Carvetii or, if not, a major town in relation to the surrounding territory, *must* be one's frame of reference.

Carlisle, with its fort and town (the most northerly town of the Roman Empire) on the south bank of the River Eden and the fort at Stanwix (as we've seen, the largest on the Wall) some five minutes away on the north bank of the river, was one of the most densely populated and most cosmopolitan places in the frontier zone. It was also the hub of a system of roads going north, south, east and west. Parts of the town and perhaps the fort at Carlisle seem to have been occupied into the fifth or sixth century.[88] As one of the Roman towns in Britain to have preserved its Roman name, we can assume that continuity of some kind was likely. Bede, writing in the eighth century, insisted on that continuity when he referred to Carlisle as '*civitatem Lugubaliam*'.[89]

Carlisle probably retained its significance as a fortified place and centre of communications in the north-west after the Roman garrisons abandoned it. If it lost that importance in the fifth and sixth centuries, which seems unlikely, it had certainly regained it by the time Cuthbert visited it as bishop of Lindisfarne in 685. By then Carlisle was sufficiently important to contain a royal monastery and strong and secure enough for Queen Iurminburg to relocate there temporarily while she waited the outcome of King Ecgfrith's campaign against the Picts. On one of several visits that Cuthbert made to Carlisle, Waga the '*civitatis praepositus*' gave him and his entourage of priests and deacons a kind of official tour during which he was, as the writer of the *Vita Sancti Cuthberti auctore anonymo*, writing between 699 and 705, put it, shown the '*murum civitatis et fontem in ea a Romanis mire olim constructum*', which Bede in his *Vita*, written around 721, gives as '*moenia civitatis fontemque ea miro quondam Romanorum opere extructum*'.[90] But what did Waga show Cuthbert? What was that '*murum civitatis*' and that '*fontem*'? As yet there is no positive archaeological evidence that the town at Carlisle was enclosed with stone walls.[91] If it were defended, it would have been with walls made of earth and timber. Archaeology has revealed a 'short stretch of an unfinished earth and timber rampart with signs of unfinished ditches' at one site[92] and, at another, 'a wide earthen bank topped with a double row of posts', which could be interpreted as a bit of the wall or as a flood defence or an aqueduct.[93]'If the town were defended by a still standing Roman earthwork it may not have been very substantial and it seems odd that it would have been considered worth showing off, even if it had been maintained. The walls of the fort, however, were made of stone. And though they would have begun to decay by the late seventh century, as had the stone walls at forts all along the frontier, they could have been more or less intact. We know that the southern defences were rebuilt, that rebuilding within the fort in stone and timber was carried out in the fourth century, and that the *principia* and some of the other buildings were still in use in the fifth century.[94] William of Malmesbury, in his *Gesta Pontificum*, written some time before 1125, referred to still-standing Roman walls and a vaulted *triclineum* arched with a stone vault.[95] The *principia* continued in use after the end of the fourth century and the *via praetoria* and *via principalis* were still in use as well.[96] Perhaps the walls were considered worthy of note because they had been maintained and still afforded Carlisle a 'continuing symbolic power', *dignitas* and real security.[97] It is likely then that Cuthbert was given a tour not of the town but of the fort. But what was that *fons*? A thing of aquatic engineering for sure. But what? A well? Drain? Water pipe? Spring tank? Sewer? Aqueduct? Or fountain?[98] We should not rule out the possibility that Cuthbert might actually have been shown a fountain. Running water was needed for flushing latrines, sewers and streets and it was usually obtained from the excess overflow from fountains.[99] One of the two aqueducts at Corbridge, a fort that had become a walled town, some forty miles east of Carlisle on the Stanegate, terminated in an impressive fountain in the centre of the town, on the *via principalis*, between the granaries (*horrea*) and the *principia*.[100] Cuthbert would probably have known about it, and may have seen it: but it may not have been working in the seventh century. Fountains, like drains, need maintaining if they are to function properly. As the fountain at Corbridge has been reconstructed, the water from the aqueduct flows into a large aeration tank where it is freshened and sweetened. It then spurts through an ornamental spout into a trough from which it can be drawn for public use before overflowing into the street drains. If Carlisle had such a fountain, and it was still working, it would have been a very impressive sight. Cuthbert would have been well known for the way he was provided with a *fontem aquae* on Farne, almost entirely by prayer.[101] If Carlisle hadn't a well to show off, a fountain with flowing piped water, which for a Christian in the Middle Ages was never merely a fountain, would have provided a wonderful metonymy for something that figured in Cuthbert's blessed *curriculum vitae*. A fountain would have done the trick, and it would have had the advantage of being more immediately and visually attractive, but no less marvellously constructed, than sewers, pipes or drains.

The point is that there must have been plenty of Rome's residual material imperial past in Northumbria, especially in the area around the Wall. William of Malmesbury certainly gives the impression in his *Gesta Pontificum* that this was so, even in the twelfth century.[102] Carlisle in the seventh century must have been a pretty impressive Roman place for Waga to have considered that a tour of its '*murum civitatis*' and '*fontem*' was just what Cuthbert would appreciate under the 'wonderful sky' of that Saturday in May 685.

If Carlisle and Birdoswald were occupied, either continuously or intermittently, into the early medieval period and persisted as sub-Roman places, local centres closely related to tribal areas, then Bewcastle may have continued as a sub-Roman place also or as the centre of a cult, shrine or sanctuary, within a sub-Roman kingdom or petty-kingdom. Back in 1934, R. G. Collingwood was alert to this possibility.[103] We need to keep it in mind and make it vivid. The fort's function, like that of the other forts and the *civitas* capitals, would have disappeared with the Roman military but its stone buildings and defensive structures would have survived into the medieval period. Roofs may have caved in, towers collapsed, barred gates broken; houses may have been gaping, tottering, fallen, undermined by age. But it would have been there to be brightened by a mind quickened with a plan of what it was before fate altered it. Even if it did not persist as a sub-Roman place with a sub-Roman way of life, we can be sure that much of its material fabric and some of its ideology would have survived until it became an Anglo-Saxon place.

As mentioned earlier, about AD 273–312, in the last period of structural change, the fort's defences were altered; perhaps its internal area was reduced; and several of its important buildings remodelled. Traces of demolition or partial demolition that were once put down to the fort's destruction by barbarians in the third century are now understood to have been occasioned by its total replanning. At its centre, in the *principia*, the *sacellum* was filled in and a new floor added to the shrine room (*aedes*). In the north-west corner of the *retentura*, the *centuriae* (put outside the fort if the north wall was brought forward) would have been demolished. And, in the south-west corner of the front portion of the fort (*praetentura*), the bath-house was given a different function.[104]

Of all the buildings in the fort, the bath-house (Fig. 8) would have been the most robustly constructed and most likely to have resisted decay and demolition. Roman buildings were constructed using methods that we now regard as traditional.[105] They would have required major refurbishment after about sixty years or so. Walls would have needed repointing; roofs would have required stripping and their tiles or slates replaced as they and the nails, laths and timber frames deteriorated. A traditional stone building tends to collapse only when it is no longer watertight. The loss of the roof leads to the decay of the supporting timber frame and, thereafter, to the collapse of the building itself. Bath-houses, however, were not constructed like other buildings. Though the timber frame roof might have been covered with tiles or slates, because of the risk of fire and the need to prevent loss of heat from the rooms of the heated suite, they were for the most part covered with various kinds of masonry vault. Apart from the disrobing room (*apodyterium*), which had masonry walls but a tile roof supported by a timber frame, the bath-house at Bewcastle was covered with a combination of barrel vaults where the walls were strong enough to support them and groin vaults where they were not.[106] It seems likely that one or two separate barrel vaults of cut stone roofed the cold room (*frigidarium*) and cold bath, and that one or two groined vaults, made of concrete supported by calcareous tufa voussoir arches, covered the hot room (*caldarium*) and first warm room (*tepidarium*).[107] The use of tufa, which was used also in the construction of the bath-house at Chesters, is noteworthy.[108] Above these masonry vaults, it seems likely that the bath-house had a pitched timber roof that integrated with the one over the *apodyterium*.[109]

Masonry vaults not only reduce the risk of fire and insulate the rooms of the hot suite but also keep a building watertight. Even if a bath-house lost the tile or slate roof over its masonry vaulted rooms it would still resist the elements for a good while longer. And at Bewcastle, as elsewhere, the external walls of the bath-house were rendered to provide a covering that protected the masonry and delayed the need for repointing. With due care and attention given to the design of those structural members that were in tension, and long-lived materials chosen for internal and external finishes, a bath-house would have a notional life of several centuries. The vaulted voussoir roof of part of the military bath-house at *Vindolanda* survived until well into the seventeenth century when it was demolished by labourers clearing land and building farmsteads.[110] The walls of the bath-house at Chesters survive to a height of 10 feet. Those of the bath-house at Ravenglass (*Tunnocelum*) not only still stand over 10 feet but also, here and there, retain their original render. The bath-house at Bewcastle was a well-designed and well-built structure. Like all Roman bath-houses, it was built to last.

As we interpret what the 1954 and 1956 excavations brought to light, the likely end of the bath-house at Bewcastle was by way of relatively careful demolition when its stone, and the stone of the other buildings in the fort, was taken away to build the castle[111] and the church[112] in the twelfth or thirteenth and fourteenth centuries.[113] Apart from the timber-frame and tile roof of the *apodyterium*, we doubt that much, *if any*, of the bath-house had collapsed by the time the Anglo-Saxons turned whatever remained of *Fanum Cocidii* into their place.

We could go further but, for now, we've essentially said what we have to say about the Roman fort. The point is, of course, that the Bewcastle monument, which was perhaps part of the deliberate appropriation and re-sanctification of a residual Romano-British cult site, *Fanum Cocidii*,[114] and which, as we'll show later in our book, could have been an obelisk at the moment of its production and first use, a very Roman monument – Ancient Roman in form and, in part, contemporarily of the Church of Rome in some of its content – was erected inside the still standing walls of a Roman fort. Not far away stood the headquarters building; commander's house; granaries; workshops; latrines; barracks that once accommodated units of between eight hundred and a thousand men, with horses; and a bath-house. *All* not yet robbed of their stone. And though, at present, we don't know where the monument was situated in relation to all the buildings in the fort, we do know that it was sited in the southern part of the *praetentura*, only about 100 feet from the south-west corner of the bath-house, perhaps in an area that the Romans had left free of buildings as a fire precaution, about the same distance from the *porta principalis dextra*, on the *via principalis*. Amongst the centuries' derelictions, in a once and still Roman place that the Anglo-Saxons made their own, and alongside whatever timber structures they erected there, the Bewcastle monument must have looked quite something.

We don't just come across a place. We're never merely in a place. We make it. We constitute it by our activity, give it an identity, and make it meaningful. At its beginning, 'place' is an intentional intervention in the orohydrography, geology, topography, and so on, of a region or in another place regarded *as if* it is not yet wholly a place or *as if* it is, in certain respects, no more than

'earth'. People make a place when they intervene in nature or in a prior intervention in nature, modifying it and themselves. Place making at Bewcastle
continued after the Anglo-Saxons. It continues in our present.

In place before the Bewcastle monument; with the historicity of that place,
even now, only glimpsed and something of the monument's circumstances
of production and first use, as yet, to be grasped, we end this chapter with
some afterwords developed from reading Martin Heidegger's essay 'Building
Dwelling Thinking'. Though Heidegger's anti-modernist conservatism and
aversion to materialist explanations of *Dasein* (the human entity in all its ways-
of-being-in-the-world) are at odds with our theoretical beginnings in Marx
and Engels, nevertheless, the importance he assigns to human intervention
in nature ('building') and its relation to forms of consciousness ('thinking')
is not incompatible with them.[115] What Heidegger says about 'building',
'dwelling', 'thinking', and thereafter about 'earth', 'sky', 'mortals' and 'divinities' seems useful when appropriated as an interpretative metaphorics with
which to make sense of the way one can be arrested by the monument and,
affected by it, attend to the complex attachments that link oneself to other
features of the material world. In front of the Bewcastle monument, sensing
and making sense of 'place', one *must* begin 'thinking' about 'dwelling' and
about being-in-the-world.

Following Heidegger, we can say that people make places when they build
and dwell on earth. 'Building as dwelling unfolds into the building that cultivates growing things and the building that erects buildings'.[116] The Bewcastle
monument is a building, which vividly illustrates how, though not all erected
buildings are constructed for human habitation, all buildings are determined
by the need to dwell. 'Building is really dwelling':the verb 'to build' means 'to
dwell ... to remain, to stay in a place'; dwelling is 'the manner in which we
humans *are* on the earth'.[117] It's how we produce our means of subsistence
and ourselves, our relations with others. And it's how we make sense of and
express our existence, how we bring 'thinking' to practical consciousness,
especially the kind of 'thinking' that is philosophical thinking, intrinsically
poetic thinking, especially about being and being-in-the-world. 'Building
and thinking are, each in its own way, inescapable for dwelling'.[118]

In one very poetic section of 'Building Dwelling Thinking', which brings the
Bewcastle monument to mind (Figs 17, 18, 19 and 20), Heidegger writes:

> Earth is the serving bearer, blossoming and fruiting, spreading out in rock and
> water, rising up into plant and animal ... The sky is the vaulted path of the sun,
> the course of the changing moon, the wandering glitter of the stars, the year's
> seasons and their changes, the light and dusk of day, the gloom and glow of
> night, the clemency and inclemency of the weather, the drifting clouds and
> blue depth of the ether ... The divinities are the beckoning messengers of the
> godhead. Out of whose holy sway the godhead, the god appears in his presence
> or withdraws into his concealment ... The mortals are the human beings. They
> are called mortals because they can die. To die means to be capable of death *as*
> death. Only man dies, and indeed continually, as long as he remains on earth,
> under the sky, before the divinities.[119]

Thinking about the *earth* effects thinking about the *sky*. And thinking about mortality, about human beings as *mortals*, effects thinking about immortality, about divinities, divine messengers of the godhead, *god*. To think of any one of these is to think of the others. This is the 'fourfold', a unified primary interplay of earth and sky (which achieve a presence that they could not have had before the thing was built), mortals (recognising the inevitability of death and developing a good attitude towards it) and gods (men and women face up to their mortality not as animals but as human beings; they need gods and await their coming because human beings are conscious of their peculiar finitude as beings as a whole and of their specialness as beings). Heidegger says that dwelling 'preserves' the fourfold, 'keeps' it 'in that with which mortals stay: in things'. It brings the essence of the fourfold into *things* by cultivating crops and constructing buildings, keeps it in place so that it remains comprehensible.[120] The Neolithic Bronze Age peoples, the Romans and the Anglo-Saxons, as would those who came after them, made earth more precise, visualised their understanding of it, built on it, enclosed it, made paths across it: they represented their understanding of it, externalised and objectified it, made its character for themselves and others more manifest: they gathered the experienced meanings of it and themselves into a kind of *imago mundi* or *microcosmos*, a concretisation of their world that must have been, itself, an existential centre. This, it seems, is what the monument was intended to do: to situate those who used it in a fixed relation with it in such a way that, before it, they might glimpse something of the fundamental character of their being-in-the-world. They looked from the earth to the sky; back to their birth, and back by yonder to their historical past; ahead to their death, and to whatever was thought to be on the far side. The monument was their response to and representation of what and who they presently thought they were, of what and who they once were, and of who and what they might become. Even now, in front of it, walking round it – attention arrested, thought focused, emotion quickened – one comes to glimpse the complex attachments that link one to the physical world, to place and dwelling, on the relatively flat-topped low hill of sand, water tickling from a spring into a bog, on the north side of a beck, above the limestone core of a post-Carboniferous domal anticline, without which there would be no place at this place we call Bewcastle, a place of cult or sanctuary, perhaps from the very moment of its coming into being to the present day.

2

Fragments[1]

⌘

Forasmuch as the Assembly is informed, that in divers places of this Kingdome, and specially in the North parts of the same, many Idolatrous Monuments, erected and made for Religious worship, are yet extant, Such as Crucifixes, Images of Christ, Mary, and Saints departed, ordaines the saids Monuments to be taken down, demolished, and destroyed, and that with all convenient diligence: And that the care of this work shall be incumbent to the Presbyteries and Provinciall Assemblies within this Kingdome: and their Commissioners to report their diligence herein to the next Generall Assembly. (*Act anent the demolishing of Idolatrous Monuments*, The General Assembly of the Church of Scotland, 1640)[2]

Anent the report of idolatrous monuments in the Kirk of Ruthw[ell] the Assemblie finds that the monument therin mentioned is idolatrous, and therefore recommends to the Presbytrie that they carefuly urge the order prescrived be the act of Parliament anent the abolishing of these monuments, to be put to execution.(*Act anent Idolatrous Monuments in Ruthwell*, The General Assembly of the Church of Scotland, 1642)[3]

Iconoclasm is never incidental and its effects are always fragmentary. Iconoclasm: the breaking or destroying of images, especially sculptures and pictures set up as objects of veneration; the destruction or removal of material things that have already been abandoned in the mind but which, because of their continued presence, are believed to be wrong or misleading of others; the expression of contempt for the objectionable; the last resort of the thwarted or frustrated reformer; vandalism. Definitions, as will become clear in what follows, are not worth much apart from given instances. However, we need not be too concerned with matters of definition here or with explaining why the General Assembly of the Church of Scotland that convened at Aberdeen on 28 July 1640 was an active iconoclastic assembly. The Episcopacy abolished in 1638, the Presbytery was dominant and aimed to rid the kingdom of any remnants of idolatry.

Though the *Act anent the demolishing of Idolatrous Monuments* of 1640 seems to have had some specific places in mind – Aberdeen and Elgin cathedrals 'in the north' were much destroyed by it[4] – it was directed at all churches where there were monuments, sculptures or paintings, that had survived the abolition of idolatry as prescribed by the *First Book of Discipline* in 1561. It seems likely that some churches would have had at least one monument that was subject to the Act. And it is clear that the Assembly expected the work of destruction to be carried out forthwith and confirmed at its next meeting.

The 1642 *Act anent Idolatrous Monuments in Ruthwell* was issued with regard to the general Act of 1640 and following the report that the Commissioners must have presented to the General Assembly at Aberdeen in 1641 or at St Andrews in 1642 on the eve of the Great Rebellion. This Act was not printed, but its terms were minuted and the minutes provide a useful glimpse of the goings-on. It seems that the Commissioners were unable to report that *all* the 'Idolatrous Monuments in Ruthwell' had been destroyed. One monument remained. Though on the face of it, since we know that it was decorated with 'images of Christ, Mary and saints departed', it clearly was 'idolatrous' in terms of the Act of 1640, there was something of a problem about its destruction that had to be reported back to the Assembly. If the wording of the Act is anything to go by, the Assembly was not unsympathetic to the reasons for the presbytery's delay. The crucial terms are 'finds', 'recommends' and 'carefully urges'. Despite deciding that 'the monument' was idolatrous, the Assembly did not, in its response, 'ordaine' that it be destroyed but, rather, suggested or advised that the presbytery, with due care (and perhaps some anxiety), press upon the attention, advocate or argue that the Act of 1640 be put into effect. As we read it, the *Act anent Idolatrous Monuments in Ruthwell* of 1642 is characterised by prudence and circumspection. Why?

Henry Duncan, Minister at Ruthwell from 1799 to 1843, was of the opinion that the monument was preserved from destruction during the Reformation for as long as it was 'probably by the influence of the Murrays of Cockpool, the ancestors of the Earl of Mansfield, who were the chief proprietors as well as the patrons of the parish, and who had espoused the cause of the Stuarts and of the Episcopal party, in opposition to that of the Presbyterians'.[5] We need to look at the Murrays and those who came after them, for 'the monument' and what it is today is very much part of their history.

So far back as the fourteenth century Ruthwell is named as being in the possession of the Murray family, first Sir Thomas Randolph, Earl of Murray, and then his nephew Sir William Murray.[6] Cuthbert Murray, who died in 1493, built the castle at Comlongon that would become the primary residence of the Murrays of Cockpool.[7] By the seventeenth century the family was one of the richest and most powerful in the Borders. In 1625, Sir Richard Murray of Cockpool was made baron and granted by sasine lands entitled the Baronetcy of Cockpool. By 1635 he had Lockerbie, Hutton, Hoddom and more.[8]

John Murray of Reidkirk, the eighth son of Charles Murray of Cockpool, was a favourite of King James VI, travelling with him to England in 1603.[9] James appointed him Gentleman of the Bedchamber and Gentleman of the Privy Chamber and made over to him large grants of land that formerly belonged to the Abbeys of Dundrennan, Linclondane (Lincluden) and more.[10] In June 1622 he was created First Lord Murray of Lochmaben and First Viscount of Annand and, in March 1624 or 1625, First Lord Murray of Tynningham and Earl of Annandale. In 1636, on the death of his brother, Sir Richard Murray, he succeeded to the Baronetcy of Cockpool, which merged with his peerage as Earl of Annandale. 'By no means nice as to whom he sold his influence, or from whom he took money, he rapidly acquired one of the best estates in Scotland.'[11] He seems to have been good at getting land.[12] After the Plantation of Ulster, he acquired over ten thousand acres in Donegal from several patentees and, in the case of the lands of George Murray of Wigton, Lord Broughton, which included all Boilagh and Brannagh, by grant of forfeit.[13]

John Murray of Cockpool, Earl of Annandale, died in September 1640 to be succeeded by his son James.[14] Not only did James inherit has father's titles and lands but, within two years, in March 1642, succeeded to the title Third Viscount of Stormont on the death of Mungo Murray of Drumcairn, First Earl of Balvaird and Second Viscount of Stormont, by way of an extended entail in favour of the kinsmen of David Murray of Gospertie, Lord of Scone, First Viscount of Stormont.[15] King Charles I, who raised his standard at Nottingham in August 1642, and with the Great Rebellion engaged in both kingdoms, made him Steward of Annandale in November 1643. After the battle of Kilsyth in August 1645, he joined the army of the Marquis of Montrose, the king's Lieutenant General in Scotland, in its campaign against the Covenanters north of the border.[16] But the next month, at Philliphaugh, Montrose's army was defeated by superior forces. Montrose managed to escape the battlefield. As did James Murray. Those peers taken prisoner were later tried and executed.[17] In July 1646 King Charles surrendered to the Covenanters and ordered Montrose to cease hostilities. In September Montrose sailed for Norway. And James Murray, if he had not done so already, left Comlongon and retired to England. In June 1647, he married Jean Carnegie, the daughter of Montrose's brother-in-law, James Carnegie, Second Earl of Southesk. He died without heirs on 28 December 1658 in the parish of St Clements Dane, Middlesex, whereupon the Viscountcy of Stormont devolved by terms of the entail on David Murray of Gospertie, Lord Balvaird and the Earldom of Annandale, Viscountcy of Annand and the Barony of Murray of Lochmaben became extinct.[18]

A little over seven months later on 9 August 1659, James Murray's widow, Jean Carnegie, married David Murray of Gospertie, now Lord Scone, Lord Balvaird and, by then, Fourth Viscount of Stormont.[19] This marriage united the late James Murray's property in Dumfriesshire and elsewhere with the Perthsire estates of the Murrays of Balvaird and Stormont.

David Murray and Jean Carnegie's son David had two sons, David and William Murray (who was born at Comlongon Castle):[20] David, the eldest son, succeeded to the title.[21] William, the youngest son, who became Solicitor-General, Attorney General, Lord Chief Justice, Leader of the House of Commons and member of the Cabinet, was made Baron Mansfield in 1756 and First Earl of Mansfield in 1776.[22] On William's death without heirs in 1793, the Earldom of Mansfield passed to his nephew David Murray, Lord

Scone, Lord Balvaird, and Seventh Viscount of Stormont – Earl of Mansfield by greater title.[23]

With that all too brief history of the Murrays of Cockpool, Earls of Annandale and pedigree of the descent of the Viscountcy of Stormont taking us to the Earldom of Mansfield, we can now see why, in 1833, Duncan referred to the Murrays of Cockpool as the ancestors of the Earl of Mansfield,[24] and Reverend J. L. Dinwiddie, Minister at Ruthwell (1890–1936), in the first of several versions of his history of the monument, referred to the Earl of Annandale as 'a remote ancestor of the present lord of the manor, the Earl of Mansfield'.[25]

Whereas Duncan privileged the influence of the proprietors and patrons of Ruthwell in explaining the survival of the monument prior to 1642, Dinwiddie privileged Gavin Young, Minister at Ruthwell from 1617 to 1671. The two are related, of course, for Young's position was dependent on the patronage of the Murrays and their successors. According to Dinwiddie, Young first delayed demolishing the monument and, after it had been toppled, 'with great secrecy, and with careful deliberation, and consummate skill ... conveniently forgot' to destroy it completely.[26] As far as Dinwiddie was concerned, Young 'rightly believed that the great Cross could not be truly described as an "Idolatrous Monument"' because 'he knew perfectly well ... that the Church of Rome could make no valid claim' to its 'authorship' or 'erection'.[27] It 'had been in existence many years before the Roman Church was established in the Kingdom of Northumbria. To the Celtic church – the Church of Columba – the Ruthwell Cross owed its existence, not to the Church of Rome. It was of St John it had to speak – rather than of St Peter – of the simple teaching of Iona and not of the doctrines of Rome.'[28] Despite his explanation of Young's praiseworthy obstinacy and far-sighted audacity in face of the General Assembly's 'ignorance of the true facts of the case', Dinwiddie could not overlook that his predecessor managed to continue in the parish 'notwithstanding the frequent changes of Government, both in Church and State' and 'suited himself to the changing circumstances of the time'.[29] Reverend Gavin Young was Scotland's 'Vicar of Bray'.[30] Dinwiddie had to admit the likelihood that patronage played some part in Young's attempts to preserve the monument. Young, who would eventually father thirty-one children, would not have wanted 'to run the risk of being deprived of his living and turned out of house and home' by the church's patrons, first John and then James Murray, Earls of Annandale, and thereafter by David Murray, Viscount of Stormont.[31]

As Dinwiddie knew the history of it, Young toppled the monument into a trench 'cut in the clay floor of the Church near the base of the Cross shaft' and then 'under the jealous supervision of the local Presbytery, yet with careful dedication and great reluctance', defaced and destroyed 'one of the largest and most accessible panels', the panel across from the crucifixion.[32] If that was the way the monument was demolished, Young did it according to the letter of the Act of 1640, with 'convenient diligence' and no more and no less damage than he could get away with. Afterwards, the largest fragment of the broken monument, as we'll see in a moment, with the Crucifixion and

Annunciation panels uppermost, remained on the spot where it fell for at least 130 years.

In 1704, on the second of two visits he made to Ruthwell, William Nicolson, Bishop of Carlisle, was able to see that part of the monument which had been toppled into the trench lying immovable in 'Murray's Quire'. He referred to Murray's Quire as 'the antient Burial place of ye Murray's Earls of Annandale now extinct'.[33] It is important for understanding the history of the Ruthwell Cross that Nicolson saw this part of the monument where he did because Murray's Quire was not added to the church until, according to Dinwiddie, some time between 1772 and 1790 when, during the ministries of Reverends Andrew Jaffray (1760–1782) and John Craig (1783–1798), extensive alterations and improvements necessitated removal of the wall that enclosed it.[34]

Even then, as is shown by the several plans on exhibition in Murray's Quire, which were made at various times either to record the arrangement of the pews and their designated occupants or preparatory to work on the fabric, the Quire seems not to have become properly conjoined to and accessible from the body of the church until 1887 when the Ruthwell Cross was installed in the apse. For centuries the pews in the Quire, which were reserved for the workers on the Murray estates, could be accessed only from the churchyard.

Duncan was largely responsible for the church as it is today. Indeed, he almost rebuilt it. Within four years of arriving at Ruthwell, he had removed the east wall to reduce the church's length by 30 feet and had removed the north wall to increase its width by 10 feet.[35] With the exception of the east and west walls of Murray's Quire, all the walls are of different thicknesses and provide evidence for the different builds – the thickest wall is that section south of the door in the west gable end, which is 4 feet thick. It is not known if Duncan changed the height of the church.

Let's look at the walls of Murray's Quire. The south wall is 3 feet 3¾ inches thick, while the west and east walls are each 2 feet 9¼ inches thick. The south and north walls were probably the original building's gable ends.

Duncan made several alterations to the structure of Murray's Quire: windows were filled in and new windows were opened: a door – probably the entrance to the original building – in the middle of the south wall was closed and a large 'heritor's Gothic' type window added: a new door in the middle of the west wall was opened, which was subsequently filled in and, perhaps at the time the apse was added in 1887 by Reverend James Mcfarlan, relocated to where the west wall meets the south wall of the main body of the church – it was subsequently bricked up in 1906 by Reverend John Dinwiddie. The works undertaken in the nineteenth century make it difficult to reconstruct what the building may have looked like three or four hundred years before.

The exterior measurements of Murray's Quire are as follows: south wall, 20 feet 5 inches; east wall, 21 feet 7½ inches; and west wall, 20 feet 10 inches. The blocked door in the west wall where it joins the south wall of the church is worth a closer look. The door's jamb is, at the moment, easily discerned about 3 feet 4 inches from the south wall; there may be some indication here, directly above it, of the quoin of the original building, which may have been independent of the church. It is easy to imagine that Murray's Quire was once a separate building 20 feet 5 inches by about 17 feet 6 inches. The exterior height of the east and west walls is 12 feet 5 inches. Again, it's not known if Duncan changed the height of the church.

The interior of the Quire, as it is now, measures: the south wall 14 feet 10½ inches and, opposite, opening to the body of the church 14 feet 10 inches; the east wall 20 feet 8 inches and the west wall 20 feet 6½ inches. Inside, the east and west walls stand to a height of 11 feet 3 inches to the cornice. The interior height of the gable end, as it is now, measures about 15 feet 11 inches.[36]

It is to the point that Nicolson, with punctiliousness and knowing that has lapsed in mentioning these matters, referred to Murray's Quire as 'the antient Burial place of ye Murray's Earls of Annandale now extinct'. As we have seen, the Earls of Annandale became extinct in 1658. The keystone of a recessed arch in the south wall of the Quire, almost certainly relocated from its original position, is decorated with a shield charged with the basic arms of Murray.[37] Also in the south wall, and certainly out of its original position, there is a coat of arms on a bordered panel bearing the date 1687 and blazoned with the arms of the Viscounts of Stormont.[38] Perhaps the Murrays of Cockpool moved the monument into the Quire. Or perhaps they built the Quire around it. Perhaps the Quire stayed intact until it was added to the church or perhaps it was rebuilt before then, perhaps around 1687, during the life of David Murray, Fifth Viscount of Stormont, who as we will see in a moment is the one Murray who can definitely be put in a relation of association with the monument. The arms of Murray is likely a survival of that ancient burial place and the arms of Stormont could be part of a funerary monument or, more likely, a memorial from the moment the Quire was appropriated by and dedicated to the memory of the Murrays of Stormont.[39]

The Church of Scotland's attitudes towards death and burial were little different from those of other Reformed Churches: in marked contrast to the observances of Catholicism, the body of the deceased was interred soberly and without ceremony. However, the Church of Scotland went further and prohibited the practice of interring corpses within the church building and in this it challenged the legal rights and prerogatives of some lairds or landowners: patrons, like the Murrays, who would have been responsible for the financial concerns of the parish, for example the church building and Reverend Gavin Young's stipend. Patronage was a heritable property right that was usually conveyed with a baronetcy and the land to which it was attached. Not surprisingly, there was opposition to the Church's attempt to prohibit burial within the church. Some landowners adapted to the change by building their own burial places. These took two forms: either a 'lair', burial enclosure or mausoleum within the churchyard, or a 'quire' or burial-aisle built on to one side of the church. A burial-aisle might be built like a transept connecting in such a way to serve both as a place of burial and as a family 'loft' or pew with external doors giving access to the vault and the loft above but no access, except by sight, to the chancel.[40] Thus separated, the burial-aisle satisfied the Church's prohibition against interment within the church. As far as the Church of Scotland was concerned, such a burial-aisle was a building by itself, unconnected and distinct from the church: one that was wholly the responsibility of the landowner. Sealed off, with access from the churchyard only, the burial-aisle was deemed properly enclosed from the church though it could be regarded as related to or part of the same building.

It is not known if Murray's Quire was a lair, burial enclosure or mausoleum in the churchyard or an annexe, that came in place as a burial-aisle in the post-Reformation period. Nicolson knew it as an 'antient Burial place', in which case, in 1640, it would have been regarded as a redundant religious building. If it were a burial-aisle, though it was annexed to the body of the church, it did not really belong to the Church and had no sanctity.

It is easy to overlook that 'the monument therein' that is the object of the 1642 *Act anent Idolatrous Monuments in Ruthwell* is the monument referred to *in* 'the report of idolatrous monuments in the Church of Ruthwell', *not* to a monument *in* the church. The wording of the Act, as with the wording of any law, not least a law drafted and passed by the Supreme Court of the Church of Scotland and national legislative assembly, would have been subject to discussion and it would have been precise. At the time it was destroyed, the monument was standing in Murray's Quire, a lair or a burial-aisle. It's important to note that Reverend John Craig, in his entry on Ruthwell in *The Statistical Account of Scotland*, recorded that the monument was 'placed in the church-yard' till it was thrown down and broken. When Craig compiled his entry on the 'Parish of Ruthwell', between 1792 and 1793, the wall enclosing Murray's Quire would have only recently been removed (assuming that the building work occurred between 1772 and 1790).[41] 'In the church-yard', albeit in the ancient burial place, lair, quire or burial-aisle of the Murrays Earls of Annandale extinct. That would explain why, when the presbytery implemented the *Act anent demolishing of Idolatrous Monuments* of 1640 with regard to the monuments 'in the church', it did not destroy the monument in Murray's Quire. The church didn't own the Quire: it wasn't part of the church: it had no special significance other than that Murrays were buried therein. Probably there was some discussion amongst the presbytery as to whether the Act of 1640 applied to the monument in Murray's Quire. If so, the decision seems to have been that it did not: either that, or it was thought best to delay matters.

These issues of Church law, the legal rights and prerogatives of proprietors, death and burial would have been especially vivid at Ruthwell in 1640 for within less than two months of the Act being passed, John Murray of Cockpool, First Earl of Annandale, major proprietor of the parish and patron of the church, died on 22 September. Perhaps Gavin Young, concerned about what his future might hold under the new proprietor, was waiting on a body that, as it turned out, was buried elsewhere.[42] The Act of 1640 and the death, bereavement, mourning and likely interment of John Murray more or less coinciding: for whatever reason, neither the burial nor the demolition took place. Moreover, that the monument stood in the ancient burial place of the Murrays could also explain why, two years later, having considered the report on it, the Assembly thought best not to *order* or command its destruction but, instead, *suggested* that 'the Presbytrie careful[l]y urge the order prescrived be the act of Parliament anent the abolishing of these monuments, to be put to execution'.

It is a moot point as to just precisely when, before Nicolson's visit in 1704, the monument was demolished but there it lay, or one very large bit of it did, broken in two, entrenched in the clay floor for a century or more, on the spot where it fell, until alterations to Murray's Quire and the church necessitated its removal.

> There appears, then, to be satisfactory evidence that the pillar has, since its first erection, undergone a great change; that it consisted at first only of one block ... the upper stone containing the cross having been added at a later period (Henry Duncan, 'An Account of the Remarkable Monument in the shape of a Cross')[43]

As it is now, in the church, the 'Ruthwell Cross' (Fig. 42) seems to be aligned incorrectly. Conventional wisdom, at least since the 1920s, takes it that the present north side, with Christ on the Beasts as its central panel, was, when the monument was produced and first used, the west side.[44] It worth noting that the photographs taken just prior to the monument's removal to the church show that, when he put it together in the manse garden (Figs 49 and 50), Duncan oriented it differently but no less incorrectly: the west side faced south and the east side faced north. When, in 1887, it was installed in the church the east side was turned to face south: perhaps lest the image of Christ in Majesty adored by the beasts should offend the eye of the Presbyterian congregation. Also, when the monument was put together in 1823, the topmost fragment was put on the wrong way round: the bird perched on the berry-bunched plant scroll on the west side should be above the archer on the east side; the figure with the large bird on the east side, which is identified as St John the Evangelist with his eagle, should be above the two figures on the west side, which are identified as St Matthew with the angel. Whenever we refer to the fragments, we will do so, as we did just then, and before that in our introduction, according to how they would have been aligned in the early Middle Ages.

As we see it, the 'Ruthwell Cross' (Col. Plate I) is an inelegant thing. What passes as reconstruction is actually an awkward mixture of five carved and inscribed Anglo-Saxon stones and six vulgar blocks of convenience from the nineteenth century (one of which is no more than a wedge) cemented together with crude pointing that here and there serves as modelling. It is an object that presents its beholders with lots of what Duncan thought of as 'peculiarities' or 'anomalies'. That is how he referred to them in the paper he presented to the Society of Antiquaries of Scotland on 10 December 1832, which was subsequently published in *Archaeologia Scotica* under the title 'An Account of the Remarkable Monument in the shape of a Cross, inscribed with Roman and Runic Letters, preserved in the Garden of the Ruthwell Manse, Dumfriesshire'.[45] Duncan's title indicates what he regarded as the main peculiarity or anomaly: that Latin and runic inscriptions should be found on the same monument. Despite that, the most obvious peculiarity or anomaly, inconsistency or oddity – it really is very striking – is that the Anglo-Saxon fragments that Duncan brought together are, as he put it, of 'dissimilar' blocks of sandstone. Although both blocks are of 'a coarse texture and of a reddish-colour inclining to gray, such as is to be found in the vicinity, the upper stone is distinctly of a deeper hue than the other'.[46] The lower part of the shaft is made of pale pinkish-grey sandstone whereas the upper part and the upper arm of the crosshead are made of pale red sandstone. Duncan assumed that both stones were 'probably taken from the neighbouring hills, but evidently from different quarries'; and, wondering why the material for one object should be taken from two places, further assumed that the upper stone was a later but still Anglo-Saxon addition 'for it is far from probable that dissimilar blocks would have been employed in its original construction, though necessity or convenience might have required this on its being remodelled'.[47] This view he saw confirmed by two further obvious differences: by the way the runic letters on the upper stone run horizontally along the borders instead of vertically as they do on the lower stone (Fig. 59);[48] and by the way the border that runs horizontally around all four sides at the top of the lower stone divides the plant-scroll on each of the narrow sides 'into two compartments, and awkwardly interrupts its elegant convolutions' – he saw it as an interruption that could be satisfactorily explained only by supposing that, in its original form, 'the pillar at this point was made to terminate'.[49] Wherever the plant-scroll with the six-lobed berry bunch and rising leaf on the lower right side of the pale red upper stone stems from, it does not come from or continue the main stem of the plant-scroll on the pale pinkish-grey lower stone, which terminates in a neatly self-contained spiral.

'The question of the provenance of the stone or rather stones ... at once presents itself', so wrote G. Baldwin Brown near the beginning of his 1920 'Report on the Ruthwell Cross' for the Royal Commission on Ancient and Historical Monuments and Constructions of Scotland.[50] Baldwin Brown was at pains to argue against the idea that the stone may have been brought to Ruthwell from somewhere general and that the monument itself had been transported ready-made from some other place.[51] He was convinced that the Ruthwell Cross had been made locally and that both stones had come from the same local quarry – though he did not say where that quarry might have been.[52] But how local was his 'local'? According to his report, both stones were from 'the geological formation known as the New Red Sandstone which occurs in the Nithsdale district, where Ruthwell is situated, as well as on the other side of the Solway in Cumberland'.[53] Leaving aside that Baldwin Brown seems not to have regarded Cumberland – about 3½ miles away across the Solway Firth from Ruthwell – as local, his geological geography is true enough but misleading (Col. Plates II and III). Ruthwell is situated on the coastal plain between, on the east, the River Annan, which enters the Solway below Annan, and on the west, the River Nith, which enters the Solway below Dumfries. To the west and north west of Ruthwell, in Nithsdale, the rock is New Red Sandstone of Permian age. The strata run roughly north–south from around Thornhill to around Bankend, and also occur under Lochmaben and Lockerbie. But in the immediate vicinity of Ruthwell, and north-eastwards towards Hoddom, the underlying strata are limestone of Carboniferous age; and the lower reaches of the Annan and the Kirtle Water are underlain by New Red Sandstone of Triassic age. This latter extends from Annan, under the Inner Solway Firth, as far to the east as Brampton and south to around Kirkoswald in Cumbria. These rocks were thus formed during three different geological periods and in different conditions, and so have different characteristics. The strata of the New Red Sandstone of Triassic age were formed by sand deposited under water, mainly in rivers; the strata are water-lain. The strata of New Red Sandstone of Permian age were formed as sand deposited under desert conditions; the strata are dune-bedded. As noted above, neither New Red Sandstone of Permian age nor New Red Sandstone of Triassic age occurs immediately in the vicinity of Ruthwell. Here the rocks comprise interbedded sandstone, limestone and siltstone of Carboniferous age. Indeed, the principal rock, as Duncan noted in his essay on the parish of Ruthwell in the *New Statistical Account*, is a coarse limestone, which was worked in the eighteenth and nineteenth centuries.[54] Wherever the stones came from, there is no obvious exposure of rock in the immediate vicinity or in the parish of Ruthwell.[55]

Even so, matters are more complicated than this for it seems that neither stone is New Red Sandstone.[56] The pale pinkish-grey lower stone is a quartz-rich, medium grained, mica-free, not obviously laminated sandstone. It is likely that it is a sandstone of the Carboniferous age from the Northumberland–Solway Basin. The pale red upper stone is also a quartz-rich, medium grained sandstone. Just the same, but compared with the lower stone, it is less well sorted, which is to say that there is a greater difference of grain sizes. The reddened hue is due to the introduction of iron oxide that coated the grains at the moment when they were cemented and compacted together. It is likely to be Carboniferous Sandstone of the Northumberland–Solway Basin also. Both stones could have been taken from different beds in the same quarry. The uniformity of grain sizes that makes the lower stone is particularly impressive. It is a prime piece of building stone, and the uniformity of grains made it an excellent stone for sculpture. Whoever chose this stone chose very well.

Beds of sandstone of the Carboniferous age occur locally across the entire outcrop of the Carboniferous Limestone that extends over about 290 square miles for a distance of about 47 miles along the border between Scotland and England from around Ruthwell on the Solway Firth, by way of around Ecclefechan, Langholm, Canonbie and Newcastleton to the Cheviot Hills in the north-east.[57] Such a large piece of high-quality stone for sculpture as the pale pinkish-grey lower stone must have been difficult to find and wherever the quarry site was it would have been unlike the modern quarries of conventional wisdom: deep, highly industrialised quarries serviced by a well-developed infrastructure. Deep quarrying is difficult. The Anglo-Saxons would have obtained their stone, like the Romans who built Hadrian's Wall, as close as possible to where they were intending to use it from fieldstones or from an outcrop or cliff-face where nature had exposed the strata. The very large size of the pale pinkish-grey lower stone suggests that, wherever it was taken from, it came from a bed of considerable height and lateral continuity. Where, one wonders, did the Anglo-Saxons find such a bed of lying near the surface, whether locally or from further away? Once they had found it, they wouldn't have taken what was exposed; they would have cut into the strata and extracted a block of the dimensions they required. There would probably have been more rock of the same quality at the same site. We cannot help wondering why they didn't take another piece of the same size or smaller.

At a time when the Anglo-Saxons were only just beginning to acquire the skills and competences of quarrying and building in stone, it would have been very difficult for them to take a block of stone from the living rock: top soil and probably subsoil would have had to be removed; then the stone split by opening any natural cracks or by making some. We wonder where the tools came from. Heavy hammers would be required, wooden and metal wedges, jumpers and crowbars, and lewis equipment for lifting the block. And once the stone had been freed, transporting it any distance without injuring or breaking it would have been equally if not more difficult – especially the pale pinkish-grey lower stone, which is a huge piece of stone by any standard. Wherever the stones for the Ruthwell Cross came from, whether from a stratum of sandstone interbedded with the limestone that had cropped out locally or from an outcrop further away, they would have been moved a considerable distance by land or by land, river and sea. We should rule out neither possibility.[58]

Occasionally one comes across an Anglo-Saxon monument made, in part at least, from a block cut across beds of different coloured stone.[59] But two sites in the same quarry, as Duncan realised, might indicate two historically specific moments of construction. If the difference between the lower and upper stones that make the Ruthwell Cross was a difference only of colour, it could be taken as of no great significance for there is evidence that some Anglo-Saxon pre-Viking stone monuments were covered with gesso and perhaps also painted.[60] If the Ruthwell Cross were covered with gesso or painted at the moment it was produced and first used, the difference in colour between its two stones wouldn't have been apparent, and the inscriptions could have been picked out with colour or even gold leaf as were the inscriptions on some Roman monuments.[61] Thus obscured, the difference may not have been a problem for those persons who produced it. But if the stone wasn't covered with gesso, it is difficult to imagine how the difference of hue could have been overlooked. It seems highly unlikely that whoever produced and used such a high-status monument would have compromised its effect by using two stones of such different hue. Notwithstanding that, the difference, as Duncan noticed, is not only of hue. We need to look at these other differences and see what they amount to.

Starting with the east side of the Cross (Fig. 61 and 62), the way the decoration has been arranged seems to conform to a certain logic. At each outside edge, a broad flat band moulding makes a continuous vertical border across the joining of the pale pinkish-grey lower stone and the pale red upper stone. A broad flat-band moulding divides each figure panel from its neighbour.

These borders are inscribed. We find something different on the west side (Fig. 54) where, instead of a single flat band moulding at the junction of the two stones, there are two mouldings each of a different width. Though this is not the only difference, it is the most obvious one.

Having noted this inconsistency between the way the decoration has been arranged on the east and west sides of the Cross, we can now return to the east side to take a closer look at the junction between the column and the cross (Fig. 61), which Duncan effected by placing a fragment of pale red stone atop the pale pinkish-grey lower stone. Robert T. Farrell saw this fragment of pale red stone, which begins the cross shaft of the cross-head, as an 'incongruous fragment' because its 'border ... does not agree with any other section of the border on the cross' – it has no trace of a Latin or runic inscription, 'the rule elsewhere on the cross' – and because the two pairs of feet that are carved on it seem to be wearing sabots, which are not seen elsewhere on the cross and 'cannot be paralleled in Anglo-Saxon carving'. Though it might have provided 'the starting point' for Duncan's 're-erection of the Ruthwell Cross', Farrell thought that it is 'very possibly not a part of the single cross we now have in Ruthwell church'.[62]

By setting this stone as he did, Duncan preserved something of the pattern established on the east side of the pale pinkish-grey lower stone with its single horizontal borders between the panels but, as we've seen, in doing so, he ended up with something different on the west side. We doubt that he mistook the area below the shoed feet on the so-called 'incongruous fragment' for a bit of border. In places it is over 4 inches wide or deep, much wider than the borders on the west side – the border on the upper stone is approximately $2\frac{3}{8}$ inches wide, that on the lower stone is approximately $3\frac{1}{8}$ inches wide.

Duncan seems to have realized that this part of the monument didn't add up as reconstruction for, when it came to making the engraving necessary to illustrate the monument in *Archaeologia Scotica* (Fig. 51), he drew something quite different from what he knew to be the case. Although he claimed that the engraving was 'an accurate representation', there are several discrepancies between it and the Ruthwell Cross. In the context of this discussion, you will notice that when he drew the stone carved with the shoed feet he changed not only its dimensions but the dimensions of all the stones that held it in place. Indeed, ignoring the cement infilling, he made it and the modern stone to its right into one stone, minimizing the degree of actual reconstruction. In other words, he graphically reconstructed the monument making the east side more like the west side than it actually was, and is.[63]

Mention of the inscriptions a moment ago brings us to the other feature that struck Duncan as peculiar. As we have seen, he noticed that the inscriptions on the two stones were laid out differently, but he didn't realise just how differently. The most obvious rule governing those on the pale pinkish-grey lower stone is that Latin and runes are segregated. Latin is used for the inscriptions on the west and east sides (Figs 55 and 62): on the east side, but not on the west side, they are fragments taken from scripture; on the west side they are more like denotative statements, labels that make the figure

panels effective as illustrations of stories told elsewhere by providing information about the action and identifying the characters by name. Runes are
used for the inscriptions on the north and south sides (Figs 59, 60 and 67,
68, 69) – verses in Northumbrian vernacular that are, as we will see in a later
chapter, in some way related to *The Dream of the Rood*, a poem that survives
in a late Anglo-Saxon manuscript in the library of Vercelli Cathedral, Italy.
Maybe, *if* one regards the west and east sides as the main sides and the
north and south sides as the minor sides, there is a hierarchy of Roman and
runic scripts and Latin and vernacular. But, *if so* one should not assume that
the runic inscriptions, thus marginalised, are mere accessory to the Latin
inscriptions.

The Latin inscriptions on the lower stone are arranged around the figure
panels in a consistent manner: they read left to right across the border above
the panel, continue down the right border, and are then completed from top
to bottom in the border on the left.[64] A resource that might have been available to the those persons who were faced with the problem of how to arrange
inscriptions around panels of relief sculpture may have been provided by
pictures or panel paintings that had been seen on or imported from the continent. Some years ago it was pointed out how the inscriptions on the lower
stone are arranged along the same lines as the inscription on the borders
around an icon of the Crucifixion that has survived from the same period on
Mount Sinai, though the letters are aligned horizontally on the monument
not vertically as they are on the painting.[65] Another example, showing the
same arrangement, is provided by the seventh-century encaustic painting of
the Virgin Mary in Sta Maria in Trastevere at Rome.[66] One is reminded of the
pictures or picture panels, mentioned by Bede, that Benedict Biscop brought
back from his trips to Rome and installed in the church at Monkwearmouth.[67]
Perhaps some of them, like the Sta Maria in Trastevere painting of the Virgin
Mary, had lettered borders.

There seem to be three exceptions to this arrangement whereby the inscriptions read left to right across the top border, top to bottom in the right border,
then top to bottom in the left border; but they are *only seeming* and can be
shown to be consistent within the pattern. The longest inscription, around
Christ and Mary Magdalen (Fig. 63) on the east side, begins at the left and
reads across the upper border, goes down the right border, resumes in the
left border reading from top to bottom and finishes reading from left to right
in the lower border. The inscription providing the textual point to Christ and
the man born blind (Fig. 64) occupies that panel's vertical borders. Here,
because the upper border was already occupied with the reference to the
Magdalen's hair, the first part of the inscription was put in the left border
and then taken to its completion in the right border. Lastly, the inscription
on the west side around Christ on the Beasts (Fig. 55) begins at the left of
the upper border – '+IHSXPS' – and goes down the right border – 'IVDEX:
AEQVITATIS' – and stops; it then continues in the left border – 'BESTIAE ·
ET · DRACONES · COGNOVERVNT · IN · DE' – and stops; and returns to the
right border – 'SERTO · SALVA?OREM · MVNDI' – where it finishes. There is
nothing clumsy about this. The way the syntagm is laid out is an important

constituent of the meaning of the text. It's a very complex arrangement that keeps to the pattern while ensuring that the 'bestiae et dracones' occupy a space apart from 'iudex aequitatis' and 'salvatorem mundi' and that a bit of the word 'deserto' is placed in the left border. In the column's original alignment, the left border or south margin of the east-facing side seems to be the border of the 'desert': Paul and Anthony (Fig. 56) are breaking bread 'in the desert' in the left border; and the Holy Family (Fig. 57) is travelling 'through the desert' in that border also. The community that came up with these inscriptions arranged them so they read from left to right and top to bottom, beginning in the horizontal border immediately above each panel, then down the right border, and then the left border, and so on.

Although the runic inscriptions on the lower stone do not, as the Latin inscriptions do, indicate the divisions between the words and are not, as the Latin inscriptions are, oriented horizontally in the vertical borders but vertically, these obvious grammatical and visual differences should not obscure the fact that both inscriptions follow the same pattern of laying out syntagms. That is to say, the runic inscriptions are arranged in the same way as the Latin inscriptions; they begin at the top left in the upper border, continue down the right border, and are completed in the left border reading from top to bottom. At least one commentator has considered that the arrangement of the runic inscription 'looks absurd and is maddeningly hard to read'.[68] We don't see the visual absurdity. Surely the inscriptions are there to rouse a medieval community to purposeful effort: Latin and vernacular, each where it is, and each treated as proper to its function. And while the modern scholar might find the runic inscriptions difficult to read he or she should not assume that they presented any difficulty for medieval rune readers. We note, in passing, that the syntagms are laid out in a quite different way on the Franks Casket – where, incidentally, two of the texts are arranged retrograde and, as it were, upside-down. Perhaps the most runic characteristic of the runic alphabet is that each character is legible and cannot be mistaken for any other character whatever way it is written, in the usual manner, retrograde or upside-down. As to the legibility of the runes on the Ruthwell Cross, as far as we're concerned the significant thing is that, at this particular moment and place of burgeoning literacy, the Latin and runic syntagms inscribed on the lower stone follow the same pattern.

If there is a hierarchy of Latin and runic scripts on the pale pinkish-grey lower stone, it does not apply on the pale red upper stone where, as Duncan noticed, the runes on the north side at the junction of the two stones (Fig. 59), which read 'dægisæf', unlike those on the lower stone, which are set vertically in the vertical borders, are laid horizontally towards the left in the manner of the Latin inscriptions. There is also an aberrant runic inscription on the east side of the upper arm of the crosshead (Fig. 53) that reads 'æfauœþo'[69] – it's on the left side of the topmost fragment carved with the bird on the berry-laden plant-scroll.

The inscriptions on the pale red upper stone also evidence some other peculiarities or anomalies. On the cross shaft, the text that borders the panel carved with the embracing figures wearing sabots (Fig. 61) is set in Latin but with some letters transliterated in runes. It seems to begin at the top of the right border – '+dominnæc' – and, lacking a lower border, continues up the left border – 'marþa' – to be completed left to right across the top border – 'mari?m?'.[70] This inscription is different from those on the east side of the pale pinkish-grey lower stone because it names the characters rather than citing scripture and because the way it is laid out departs from the pattern set by the way the inscriptions are laid out on the lower stone. Another difference may be that, unlike the Latin on the lower stone, this text may contain at least one lapse or error.[71]

It is difficult to reconstruct the inscription in the borders surrounding the large panel on the west side of the pale red upper stone (Fig. 54). The edges are badly damaged and only the lower part of the left border and part of the bottom border preserve any inscription. What survives can be transcribed as '...DORAMVSVTNONCVM'[72] and read as '[a]doramus ut non cum' – significantly with no mention of the 'desert', and with forms of 'N' and 'O' in 'VTNONCVM' not found on the lower stone.[73] The 'V' of 'VT', set on its side in the lowest part of the left border, may have been added later to correct an omitted letter, but it should be noted that, if so, the correction accords with the 'V' of '[A]DORAMVS' above it. It is difficult to know what to make of this inscription. If it were arranged so that it began in the top of the left border and descended – '[..A]DORAMVS' – to continue left to right along the lower border – 'VT NON CVM' – before travelling in whichever way to completion, it would have been laid out unlike any syntagm found elsewhere on the monument.[74]

What do these deviations from good Latin, and the runes that resist our best efforts to make them meaningful, amount to in relation to the inscriptions on the lower stone? Does it come down to different moments of literacy and linguistic skill within the same community – moments of competence and incompetence – or that the same literate and linguistically skillful community employed stone carvers of mixed linguistic competence? Of course, the differences may also be taken for evidence of two historically and culturally different communities, two different moments of production: in which case, the questions multiply.

There are more 'inconsistencies' and 'peculiarities', problems of form, content and facture, but those we have just discussed are sufficient for the purposes of this chapter. All the material and pictorial, logical and ideological inconsistencies between the lower and upper stones should encourage us to see them as different and keep them apart even as their very togetherness forces us to see them as a unity.

Rereading Duncan's 'An Account of the Remarkable Monument in the shape of a Cross', it is striking how scrupulous he was in always referring to the lower stone as 'the column' or 'the pillar' and to the upper stone as 'the cross'. When he refers to both stones together, to the material entity he put together, he calls it 'the monument' and, on one occasion, 'the Ruthwell Monument'.[75] Almost two hundred years after its destruction, Duncan thought that he had reconstructed an object that had been first erected as a 'column' and that, subsequently, 'at a later date', had been 'remodelled' with the addition of a cross. It is not known whether the 'column' or 'pillar' and the 'cross' first came together in medieval Northumbria, a composite of two moments of production, or in nineteenth-century Dumfriesshire, as a composite of Duncan's ingenuity.[76]

'Column' or 'cross'? Column and cross? Our object of study became a 'fact' just over forty years before its destruction was ordered by the General Assembly of the Church of Scotland. That was when, in 1599, Reginald Bainbrigg, headmaster of Appleby Grammar School and pioneer antiquarian, visited the church at Ruthwell and made a note of what he regarded as notable, represented what he thought was worthy of note.[77] Bainbrigg's note (Fig. 43), which gives us the only description we have of the monument before it was toppled, introduced memory to a material object whose life, in as much as we have the archive of the written word, was until that moment outside language in the 'real'. It refers to what was in that 'real'. But, be that as it may, it would be wrong to take Bainbrigg's note for what was in the real *or* for the object that Duncan erected in his garden *or* for the object that is now installed in the church, which, following Duncan, we henceforth call the 'Ruthwell monument'.

Bainbrigg's note seems to have been sent, probably in 1600, to William Camden who was collecting material for publication in a new edition of his 1586 *Britannia*. It reads:

> Behold unexpectedly I came across a cross of wonderful height which is in the church at Ruthwell with beautiful images telling the story of Christ, decorated elegantly with vines, animals and on two sides with foreign but fluent letters ascending from the base to the very top and also descending from the very top to the base. The inscription is such.[78]

Bainbrigg, who collected inscribed Roman stones and, if not actual stones, inscriptions on such stones, on this occasion was less interested in the Latin texts on the monument's west and east sides than in the texts on its north and south sides that were written in 'fluent letters' which were 'foreign' to him. His note provided Camden with a sample of these letters, which he arranged along the top of his note and down its right margin: 'literae transversae' and 'literae perpendiculares ab apice ad basim'. What Bainbrigg saw as worthy of note, 'in the church', and what his note represents are the runes in the border at the top of the north side of the pale pinkish-grey lower stone and the first fourteen lines of runes (minus the fifth line) in its right border.

True, Bainbrigg's note tells us that he saw the monument 'in the church', but we've seen how problematic it may have been to see it as properly *in* the church. However, we can be certain that Bainbrigg knew '*apex*/very top' from '*basis*/bottom'; he attached some importance to those terms, which as a good Latinist he would have chosen carefully; he insisted on them three times. But when it came to representing what he regarded was worthy of note he did not include any of the runic inscriptions from the east side of the pale red upper stone. If he had, we might have been able to make more sense than we can of the meaning of the still legible but, as we mentioned a moment ago, seemingly meaningless 'dægisæf' at the junction of the upper and lower stones and, on the *very top* of the crosshead, 'æfauœþo'. It seems that the 'very top' of what Bainbrigg considered notable did not include the pale red upper stone or cross. Why? We doubt it was a case of ignoring some of what was worthy of note – Bainbrigg had, after all, decided that what was worthy of note were the 'fluent letters' that were 'foreign' to him – or of not being able to see the runes on the upper stone – the 'dægisæf' runes are, after all, very clear – but that the upper stone or 'cross' was not notable. Why? The most obvious answer is that it wasn't there to be seen and noted for, by definition, an 'apex' is the highest or culminating point, the narrowed or pointed uppermost part of something. As he described and represented it, 'literae transversae' and 'literae perpendiculares ab apice ad basim', the very top of the monument coincided with the very top of the column. Apparently, Bainbrigg saw a column, which he referred to as a 'cross'. And in this respect he was doing something that was and is neither unique nor unusual.[79]

You may find this explanation (which reads nothing into Bainbrigg's note that is not there to be read) unconvincing, but Murray's Quire could not have accommodated the monument as it now is, over 19 feet high: nor, and this is more significant in that the height of the Quire could have been changed, given the available floor area, could the monument have been toppled in it. Unless, of course, it was sunk, as it was sunk by Duncan in the manse garden, up to its flared set-offs, and had a height of about 15 feet 6 inches.[80] In which case, it is still far from clear why Bainbrigg accounted for the monument in the way he did. As we said in our introduction, sometimes it is very difficult to establish even a simple 'fact' beyond question.

William Nicolson who, in 1697 after his first visit to Ruthwell, made when he was Archdeacon but not yet Bishop of Carlisle, wrote in a letter to his friend Edward Lhwyd, keeper of the Ashmolean Museum, Oxford, that 'I took a progress (last week) into Scotland to view a famous cross in a church near Dumfries. I was surprised with the inscriptions, very fair and legible on all its four sides. They were Latin and Runic intermixed.'[81] These inscriptions were eventually published in 1703 by George Hickes as illustrations for his *Linguarum Veterum Septentrionalium Thesaurus Grammatico-Criticus et Archaeologicus* (Fig. 44).[82] Nicolson went expecting to see a 'cross' but what he saw was not a cross. He saw only the top fragment of the pale pinkish-grey lower stone that, by then, must been removed from Murray's Quire to the body of the church. Nicolson's letter may provide us with textual confirmation of the conjecture that Murray's Quire was remodelled or rebuilt some time before 1687. Work on the Quire would have provided an opportunity to remove at least the upper fragment of the monument – the part that could most easily be moved – to the body of the church. Nicolson did not see the other fragment of the lower stone until he returned to Ruthwell with three companions in July 1704, the year after the publication of *Linguarum Veterum Septentrionalium Thesaurus Grammatico-Criticus*, to compare his 'Transcriptions (once more) with the Original'.[83] This time, thanks to the parish clerk, who brought him the key to the church, he was able to see that bit of the monument that was still embedded in the floor of Murray's Quire.[84] Nicolson recorded this visit in his diary, 5 July, wherein he gave a description of the fragment in Murray's Quire and noted the words 'ET.INGRESSVS. ANGELVS' in the inscription around the Annunciation scene carved on its east side, 'y[t] side w[ch] lay to view', but the stone was 'so clumsy and unwieldy' that they 'could not (wth out Crows or Levers) remove it'.[85] Having seen the upper fragment of the lower stone in the church and 'some lesser pieces, which seem to have been in y[e] middle', which he found 'thrown under Thoughstones in y[e] Church-yard', he referred to the fragment in Murray's Quire as the 'heavy pedestal' of the 'Cross'.

Though Nicolson's letter of 1697 has him going to the church at Ruthwell to see a cross and finding a fragment that he described as a cross, other accounts represent things differently. The second English translation, with additional materials, of *Camden's Britannia* by Edmund Gibson, published in 1695, for example, tells us that the 'most ancient monument remarkable hereabouts is St. *Ruth's* Church, where is a Pillar curiously engraven; with some Inscription upon it'.[86] This was the first mention of the monument in the *Britannia*. Dr George Archibald's 'Account of the Curiosities at Dumfries', which was written to a third party in response to an advertisement and a series of queries that were circulated throughout Scotland in 1682 by Sir Robert Sibbald, Geographer Royal, for the purpose of gathering information for a *Scottish Atlas*, also describes the monument as a pillar: 'Here is also in this County, St. Ruths Church, called Ruthwall, where lyes a Monument broken in two pieces, which was a Pillar quadrangle of stone, reaching from the bottom of the Church unto the roof.'[87] This account, which must have been written within a few years of the advertisement, goes on to describe the west side of the upper fragment of the pale pinkish-grey lower stone, which we assume was lying on the floor and could not be examined on all four sides. Perhaps Archibald couldn't get into Murray's Quire, not yet added to the church, to examine the other fragment of the pale pinkish-grey lower stone. Archibald, the son of the minister of Dunscore, about twenty miles north-west of Ruthwell above Dumfries, was general practitioner in Dumfries from about 1688 until his death in 1715.[88] We wonder, when he described the monument as a 'Pillar ... reaching from the bottom of the Church unto the roof', whether he was giving as accurate as possible description of what seemed to be the case or if he really knew what the monument was before it was toppled. W. Hamilton of Orbeston saw the fragments otherwise. In a note that he gave to Walter Macfarlane in 1695 he mentions both fragments of the lower stone: 'A Broken Cross in the Revel Church. The Length 4 foot three inches. Breadth at top one foot three Inches; at bottom 1 foot and six Inches. The Pedestal in Murray's Quire, hath the bottome of the Inscriptions with some few more Images on the Latin side.'[89] Of course, what Hamilton saw was not a cross but two fragments of stone that he referred to as a cross.

Of the accounts that post-date Nicolson's, Alexander Gordon's *Itinerarium Septentrionale* of 1726 refers to the monument as an 'obelisk' that 'lies flat on the ground within the Church', which 'some think was originally of one entire stone, but is now broken into three parts'. Because the base fragment of the pale pinkish-grey lower stone was still immovable in Murray's Quire, Gordon managed to provide illustrations (Figs 45 and 46) – very poor illustrations – only of the upper fragment of the lower stone.[90] The plate showing the west and east sides is inscribed for the Honourable David Murray, Fifth Viscount Stormont.[91] It is possible that the third fragment mentioned by Gordon was one of the 'lesser pieces' that Nicolson had seen in 1704 thrown under throughstones in the churchyard. It wasn't until Thomas Pennant visited Ruthwell in 1772 and recorded what he saw in his *A Tour in Scotland and Voyage to the Hebrides* of 1774, that any fragments definitely of the pale red upper stone entered published discourse.[92] Pennant saw two fragments of this stone: the very top fragment 'on each opposite side an eagle, neatly cut in relief'; and the base fragment with 'the lower part of a human figure, in long vestments, with his foot on a pair of small globes'. At the time of his visit, the largest fragment of the pale pinkish-grey lower stone was still 'buried beneath the floor of the church', which is to say Murray's Quire. Pennant, perhaps following Gordon, saw the monument as broken into three pieces. He also referred to it as an 'obelisk' but associated only one of the smaller fragments with it, the fragment with an eagle on each side. Adam Mansfeldt de Cardonnell-Lawson, who visited Ruthwell in 1788 to make the drawings from which to produce the engravings that would illustrate the monument in Gough's *Vetusta Monumenta* (Figs 47 and 48), 1789, followed either Gordon or Pennant or both when, changing their dimensions, he arranged the fragments in the shape of an obelisk.[93]

While it is reasonable when one sees an object that is actually in the shape of a cross to maintain that a cross *is* what one sees, it is not so reasonable, when one sees an object that does not have the shape of a cross to maintain that what one sees *is* a cross. And while it might be reasonable when one sees an object that has the shape of a column to *see* it *as* having once been a cross or as having once been intended to be *seen* and understood *as* a cross, it is not so reasonable when one sees an object that very definitely has the shape of a cross to *see* it *as* a column. Though there are few persons who would admit to *seeing* crosses *as* columns, there are many who tend to *see* columns *as* crosses, rather than as objects that may or may not once have been crosses. These are matters of 'seeing ... as', which we will return to in the next chapter. Here, it is important only to stress that nothing in the foregoing puzzling about what kind of monument was demolished in 1642 should be taken for an argument that there was not once an Anglo-Saxon monument – or, indeed, several Anglo-Saxon monuments – in the shape of a cross at Ruthwell.

The first step in any scientific or quasi-scientific discourse is that of defining its object. Art history concerned with the Ruthwell monument must be clear as to what its material object of study is and hold to the differences between the lower and upper stones. Which is to say that it ought to be clear as to what kind of object Duncan put together between 1802 and 1823, first as a column of pale pinkish-grey sandstone and subsequently, after a fifth fragment of the pale red upper stone came to light whilst digging a grave, as a cross:[94] an object that, mindful of its 'inconsistencies' and 'peculiarities', he saw not as a 'cross' but as a 'monument' that he had erected 'in the shape of a cross'. Duncan was in no doubt: the monument in his garden was not ontologically secure as a 'cross'.

Inconsistencies and peculiarities there are: inconsistencies and peculiarities that are of the Ruthwell monument, and of the discourse that has determined our knowledge of it. It is easy to overlook these *as if* they are not there or, if seen, to assimilate them to the gestalt of a long-established standard and organising principle governing perception and *see* them *as* the 'Ruthwell Cross'. These inconsistencies and peculiarities have to be taken as worthy of note and attended to because, in a very real way, they are what constitute our material object of study – the Ruthwell monument: column *and* cross.

The common Tradition of ye Original of this stone is this ... (William Nicolson, 'Bishop Nicolson's Diaries', 5 July 1704)[95]

Since the development of 'objective history' and the techniques, narrative forms and institutions that are based in the need to produce, disseminate and authenticate it, the idea of a 'common tradition' has become devalued.[96] Think of the common tradition of the Ruthwell monument as an invention based on insubstantial evidence or as a product of enthusiasm and imagination more than knowledge, and it needn't be taken seriously: it isn't history; it's fiction. And regarded as fictional and irrational, it's brought into the narrative of the seemingly non-fictional, rational, objective history of the monument only to be dismissed.[97]

Given the growth of interest in the study of oral history and the analysis of oral traditions it hardly seems legitimate to oppose 'common tradition' to 'objective history'.[98] The two kinds of history may have different forms and may be dispersed in different ways but, in the case of the Ruthwell monument, they seem to be trying to make sense of the same actual, material object. Each history effects an idea of that object according to its different interests and competences drawing on the resources available in its culture. Common tradition and objective history are different kinds of narrative recollecting, transforming and using the past. Each one is able to see and explain certain things and not others; and each one makes decisions about what should be and should not be remembered. The one is not necessarily more or less fictional than the other. As one commentator pointed out forty years ago, 'by its very structure and without there being any need to appeal to the substance of the content, historical discourse is essentially an ideological elaboration or, to be more specific, an imaginary elaboration'.[99] Our point is simply that the common tradition of the Ruthwell monument has to be taken seriously as one of several kinds of historical discourse and that it *is* possible to put that kind of stress on it.

Once again we are indebted to Nicolson, who came across the tradition of the monument on each of his two trips to Ruthwell. After the first trip in April 1697, in the second of two letters he wrote about the monument, he noted

that: 'They have a long traditional legend about its being brought thither from the sea-shore, not far-distant.'[100] On his second trip, in 1704, he compared the transcriptions he'd made of the inscriptions on his previous visit against the originals; located as many fragments of the monument as he could – this was when he found 'some lesser pieces ... thrown under Throughstones' – and measured them; and recorded more of the monument's history.

> The common Tradition of ye Original of this stone is this: It was found, letter'd and entire, in a Stone-Quarry on this Shore (a good way within ye Sea-mark) call'd Rough-Scarr. Here it had lain long admir'd, when (in a Dream) a neighbouring Labourer was directed to yoke four Heifers of a certain Widow y^t liv'd near him; and, where they stop'd with y^ir Burthen, there to slack his Team, erect ye Cross & build a Church over it: All which was done accordingly. I wonder'd to see a Company of Modern Presbyterians (as ye present parishioners profess y^mselves to be) so steady in this Faith; and even to believe, yet farther, y^t the Cross was not altogether so long (at its first erection) as it was afterwards: But that it miraculously grew, like a Tree, till it touched the Roof of the Church.[101]

Our next version of the common tradition was noted by Pennant in 1772:

> Tradition says that the church was built over this obelisk, long after its erection; and as it was reported to have been transported here by angels, it was probably so secured for the same reason as the *santa casa* at Loretto was, least it should take another flight.[102]

Twenty years later in 1792 Craig included what he knew of it in the material he gathered for Sinclair's *Statistical Account*.

> Tradition says, that this obelisk, in remote times, was set up at a place called Priestwoodside near the sea, in order to assist the vulgar, by sensible images, to form some notions of religion, but was drawn from thence by a teem of oxen belonging to a widow, and placed in the church-yard, where it remained till the reformation, when, by Act of the General Assembly, it was ordered to be thrown down and broken, as a remnant of idolatry.[103]

And last there's the version that Duncan recorded in 1833.

> The later history of this remarkable column is not much more indebted to tradition than that of an early date. In Sir John Sinclair's Statistical Account of the parish of Ruthwell, a report is mentioned of its having been set up in remote times, at a place called Priestwoodside (now Priestside), near the sea, from whence it is said to have been drawn by a team of oxen belonging to a widow. This tradition is still common in the parish, with some additional particulars. The pillar is said to have been brought by sea from some distant country, and to have been cast on shore by shipwreck; and while it was in the act of being conveyed in the manner described, into the interior, the tackling is reported to have given way, which was believed, in that superstitious age, to indicate the will of heaven that it was to proceed no farther. It was accordingly erected, if we are to credit the report, on the spot where it fell, and a place of worship was built over it, which became the parish-church of Ruthwell. It is not improbable that this tradition may bear some vague reference to the period when the alteration took place in the form, and perhaps also in the object, of the column, at which time its site may possibly have been changed. It is

remarkable that the remains of an ancient road, founded on piles of wood, leading through a morass to the Priestside (which is a stripe of arable land inclosed between this morass and the shore of the Solway Frith), were in existence within the last thirty or forty years.[104]

Any kind of story is a 'multi-dimensional space in which a variety of writings, none of them original, blend and clash. The text is a tissue of quotations drawn from the innumerable centres of culture.'[105] Some of the commixture that is the common tradition of the Ruthwell monument seems to have been taken from stories about the community of St Cuthbert and its wanderings through Northumbria after the Viking raid on Lindisfarne in 875. These are stories about a monastery on the move along with the relics and other things that were its most precious possessions: an aborted journey by boat down the Solway; the loss of a relic overboard and its later recovery from the tidal flat off Whithorn; the refusal of the cart carrying the body of the saint to move; and, at the end, the erection of a broken and repaired cross that had travelled with the relics.[106] The correspondence between these stories and the common tradition of the Ruthwell monument seems hardly coincidental, which is not to say that we must take it as necessarily intentional.

When trying to understand the tradition's value as historical discourse, we should put aside the stories that seem to have been taken from the wanderings of St Cuthbert's community for the more or less obvious devices that provide and elaborate its narrative structure. Likewise the references to divine intervention (but perhaps not the references to accident or chance, for accidents do happen). We should also put aside those details that are superfluous in relation to the narrative's predictive function and are there only to effect its realism: the 'neighbouring labourer'; the 'widow'; and the 'four heifers' or 'team of oxen'.[107] Once we have done that, we're left with the story of an object – 'this stone', 'this obelisk', 'this remarkable column' – that travelled down the Solway and was first seen at Rough-Scarr or was first located at Priestwoodside, now Priestside. It is very unlikely that the monument was transported ready-made, carved and inscribed but, as we have seen, it is possible that undressed or dressed stone could have been transported down the Solway for part of its journey to Ruthwell. The stone for the monument, or the monument itself, would then have been transported inland and erected, or re-erected, where its journey ended. A church was built over the monument and, once inside, the monument's height increased till it almost touched the roof. It's a story that fits very well with what we know about the possible provenance of the stone and what we've surmised about the monument's relation with Murray's Quire and the church. More than that, the common tradition gives us two sites to think about: Rough-Scarr and Priestside (Col. Plates II and III).

The parish of Ruthwell is about five and a half miles long east-south-east; its greatest breadth is about three miles east–west: an area of about thirteen square miles. Its surface is generally flat, nowhere rising to more than 80 or 90 feet above sea level. At the coast, the sea-beach of mud and sand extends as inter-tidal flat far into and seemingly across the Solway Firth to the Cumbrian shore – the Solway was, and perhaps is still, fordable between Annan and Bowness; that's the route that Nicolson took when he visited Ruthwell in 1704.[108] A considerable tract in the west of the parish, named Priestside Bank, is made up of this mud and sand. Priestside Bank extends towards the estuary of the River Annan in the east and is separated from Blackshaw Bank and the parish of Caerlaverock in the west by the Channel of Lochar Water. Rough-Scarr, about one and a half miles out on Priestside Bank, marks the confluence of the Channel of Lochar Water and the Channel of the River Eden. At the shoreline, the mud and sand of Priestside Bank becomes salt marsh. Beyond the shoreline, between it and Ruthwell Church, almost level with the sea and extending west to the River Nith, north from there to Locharbriggs, and to the east almost as far as the estuary of the River Annan, is an area of morass, black top and bog, known in Ruthwell and in the parish of Cummertrees as Priestside Flow and, more generally, as Lochar Moss. The Lochar Water divides Lochar Moss lengthways into nearly equal parts. Once good for grouse and peat, Priestside Flow's recent history has been one of various attempts, successful and unsuccessful, to drain and claim it for arable and pasture.

Sinclair's *Statistical Account* recorded the common tradition of Lochar Moss, since confirmed by geological survey. The area was first covered with wood, which was then overflowed by the sea and made so deep as to be navigable to nearly its head at Tinwald; it then became choked with silt, mud and aquatic vegetation, till it became successively a marsh and a bog.[109] The tradition was preserved in the following couplet:

> First a wood, and next a sea,
> Now a moss, and ever will be.[110]

Beneath the morass is a stratum of sea-sand, occasionally mixed with shells and other marine deposits. From this stratum have been dug 'sometimes boats, almost entire, with anchors, cables, and oars'.[111] Trees have been found in the peat above the sea-sand: chiefly fir, but also oak, birch and hazel (with their nuts and husks); it is said that timber from several of these trees was worked by carpenters and that, cut into small pieces, it made fine kindling.[112]

Rough-Scarr, 'a good way within yᵉ sea-mark', must once have been sufficiently conspicuous to be used by sailors as a guide or warning in navigation. The area has not been surveyed: it might be made up of boulders washed out of the clay beneath the mud and sand, or it might be an outcrop of rock; if it's the latter the stone is likely New Red Triassic Sandstone, not Carboniferous Sandstone. We think it unlikely that anything was ever quarried at Rough-Scarr; and if anything travelling on the Solway arrived there, it would have been by way of negligence or accident not by intention.

Priestside is a narrow strip of land enclosed between the shoreline and the morass of Priestside Flow. It is about one and a half miles south of Ruthwell church and about equal distant between the church and Rough-Scarr. It has become possible to construct buildings on it, more in the last eighty years or so, during which time it has been made increasingly suitable for agriculture and forestry. One common tradition cites Priestside as an ancient place of salt working: Robert the Bruce is said to have granted the people in the area a charter to make salt, duty free; it's not known if the salt works were there in the early Middle Ages, or earlier.[113] Any stone transported on the Solway could have come ashore intentionally on the high tide at Priestside.

If the stone or the monument were once at Priestside, transporting it across the morass would have presented certain difficulties. Even on a wagon pulled by four heifers or a team of oxen it would have got bogged down. We suppose that it could have been moved in winter when the ground was frozen; or it could have been moved over a road. And *if* there were a road, perhaps it was like the 'lately discovered ... singular road through a morass' that Pennant recorded in 1772. This was 'made of wood, consisting of split oak planks, eight feet long, fastened down by long pins or stakes, driven through the boards into the earth. It was found out by digging of peat, and at that time lay six feet beneath the surface. It pointed towards the sea, and in old times was the road to it; but no tradition remains of the place it came from.'[114] We wonder whether the line of this road, deep in the peat, bore any relation to 'the remains of an ancient road, founded on piles of wood, leading through a morass to Priestside' that Duncan associated with the common tradition of the monument and which was in existence at the beginning of the nineteenth century.[115]

If the stone or the monument were transported across the morass over a corduroy road of the kind described by Pennant and Duncan, it would have passed by the, as yet, unexcavated Roman temporary fort (NGR 102 677) midway between Priestside and the site of Ruthwell church. The fort was located just above the shore where ditches could be dug and foundations established in the boulder clay or till. It was one of a line of military bases along the north shore of the Solway that terminated at a permanent fort at Lantonside on the estuary of the River Nith.[116] Unlike those persons who produced and first used the monument at Bewcastle, whoever produced the Ruthwell monument chose not to locate it within whatever traces remained of this Roman fort. Nor did they locate it inside the other place in the immediate area that is known to have pre-existed it. This seems to have been a large defended ring enclosure, probably contemporaneous with the period of Roman occupation, which was used for iron working.[117] Whether the enclosure was still used or not, the stone or monument, whether by intention or accident, came to its journey's end just outside it. The monument was erected there. A church was built over it. Or it was in the churchyard till it was demolished. Or it was in a building that was a place of worship that became the parish church.

What the common tradition gives us, albeit by appropriating other traditions and other memories, is a history of what might have been real changes in the circumstances of the monument's production and use. It also provides us with a history of the monument's continual displacement, of its lack of place. Even now, an 'idolatrous monument' back in the Church of Scotland whence it was abolished; tolerated; misaligned. The monument seems always to have been out of place, or not quite in place, and to have never quite made a place. In whatever way we explain its circumstances of production and whatever it may have meant to those persons who first used it, the Ruthwell monument is a peculiarly homeless representation.

Amongst those contemporary scholars of Anglo-Saxon stone sculpture who have concerned themselves with it, Robert B. K. Stevenson was convinced that the 'Ruthwell Cross' was a monument that, if it had not been transported from one place to another, had been, as he put it, 'heightened'.[118] Stevenson seems not to have been interested in the common tradition but he was very interested in the monument's base, which as he pointed out had been more or less completely ignored except for consideration of the Crucifixion panel (Fig. 66) on its east side. Stevenson was puzzled by the way that the Ruthwell designer separated off the base distinctly by a strong outward flare at the sides of the shaft immediately above it, thus effecting what he considered to be an awkward transition from base to shaft. He also wondered whether, with the exception of the Crucifixion panel, which he thought might have been abandoned unfinished, and the stock from which the plant-scroll starts on the north and south sides, the base had ever been carved. He further speculated that the damage caused to the Crucifixion panel might have been accidental rather than deliberate – the work of cattle rather than seventeenth-century iconoclasts. He considered that the crucifixion was subordinately positioned and that it made more sense when seen as a work of the late ninth century, which made it unexpected at the believed date. In other words, he was puzzled as to how the base related to the shaft, and to the monument as a whole, in terms of its form, content and condition. It didn't add up. In much the same vein as Elizabeth Coatsworth, who argued 'there is at least the possibility that the lower portion of the cross was utilised at a different date', Stevenson concluded that it

> had originally a roughly flaked bulbous base, intended to be entirely sunk in the ground ... After a while the Ruthwell cross was heightened by squaring off the base and rounding its corners, all by levelling the surfaces, least success-fully at the back where there had been more hollows. The very bottom was chiselled to produce a tenon 9 inches (23 cm) high and over a foot (30 cm) wide for insertion into a socket of stone. The tenon is what is now sunk in the concrete floor in the church, as the sculptor [J. W. Dods] who re-erected the cross in 1887 has recorded.[119]

The evidence provided by the base and the transition from base to shaft suggested to Stevenson that the column was originally buried up to its outward flares, much as Duncan set it up in his garden (Figs 49 and 50), and that subsequently it was raised and then carved with a representation of the crucifixion. In view of our discussion of the monument's inconsistencies and peculiarities, and mindful of how we have always to keep sight of a column and a cross, it seems to make more sense to see the Ruthwell monument as originally having been a column that was sunk into the ground; that was then raised and amended with the addition of a crucifixion scene; at which time or subsequently it was further amended with the addition of a cross-head (Figs 70 and 71). *If* this is the history of the Ruthwell monument, then Duncan's account is more or less correct and the common tradition has been telling its history more or less accurately for a very long time.

> The joint has been made in the most approved Masonic form with a socket and tongue. (John W. Dods, Dumfries 14 Feb 1913)[120]

A good deal rests on what John W. Dods did or did not do when he took apart Duncan's 'remarkable monument in the shape of a cross' and moved it into the church in 1887. We can surmise something of this from the contents of a letter he sent in reply to some enquiries from J. K. Hewison in 1913. Not all the letter is relevant here, only the first of its eight pages:

> I was at Ruthwell ye*ster*day (13th. The Cross has originally been made in two pieces the joint is shown on the enclosed sketch. The shaft or lower section is fully 12 feet in height. The upper or Cross section is about 6.3 in height. The joint has been made in the most approved Masonic form with a socket and tongue.

Thus

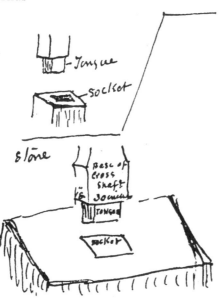

The shaft of Cross is was fixed by me in the same manner into a base block below the floor line. I have no doubt the cross originally would be fixed into a large flate base stone like a step standing a few inches above the ground line thus

In June 1912, Hewison had visited Ruthwell in the company of Dods and eight months later, in the last stages of completing his book *The Runic Roods of Ruthwell and Bewcastle with a Short History of the Cross and Crucifix in Scotland*, had written to Dods requesting information about the Ruthwell monument that would help him establish that it was originally a wheel-head cross.[121] Since Dods thought that the monument showed no signs of ever having had a wheel cross-head, most of what he wrote went against what Hewison hoped for.

As the references in Dods's letter make clear, it was accompanied by several sketches on tracing paper. One of these tracings is of special interest to us. It may be the 'enclosed sketch' mentioned in the first sentence (though that could also refer to the sketch in the body of the text). Most likely it is the drawing (Fig. 52) that 'will measure to 1 inch scale' where 'the separate stones belonging to the original cross' are numbered 1–5 'with blue pencil', and which shows the breaks, the 'original joint tongued in' between 'the shaft or lower section' and 'the upper or cross section', and the tongue at the base of the lower stone lodged in a socket below the floor of the church.

Dods's drawing, which, contrary to what his note says, is not always to scale, measures the Ruthwell monument, as he reconstructed it, 17 feet 6 inches above ground. He points out that it was 'originally in 2 pieces', and assumes that the upper stone, as Duncan had constructed it, with its various 'packing pieces', was originally 'one piece 6´ 3"', comprising the visible cross of 5 feet 6 inches and a concealed tongue of 9 inches. The shaft or column measures above ground 'fully 12 feet': the base fragment from ground '7 feet to Break'. We measure it about 7 feet 2½ inches to the break, but measurements depend on whether the high point or low point of the fracture is taken as the limit.

We should now consider the tongue at the base of the column, which secures it and keeps the whole monument upright. The hard evidence is hidden, of course. We must rely on what the antiquarians recorded. De Cardonnell, who visited Ruthwell in 1788, was the first person to account for this fragment after it had been prised free from the floor in Murray's Quire. Unfortunately, his engravings (Figs 47 and 48) in Gough's *Vetusta Monumenta*, 1789, are so abbreviated that they show nothing of what was at its base. Both Nicolson and Duncan measured this fragment. Nicolson reckoned it was 'about two yards & a half long', and Duncan 'about seven feet eleven inches'.[122] Neither of them suggested that it was fashioned with a tongue. If it were there, we feel sure that Duncan would have mentioned it in his account and perhaps taken advantage of it when he erected the monument in his garden.

Given that the bottom fragment of the pinkish-grey lower stone now measures about 7 feet 2½ inches from floor to break, Dods must have cut away stone from its base sufficient to make a tongue with a length of between 4 and 9 inches. That Duncan's 'about seven feet eleven inches' was correct and that Dods did, indeed, cut away the stone to make a tongue of nine inches seems to be confirmed by this entry in Reverend James McFarlan's pocket book, 25 August 1887:

> The Cross completed in its new site by Mr. Dods, Dumfries :–
> Complete height,   18 feet, 1 inch.
> In socket,   9 inches.
> It stands 17 ft. 4 inches, showing all that was originally shown on the base. It stood before, 15 ft. 6 inches from the grass.[123]

McFarlan was the minister who, having gained the consent of the heritors and presbytery and raised the necessary money, was responsible for adding the semi-circular apse to the north side of the church and for bringing the cross into it as an ancient monument. He may have got his figures from Dods and but he could easily have taken them for himself.

A correction that Dods made to his letter might be taken to corroborate that he cut away stone from the base of the column. He seems to want to distinguish the joint between the column and the cross from the tongue by which the column is fixed into the floor. He first wrote: 'The cross has originally been made in two pieces the joint is shown on the enclosed sketch ... The joint has been made in the most approved Masonic form with a tongue and socket ... The shaft of [the] cross is fixed in the same manner into a base block below the floor line.' He then changed 'is fixed' to 'was fixed', and inserted 'by me' so that the sentence read: 'The shaft of [the] cross was fixed by me into a base block below the floor line.' It is germane that no mention is made of a base-block or fragments of a base-block – for it would surely have come to light when the monument was toppled – by any of the seventeenth- and eighteenth-century antiquaries.

Then there's the joint between the column and the cross. Again, the hard evidence is hidden. Neither Dods's letter or its intratextual sketch nor the scale drawing makes it clear whether the 'original joint tongued in', which keeps the column and the cross together, was an 'original joint tongued in' by Anglo-Saxon masons or an 'original joint tongued in' by Duncan's mason when he erected the monument in the garden or by Dods when he moved it into the church. Dods's use of the past progressive 'has been made' makes an ambiguity we could well do without. It is a construction he seems to favour, almost a speech-pattern: '[t]he breaking of the lower shaft & the upper section has been caused'; '[a]nother argument I would use which bears great weight with me in saying it has not been a wheel cross is'; '[a]ll the stones the cross has been made from is real sandstone'. When he writes 'the cross has originally been made in two pieces', he means that the cross was originally made of two pieces of stone. But when he writes that the joint between the column and the cross 'has been made in the most approved Masonic form with a socket and a tongue', does he mean that the joint was originally made that way or that he himself made it that way? Whichever it was, he writes 'the shaft of [the] cross was fixed by me in the same manner into a base block below the floor line'. And that joint must have been Dods's work. We wonder whether the tongue and socket joint between the column and the cross was Dods's work also.

W. Hamilton, who visited Ruthwell in or before 1695, measured the upper fragment of the lower stone but made no mention of a socket in it.[124] Nor did Richard Pococke, Bishop of Meath, who measured both fragments when he visited Ruthwell in 1760.[125] Thomas Pennant, who visited Ruthwell in 1772, seems to record a socket in the top of the upper fragment of the pinkish-grey lower stone but makes no mention of a tongue at the base of the fragment of the pale red upper stone, which, as we've seen, he described as decorated 'with Saxon letters round the lower part of a human figure, in long vestments, with his foot on a pair of small globes', and which he didn't associate with the monument.[126] De Cardonnell's engravings of the west and east sides of the monument seem to show a tongue at the base of the fragment carved with the feet on globes but his engravings of the north and south sides do not. Perhaps the most one can say with any certainty is that, at the moment a socket in the top of the pale pinkish-grey lower stone and a tongue at the base of the fragment of the pale red upper stone that is carved with the feet on globes seem to come in place, they immediately disappear.

Assuming that, when he drew the fragments at Ruthwell, what de Cardonnell *saw* and represented *as* a tongue *was* a tongue, it would not have been intact. According to Duncan's scale drawing, the fragment carved with the feet on globes measures on its west side about 1 foot and on its east side about 9 inches. Dods's scale drawing gives this fragment a tongue with a width of about 9 inches and a length of 9 inches. Unlike his drawing of the tongue at the base of the column, which is done with straight lines like the rest of the drawing and measures to scale, his drawing of the tongue and socket between the column and the cross does not measure to scale and is drawn with a wavy line, a bit like that used to indicate the break in the pale pinkish-grey lower stone. Dods seems to have added the wavy line as an afterthought by way of giving a bit more detail to make the whole drawing more or less useful for Hewison. Its graphic difference might be significant. If the fragment carved with the feet on globes ever possessed a tongue it may have needed some extra jointing to provide sufficient support for the other stones, ancient and modern, that Duncan assembled above and around it. We wonder why or whether it needed a tongue of the same size as that which keeps the whole monument upright.

Comparing the photographs that J. Rutherford took of the monument in the manse garden with what it looks like today in the church, one can see that, during the process of taking it apart and reconstructing it, the monument became misaligned around the join between the column and the cross. Helen McFarlan, Reverend James McFarlan's wife, has given us a vivid eyewitness account of its relocation.

> The skill and ingenuity of Dr. Henry Duncan, in piecing together the many fragments called forth admiration and grateful remembrance, as they were one by one detached and laid carefully on the grass ... Next day, the socket having been prepared, and a gentle slope arranged towards it, the base of the Cross – the large block which forms the lower half of it – was wheeled round into position. The rope, fastened around the stone, was passed over a pulley and grasped by men inside the church, the minister and his boys laying hold of it too ... At a given signal the rope was pulled with a will, the grand old block rose forwards, and, guided by the sculptor's hand, slid unscathed into its resting-place.
>
> A scaffolding was quickly erected, and the other parts of the monument restored to their places.[127]

It seems that when he restored the fragments to their previous positions, Dods was unable to bring everything together as neatly as had Duncan's mason. He couldn't replicate either the fit or the good line that can be seen in Rutherford's photographs. Dods placed the fragment carved with the feet on globes on top of the column, and then stacked the packing pieces around it, in such a way that everything is noticeably out of true and shifted to one side. Duncan's drawing of the monument in *Archaeologia Scotica* is certainly inaccurate and misleading in several respects but it does not, as some commentators have claimed, amend this misalignment for the misalignment was not part of his construction.

Some time before 1858, Hannah Mary Wright, the daughter of Reverend H. W. Wright, Vicar of St John's Newcastle-upon-Tyne, visited Ruthwell to see the monument. Her thoughts on it, a delicate almost hesitant pencil sketch of it, perhaps her own, together with some other items, including her own translation of *The Dream of the Rood*, were published posthumously in commemoration of her as *The Ruthwell Cross and Other Remains of the Late Hannah Mary Wright* in 1873. When she saw it, the monument was, of course, sunk up to its outward flares in the garden. Perhaps she'd spoken to Duncan's successor about it, or to someone who knew how Duncan and his mason had put it together. No matter who told her, she recorded that when Duncan 'had it ... removed to his garden ... he ordered the cross to be hollowed, and an iron stem inserted throughout its length'.[128] Surely not 'throughout its length' but possibly where the fragment of the pale red upper stone rested on top of the pinkish-grey lower stone – with possibly another iron stem inserted across the break in that lower stone. A joint like that would make sense. Hardly something of which Dods would have approved but not altogether contrary to the way that some Anglo-Saxon monuments seem to have been jointed.[129] *If* that was how Duncan's mason jointed the monument, Dods would have had to remove at least the iron stem between the column and the cross when he took them apart.

There is something obscure and intractable at this part of the Ruthwell monument. We truly don't know how it was first jointed or when it was first jointed. Or if the pinkish-grey lower stone and pale red upper stone, the column and the cross that make the monument what it is, were ever joined to each other before Duncan's mason put them together and Dods put them together again. Nevertheless, though we can't see it, we can be sure about the tongue at the base. That must have been added in the nineteenth century by cutting away stone from the original monument, the first freestanding 'ancient monument' of Scotland. Dods made the tongue at the base of the lower stone, and this knowledge affects how we should think about the joint between the column and the cross. We guess that Dods, because he was prepared to cut away the lower stone in the way he did, would also have been prepared to make a joint between the upper and lower stones that was in some way different from the joint that Duncan's mason had made, and different from whatever may or may not have been there before that. *If* this guess is correct then Dods followed the very precedent that he himself had established when he 'fixed the shaft ... in the same manner into a base block below the floor line'. And *if* that is, indeed, how the Ruthwell monument's lower stone and upper stone became secured in history, with two nineteenth-century joints made 'in the most approved Masonic form', we will, almost certainly, never know their full measure. Which is to say that when Dods secured Duncan's two stones, the pinkish-grey lower stone and the pale red upper stone, the *column* and the *cross*, together with all the packing pieces, in the church, he secured not only the Ruthwell monument's material resistance to history but also its resistance to theory.

3

Style, and seeing ... as[1]

⌘

BY STYLE is meant the constant form – and sometimes the constant elements, qualities and expression – in the art of individual or group. The term is also applied to the whole activity of an individual or society, as in speaking of a 'life-style' or the 'style of a civilisation'. (Meyer Schapiro, 'Style')[2]

A book about Anglo-Saxon stone sculpture will inevitably engage with style. It is as unavoidable as it is questionable. Though it has long been the art historian's principal way of selecting and shaping the history of art, its use-value bears little systematic relation to its value in cognition. One along with several characteristically unsettling aspects of the now outdated but still fecund modern texts that laid the foundations for studying Anglo-Saxon stone sculpture of the pre-Norman age is that, though their authors were inclined to use the idea of style to denote and group, identify and order, shape and limit, interpret and explain their objects of study, they all too frequently were at odds with each other as to which of those objects exemplified the same style. This is especially so with regard to the Ruthwell and Bewcastle monuments, which have been variously seen as exemplifying the same style, or two tendencies or variations within a style, or different styles.[3] So, what are scholars doing when they work with style? What unacknowledged or unexplained assumptions are they appropriating and organising? To what effect? And what can we make of it?

Meyer Schapiro's 'Style' of 1953 is still the most judicious, inclusive and committed consideration of style that we have.[4] As Schapiro defines it, teasing out the related concepts that inhere it, style refers to the constant, regular, stable, invariable, unvarying, unchanging form or external shape of an intentional object or to the way its parts are arranged; sometimes it refers to the constant elements, component parts or motifs of form and the way they've been combined; and sometimes it refers to the qualities – the characteristic distinguishing features, excellence or distinctive effect – of form. Style might also be used refer to the actual material from which the constant form has been made, or to the technique by which it has been made, or to subject matter. Over and above that, we deploy the idea of style when we refer to the entire material and mental production of an individual or a society, an epoch defined by a dominant mode of production or an individual's production within it.

In the discussion that follows this definition, Schapiro attends to the ways in which the idea of style has been appropriated as an aid to interpretation and explanation by the archaeologist, the historian of art, the synthesising historian of culture and the critic of art or literature. As used by the critic, style is a value term, a standard of quality and a measure of accomplishment. The historian of culture regards style as the representation of a whole way of life, the visible sign of a society's unity, of its sense and sensibility. The art historian regards it as a necessary aid to interpretation and explanation and the object of interpretation and explanation. He or she attends to the way a style comes into being, changes and develops, and uses it to allocate a particular object to a particular time and place and to track the relations of association between it and other objects in other spaces. Above all, the art historian regards style as an expression of the state of mind of an individual artist and as a representation of the ideas, conceptions and consciousness of a group of artists. As understood by the archaeologist, style is exemplified in a fragment, in a bit of motif or pattern, material or technique, and so on, that is taken as a synecdoche of the absent whole and used to situate that whole in a general or specific time and place and in relation to others of its kind.

The assumption that there will be only one or a limited range of styles at any given time or place is, Schapiro points out, common to all these ways of using the idea of style. There's a connection between a style and a period of time: objects in a style that seems out of time are usually explained as survivals or revivals; objects in a style that seems out of place are usually explained by reference to trade or migration. It's in this way that style is used to establish the time and place of origin of an object. Given that the desire to locate the 'origin' of something must necessarily be unsatisfied, the main problem for the art historian who is committed to using style is how to move from identifying and describing the constant form, its materials and techniques, elements and qualities, themes and expression, to explaining how it might relate to and represent its historically and culturally specific moment of production. Few art historians, especially those concerned with Anglo-Saxon stone sculpture, manage to make this move.[5]

Modern scholarship of Anglo-Saxon stone sculpture can be said to have begun in 1927 with the publication of W. G. Collingwood's *Northumbrian Crosses of the Pre-Norman Age*. It was in this book that Collingwood tried to locate the origin of the freestanding 'tall stone cross', the 'ordinary type of stone cross, that with a rectangular section',[6] 'carved with ornament and showing a cross-head standing free against the sky', which he regarded as a 'Northumbrian invention';[7] this he did by deploying style understood as constant form and constant activity, the cross and the 'stone cutter's craft'.[8] His aim, as stated in the preface, was 'to consider ancient styles as phases of a process and to place the examples in series'.[9] Although Collingwood thought that detailed studies of individual monuments, or the 'more famous' of them, were valuable, and 'descriptive catalogues' also, because they provided 'material for classification', his focus was on the 'general character' of a monument and 'typology'.[10] What was required was 'a corpus of the whole body of known fragments'.[11] Scholars would not have done all that they could do until the 'classes' had been formed and 'then connected into some reasonable scheme'.[12] In order to produce the classes and put them in connection and series, 'science' and 'history' had to consider 'all the examples'.[13] Collingwood thought that, if this could be done, if all the surviving fragments could be classified and connected in series, the examples would then 'explain themselves'.[14] But this is precisely what they could not do, if only because examples can't explain anything: the most they can do is illustrate general rules, in this case the very principles governing their formation into classes and connection into series – the principles of style.

It is not surprising, then, that when an art historian's practice is based in or structured by the idea of style little or no attention can be given to interpreting and explaining any individual object with regard to the historically and culturally specific circumstances of its production and first use. The protocols and procedures that guide the description, discussion and classification of form are of a different order and kind from those that guide the interpretation and explanation of the meaning of an individual form, element, quality, expression or whatever, which are essentially causal with regard to some psychological or sociological determination. For the art historian whose practice is structured by style, questions about why any individual object was made, about who made it and who first used it, about why the materials and ideas that made it were used and not others, about how it might have been understood by those who made it and those who used it, about how people may have been affected by it and what its cognitive effects might have been, if they are in mind, must give way to judgements about form, precedence and posteriority. This is not to say that the art historian whose practice is based in or structured by style is prevented from engaging with the individual object but, if and when he or she does so, he or she will, almost invariably, see the object in relation to other objects and emphasise formal and technical matters. And if he or she does proceed beyond the description and discussion of form and technique to the identification of the motif, or the combination of motifs that inheres in it and represents something, he or she rarely goes on to explain how any particular form and what it means also represents the 'symbolic values' of the moment of its production and first use, 'the basic attitude of a nation, a period, a class, a religious or philosophical persuasion' that, modified by its producer or producers, is 'condensed' – the word can bear a Freudian load – within it.[15] This is not to say that interpretation and explanation can dispense with matters of form and motif *as if* they are irrelevant or that the study of one monument might not be enhanced by an awareness of others and the possible relationships between them. Nor can it or should it try to avoid or ignore style and the language of style. Of course not. But it can and should avoid being structured by or reduced to an uncritical idea of style.

One common misconception amongst those who deploy style is that a type of form or bit of form, and also a kind of technique, is seen and understood as a possession of an object that, in some way, exists prior to description and interpretation. It was pointed out some time ago that formal patterns, and we would add form itself, are themselves products of interpretation, that there are no such things as form and formal patterns, in the sense necessary to the definition of style.[16] This is not to say that there are no such things as forms and formal patterns. There are; but they are always products of a prior interpretative act. Their identification is always an interpretation: 'description' is always 'discussion'. The art historian who is concerned with style proceeds *as if* by first observing and describing 'facts' – form, formal elements, technique or whatever – and then moves to the discussion or interpretation of those facts. It is important to note the practical fiction here because the art historian is really concerned not with observing facts but with deciding what counts as observable facts, with identifying what is 'worthy of memory' or 'worthy to be noted'. Or to put that another way: rational procedure and language are involved; seeing some thing connects with our knowledge and language; 'observation of x is shaped by prior knowledge of x' and by 'the language or notation used to express what we know, and without which there would be little we could recognise as knowledge'.[17] The scholar of Anglo-Saxon stone sculpture seeing, for example, an upright or recumbent fragment or fragments of what was once a freestanding object, attempts to get his or her observation to cohere in the context of established knowledge and a now extensive vocabulary that is considered necessary to express its form adequately: cross-shafts (angular or round); cross-heads (with arm terminals that are squared, wedge-shaped, or whatever, and pits of various types); tombs and grave markers (upright and recumbent slabs, and so on); architectural sculpture and church furnishings.[18]

Though style is used as an aid to interpreting and explaining how form comes into being and then changes and develops, the circumscribing characteristic of style, according to the conventional wisdom encapsulated in Schapiro's definition, is neither form nor how form must and does develop and change. It is, to the contrary, the perceived constancy, uniformity, regularity, stability, and immutability of form. The idea of style implies a much greater stability of form than can ever be the case. At several points in his essay, Schapiro raises just this issue: that the constant is less constant than it is assumed to be.[19] Hence the search for forms that can be seen as the same or similar but which, once found, are described not as the same or similar but as 'practically identical' or 'obviously derived from' or 'most closely associated with' or 'very reminiscent' or 'corresponding' or 'analogous'. The 'constant' forms of style seem never to be the same or similar. In the art history of Anglo-Saxon stone sculpture the survivals only ever 'resemble' or 'parallel' each other. The terms indicate a kind of frustration: the art historian's need to make out and locate the constant form possessed by several objects produced by an individual or several individuals within a place or across a period of time, like the desire to locate the origin, can never be satisfied. In other words, the idea of style undoes itself in the emphasis it puts on continuity over discontinuity and, thereafter, in the inevitable discursive inequality that makes it privilege similarity over difference. The most useful aspect of working with style might be that the imagined continuities established with it enable one to recognise actual differences and disjunctions, which might otherwise be overlooked.

In everyday life and social intercourse, we're in the habit of *seeing* things *as* similar to other things. And similarity is all the more likely to be attended to when, somewhat removed from everyday life and consciousness with its limited connections of persons and things with other persons and things, in the rarefied study of Anglo-Saxon stone sculpture, one's objects are incomplete and when one does not know or doesn't understand the moment of their production and first use.

The idea of style relies on similarity, but similarity, as Nelson Goodman demonstrated in his essay 'Seven Strictures on Similarity', is a thoroughly problematic concept.[20] Though it is sufficiently clear 'when closely confined by context and circumstance in ordinary discourse, it is hopelessly ambiguous when torn loose'.[21] Some of Goodman's cautions against statements of similarity seem pertinent to the study of surviving Anglo-Saxon stone sculpture, painting, manuscripts, metalwork and ivories, or whatever, for similarity 'does not pick out inscriptions that are "tokens of a common type", or replicas of each other';[22] it 'does not provide the grounds for accounting two occurrences performances of the same work, or repetitions of the same behaviour';[23] it 'does not suffice to define qualities';[24] and it 'cannot be equated with, or measured in terms of, possession of common characteristics'.[25] 'Since every two things have some property in common, this will make similarity a universal and hence useless relation.'[26] To the question 'Are two things similar, then, only if they have all their properties in common?' Goodman answers, 'of course no two things have all their properties in common'.[27] To this we add the caveat that even if, as Jorge Luis Borges demonstrated in his story about Pierre Menard's *Don Quixote*, which was not another *Quixote* but *the Quixote itself*, two objects (two texts) could have precisely the same structure and form (be word for word, and line for line the same), the difference between them would be that they are different in both cause and effect.[28] Goodman next considers whether two things are more alike than two other things if the former pair has more properties in common than the latter pair. In this case, the count is what is important. But this comparative counting will not establish similarity because 'any two things have exactly as many properties in common as any other two'.[29] Finally, Goodman considers whether it would be more pertinent to count not all the properties common to objects but 'only the *important* properties' or, better still, consider 'not the count but the overall importance of the shared properties'.[30] He rightly dismisses this in the knowledge that 'importance is a highly volatile matter, varying with every shift of context and interest, and quite incapable of supporting the fixed distinctions that philosophers so often seek to rest on it'.[31]

Goodman's cautions should alert us to the possibility that, while we usually take similarity as offering empirical evidence on which to base metaphors or principles of classification and discrimination, judgements of similarity may actually follow from metaphorical modes or principles of classification and discrimination already established. Classification of Anglo-Saxon stone sculpture is supposed to be established on the basis of observation of stylistic similarities. With Goodman's strictures in mind, we might suspect that finding similarities or the invocation of parallels is a sign that some principle of classification has already been applied or that some interest is already at work. Goodman asserts that similarity is relative to culture, to purposes and interests, to inductive practices and principles, to significance and circumstance. It is not a reliable basis upon which to form a picture of any thing because it 'tends under analysis either to vanish entirely or to require for its explanation just what it purports to explain'.[32] No wonder, then, that it is usual for a similarity to be stated and then withdrawn once its superficiality has been acknowledged.[33] If the art historian is going to make the statements of similarity that are so necessary for identifying style then he or she needs to keep in mind that 'similarity is relative and variable, as undependable as indispensable',[34] and be very clear in defining the kind of similarity he or she is interested in and as clear as possible about how it functions in interpretation and explanation.

> What does anyone tell me by saying 'Now I see it as ...?' What consequences has this information? What can I do with it? (Ludwig Wittgenstein, *Philosophical Investigations*)[35]

Seeing and 'seeing ... as'. What is really seen? We see an object as a thing or as another thing. 'So we interpret it, and see it as we interpret it ... The description of what is got immediately, i.e. of the visual experience, by means of an interpretation – is an indirect description.'[36] We see an object and interpret it, and see it as we interpret it. 'Seeing it as' or 'seeing ... as' is a problem of representation. Coming across a fragment of carved stone in or near or in relation to a church and seeing it as, for example, a 'cross' would be to see it as an upright post or shaft with a transverse bar. The idea of a stone cross, perhaps with an angular shaft and a cross-head with squared arm terminals and half-round arm-pits, is there in seeing it and in the language and notation needed to bring it to practical consciousness. Seeing it as that would not be unusual – especially if one had an interest in Anglo-Saxon stone sculpture. Our point is, however, that we are easily misled or are misleading of others if our accounts of what we see are governed by assumptions, ideas and beliefs, language and notation, and so on, which others do not share.

In 1599 Reginald Bainbrigg visited the church at Ruthwell where he came upon 'a cross of wonderful height' but, as we saw in the previous chapter, what he was faced with may not have been a cross: it may have been another kind of object that he brought to practical consciousness by seeing it as a cross. In 1697, William Nicolson visited the church at Ruthwell to see a cross but what he saw was certainly not a cross: it was a fragment of something that he saw as a cross. Wittgenstein is right: 'seeing' makes a 'tangled impression' and there can never be *'one genuine* proper case' of the 'description of what is seen'.[37]

So, we return to the Bewcastle monument (Figs 17, 18, 19 and 20) faced with a problem of 'seeing' and 'seeing ... as'.

Bewcastle 1. Cross-shaft and -base.
Present location: Churchyard, south of west end of church.
Evidence for discovery: First recorded, in present position, in 1601 by Reginald Bainbrigg.[38]

Bewcastle 2. Cross-head.
Present location: Lost.
Evidence for discovery: None. First recorded in unpublished drawing (Society of Antiquaries of London, [Cumberland] red portfolio, no. 3).[39]

Bewcastle 7. Rune-inscribed fragment, probably of cross-head.
Evidence for discovery: There is no find-report as such. Four manuscript copies of the runes provide the only evidence for discovery.[40]

Seeing an object combines with, or is consolidated in the knowledge of, past representations of what it might be seen as and according to the descriptions that can be used to bring it to practical consciousness. The *Corpus of Anglo-Saxon Stone Sculpture* describes 'Bewcastle 1' as a 'cross-shaft' and discusses it as a 'cross' because that is what the editors 'judged it to be'.[41] This judgement seems to have been 'firmly based on several pieces of evidence,'[42] which can be summarily presented thus: there is clear indication that something was once mortised to the top of Bewcastle 1; the first known accounts of the monument see it as a cross; there are four manuscript copies of a runic inscription on a stone that was associated with it; there's a mention by someone who visited Bewcastle in 1775 that 'part' of a cross was being used as a gravestone in the churchyard, which like the rune-inscribed stone was also associated with the monument; and, last of all, there's a drawing that shows Bewcastle 1 with a broken cross or cross-head lying on the ground close by, propped up against a rock. Since it is clear that there was once a socket in the top of Bewcastle 1 – it's now filled with cement – it is safe to assume that something fitted into it.[43] It's also safe to assume that whatever fitted into it was lost either intentionally by way of vandalism or some other less malign alteration to its form or unintentionally by accident or some other contingency.[44] But why, on the basis of these several pieces of evidence, should we think that, at the moment of the monument's production and first use, it was a cross? Art historians have worked so hard to maintain that the massive fragment of Anglo-Saxon stone sculpture at Bewcastle is a cross, and thus that a cross was intended to top it off, that we owe it to the record to bring to the fore that, when read closely, it tells us no such thing.

As with the earliest known reference to the monument at Ruthwell, we are indebted to Reginald Bainbrigg for the earliest known reference to the monument at Bewcastle. Bainbrigg visited Bewcastle during a tour of Hadrian's Wall in 1601 and sent William Camden a collection of notes recording the inscriptions he'd come across. The note of what he found at Bewcastle, along with notes of what he found at some other Roman forts along Hadrian's Wall – his tour took in Bowness, Netherby, Castlesteads, Birdoswald, Risingham and High Rochester – is preserved amongst the materials that Camden collected whilst preparing a revised edition of his *Britannia*, which was published in 1607.[45]

> I had this monument at Beawcastle; the stone lyes in the church.
> LEG II AVG
FECIT
> The cross, which is in the cemetery, is about twenty feet (viginti fere pedum), made of one squared stone finely carved with this inscription

ID † IBOROX·

The first inscription, on a fragment of a dedication stone from the Roman fort, 'the second legion Augusta built this', was easy to transcribe. The other inscription is the single line of runes between the plant-scroll and chequer pattern on the north side of the monument (Fig. 26). Bainbrigg seems not to have realised that this was in the same kind of 'foreign but fluent letters' he'd come across and so successfully transcribed at Ruthwell. Instead, he saw it as cut with roman characters.

Camden took some of what Bainbrigg sent him into his 1607 *Britannia*.[46]

> In the church, which is somewhat ruinous, lies this old inscription, somewhat like a gravestone, carried there from elsewhere:
> LEG II AVG
FECIT.
> In the cemetery a cross rises to more or less twenty feet (viginti plùs minùs pedes), finely cut out of a squared stone and inscribed, but the letters so decaying that they cannot be read. And that cross is chequered like the shield of the noble family of Vaulx, that some may think it was their work.

An object 'about' or 'more or less' twenty feet tall would be about five and a half feet taller than Bewcastle 1 is now, which suggests that what Bainbrigg saw was perhaps the complete object. In this case the statement that it was 'ex uno quadrato saxo ... excisa', which Camden leaves intact, must be incorrect because, whatever it was, we know that it was made of at least two stones.[47] Unless, of course, what Bainbrigg saw was Bewcastle 1, which he interpreted or judged as having been a cross and so referred to it seeing it as a cross. (He may have been overgenerous in his estimate of its height – as was, for example, Sir John Clerk when, in 1741, he reckoned Bewcastle 1 to be 'about 18 or 20 feet high'.)[48]

Camden accepted Bainbrigg's transcription of the Roman inscription on the fragment in the church but chose not to include his transcription of the inscription on the 'cross'. Given the additional material about the ruined state of the church, that the inscriptions on the cross were 'so decaying' as to be illegible and that it was decorated with a chequer pattern like the arms of the Vaux family, none of which appears in Bainbrigg's note, and bearing in mind that Camden had not visited Bewcastle,[49] it is clear that Bainbrigg was not his sole informant. It's likely that one of his informants was the Catholic scholar Nicolas Roscarrock. We know that, while he was preparing the new edition of *Britannia*, Camden received a letter dated 7 August 1607 from Roscarrock, by then a permanent house guest of the antiquarian, collector of books, manuscripts and Roman stones, and one of the main characters in James I's pacification of the Borders, Lord William Howard recently installed at Naworth Castle, 7 miles south of Bewcastle.[50] In his letter to Camden, Roscarrock gave notice of 'two escapes in the last edition'. This is how he captured the one he came across at Bewcastle, some of which Camden may have used:

> Yf you have any occasion to speake of the Crosse of Buechastell, I assure myselfe the inscription of one syde ys, *Hubert de Vaux*; the rather, for that the checky coate ys above that on the same syde; and on the other the name of the Ermyt that made yt, & I canne in no sorte be brought to thincke it *Eborax*, as I perceave you have been advertised.[51]

Perhaps Roscarrock was aware of Bainbrigg's note to Camden, or of its contents, and was trying to correct its version of the inscription. Roscarrock cannot read the inscription as 'Eborax,' which is to say, we guess, he could not see it as Bainbrigg's 'D+IBOROX'.

Both Bainbrigg and Roscarrock were very learned men. They certainly knew what a cross was; but knowing what a cross *is* and *seeing* an object *as* a cross, referring to it as a cross, are not the same kinds of knowledge. We need to keep that in mind when considering what their notes, especially Bainbrigg's, contribute to the historical record. Let's assume that Bainbrigg was precise in his choice of words and that it was as important for him to describe the object as made 'ex uno quadrato saxo … excisa' as it was to use the word 'crux' to describe its form. We're scrutinising the record, reading texts. And our point is that, whether in and of itself or supplemented by Roscarrock's note, which seems to make reference to it and to have been partly written by it, Bainbrigg's note effects not certainty about what kind of actual, material object its author saw in the churchyard, but doubt.

We need now look at the four manuscript copies of the inscription on the lost stone for which no illustration has survived, Bewcastle 7, that is interpreted as having been on, or on something related to, the assumed 'lost cross-head', Bewcastle 2.[52] Three of these copies were amongst the notes that Camden collected for the revised *Britannia*. Two of them, ended up in the library of Sir Robert Cotton, collector of Roman antiquities and inscribed Roman stones; the other is found interleaved in Camden's own copy of the *Britannia* of 1607.

One of the notes from the Cotton library (BL MS. Cotton Domitian A.xviii, fol. 37r), perhaps penned by Cotton himself,[53] has:

ᚱᛁᛚᚠᛋᚻᚱᛦᚿᛏ᛭ᚠᛋ.

This Inscription was on the head of a crose found at Beucastell in 1615.
The length of the stone. bein the head of the Crosse – 16.inches
The breadth at the vpper end – 12. ynches
The Thickness – 4.inches[54]

The other note (BL MS. Cotton Julius F.vi, fol. 313), which seems to be in a different hand[55] – perhaps it was penned by a secretary, possibly as a rough draft or abbreviation of the above – after the inscription has:

The length of the stone
beinge the head of a Cross   16.ynches
The b[rea]dth at the vpper end   12.ynches
The [thick]nes   4.ynches
Bucastle inscription For Mᵣ Clarenceaulx [for Camden, addressed by his title as King of Arms in the Heralds' College][56]

These notes tell us that the inscription was on the head of *a* cross. They do not tell us that it was once on the head of *the* cross. Both Camden who, as we have seen, thanks to Bainbrigg amongst others, had mentioned it in the 1607 *Britannia*, and Cotton who, if he hadn't known about it before by word of mouth or otherwise, would have read about it in *Britannia*, knew about the monument in the cemetery at Bewcastle. The note seems to present Camden with something he was not aware of, something newly discovered: the head of *a* cross. Whatever it was, the dimensions of the stone indicate that it was probably a fragment of something – though the terms 'length' and 'breadth' are difficult to grasp[57] and some imagination is required to project from it a whole that would sit atop Bewcastle 1.[58]

Cotton probably sent the third note (MS Smith I, Boldleian Library, Oxford), the one interleaved in Camden's own copy of the 1607 *Britannia*. It has the inscription but with a significant variant: it gives not

ᚱᛁᛚᚠᛋᚻᚱᛦᚿᛏ᛭ᚠᛋ.

but

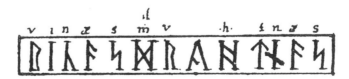

Beneath the inscription is written:

I receaued this morning a ston from my lord of Arundell sent him from my lord William it was the head of a Cross at Bewcastell All the lettres legable ar

thes in on Line And I hau sett to them such as I can gather out of my Alpha-
betts that lyk an .A. I can find in non But wether thes be only lettres or words
I somwhatt dout ...[59]

'Lord William' is, of course, William Howard of Naworth. 'My lord of
Arundell' is Howard's half-nephew Thomas Howard, Earl of Arundel, who
amassed famous collections of paintings by Dürer and Holbein, Rubens and
Van Dyck, Greek and Roman sculptures, and books and manuscripts. This
note does not give the dimensions of the 'stone', which it refers to as having
been 'the head of a cross'. It is not clear whether this was intended to mean
that the stone was a fragment of the head of a cross or that it was the head
of a cross entire. Nor is it clear that the reference to 'a stone' should be taken
literally; it could be that an inscription is being referred to metonymically by
way of the thing on which it was inscribed.[60]

And then there is the fourth note of the inscription, more or less as
Camden had it interleaved between the pages of his *Britannia*, in a letter
dated 18 April 1629 that Sir Henry Spelman, antiquarian, historian, philologist and prime mover in the field of Old English studies, wrote to Palæmon
Rosencrantz, the Danish ambassador to England, part of which Rosencrantz
passed to his countryman Ole Worm, Chair of Medicine and several times
Rector at the University of Copenhagen, naturalist, early archaeologist and
innovator of research into Danish runic inscriptions. Spelman would like to
know something about runes. For instance, to what country and people they
properly belong. He included a runic inscription that he would have Worm
translate. Worm replied to Spelman on 18 July 1629: he wished that Spelman
would have the inscription more accurately copied by someone not wholly
ignorant of the literature, in which case he would do what he could with it.
The original letter seems not to have survived but, fourteen years later in 1643,
Worm published some of it, along with the runic inscription enclosed with
it, in his *Danicorum monumentorum libri sex*. His version of the inscription is
related to the version interleaved in Camden's 1607 *Britannia*, the one that is
thought to have been supplied by Cotton. The published version differs from
the text in Camden's copy of his *Britannia* 'only in inessentials'.[61]

ᚱᛁᛚᚠᛋᛞᚱᚪᚻᛏᛣ ᚠᛋ.

This inscription was carved on 'epistylio crucis lapidæ' at Bewcastle in the
northern parts of England (where the Danes lived). It was shown to Camden
and myself at the same time, AD 1618, by the most learned antiquarian amongst
the lords of England, William Howard, the son of the Duke of Norfolk.[62]

It is hard to understand just what Spelman is describing. Strictly speaking,
an epistyle is the lowest division of an entablature consisting of the main
beam that rests immediately on the capital of a column, a squared stone
resting on top of a column and supporting something. It is difficult to *see* this
'epistylio crucis' *as* something in the shape of a cross or a cross-head. One
could, of course, *see* it *as* a bit of something that was intended to support a

cross or a cross-head, especially *if* one saw Bewcastle 1 as a cross. But would Bainbrigg have described the monument as 'ex uno quadrato saxo ... excisa' if he had seen this 'epistylio crucis', perhaps supporting some terminal feature above it? We doubt it.

Very little of what is signified by these four notes is certain. They seem to tell us that some person or persons unnamed found a rune-inscribed stone at Bewcastle in 1615. It is not clear whether this was a fragment of Bainbrigg's 'cross' or Roscarrock's 'the crosse of Buechastell' or something previously unknown that came to light only then. In 1618 William Howard showed it or only a drawing of its inscription to Henry Spelman and William Camden. The latter also received a note of its inscription and its dimensions at an unspecified date and from an unspecified informant. William Howard sent the actual stone or a copy of its inscription to Thomas Howard who, in turn, sent it to Robert Cotton who, in his turn, informed Camden about it. Somewhere along the line, the actual stone, whatever it was and from wherever it came, disappeared.

William Nicolson, who was to visit Ruthwell in 1697 and 1704, also visited Bewcastle. We should take a look at his description of Bewcastle 1. There is an entry in his diary for 20 October 1684 that records the writing of a letter to Obadiah Walker, Master of University College, Oxford, about the Bridekirk font, in which he promises 'ere long a fuller account of [it] and the Pedestal at Bewcastle'.[63] In the promised letter, 2 November 1685, Nicolson not quite accurately transcribed the inscription on the north side of the monument that had flummoxed Bainbrigg, 'the following Characters, fairly legible'

and attempted, less successfully, to make sense of some of the other inscriptions.[64]

Nicolson's description of the monument is very definitely a description of Bewcastle 1. It is not a cross. It is 'one entire Free-Stone of about five yards in height' that 'inclines to a square Pyramid; each side whereof is near two foot broad at bottom, but upwards more tapering'.[65] Though it inclines to a 'pyramid', and was in the promissory note of the previous year referred to as a 'pedestal', in the letter of 1685, Nicolson *sees* it somewhat less securely neither *as* a pedestal nor as something approaching a pyramid but as an 'epistilium crucis', which he goes on to refer to as 'the Cross'. Nicolson referred to it as an 'epistilium crucis' in the knowledge that *that* was what 'Sr *H. Spellman*, in his Letter to *Wormius*, has called it'[66] – which he'd read in Worm's *Danicorum monumentorum libri sex*, by then a canonical text for English antiquarians. But, because Spelman's letter, as cited by Worm, doesn't mention it, Nicolson knew nothing of the cross, cross-head or stone, 16 by 12 by 4 inches, that had come to light only in 1615. Writing to Walker, trying to make sense of Bewcastle 1 in terms of what he'd read in Worm's book, Nicolson is flummoxed. Amongst other things, he is confused about where Spelman's inscription came from. (He thought it had been copied from the large inscription above the figure panel at the base of the west side of the monument.) Nicolson was trying to *see* Spelman's 'epistilium crucis' *as* Bewcastle 1; or, rather, he was trying to *see* Bewcastle 1 *as* Spelman's 'epistilium crucis'.

Confused and confusing as Nicolson's description is, it became public knowledge when, almost immediately, his letter to Walker was published in the *Philosophical Transactions of the Royal Society of London* in 1685. Thereafter, it was taken into William Hutchinson's *History of the County of Cumberland, 1794,*[67] and, before that, provided the basis of the description of Bewcastle 1 that was published in the *Magna Britannia et Hibernia, Antiqua et Nova*, edited by Thomas Cox, 1720.[68] The *Magna Britannia et Hibernia* also contained a crude, thoroughly imaginary representation of the 'Bewcastle Cross', made up from Nicolson's transcription of the legible runic inscription on the north side of the monument and the reference to a 'great deal of Chequer-work' on that side also.  This representation so offended George Smith, antiquarian, topographer and geographer of Brampton, who, in order to correct its 'imperfect Account', made his own 'prospects of the famous Runic Obelisk' (Fig. 13) that along with a description were published as a letter to *Gentleman's Magazine* in 1742.[69] One of Smith's 'prospects' included 'A perspective View Top, wherein the Cross was fixt, from an Elevation of the Ocular Horizon', a cross that, as he knew the history, 'has been demolished long ago, by Popular Frenzy and Enthusiasm; and probably its Situation in these unfrequented Desarts has preserved the Remainder from their Fury'.[70] If whatever was on the top of Bewcastle 1 was broken off 'by Popular Frenzy and Enthusiasm' sometime between 1607 and 1615 then one might have expected that moment of iconoclasm to be part of the historical record – which is not one of an unfrequented desert: for the first time in a hundred years or so Bewcastle was a frequentable and frequented place. The pacification of the Borders had been achieved between 1603 and 1608.[71] And though, in 1611, Bewcastle still had the reputation of being 'the theyvished place in oure Countrye', it seems to have been peaceable enough and visited by outsiders.[72] In 1607 Thomas Musgrave, who had, since 1570, held the position of deputy captain of Bewcastle under his father Sir Simon Musgrave as Constable, was reappointed for life as Constable by James I.[73] The demesnes of Bewcastle, a Crown property, were by then at the Earl of Cumberland's disposal and his estate officers were at work surveying, valuing and rack renting them.[74] In 1614 Cumberland, as governor of Carlisle, obtained the castle and lordship of Bewcastle from the Crown but took no special action there.[75] King James's survey of the Crown lands adjoining Scotland, undertaken in 1604, noted that the castle and the church were in ruinous condition and that services were held in the latter only in dry weather, but in 1606 the Church began a gradual return to the Borders.[76] Henry Hudson, Vicar of Brampton, served as rector at Stapleton and Bewcastle from then until October 1607 when he was replaced by Dr Henry Sibson who stayed in post until the Civil War (he was still rector in 1644).[77] The historical record, such as we are aware of it, makes mention of some alleged thievery and cattle rustling, and William Howard's low opinion of the Musgraves, but has nothing about any acts of iconoclasm committed by 'Popular Frenzy and Enthusiasm'.

The penultimate piece of evidence for the assumed 'lost cross-head', Bewcastle 2, is part of the description that accompanied a drawing made by George Armstrong, retired army officer, land surveyor and native of the parish, under the head 'An Account of a curious OBELISK, of one Stone, standing in the Church Yard of Bewcastle', *London Magazine*, August 1775: 'What is here represented is 15 feet high; besides there has been on the top a cross, now broken off, part of which may be seen as a grave stone in the same church yard.'[78] Unfortunately, though the description, which may or may not have been penned by Armstrong, mentions the chequer pattern on the monument's north side, it fails to provide any information about the fragment that was then being used as a gravestone. Nor is it illustrated in the 'elegant engraving' that accompanied Armstrong's 'Account'. It couldn't have been the 16 x 12 x 4 inches stone that was found in 1615 – that was long gone. Was it another 'part' of whatever that stone came from? Perhaps. It could have been part of anything that could be seen as having a relation of association with the truncated top of Bewcastle 1. Armstrong's is the only mention we have of this fragment, which, as soon as it enters published discourse, disappears or is not taken forward.

And, finally, what are we to make of the undated drawing (Fig. 14) in the collection of the Society of Antiquaries, London, of the monument with, on the ground nearby, propped against a rock, what seems to be a cross-head?[79] It is one of three in the Society's collection, kept together in the same folder, that seem to have been made by the same hand, in the same media – pale grey wash, here and there picked out by sepia, on heavy (watercolour) paper – and probably around the same time.[80] One of the other two is of the 'Monuments at Penrith', Giant's Grave, and the other (Fig. 11) is the drawing – we referred to it in our introduction – of the Roman sculptural relief (Fig. 10) of the 'Seated Mother Goddess', in the collection of Tullie House Museum and Art Gallery, Carlisle, 'A Stone found lately at Bewcastle – in Cumberland – 1765. now removed to Netherby'. Charles Lyttelton, President of the Society of Antiquaries of London, probably commissioned these drawings while he was Bishop of Carlisle from 1762 to his death in 1768.[81] (The drawing of the Giant's Grave was made into an engraving to illustrate the posthumous publication of Lyttelton's 'An Account of a Remarkable Monument in Penrith Church Yard, Cumberland' in *Archaeologia* in 1773.)[82] The 'Seated Mother Goddess' may well have been acquired by Reverend Robert Graham, who inherited the Graham estates at Netherby in 1757 and built Netherby Hall by adding on to existing buildings, probably in 1765.[83] There seems to be no way of telling if the drawing was made at Bewcastle or Netherby. The 'now removed to Netherby' in the note on the drawing could be a later addition in another hand. If the drawing of the Bewcastle monument and the 'Seated Mother Goddess' were drawn at the same time, on the same visit, then the cross-head was there in the churchyard in 1765.

The 'Seated Mother Goddess' may not have been the only Roman stone that was transferred from Bewcastle to Netherby. An altar of whitish sandstone dedicated to Cocidius, which was drawn by R. G. Collingwood and is catalogued and illustrated in his and R. P. Wright's *The Roman Inscriptions of Britain*, 1965, may likewise have been removed.[84] There is no record for the discovery of this altar, now also in the collection of Tullie House Museum and Art Gallery, but since 1953 it has been thought, because the stone is unlike that usually employed for the Netherby inscriptions, because Cocidius was a god associated with Bewcastle, because the dedication is on behalf of the *cohors I Nervana* that was garrisoned at Bewcastle, and because of the recorded transfer of the 'Seated Mother Goddess' in 1765, that it was originally at Bewcastle.[85] What is certain is that Thomas Pennant recorded seeing the altar at Netherby during his tour of Scotland in 1772, which was published as *A Tour in Scotland and A Voyage to the Hebrides* in 1774.[86] We make this brief excursion to Netherby and Pennant's mention of the altar to point out that Pennant visited Bewcastle in 1773, a visit seemingly overlooked in studies of the Bewcastle monument. *If* the cross-head were still there in the churchyard then, it seems strange that he did not record it in the entry on Bewcastle, which described the castle, the church and the monument (Fig. 2), when his journey of 1773 was written up and published as the *Tour from Downing to Alston-Moor* in 1801.[87] Perhaps it was there, but he decided not to mention it. Perhaps he overlooked it. Perhaps the cross-head in the drawing *is* the fragment that Armstrong saw being used as a gravestone in the churchyard at Bewcastle in 1775. Nothing is certain. The whole matter remains open to opinion pending further 'evidence'.

The Society's drawing is somewhat peculiar. The cross-head is rendered in a slightly different manner to the monument: the wash is heavier and it lacks the flicking and flecking strokes that characterise the other drawings; also it seems out of scale beside the two drawings of the monument or, if to scale, too large to fit comfortably on top of either. These differences could be intended to signify differences of material and facture or to establish a sense that the two fragments, monument and cross-head, don't quite belong together. Is it likely that what's represented in the drawing is a thoroughly spurious representation resourced by knowledge of the illustration in *Magna Britannia*? Given the likely circumstances of its making, one might agree with the *Corpus* that 'it is unlikely that the artist would have made up a head'.[88] But can we be sure of that? As the *Corpus* goes on to to point out, its 'shape ... is not that of an early type'.[89] Though it 'would be perfectly appropriate in a Cumbrian setting in the Anglian period', it is of a type that is about a hundred years later than the likely date of Bewcastle 1, 700–750.[90] The *Corpus* compares it with the head of the cross at Irton.[91] (But wouldn't one expect a cross-head like that in the drawing, decorated across its broad face, to have been edged, as is the head of the cross at Irton, and as are the majority of the surviving cross-heads of high-status crosses, with some kind of moulding? On the basis of stylistic judgement alone, one might sense that there's something not quite 'Anglo-Saxon' about this head.) If it or something like it were ever on the top of Bewcastle 1, it was likely a later addition – perhaps a very late addition – that was subsequently broken off. In which case, how do we explain that later addition?

Faced with the problem of consolidating Bewcastle 1 (Figs 17, 18, 19 and 20), what it is and what it may have been, as an object of knowledge in relation to the earliest writings and pictures that represent ideas about it – the 'several pieces of evidence' – one could very easily mistake those *ideas* for what the monument was and *is*. We are looking at Bewcastle 1 and rereading the evidence that has been taken to effect the fact of it in discourse. And taken as evidence, the writings and pictures on which firm judgements have been based, when read attentively, seem to confirm nothing so much as how unreliable they are as evidence for *seeing* Bewcastle 1 *as* a cross. The earliest surviving representations of the monument in the churchyard at Bewcastle cannot secure it in the knowledge that, at the moment of its production and first use, it was a cross. And that is why we think it is possible to bring it into practical consciousness under another description. We could *see* Bewcastle 1 *as* the major part of an object that was, at the moment of its production and first use, a column, obelisk or, though not quite in the way Nicolson described it, something inclining towards a 'pyramid'.

It is possible that several fragmentary survivals of Anglo-Saxon stone sculpture, which might be seen as cross-shafts or crosses, could be seen as having been columns or obelisks at the moment of their production and first use. The round columnar survivals at Reculver, Dewsbury, Masham and Wolverhampton, which come immediately to mind, were probably columns produced of an awareness of the columns which were erected all over the Roman world.[92] Triumphal columns had been set up in Britain at Chichester (*Noviomagus Regensium*), Cirencester (*Corinium Dobunnorum*), Catterick (*Cataractonium*) and York (*Eburacum*).[93] The most famous triumphal columns, of course, were Trajan's column and the column of Marcus Aurelius in Rome.[94] Less famous were the several memorial columns that were in place throughout the Middle Ages: the column of Antoninus Pius, which stood in the Campus Martius and featured in the anonymous eighth-century *Einsiedeln Itinerary*;[95] the column of Duilius erected on the Rostra in honour of the consul's naval victory over Carthage in 206 BC; and the column of Phocas, erected in honour of the Byzantine emperor Phocas, which stood in front of the Rostra and was unusual for being surrounded by a base-like pyramid of steps (the only memorial column to have survived).[96] Anglo-Saxon visitors to Rome would no doubt have been acquainted with some if not all of these monuments. They would surely have known the column of Phocas – it was Phocas who gave the Pantheon to Pope Boniface IV for use a church.[97] Erected in AD 608, this column was the last addition to the Forum before it was abandoned. It would have been one of several important building projects begun and completed in the seventh century – the church of S Agnese fuori le Mura, which was reconstructed by Pope Honorius I (625–638), would have been another – that might have attracted the attention of Anglo-Saxon visitors from Northumbria like Wilfrid, who first visited Rome in AD 653, who may have fancied themselves as builders.[98] They would also have been familiar with the three Egyptian obelisks that were still standing in the city: the obelisk of Augustus on the Campus Martius and the obelisk that stood on the Collis Hortorum between the Porta Salaria and the Porta Pinciana, both of which featured in the *Einsiedeln Itinerary*;[99] and the obelisk that, until the sixteenth century, stood to the south-west of St Peter's.[100] It is likely that some of the other eleven known ancient obelisks in Rome could also be seen, though they were probably recumbent, broken and partially buried. These Roman columns and obelisks provide us with examples of some of the resources available in the visual culture of the Anglo-Saxons that could have been appropriated directly to the idea of making a column or an obelisk or, indirectly, to the idea of making a stone monument in the shape of a cross, column and cross.

Some of the written sources from the immediate post-Conquest period refer to several monuments that seem to have been produced before the Conquest that were not crosses and which were columnar in form, in part or whole. These Anglo-Saxon monuments are referred to as 'pyramids'.[101]

Eadmer (c.1064–1124) described two pyramids at Christ Church, Canterbury. A 'large and lofty pyramid' stood above the grave of St Dunstan, which was set before the steps up to the altar of Christ: this pyramid must have been columnar in form otherwise it would have interrupted traffic and obscured the view.[102] It seems safe to assume that the other pyramid, which marked the grave of Bishop Odo, at the south of the same altar, was a column too.[103]

William of Malmesbury (c.1090–1143) also recorded several pyramids, including one at Worcester and two at Glastonbury. He tells us that St Wulfstan, bishop of Worcester from 1062 till his death in 1095, the last Anglo-Saxon bishop to survive the Conquest, was buried 'between two pyramids, with a beautiful stone arch curving above him ... a wooden cover projecting out over his grave, held firm by iron clamps called "spiders"'.[104] However, the two pyramids at Glastonbury, which were outside the church at the edge of the monks' cemetery a few feet from the old church, were different in form from the one at Worcester: they were also much older and in a ruinous condition.[105] The taller, which was nearer the church, had five tiers and was 26 feet high. In the uppermost tier there was a figure dressed like a bishop. In the second tier there was a figure like a king in state, and the inscription: 'Sexi' and 'Bliswerh'. There were names in the third tier also: 'Wemcrest', 'Bantomp' and 'Winethegn'. And in the fourth: 'Bate', 'Wulfred' and 'Eanfled'. In the fifth and lowest tier there was a figure and the inscription: 'Logor', 'Weaslieas', 'Bregden', 'Swelwes', 'Hiwingendes' and 'Bearn'. The other pyramid was 18 feet high, and had four tiers, on which were inscribed the names: 'Centwine', 'Bishop Hedde', 'Bregored' and 'Beorward'. There was something about these monuments that made William think that they were hollow and contained the bones of those persons named on the outside. The arrangement of the figures and inscriptions on the largest pyramid, a single figure at the top and a single figure accompanied by a long inscription at the bottom, might suggest that these were monuments with tapering forms. They are easily brought to mind as columns or obelisks and have occasionally been put in a relation of association with the Ruthwell and Bewcastle monuments.[106]

Visitors to Rome throughout the Middle Ages would have come across several monuments that we would now refer to as pyramids, Roman imitations of the Egyptian pyramid, each with a square ground plan and rising in stepped or flat triangular sides to a point at the top. One of these, the Meta Romuli, stood at the intersection of the ancient Via Cornelia and Via Triumphalis near the Mausoleum Hadriani.[107] Another, the Meta Remi, which is to say the tomb of C. Cestii, stood on the Via Ostiensis.[108] The former disappeared sometime in the fifteenth century – in the early Middle Ages it may have contained its sarcophagus; the latter has survived, incorporated into the Aurelian fortifications next to the Porta Ostiensis. Yet another stood at the side of the Via Flaminia, by the site of the modern church of Sta Maria dei Miracoli in the Piazza del Popolo – it disappeared in the sixteenth century.[109] Magister Gregorius, an Englishman who visited Rome in the twelfth century and left a record of the 'wonders' he saw there, referred to the Meta Romuli and Meta Remus as 'pyramidibus seplucris potentum'.[110] He also referred to the obelisks – of which, he commented, Rome contained many – as 'pyramids'. These, too, were deemed 'sepulchres of the mighty'.[111]

All the references we have cited so far come from the eleventh and twelfth centuries but, three hundred years before, the author of the *Einsiedeln Itinerary*, who would have been familiar with the Meta Romuli, referred to the obelisk on the Collis Hortorum as a 'pyramid' also.[112] The term seems to have had this usage throughout the Middle Ages, but the object to which it referred held to no grand form. It could be columnar but, apart from that, took several forms and was defined not so much necessarily by its form as by its function. As far as the sources are concerned, and on this they're clear, a pyramid was usually a kind of high-status funerary monument.[113]

It is worth recalling the record left by William Hutchinson who seems to have 'excavated' the monument at Bewcastle in the eighteenth century and who was in

> no doubt that this was a place of sepulchre, for on opening the ground on the east and west sides, above the depth of six feet, human bones were found of a large size, but much broken and disturbed, together with several pieces of rusty iron. The ground had been broken up before, by persons who either searched for treasure, or like us, laboured with curiosity.[114]

Of course, digging in a cemetery one would expect to find bones but that mention of 'several pieces of rusty iron' is intriguing. It's easy to get carried away but they could indicate that Hutchinson had turned up an iron-bound coffin burial like those found at York.[115]

One of the things we've been concerned to do in this chapter is show that it is possible to see the Bewcastle monument as having been a column or an obelisk at the moment it was produced and first used. No more than that. To which we would add that, in view of the foregoing, we should not ignore the possibility that Bewcastle was a place of sepulchre and that the monument was a pyramid set up in memory of someone who was buried close by:

[+]þissigb[*e*]c[*n*]
*[.]setto/nh
wætre[*d*..]þ
gæra[.]w[.]wo[.]
*[œ]ft[.]lfri
*m[.]n[*g*]u[.]ŋ
[.]cb[....]u/ŋ
[.]gebid[.]
[..]so[.]o

'This token of victory (alternatively victory cross, victory memorial) Hwætred, ... gear and ... set up in memory of .lcfri'. And, at the end, an invocation to prayer.[116]

We are now some way removed from thinking about style as constant form and from *seeing* the Bewcastle monument *as* necessarily a tall stone cross: which, mindful of the cross-head recorded in the drawing in the Society of Antiquaries' collection, is not to say that it was not once made up with a cross-head. And, though we've not dispensed with the principles of style *as if* they were an irrelevance or with form as such, we have moved towards *seeing* the surviving fragments of Anglo-Saxon stone sculpture *as* defined not by form but by function. We can now bring the Bewcastle and Ruthwell monuments together in the same chapter, mindful that, as Bishop Butler put it, 'Everything is what it is, and not another thing'.

4

Forms of difference[1]

⌘

Difference is of two kinds as oppos'd either to identity or resemblance. The first is called the difference of *number*; the other of *kind*. (David Hume, *A Treatise of Human Nature*)[2]

Over forty years ago, Rosemary Cramp, in her first published essay on Anglo-Saxon stone sculpture, noted that the Ruthwell monument, 'a highly individual monument', and 'the related monument at Bewcastle' were 'different in intention and thus difficult to compare in their complete schemes'.[3] It's necessary to stress this difference, if only because the important questions have remained unasked.[4] What were those different intentions or functions? Why *those* intentions? How do the form and content of each monument relate to its purpose and the way it fulfilled that purpose? We do not come close to understanding the Ruthwell and Bewcastle monuments unless we, at least, try to answer these questions.

By way of preliminary we follow the *Corpus of Anglo-Saxon Stone Sculpture* as it directs us to some of the differences between one of the two figure panels that are shared by the Ruthwell and Bewcastle monuments: the one representing Christ on the Beasts (Figs 23 and 55). This panel presents the beholder with what is arguably the most complex image on each monument. As we saw in a previous chapter, on the Ruthwell monument it is provided with an inscription: +IHSXPS·IVDEX·AEQVITATIS·BESTIAE·ET·DRAC ONES·COGNOVERVNT·IN·DESERTO·SALVAꝰOREM·MVNDI. Christ is in the desert where, in this instance, he has no need to trample on the beasts for they recognise and submit to him without violence as *iudex aequitatis* and *salvator mundi*. There is something about the two beasts – perhaps it's their size, more or less the same, and their affection for each other, which seems not that of mother and child – which suggests that their relation is not familial but ethical. As to the differences, and ignoring for the moment that there is no inscription around the panel on the Bewcastle monument, the *Corpus* points out there is less of the animals on the Bewcastle monument than on the monument at Ruthwell (though the former, unlike the latter, manages to accommodate a forelimb at each side of the panel); that at Bewcastle Christ's halo is plain whereas at Ruthwell it is cruciferous; and that, whatever Christ is wearing, the 'drapery arrangements differ'.[5]

That last difference used to exercise art historians more than it does today, especially those committed to form and iconography as they relate to the principles of style. It was assumed that the figure panels were based on the 'patterns' of an unknown 'foreign model' of 'Mediterranean origin' that could best be understood by puzzling 'certain peculiarities of form' such as 'the strange "loop" of the robes of the Bewcastle Christ' and 'the little "bag" under the right arm [of the Ruthwell Christ]'.[6] These peculiarities pertained to what kind of 'Mediterranean' or 'southern dress' Christ is wearing; though 'only the motive of the drapery tucked under the elbow' of the Ruthwell Christ was deemed to have 'Mediterranean parallels'.[7] Christ seems to wear a full-length long-sleeved *tunica* with a round neck. But what's that cloak over the *tunica*? A *pallium* or a *paenula*? And which of the two monuments gives us the most accurate representation of whatever it is? *As if* the answer to that question would tell us which monument was closest to the model or origin, and so which was produced first.[8] Nevertheless, there might be some gain in returning to these 'peculiarities of form', if only to begin puzzling the difference between the two panels.

This is a matter of what kind of late Roman civilian attire Christ is supposed to be wearing, not whether he is wearing the ecclesiastical *pallium*, the thin band of white wool worn by the Pope in the performance of the liturgy, the use of which could be conferred on approved metropolitan bishops. Nothing on either monument affords a glimpse of this.

The *paenula* was a semicircular or circular cloak, knee length or longer, with a hole in the centre so that it could be pulled on over the head. Sometimes it was provided with a hood. To begin with, the *pallium* was a simpler version of the toga, which was restricted to citizens of Rome. In the Empire, it was adopted as the dignified dress of the ordinary citizen; the toga appearing only in the official dress of consuls: it was made of less cloth, easier to wrap around the body, lighter and more convenient for everyday wear. To put it on, one first draped a little less than a third of the length of the cloth against the centre of the body and threw the rest over the left shoulder. What went over the shoulder was passed across the back and brought round under the right arm to the front of the body. The remaining cloth was, once again, thrown over the left shoulder. The right arm could remain free or rest in a gather like a sling. The cloth could also be pouched at the front and drawn up over the head as a hood. In early Christian art, the *pallium*, with the full-length long-sleeved *tunica*, became the costume that was used to signify Christ and his disciples. More often than not Christ is shown wearing it in the manner of a philosopher, his left hand holding a small *volumen* or scroll, his right arm in the sling or raised with the hand gesturing speech or blessing. Christ on the beasts at Ruthwell is probably supposed to be wearing this kind of *pallium*. At Bewcastle he could be seen as wearing an open cloak that falls in a loop as it gathers over the elbow of the left arm. *If* it is supposed to be a *pallium* then both monuments represent it differently and neither represents it conventionally for, no matter how one imagines it is draped, it does not cross the body for the return throw over the left shoulder; and, at Ruthwell, it is the left arm that rests in the sling, not the right one. It might be that whoever was responsible for bringing these panels into being had little understanding of what it was they were supposed to be representing. Or, *if* they did understand it, had studied it on survivals of Roman sculpture and intended to represent it accurately, then perhaps the peculiarities came into play as other aspects of the panels' production became more pressing, especially those pertaining to the urgencies of sculptural form, namely technical problems of facture, affect and effect.

What we are after are clues to what was there when the panels were produced: clues to sculptural decision-making. Despite being badly damaged, sufficient remains to call attention to some differences between them that pertain to sculptural form and facture.

Form: the shape and order in which ideas are presented. In the third and fourth centuries, after Constantine's victory at the battle of the Milvian Bridge in 312 when it was permitted that Christian ideas could be expressed publicly and forms of devotion practiced freely and openly, the artists of the new sect were faced with the problem of imaging their new god.[9] They had to think about what aspects to represent and how to represent them. Any single representation will be made of any number of possibilities that the resources of a culture make available, and the image of the philosopher was not the only resource appropriated to imaging the figure of Christ. Another resource was provided by images of old gods. One that was especially good for effecting a sense of Christ's dignity, authority and royal power was the image of the emperor as sovereign. Though early Christian artists had little or no use for the insignia of the emperor's supreme authority – the jewel-studded diadem, *chlamys*, purple boots and sceptre – they did realise how the frontality and symmetry that were associated with an imperial mode of composition could be adapted to form a vivid image of Christ's divine sovereignty. Making the figure of Christ in majesty a frontal, just about symmetrical form contained within its own outline, gave it the rigidity, fixity and inflexibility that were indispensable for the representation of imperial authority.[10] Perhaps not surprisingly these formal, compositional traits were in accord with what seem to have been a dominant set of principles determining and expressed in late-Antique visual art: strikingly in the relief sculpture that was everywhere in the visual culture of the Empire. We take it that whoever designed and carved Christ on the beasts at Bewcastle and at Ruthwell had this mode of imperial composition and some idea of late-Antique relief sculpture, if not actual examples, in mind when they did so.

According to the most enabling account we have of it, 'the visual art of the whole of antiquity had sought its ultimate goal in the representation of external objects in their clear material individuality, and in contrast to the accidental appearance of things in nature, avoided everything which might disturb or weaken the immediately convincing impression of material separateness'.[11] This fundamental aim found its ideal in relief sculpture where each object had to be represented as a continuous form within a boundary, unconnected with any other object. To that end, it was conceived as a self-contained unity not only in relation to the other objects in the relief but in relation to the beholder also. By way of achieving this effect, the sculptor had, as far as possible, to suppress suggestions of space. He had to arrange the objects in the relief as individual forms placed one beside the other or carved in different planes on top of each other but not actually behind each other. If they were placed behind each other, some of them would escape the eye of the beholder and so not be grasped promptly as individual self-contained forms.

Facture: the action or manner of making a thing and the framing of its parts. Like a painting, a relief sculpture creates an image of a world within the edges of a plane surface. A picture and a relief sculpture must organise that image according to the play of distance and proximity, dividing the objects represented into foreground and background. Painting does this by illusion. Relief sculpture does it by illusion and in reality. A carved relief is cut back into the stone from the surface in parallel planes. Each plane has a real depth, an actual distance from the surface, and, as fashioned into form, brings about an illusion of depth in relation to other forms. If the sculptor cuts too deeply, through too many planes, he will deny himself the material necessary to maintain the illusion. This illusion is largely the result of the play of light and shadow, which has as much to do with the absence of form as with form as such. The plastic characteristic of relief sculpture lies in its flatness and in its treatment of planes. The sculptor must have command over the planes. Antique relief sculpture was composed in the plane and carved in such a way as to avoid the representation of depth and, just about immediately, to excite the sense of an interconnected, coherent unity.

The main difference between Christ on the Beasts at Bewcastle and Ruthwell seems, initially, to lie in the ways the sculptors worked to different effect within the material limits of the circumscribed framing edge of the plane – an arched trapezium at Bewcastle; a parallelogram at Ruthwell, narrower at the top than the bottom – and within the self-contained figure of Christ.

Let us start with the panel on the Bewcastle monument. On the left, the edge of this panel was cut in at ninety degrees to a depth of about 1¼ inches but on the right, in the arch, it was cut to that depth on an incline. A depth of about 1¼ inches seems to have been maintained across the relief. There's very little actual excavated or illusory space around the figures: reduced to the least disturbing measure, it is just sufficient to define their forms in the plane of vision. Whatever Christ is wearing, all the draperies have their identities as sculptural forms in relation to the outline of the figure, the shape of the panel, and the plane. (We could see the arch as shaped to echo Christ's halo.) Though we can no longer make out everything, we feel sure that each form is just about in its proper planar relation to every other form. The pictorial qualities of sculptural relief make it possible to talk of a picture plane: the illusory plane in the narrated world of the relief that is closest to the beholder. As far as we can make out, the backs of the beasts, Christ's toes and the hand holding the scroll – perhaps also the gathered draperies falling from Christ's arms and his right hand – lie on the picture plane. The plane at the back of the panel, the background plane, establishes the distance plane: the illusory and real plane in the narrated world of the relief that is furthest from the beholder. The sculptor has provided just sufficient perceptual clues to represent the forms that needed to be represented and, at the same time, sustain them as forms parallel to the surface. The neatest and subtlest carving made the halo. It is cut away on its front surface to strike the beholder as if it is radiating from behind Christ's head. The *Corpus* describes it as 'a large dished halo'.[12] It almost merges with the background plane at Christ's shoulders. At the top of the arch it merges with the actual plane surface of the mass of the monument, but in such a way as not to break the illusion of the picture plane. Instead, it confirms the plane's coherence. Christ's feet and the beasts, though their forms are gently rounded, have been flattened on to the plane. The figure of Christ lies securely within the planes, between the surface of the actual stone that's been cut away and the background plane beyond which the chisel did not cut and the eye cannot pass.

The vertical axis of the composition is slightly to the right of the panel's vertical axis. The difference is slight and does not disrupt the composition's symmetry. The greatest asymmetry is established by the shape of the edge of the arch, which makes an abrupt and definite spring from the roll moulding on the left side and makes a long gently curving transition on the right – the same asymmetry characterises the arch over the panel at the base of the monument. The halo is also asymmetrical, though the asymmetry is hardly striking. Together, the two vertical axes and the halo's asymmetry – and, it should be added, the different ways that the arch has been cut away at each side of the halo – enliven the overall stability of the composition and the framing edge of the panel but do not disrupt it. The asymmetries add an interest that is registered in seeing but makes little effect in seeing ... as.

No matter what Christ is supposed to be wearing, the formal elements have been arranged in a predominantly vertical pattern within the outline of the figure and across the panel. The formal elements direct the eye to the bottom of the panel. The non-vertical forms conform to this pattern. The edges of Christ's cloak, for example, tight across his chest, converge in two diagonals *down* towards the scroll. Below the scroll, balancing the diagonals, the looped drapery – which may have become 'strange' to the extent that, as sculptural form, it was turned to emphasise or exaggerate the way it hangs rather than the way it curves – *weighs down* between the falling draperies on each side of it. Even the zigzags that suggest the hem of the cloak, and describe how the cloth falls across the arms, are so disposed to direct the eye *down* rather than across the panel; such diversions from the vertical that they provide are returned to it when they meet the outline of the figure. The arrangement of the draperies and the emphatic verticality of the composition, different above and below the horizontal axis of the figure, but nevertheless balanced, ensures that almost everything within the outline of the figure bears down on the beasts so that they hardly make it into the panel.

It's the clothes that disclose the figure of Christ. Though one does not see it, one is convinced that, under the *tunica* and cloak, there is a body possessed of a naturalism and substantial corporeality.

There's a connection between touch and the elusiveness of carved detail that evokes an awareness of the actions of the sculptor. Lines, which here are formed by shadows at the edges where shallow planes meet, not by actual lines cut into the stone, seem to cling to the body. They quicken the eye across the surface. Line is predominant in the upper part of the figure, rounded forms in the lower. Deeply cut rounded forms, which trap more light and produce more shadow, affect us differently. Shadows, which have no form, are apt to effect uncertainty. They generate a vitality different to that of line: one that takes more time to penetrate. We must look into shadow to perceive what's there; shadows slow the way we come to an understanding of form. More than anything, it is the economy of carving and the balanced play of the two-dimensionality of line and the three-dimensionality of rounded form, here and there relatively deeply cut, and the different kinds of shadow cast by them, that give this figure a balanced actual and an illusory materiality and weight, such that it seems subject to the force of gravity.

This Christ has his self-contained divine majesty on earth but he is not firmly grounded on the beasts. Only his toes make contact with them. It is not clear if he is arriving or departing, descending or ascending. Though he has weight and mass, he is light on his feet: neither down nor up, he is, as it were, up and down at the same time – suspended. And without the beasts there he would remain – suspended. Like the figure of Christ, the beasts are arranged symmetrically and, as formal elements, balance each other across the vertical axes. They fill the corners at the bottom of the panel and provide the necessary resistance to support Christ and, in the narrated world of the relief, taking over from the angels, keep him off the earth by lifting him up. However, Christ is not just uplifted. At the edges of the panel, the beasts' outside forelimbs, raised in praise no doubt, are important but easily overlooked formal elements that redirect and elevate Christ's mass, and the beholder's eye, back along the outline of his body to the arch at the top of the panel.

Let's now look at the panel on the Ruthwell monument. The vertical sides and top edge have been cut away on a conspicuous curving incline to various depths, greater at the bottom of the panel than at the top. The halo has been excavated from the corners of the panel to a depth of probably 2 inches. The area between the beasts and between the beasts and the hem of Christ's *tunica* has been removed to a depth of about 2½ inches. Here at Ruthwell, it makes little sense to talk about the background plane in relation to the material plane surface of the mass of the monument. Nor does it make much sense to talk of a self-contained figure within an outline in the plane of vision. The figure of Christ, in particular, is not bounded in the plane of vision as a distinct form in relation to the circumscribed edge of the panel. Some of what's there to be seen is not immediately accessible to sight: it disappears from view. The amount of excavated space around the figure has given it something more like a contour in relation to an actual mass. It is *as if* the sculptor wanted to break with the fact of the plane. To this end, he secured and freed an actual spatial zone within the surface of the monument and carved, or tried to carve, figures that would seem really to occupy that actual space. It's a niche-like panel.

Though the sculptor was carving a relief, and had to be careful how he cut through the planes, much followed from the decision to have the figure of Christ positioned in an actual space excavated from the surface of the monument. Though the plastic character of a relief lies in its flatness, the sculptor had decided that his would be a work that did not avoid the representation of depth. And, since the arrangement of the formal elements could no longer be determined and held together by the external relation that would have been established by the shape of the panel's circumscribed edge – at least not to the extent that it was at Bewcastle – it had to be held together by other relations. Wherever possible, those relations would be internal relations established between striking space-revealing forms.

If there is a picture plane in the narrated world of this relief it seems not to have been adhered to, at least not as rigorously as in the relief at Bewcastle. The back of the beast on the left and the shoulder of the beast on the right can be seen as closest to it. They are materially and illusorily closer to us than the figure of Christ, which stands, one foot completely and firmly on the snout of each beast, some distance behind the picture plane. The scroll must lie close to the same plane as Christ's toes; the raised hand perhaps on that plane also. But the halo must be radiating from around or behind Christ's head at some distance behind the picture plane. It effects the sense not so much of an immaterial disk of light as of something solid and three-dimensional. At the top edge of the panel, where it coincides with the actual material plane surface of the excavated stone, it establishes another picture plane, one in front of the picture plane at the bottom of the panel. The halo cannot be on the picture plane at both places unless it was intended to have or came to have the form of a funnel or a deep dish – the preferred form of halo on the Ruthwell monument's pinkish-grey lower stone; on the pale red upper stone, the halo of the figure that is usually seen as John the Baptist is a more two-dimensional form.

As at Bewcastle, there are two vertical axes in the panel at Ruthwell: the panel's vertical axis and the composition's vertical axis. The vertical compositional axis is a little to the right of the panel's vertical axis. This partly explains why Christ's halo seems unbalanced – as it is at Bewcastle, its left side is broader than its right – but not why it seems somewhat out of proportion in relation to the figure. It is a very large halo. The beasts are arranged on either side of the panel's vertical axis but they, too, are unbalanced. And so is the figure of Christ. Self-contained and frontal, the edge of the figure at Ruthwell, compared to edge of the figure at Bewcastle, because it has the characteristics of a contour rather than an outline, is much more animated. It's a springing, bouncing, rounded form that moves differently at each side of the figure, where the transitions of height are different. Compared with the figure of Christ at Bewcastle, it has veered away from the rigid stability that is associated with the stereotypical late-Antique and early figure of Christian Majesty. We see the same thing within the boundary of the figure. Whatever Christ is wearing, the drapery has not been arranged in a symmetrical pattern across the vertical axis of the panel or the composition, or across the horizontal axis of the figure itself. It seems most to relate to the way the accompanying inscription has been arranged around the sides of the panel. It makes a pattern that directs the eye in a play of directions back *and* forth and across *and* around the figure. Very little in the way that the formal elements have been arranged directs the eye down the panel – not with any force.

The most literally roundabout form in the composition is the halo. The lines that are cut into it – there's another asymmetry here – direct the eye across its concavity to Christ's face. For a moment, we focus on Christ who would once have been looking at us, but his attention does not hold ours. The eye moves to the sling, which creates a movement over his left shoulder and down the arm; across the chest; around the neck and down the left shoulder again; and so on – roundabout. These formal elements seem to be part of a larger pattern in the upper part of the body that takes in the sling, the left arm, the scroll, the raised right arm and hand, the edge of the halo – and roundabout again. The two draperies on Christ's chest, both carved with the same dynamic striated pattern as the sling – we might see the sling as made of the same piece of cloth if the *tunica*'s right sleeve were not also carved with the same pattern – direct the eye down, across the chest, to the right forearm, hand and scroll, but no further. The drapery, on the left of the panel, which is not part of the sling, goes nowhere, unless you *see* it *as* passing under the scroll to turn into the 'little "bag" under the right arm'. Its outside edge disappears behind the hand and the scroll at the panel's vertical axis. Perhaps the 'little "bag"' is supposed to represent a pouch in the folds of a *pallium*. The pattern in the lower part of the body is much more vertical, though not as vertical as it might at first appear. Something about the forms that describe the cloak and the *tunica* as they fall free of the body seems to resist the force of gravity or, if not resist it, interrupt it. Below the hand holding the scroll, there's that 'little "bag"' under Christ's right arm. Once seen, it is endlessly absorbing. It's positioned in a deep space that has been excavated from between the edges of the cloak as it falls from wherever it falls. The 'bag' has a furled look that forms a brief but prominent salience away from the vertical just where, if it were not there, the eye would move in free fall down the figure directly to the hem of the *tunica*, and, for some distance, in deep space. It interrupts that downward movement, suspends gravity with a turn to the right, to the panel's vertical axis and to the folds of the cloak, which take up more space on this side of the panel than on the other and are arranged differently. The movement down the folds in the cloak is converted into another movement sideways at the hem, one at each side: two coiling, curling zigzags signifying folds in drapery that seems to fall from nowhere in particular, asymmetrical across the panel's vertical axis, that direct the eye to the right and to the left, across the figure to its bounding contour, then around it, and back into space. Below the hem of the cloak, the *tunica* hangs in four emphatic almost vertical folds. Neither the drapery nor the eye can ignore the pull of gravity in this part of the figure. Finally, some distance away from the bottom of the panel, the more or less horizontal hem of the *tunica* establishes the lowest limit of the bulk of the figure and terminates all downward forces within and across it.

The farther we go in describing the figure of Christ, the more difficult it becomes to do so adequately. The figure is, as a self-contained form, composed of lots of formal elements, each one a detail demanding attention for the quality of its carving alone. To give just two examples: notice how Christ's raised hand must have been almost free of the block; and how the hem of the *tunica* has been drilled out to hollow the folds – and, here and there, the hem of the cloak also. We're supposed to take note of these details, admire and value them as carving. But so many are they that it is impossible to lay hold of them completely and aggregate them. At Bewcastle the underlying principle structuring the panel was directed towards ensuring that the individual forms and formal elements in the relief presented the beholder with a unified totality. That is not the underlying principle structuring the panel at Ruthwell.

At Bewcastle, form and facture disclosed the figure and gave it a substantial corporeality. At Ruthwell, form and facture do not always bring about the sense that there is a body beneath the draperies. Generally, they convey a sense of changing action: they disclose space, not a body. Around the 'little "bag"', for example, and below it, in the area on the left side of the panel's vertical axis, and perhaps on Christ's chest, next to the arm in the sling, the need to find forms that move freely through space has robbed the figure of some actual or illusory materiality and corporeality. In these areas, and elsewhere, which required the sculptor to negotiate abrupt changes of plane, the carving of limbs and draperies has cut so deeply that it, and the effects of light and shadow that are effected by it, begins to dissolve the unity of the body. These effects are greatly exaggerated or enhanced, and become quite emotive, when seen by artificial light, which might suggest that the monument was intended to be sited inside where it would have been seen by the tremulous light of candles and torches distributed throughout the church.[13]

At Ruthwell, Christ's feet are *on* the beasts. We mustn't overlook the beasts. As we've seen, they are arranged symmetrically across the panel, but as asymmetrical forms. More of the beast on the left makes it into the panel. By way of introducing some distinctions between them, the sculptor has provided them with different kinds of ears. More details. The beasts turn towards each other from the shoulders and up to Christ – the beast on the right almost anthropomorphising at its shoulder as it does so. Some attempt has been made to foreshorten them. Perhaps they are supposed to be rising up to Christ, not moving along the ground on all fours but standing on their hind legs. Their heads must, in the narrated world of the relief, recede in depth so that Christ can stand on them. The inner forelimbs move to cross below their heads, the paw of the beast on the left seemingly holding the leg of the beast on the right – three digits still clearly there: another detail. Their noses touch, almost on the panel's vertical axis. They could be animated like this, and so made to illustrate a series of complex actions, because the increased width at the bottom of the panel provided sufficient material out of which the sculptor could carve forms in depth that could be turned in space. Unlike the beasts on the Bewcastle monument, which hardly make it into the panel and, as forms, adhere to the plane, these beasts have a substantial materiality and a kind of mobility. Also, they are much larger in relation to the size of the panel and in relation to the narrated world of the relief. Christ is a relatively slight figure. He is small in relation to the overall size of the panel and in relation to the beasts. *If* the sculptor had wanted to, and it seems he did not, he had no need to make the beasts symmetrical immobile forms as a way bringing about the feeling that they could support Christ, ground him on earth.

Maybe this is the moment to take stock and sum the differences of form and facture. The relief at Ruthwell is held together by narrative form as much as it is by sculptural form. Christ relates to the beasts in an active way and they relate to him and each other in an active way also. The figures have their being in a space that the sculptor has literally removed from the mass of the stone: they move relatively freely within it. That space is their world, and it is a space removed from ours. It takes time to see and understand this world, to grasp its sculptural and narrative forms. It has a fluid, discontinuous complexity. The figures at Bewcastle are held close between two planes and fast within the circumscribed shape of the edge of the panel. They have their existence in the plane and have no need of any more space than was sufficient to establish their outlines within and apart from the circumscribed edge of the panel. Their forms and formal components are arranged in a vertical pattern across the panel's vertical axes and assert the planar quality of relief and the flat surface of the monument on which they're carved. This pattern effects a fixed, inflexible, coherent unity. It was designed to have a direct impact on the beholder. One can easily imagine that, when the monument was produced and first used, its effect was more or less immediate. The unmistakable focus is the self-contained figure of Christ who, engaged in an action that involves the beasts, addresses himself first and foremost to the beholder from a plane more or less immediately in and of our world, not from a space apart from it. In the end, it comes down to space, to different ideas, conceptions and consciousness of space and of the bodily in relation to space. These are more matters of psychophysical being-in-the-world than of relief sculpture, which was but the means of bringing them to practical consciousness.

We could see these different ways that Christ and the beasts on the Ruthwell and Bewcastle monuments were brought to sculptural form – the way that solids and voids, beings and non-beings were distributed in and across the relief – as expressing or representing each community's sense of space, its sense of place and time. If we did, we might see the kind of space that characterises the panel at Ruthwell as made of material that has been literally and metaphorically removed from the mass of the monument. This space is 'inside' the monument. It is a self-contained and seemingly self-sufficient narrative space in which actions and events occur. Beings have their existence within it at a distance removed from the beholder 'outside' in the actual world. We could see this space as expressing or representing the bodily in relation to the space of a monastic community. At Bewcastle, however, though there is space 'inside' the panel, Christ and the beasts are more or less coexistent with the mass of the monument: it's their world; they're made of and out of it, but not so obviously installed within it; and it's a world not so far removed or set apart from the actual world of the beholder. This panel effects a different sense of space, and of the bodily in relation to space. We could assume that it was made of a different kind of community, one mentally and materially closer to and more connected with the world around it. But how could we test these ways of seeing? What could we test them against? We know nothing of the lived reality of the communities that produced and first used these monuments: except what we can glean from the monuments themselves. And, in the end, though these ways of seeing might strike one as useful, in as much as they seem to open up the field of study, it is easy to overestimate their use-value. They are, after all, little more than intuitive analogies of form and content based on comparisons between the apprehension of sculptural form and ideas about different kinds of communities, and as such are but one more type of similarity subject to the same strictures on similarity that we raised with regard to style. So, engaging with matters that touch on stylistic analysis, we use them, but make our prejudices clear.

Whatever the differences between the panels representing Christ on the Beasts at Bewcastle and Ruthwell signify, we now recognise them as more than what might be considered 'minor differences of style'.[14] But even if we were to think of them in that way we would still have to bear in mind that the meaning of each panel is contextualised by the formal, iconographical and textual programmes of which it is an affective and effective part. No matter how we make sense of the Christ on the Beasts panel at Ruthwell, it effects its meanings and expressive qualities within a complex theological programme that isn't there on the monument at Bewcastle.

The point, however, is not just to accumulate differences. We're wondering what kind of knowledge we would gain of the two monuments if we insisted, contra the principles of style, on their dissimilarity and concentrated on interpreting the differences of form, facture and iconography as signs of different intentions or functions and different circumstances of production and first use. We need to look at some of these differences.

However, before we do, we must not forget the different place *of* each monument. Whereas we can be almost certain that the monument at Bewcastle occupies the site for which it was intended, we can be certain that the monument at Ruthwell does not. Whatever else it was intended to do, the Bewcastle monument was built to bring about, represent and express the relation between a community and a place. It seems to have been intended as a focus of a settlement: a material thing that kept building, dwelling, thinking *in* place. What survives is still capable of exciting an embodied relation between earth and sky, past, present and future, and of gathering them into a heightened sense of being-in-the-world, a heightened sense of place, such that it is very difficult to imagine Bewcastle without it. One could say that the monument preserves place at Bewcastle. The Ruthwell monument would have been intended to do most if not all of that, but we have no idea where it was intended to do it. The monument has no immediate connection with the historical landscape around it. It is especially poignant that the place where it now *is* has none of the experiential depth of time and place that characterises Bewcastle. We know that it was moved about and came to rest contingently, and arbitrarily. Preserved but not preserving, it is removed from wherein it now is: displaced; compromised; tolerated.

As we saw in the previous chapters when we looked at what survives of the actual monuments and how that was taken into discourse, the Bewcastle monument is likely to have been a column at the moment of its production and first use and may never have had a cross-head, whereas the Ruthwell monument seems to have been a column that came to have the shape of a cross. Resourced, as these columns must have been, by knowledge of the Egyptian obelisks and the triumphal and memorial columns in Rome and elsewhere that caught the attention of Anglo-Saxons, they would have been intended as monuments that represented or evoked a kind of Romanness.[15] It is germane that Bede's *Historia ecclesiastica* begins with Julius Caesar's crossing into Britain.[16] Bede's historical and geographical worldview was unavoidably appropriated from the legacy of the Roman *imperium*.[17] Northumbria's Roman past, filled with the contemporary, was there to be used and turned to the work of the Northumbrian present – in different ways. In the latter half of the seventh century and in the eighth century, Northumbria represented itself as being in various kinds of relations of association with an imaginary and real Rome, both ancient and modern. When it came to making the Ruthwell and Bewcastle monuments, Northumbria appropriated the form of an important type of Roman monument, an obelisk or a column, to its own imperial project in very much the same way that it built churches in stone *iuxta morem Romanorum*, which were often erected in or close by the surviving remains of Roman fortifications.[18] These 'Roman' churches and monuments may not have been many but within or alongside a ruined ancient Rome, which was still very much part of the lived reality of Northumbria in the eighth century, they would have marked the landscape very effectively. We should keep in mind that the Bewcastle monument was erected within the probably substantial remains of a Roman fort, *Fanum Cocidii*, the temple or shrine of Cocidius, and that the Ruthwell monument is sited only a hundred yards or so from an unexcavated Roman marching camp or temporary fort (NY 102 677). A difference to be noted here is that whoever sited the monument at Ruthwell did not want it in the remains of Rome, no matter how substantial or insubstantial. That would be the case even *if* it were once sited in or near the fort. It was a Roman monument but one always or in the end intended for another place: a Roman place apart from the place of old Rome. The monument at Bewcastle made a close material and ideological relation with what survived of the old Rome. The monument at Ruthwell made a different relation somewhat removed from whatever of Rome survived there.

Though the columnar form of both monuments (Figs 15 and 42) would have connoted Romanness, at its beginning the monument at Ruthwell would have been a different kind of column to that at Bewcastle. The two columns are not the same shape nor are they decorated in the same way, and so they affect us, as we assume they would have affected their medieval beholders, differently. The Bewcastle monument is square in section at the bottom and oblong at the top.[19] The Ruthwell monument's pale pinkish-grey lower stone or column is oblong in section throughout. Each side of the Bewcastle monument is edged with a plain broad outer roll moulding that is echoed by a fine plain inner roll moulding. Uninscribed, nothing delays the eye in travelling up and down these roll mouldings. Flat band mouldings are a distinctive feature of the Ruthwell monument: its sides are edged with flat band mouldings, and flat band mouldings separate the figure panels on its west and east sides. All these mouldings are inscribed with textual matter that must be weighed up. It takes time to do this. The slender, tapering form of the Bewcastle column, neatly supplemented by the shapes of its decorative panels, two springing to arches, enhances the dynamic upward movement characteristic of an obelisk. The Ruthwell column seems less slender, less free of the ground, less upwardly mobile. Each monument supports its form and iconography differently and to different effect.

We have seen how very different are the panels representing Christ on the Beasts. These differences characterise the other panels also. At Ruthwell, the figures occupy actual spaces excavated from the mass of the monument. They move in and across them with a kind of freedom. The panels are composed of space-revealing forms, several of them very deeply carved. Some especially noticeable details on the east side of the Ruthwell monument include the cruciform dished haloes that, like the one on the west side, are hollowed on the surface and deeply undercut behind. The halo around Christ healing the bind man (Fig. 64) is a neatly carved ellipse, deeply cut away at the top left of the panel, where it approaches the picture plane, delicately receding until it merges with the background plane on the right. Some now missing details seem to have been free or almost free of the supporting block. You'll notice, for example, the wand that Christ is using to heal the blind man, which is now but the feint trace of a scar on the background plane, and the blind man's left forearm; Christ's hand raised in speech or blessing above the beasts (Fig. 55) and Mary Magdalen (Fig. 63); and the left foreleg of the donkey carrying the Holy Family (Fig. 57).

The need to represent figures interacting with other figures, their forms moving in space, necessitated an increase of modelling and in the Annunciation panel (Fig. 65), where dynamic changes of plane were required, to a need to have forms, which, as far as can be made out from what survives, move out beyond the edges of the panel, not by much but by sufficient to be worthy of note. On the left, whatever the angel is wearing seems to move out on to the flat band moulding. On the right, it looks as if Mary's cloak moves out on to the moulding at the side of the panel; her feet seem to move on to the moulding at the bottom of the panel. Form and facture are different at Bewcastle. Forms and formal elements are outlined in the plane and, whether they're making figures, interlace patterns, plant trails, medallion plant-scrolls or inhabited plant-scrolls, are situated between the material plane surface of the monument and the background plane of the panel. Everything adheres to the plane and the circumscribed edge of the panel. Despite the effects of movement, it's a more stable, two-dimensional world on the Bewcastle monument. *If* the figure in the panel at the bottom of the west side, the secular aristocrat with a hawk (Fig. 21),[20] turns to the left, then it makes a stiff turn that holds somewhat awkwardly to the plane and generates little or no sense of the space in which it turns.

The single panel of chequers (Fig. 27) and the five individual panels of plain interlace (Figs 26, 27, 32, 34 and 35) on the Bewcastle monument and their absence from the monument at Ruthwell must also be taken into consideration when a relation of similarity is asserted between the two monuments. Plain interlace, as distinct from zoomorphic lacing patterns, is a very common decoration in Anglo-Saxon visual culture from the mid seventh century onwards. Sometimes, because of the way a strand changes direction and, instead of crossing, breaks a pattern into sections, any 'basic pattern', when set as a 'mirror image' of itself to make a 'complete pattern', can form a cross shape in the areas between the sections.[21] Any individual pattern might contain several of these cross shapes. They seem to have a special value. They arrive within the pattern and, having been recognised, and fulfilled their purpose, they return within it. Though they are there, they are never obviously and immediately there. It is impossible to see them and the pattern around them at the same time. One has to turn from one kind of seeing to another: from *seeing* them *as* basic patterns to seeing and understanding what is being formed in the sections between them. It takes awhile to do this. The cross shapes in the sections between the mirrored patterns are real enough but not quite as securely in the same space – the same place and time – of the world as are the strands of interlace themselves and the patterns made by them. Each one takes the form of an ambiguous absent presence. Neither present nor absent, neither in the world nor not in the world, it is both present and absent, both in the world and not in it. The world of plain interlace is, at these moments, not an either/or world.

Interlace was surely designed to elicit this mode of attention. It imagines a beholder who is able to follow its particulars of articulation wherever they might lead and to whatever they might form. The patterns were designed to bring into being a very active kind of seeing ... as. One is supposed to go over each panel thoroughly and attend to the sections between the patterns: to see the obvious significance and to look for whatever might be revealed between the patterns. Within the overall scheme of things on the Bewcastle monument, the interlace patterns – and perhaps the chequer panel – possess an especially vivid heuristic value. But how many crosses can you see in the sections between the patterns of any one panel? In some panels you can see a cross. In others you can see several crosses. But in others you can't see any. For the beholder: seeing, and *seeing* something *as* form between-the-patterns. For the designer: representing something by drawing attention to it *as if* you're hiding it: 'looming', 'intriguing' or 'riddling' it to awareness.

The kind of plain interlace pattern that appears on the Bewcastle monument seems to have had its beginnings in the ecclesiastical centres of Anglo-Saxon England.[22] It has been suggested that the cross shapes in the sections between the patterns might be seen as representing the hidden pattern that early Christians took to exist in God's creation.[23] We should, however, beware reducing the meaning and value of plain interlace to the use that was made of it by Christian institutions. There's probably more to it than that, for making significant shapes within decorative patterns seems always to have been an aspect of Anglo-Saxon visual culture.[24]

Ornament supplements form, makes it more fluent and coherent, adds visual interest to it and increases its attraction to the eye. It heightens form's aesthetic interest, if not always its aesthetic value. Ornament is usually, and certainly at its best, more than mere decoration. The Anglo-Saxons valued ornament and attributed apotropaic power to it: a helmet might be decorated with wild boars so that no sword should cut through it; a sword might be decorated with spiral patterns, worm-looped to ensure it did precisely that.[25] No doubt the interlace patterns on the monument at Bewcastle boded well for some and not for others. Tracing 'magic' lines that embodied thought, the Anglo-Saxons were putting aspects of their world on to the surfaces of their monuments, bringing them to the general eye. In ways we have hardly begun to glimpse, ornament represents the general consciousness of the living shape, the material production and general processes of the social, political and intellectual life of the community that produced and used it. Perhaps it signified a way of dealing with the world, of working out how it was ordered and how it might be thought of as a whole. Something was being recovered as a striking fact by the people who designed these panels of plain interlace, some particular and substantial set of qualities and values which was necessarily derived from elsewhere. It's difficult to know just what. Recourse to the idea of the apotropaic or a predilection for ambiguity or hiding things or riddling doesn't seem to get us very far.[26] A new form of visuality was being accommodated, contained, or manifesting itself in an old form.

Looking at the differences between the Bewcastle and Ruthwell monuments, however, the important thing is not to puzzle the meaning of interlace or how it might be seen as representing the material and mental life of the community that produced and first used it. The point is, granted that interlace is one of the most common types of ornament on Anglo-Saxon sculpture, that we should note the value of the patterns on the Bewcastle monument in relation to the absence of any such patterns on the monument at Ruthwell. If those persons who produced and first used the Ruthwell monument knew how to pattern interlace and to see what lay within it then why were they not concerned to display that knowledge on their monument? If they didn't possess those patterns: why not? Or perhaps their interest in riddling things to awareness is represented otherwise. Perhaps it's there in the language of the Old English runic inscriptions on the monument's narrow north and east sides:

> Almighty god unclothed himself when he wished to climb the gallows brave [before all] men. [I dared not] bow ...

> [I raised] up a powerful king, lord of heaven, I did not dare bend. Men mocked us both together, I [was] with blood drenched [poured] ...

> Christ was on the cross but eager ones came from afar nobles to the one. I [beheld] it all. Sorely I was with sorrows troubled, [I] bowed ...

> Wounded with arrows they laid him down limb-spent, they placed themselves at the head of his body [they beheld there] ...

We will look at the riddlic quality of these inscriptions in Chapter 7.

It is difficult to maintain a sharp distinction between form, ornamentation and iconography, especially with regard to the sundial on the Bewcastle monument (Fig. 35). There's no sundial on the Ruthwell monument. We can be sure that the monument at Bewcastle was intended to function in the open air. We can't be sure that that was the case with the monument at Ruthwell.

The sundial is no insignificant detail for it is probably our earliest surviving English instrument for calculating the passage of time. It is also unique amongst the surviving post-Roman, European medieval dials that can be dated before 1066, and with only three or four exceptions all post-Conquest medieval dials, because it marks not only the daytime liturgical hours but all twelve hours of daylight. It is *as if* whoever produced and first used the monument wanted, in a peculiarly modern way, to know what time of day it was and were concerned to represent an interest in how the passage of time, controlled by the sun, could be shown and conjoined, by the gnomon and its shadow, to the persons who consulted it. We will have more to say about the sundial in Chapter 6; suffice to say here that it puts a big difference between the Bewcastle and Ruthwell monuments. The monument at Ruthwell was not a timepiece. If those persons who produced and first used it had an interest in time, such is the sophistication of their theology, it was in the institutional and ultimately political aspects of time as mediated by and controlled by the Christian calendar, Easter tables and liturgy. Calendars do not measure the passage of time as sundials do. The Ruthwell monument functioned with reference to a calendar. The Bewcastle monument functioned, almost immediately, with regard to a sundial.

Both columns exhibit an abundance of inscriptions. Those surviving on the Bewcastle monument are all runic; those on the Ruthwell monument are runic and Roman.

The longest inscription (Fig. 22) on the Bewcastle monument is located on the west side between the secular aristocrat with a hawk and Christ on the Beasts. This inscription tells us that the monument was erected as a 'sigbecn' by 'Hwætred' and at least one other to the memory of someone called '[A]lcfri[th]'. It's a memorial text that, in its penultimate line, seems to invoke the reader to prayer.[27] The runic inscriptions (Figs 59, 60, 67, 68 and 69) on the Ruthwell monument – we referred to them a moment ago – are laid out on the flat-band mouldings around the inhabited plant-scrolls on its narrow north and south sides. They give us four lines of Old English representing the crucifixion. The Latin inscriptions are arranged around the figure panels on the east and west sides. We will look at these and the ways they relate to the figure panels in Chapter 9 when we consider the special significance that the stone cross seems to have had in Northumbria in the early Middle Ages.

Latin, the language in which the mysteries of Christianity were recited to increasing numbers of people whose native language was Old English and who could understand almost not a word of it, was the privileged instrument of Church if not state bureaucracies. But whereas Latin is the language on the main sides of the Ruthwell monument, with Old English doing its signifying on the narrow sides, the Bewcastle monument's dominant textual language is Old English, and it does its signifying wherever text was deemed necessary.

Both monuments are inscribed with the *nomen sacrum*. At Bewcastle it is given as the Latin 'Jesus Christus' translated into Old English and transliterated in runes. On the west side, in the area between the Christ on the Beasts and John the Baptist panels (Fig. 24), there's 'G[E]SSUS KRISTTUS'. And at the top of the north side (Fig. 28) there's '[GE]SSUS'. The use of double runes where single runes would be expected needs comment. It would be easy to put these double runes down to 'scribal errors' or the 'rune master's mistakes' but this wouldn't be generally satisfactory.[28] Nor is the suggestion very convincing that runes may have been doubled so that an inscription might fill a panel more satisfactorily – that explanation tends towards imposing a modern sense of balance and order, or modern ideas of what constitutes adequate typography, on to a historically and culturally specific community that seems to have had other standards of satisfaction. Whoever was responsible for inscribing 'GESSUS' on the monument must have thought that *that* was how you spelt 'Jesus' when you took it into Old English and runes. As one of the most astute commentators on these matters has pointed out, 'spellings like these are only errors in the sense that they do not conform to the usual orthography of written texts. It could be suggested, however, that the Old English rune-masters worked within a less rigid, perhaps even a quite different, orthographical tradition from the Old English scribes, and so used spellings not acceptable to the latter.'[29]

Whoever produced and first used the Bewcastle monument knew some Latin but chose to have the inscriptions cut in Old English. Whoever produced and first used the Ruthwell monument's lower stone or column knew Latin and Old English and wanted both languages represented, each in its proper place and communicating an apt content. It may be that the community at Bewcastle was accomplished in both languages but chose not to represent its accomplishment. Though the form of its monument was Roman, it retained its mother tongue when communicating its textual message. The community that produced the Ruthwell monument was accomplished and chose to represent that accomplishment and, perhaps, to take delight and signify its sophistication in it.

Just how accomplished and sophisticated it was can be measured by the way that it plays with the visual form of the *nomen sacrum*: IhS XPS (Fig. 55). The six letters are the abbreviations of the *nomen sacrum* as rendered in Greek capitals ΙΗΣΟΥΣ ΧΡΙΣΤΟΣ. Medieval scribes took the Greek Eta (H) for the Latin aspirate (H), which could be figured as a minuscule 'h'. The Greek Rho (P) was taken for the Latin P (P); and the Greek Chi (X, χ) was replaced with the Latin X (X) to which it was seen as similar though it had a different phonetic value. As it is inscribed on the Ruthwell monument, with 'Eta' given as a minuscule 'h' and 'chi', retaining its Greek form and given as an enlarged insular half-uncial χ, the value given to the *nomen sacrum* is such that any beholder who had seen the Chi Rho at Matthew 1.18 in a high-status gospel book, or knew about the decorative calligraphic conventions of the display pages of those books, would call it to mind. The insular half-uncial χ is one of several letter forms on the Ruthwell monument that must have been resourced by the calligraphic conventions of a manuscript culture.[30] This form of the *nomen sacrum* puts another difference between the two monuments. Along with the other different epigraphical and linguistic preferences, it may represent differences of tradition and of Church politics.

The use of IhS χPS in the inscription around the Christ on the Beasts panel at Ruthwell can also be explained by the opportunity that the Greek letter Chi, associated with the cross, and known as the "crux decussata," presented to make a visual rhyme with the crossed paws of the beasts and the cross on Christ's halo in the panel below. But it can only be partly explained in this way because it is used twice in the same inscription, the second time where a visual rhyme with sculptural form was not required: 'IhS χPS IVDEχ AEQVITATIS'. Its second instance of use, in IVDEχ, is perhaps more suggestive. *If*, as seems likely, whoever designed the Latin inscriptions on the lower stone knew that they were using the Greek abbreviation of the Latin Christus and that the Greek Chi (X, χ) could be either retained or replaced with the Latin X, they also realised that, in certain contexts of use, the visual form of the Greek letter Chi could be used to represent the Latin X and still make sense, despite its different phonetic value. Having grasped this, they figured IVDEX as IVDEχ and so put a synecdoche of 'Christ' into 'Judge'.

Names and the idea of naming were important to the persons who produced and first used the Ruthwell and Bewcastle monuments. On the latter, some individual names actually fill what would otherwise be empty fillets. But whereas all the names on the Ruthwell monument, with the exception of Paul and Anthony, are of persons mentioned in the Bible and are of very distant places and a very distant past, the names on the Bewcastle monument, with the exception of 'Jesus Christ', are, as they have survived, all Anglo-Saxon names.

Names and persons are being remembered on the monuments, brought and kept in the general eye but each monument presents us with different kinds of names, which have different values and significance. One value and significance that's easily overlooked is that only on the monument at Bewcastle are we given the names of the persons doing the remembering.

The prominence and importance of the long commemorative inscription on the west side of the Bewcastle monument suggests that the monument was erected to function as much as a locus of Anglo-Saxon memory as for any other reason. Memory, like wisdom, rests in places. Memory is incarnate at Bewcastle: the monument is its material form: its shape, images and texts functioning as a kind of 'tool for remembering'. Bewcastle was a 'place of lived memory': the inscription provides us with its 'documentary continuity.'[31] The idea of the epitaph evidences not only a need to mark but also a desire to overcome the difference between life and death. That could mark an agnostic or non-Christian desire but, as it's represented here, along with representations of Christian ideas and beliefs, it is given some theological and perhaps ecclesiastical significance as well.

We have not described and discussed all the ways in which the Ruthwell and Bewcastle monuments can be seen as different. For example, we have not pointed to the differences between the inhabited plant scrolls (Figs 59, 60 and 67, 68 and 69). Just the same, the foregoing should suffice for our present purpose. We need now to say something about the seemingly shared concern with certain themes that are signified through different material forms. The Ruthwell and Bewcastle monuments seem to share a concern with certain systems of ideas and beliefs, which they represent in different ways and to different effect. We will restrict ourselves to mentioning only what is obvious.

Both monuments are carved and inscribed with representations of different ideas about death and dying heroically: for example, the biblical death as it is represented by the Crucifixion panel on the Ruthwell monument and the not-quite-biblical crucifixion represented in the runic texts on its north and south sides. The persons who composed these texts represented the biblical crucifixion using their native language and their ideas about how an Anglo-Saxon warrior should die, and made Christ a 'ricnæ kyninc' and 'hlafard' who, about to be executed, 'brave [before all] men', goes to the gallows with no loss of his commanding authority. In the choice of words – those most sensitive indices of social change – that were used to make the texts, we see how the novel ideas of Christ's kingship could not quite be represented with the currently available signifiers of Germanic kingship. Words such as 'kyninc', 'hlafard' and 'dryhten', which may have been in the Ruthwell verses as well,[32] used to describe the Christian God, would still have signified not necessarily compatible Anglo-Saxon standards of moral excellence, ideas of uprightness and goodness that inhered in Germanic notions of what constituted courage, loyalty and generosity. The value of the Old English inscriptions is probably demeaned if reduced to a kind of harmonious continuity between different values achieved by means of words. It is better to stress the way the texts mark the linguistic difficulty that must have been experienced by persons trying to synthesise their commitment to a Germanic warrior mentality with ideas of Christianity. The texts give us a sense of a praiseworthy death, and a supreme confidence in death, but nothing, it seems, that signifies a triumph over death. The biblical death of Christ is there on the Bewcastle monument also, as it is on the monument at Ruthwell, in the form of the Agnus Dei: Christ as ruler of Heaven and Earth, sacrificial and holding out the promise of eternal life. As at Ruthwell, this biblical reference to Christ's death has its place in a relation of association with an Anglo-Saxon death, the death of '[A]lcfri[th]', an aristocrat and, perhaps, a king. The Ruthwell monument was erected primarily to commemorate, preserve and transmit the memory of the human life and afterlife of a divinity. The Bewcastle monument, which, as we saw in Chapter 3, was perhaps a 'pyramid' that marked the sepulchre of a pious warrior and powerful aristocrat, commemorated, preserved and transmitted the memory of a human being.

These residual and emerging ideas and beliefs about dying, the right ways to live and die, are inseparably bound up with ideas about kingship and nobility. There is the representation of Christ in majesty on the Ruthwell monument's west and east sides: made of Roman resources, a philosopher-judge formed in the imperial mode, albeit one with a Germanic moustache; and, in the inscriptions on its north and south sides, a different kind of character, an Anglo-Saxon military aristocrat, possessing all the virtues that attached to a *kyninc*, *hlafard* and *dryhten*, imperial perhaps (though, if so, in an Anglo-Saxon not Roman way), commanding unswerving loyalty and respect in life, and, in death, causing noblemen, 'æþþilæ', presumably his own kith and kin, tribe or clan, to hasten to his corpse. As at Ruthwell, so it is at Bewcastle, two lords, the one divine and the other human, have their metaphorical and metonymical places on the monument: each represented in sculpture and words: 'G[E]SSUS KRISTTUS' and '[A]lcfri[th]'.

And last but not least, we have in mind the way that ideas about women, about what it was to be a woman, are represented on the two monuments. On the Ruthwell monument images of women function not only in illustrations of Bible stories but also as signs of vivid types of female identity: on the pale pinkish-grey lower stone, the penitent Mary Magdalen (Fig. 63) and the Virgin Mary at the Annunciation (Fig. 65) and during the journey into or out of Egypt (Fig. 57); and on the pale red upper stone the image (Fig. 61) of *either* Mary and Martha, the good woman in secular society and the good woman in the monastic community, *or* Elizabeth and Mary at the visitation, two humble pregnant women. Penitence. Probity and virtue. Pregnancy. Maternity.

Yet while women proliferate among the Ruthwell monument's visual imagery, they are significant absent others in the Old English inscriptions on its narrow sides. There may well have been theological, grammatical and rhetorical reasons for telling the story of the crucifixion in this way but it omits many events and characters and privileges the kind of masculinity associated with an Anglo-Saxon warrior king. The representations of women on the Ruthwell monument have their value more in relation to presented biblical males and Paul and Anthony than in relation to the Anglo-Saxon *kyninc, hlafard* or *dryhten* Christ.

The significance of women on the monument at Bewcastle seems different. Woman is unformed as sculpture, but, nevertheless, present. In text, the name 'Kynibur*g' (where the asterisk indicates a rune of unknown value), on the monument's north side (Figs 25 and 26), is inscribed in a contiguous relation of association with 'g[e]ssus' above and with the aristocrat with a hawk and the men remembered in the inscription on its west side. Though, as we've seen, some names in the main inscription are lost to us, given that masculinity and femininity are socially constructed and historically specific ideas, perhaps the monument's north side is gendered in the feminine.[33]

Women seem to have played a major role in remembering, preserving and transmitting, structuring and moulding the past for families, institutions and places. In some parts of Europe across the Channel, and perhaps in Northumbria also, they were responsible for the preservation of family memory, for ensuring that the names of their dead men folk were kept alive by mourning, fasting, acts of penance, keeping and protecting the family necrology, and by making the necessary arrangements with a monastery to ensure the celebration of liturgical memory.[34] Perhaps 'Kynibur*g' was the monument's patron or one of its patrons. A rememberer remembering perhaps. Or, *if* Hwætred and his companions or kin erected the monument, perhaps 'Kynibur*g' is a rememberer remembered by others. As was observed earlier, it is to the point that no one is remembered as a rememberer on the monument at Ruthwell.

In the next chapter we will have something to say about the coincidence of the historical names '[A]lcfri[th]' and 'Kynibur*g'. The importance of 'Kynibur*g' in this discussion of difference is that it brings an important and valuable female name into view.

The differences between the Ruthwell and Bewcastle monuments: that one came to be a remarkable monument in the shape of a cross while the other, at the moment of its production and first use, may have been a column, obelisk or pyramid; that their schemes of ornamentation and decoration, textuality and language are different; that form and facture are different and would have signified different meanings. But there is also 'similarity' in difference, some shared themes that are represented in and by the different material forms, such as the concern with ideas and beliefs about death, eternal and temporal kingship, and the function and significance of women. What can we make of this?

One explanation would be that whatever establishment, institution or formation produced and first used each monument wanted to find terms and come to terms with, make sense of and represent, traditional Anglo-Saxon ideas about death, kingship and perhaps kinship, masculinity and femininity alongside its commitment to a kind of Christianity, institutionally powerful and owing its allegiance to Rome, that in the seventh and eighth centuries was causing those ideas to be changed, amended and abandoned.

The gender specificity of what it was to be a noble woman seems to have been redefined and redescribed by the assimilation of Roman Christianity.[35] Over a period of time, double monasteries containing male and female religious and presided over by an abbess declined with the more rigid enclosure of women in segregated houses. The power that enabled royal abbesses to share the status and some of the powers and offices of bishops gave way before the male sacerdotal idea and the increasing number of priests. Marriage became subject to complex rules that prohibited degrees of consanguinity. Monks were disputing the role traditionally assigned to women for the preservation of family memory. How would it alter things if we saw the representation of women on the Ruthwell and Bewcastle monuments as different, site-specific attempts to hang on to and assert the power and presence of women in the monastery and at court at the moment when that power and presence was being challenged and successfully diminished by the burgeoning power and presence of the Church of Rome? We would have to understand the different ways that women are represented on the two monuments as different aspects and effects of that process. When the upper stone or cross was added to the lower stone or column at Ruthwell, Mary and Elizabeth or Martha and Mary would have doubled the number of women represented on the monument.[36] The addition could imply an attempt to strengthen the position of women or the idea of what it was to be a woman. On the monument, of course, but also amongst those who produced and used it. *If* one assumes that 'Kynibur*g' was kin or had affinity to one or more of the persons recorded in the main inscription, then female kin or affinity relations are there, in the general view, on a very high-status monument. So, when we said 'make sense of' and 'find terms and come to terms with' we also meant contest and struggle against, and not only *contest* and *struggle* in the realm of the imagination, in mental life, but also in life as it is lived, in material existence.

There is a tendency amongst scholars of Anglo-Saxon stone sculpture to see and understand the Ruthwell and Bewcastle monuments as harmonious unities of form and content, shape and meaning. Given what is known about the way signs are constructed by socially organised persons in the process of their interaction, it makes more sense to see the Ruthwell and Bewcastle monuments as different signs of multi-accentuality between territorial and national interests, national interests and international interests, between secular and theological or ecclesiastical themes, between masculine and feminine identities, different notions of time and place, and so on – to see each monument as determined not by unified and harmonious interests but by conflictual interests in process of change.

Insisting on difference opens a gap between the Ruthwell and Bewcastle monuments in such a way that, once seen and understood as closely related in series and connection, they might now be seen as more complexly related and perhaps even as almost unrelated through date and circumstance, time and place. Of course, some scholars will resist seeing and understanding them in this way. From a certain point of view too much difference puts the order of things in doubt, makes it incoherent, irrational and discontinuous but it must lead to a closer and less obfuscated engagement with the historical and cultural specificity of each individual monument.

Different intentions and functions. Different kinds of form and facture, ornamentation and iconography. Different circumstances of production and first use. Different historical moments, perhaps. Different places, certainly. A place without a date and a date without a place is more or less useless for history. Various methods have been devised to date and place the survivals of Anglo-Saxon stone sculpture on the basis of their 'inscriptions', 'associations', 'historical context' and 'style'.[37] But the Anglo-Saxon associations of Bewcastle and Ruthwell as places are, at the moment, less than scant. Much depends on what the *Corpus* refers to as 'historical context', on being able to relate the monument to 'historical events ... reigns of kings, foundations of bishoprics, monasteries, churches; travels of craftsmen or individuals'.[38] And this is precisely what we cannot do. Hence, the various attempts that have been made to link them to the known ecclesiastical centres of Wearmouth–Jarrow and Hexham, or wherever. It's been all too easy to call up the picture of a dusty band of stonemasons, perhaps trained at Jarrow, trudging along Hadrian's Wall to the headwaters of the Solway and setting up the monument at Ruthwell, after having made the monument at Bewcastle on their way or perhaps constructing it on their return journey.[39] That story establishes its links between Ruthwell–Bewcastle–Jarrow on the basis of perceived stylistic similarities between what survives at each site. Given Nelson Goodman's strictures on similarity, however, we should be suspicious of any attempt to link the Ruthwell or the Bewcastle monument to a known historical context on the basis of claimed similarities between it and what survives at another place. The finding of such stylistic similarities may well be evidence that some principle of classification has already been applied or that some interest is at work. Ruthwell–Bewcastle–Jarrow-or-wherever: 'similarity tends under analysis either to vanish entirely or to require for its explanation just what it purports to explain'.[40]

Matters of stylistic similarity aside, there are also several reasons why we should be sceptical of any attempt to link the monuments to what might be referred to as a 'reliably recorded' historical context.[41] We will give just three reasons by way of example. Firstly, when scholars try to link the Ruthwell monument or the Bewcastle monument to Jarrow or wherever, they are doing no more than trying to provide it with a name and description of its origin, a frame of reference for its complex signification, a value and mode of existence for its time and place in the discourse of Anglo-Saxon stone sculpture specifically and in the history of Anglo-Saxon England generally. They are classifying it as caused or determined by an Other place, and in so doing they are denying it its own historically and culturally specific circumstances of production and first use. Secondly, the very idea of a reliably recorded historical context is one that should not be used uncritically. We know a 'context' only by way of the 'texts' – the stone sculptures, buildings, references in manuscripts; the records of antiquarians and the reports of archaeologists; the common traditions and objective histories; and so on – that are deposited as survivals in our present. As we have seen, that record can never be taken as thoroughly reliable. Any context is a construction of many texts, complex and interacting, all in variable and problematic relations with each other, raising difficulties of interpretation.[42] Thirdly, the idea of 'context' assumes that a distinction pertains between the object and what is around it, between the monument and the intentions of the persons who produced it, the monument and society, the monument in the foreground and history in the background *as if* history is something essentially absent from it and its production and use, which needs to be found and put back in order to provide its point of reference.[43] These distinctions do not pertain: they assume that text and context are separate and independent of each other – which they are not. Various contexts and texts came together to make each monument what it was and *is*. The Ruthwell and Bewcastle monuments: each one an intentional object determined by the specific circumstances of its moment of production and use, made of and inscribed with the aims and objectives, interests and competences of the persons who made it and who were affected by it. Each one an action *in* history and *on* history,[44] most especially *in* and *on* the history of 'Northumbria', which is, itself, a broad historical 'context' determined by a knowledge of any number of different 'texts', each one a different fragment of history.

5

Fragments of Northumbria[1]

⌘

Northumbria, State and Church

The Ruthwell and Bewcastle monuments are survivals of the pre-Viking Age. The 'context' of their moments of production and first use, as opposed to that of their rediscovery and interpretation, is the kingdom of Northumbria. A knowledge of the history of the Northumbrian kingdom must help in interpreting their meaning, and, indeed, the monuments themselves must cast some light on that very history. They are historical documents just as much as is Bede's *Historia ecclesiastica*, or the archaeology of Yeavering, Wearmouth and Jarrow, or of West Heslerton on the north side of the Yorkshire Wolds, and they should be included within what counts as the historical record.

To say that Ruthwell and Bewcastle are Northumbrian, however, is not to say anything very precise. An Anglian kingdom of Northumbria, albeit varying in size and strength, was in existence for the whole of the seventh and eighth centuries and for much of the ninth. Although the first Viking raids took place in the 790s, the Viking Age proper began only with the seizure of York in 867. Within the period of the Anglian kingdom there were considerable changes in the region,[2] to the extent that a reconstructed seventh-century moment for the production of the Ruthwell and Bewcastle monuments would look very different from an eighth- or ninth-century one. In the nineteenth century most scholars, enchanted by the magic of the runes on the Bewcastle monument, placed it and the cross at Ruthwell in the second half of the seventh century.[3] Nowadays the consensus, formed largely on the basis of stylistic judgement, as well as for linguistic and epigraphic reasons, is that they were produced in the eighth century,[4] although the early ninth should not be excluded.[5] This, however, still leaves a number of radically different possible moments of production. Even the fragmentary evidence that we have for the eighth century suggests that the period saw considerable changes in the political and social structure, as well as the material, mental and spiritual culture of the Northumbrian kingdom. Aldfrith (686–705) and Ceolwulf (729–37) at the start of the century were faced with problems very different from those occasioned by the early Viking raids which troubled King Æthelraed (774–778/9, 790–796): different again were the dangers of the mid ninth century.

In eighth-century Northumbria kings gained power and lost it quickly. The succession was fluid and uncertain, with several dynastic factions competing for the throne.[6] Aldfrith's son Osred was murdered in 716. He was succeeded by Coenred, who reigned for two years before giving way to Osred's brother Osric. Osric ruled for eleven years before appointing as his successor Coenred's brother Ceolwulf, the dedicatee of Bede's *Ecclesiastical History*, in 729. After three years on the throne, Ceolwulf was forcibly tonsured, and abdicated, but he seems to have returned shortly thereafter and reigned until 737 when he resigned in favour of, or was ousted by, Eadbert, and then retired to the monastery of Lindisfarne.[7] Eadbert, who reigned for twenty years, until 758, brought some stability to the throne. He was well remembered not only by Alcuin[8] but also, centuries later, by Symeon of Durham.[9] As well as having a good deal of political and diplomatic acumen, he also pursued aggressive military policies in the north. According to an addition to Bede's *History*, in 750, but possibly in 752, he tried to strengthen the kingdom by expanding the frontier north into the Plain of Kyle in the territory of Strathclyde.[10] Among his more peaceful activities was a reform of the currency.[11] Perhaps most importantly, he worked together with his brother Ecgbert, bishop (734) and then archbishop of York (735–766).[12] As archbishop, Ecgbert controlled ecclesiastical patronage and policies. Working jointly with his brother, he seems to have addressed some of the problems of the Northumbrian Church that, as we will see, worried Bede at the end of his life.[13] However, after Eadbert abdicated in favour of his son Oswulf, Northumbria once again became a land of insecure and rapidly changing kings. Within a year of coming to the throne, Oswulf was murdered by members of his own household, and Æthelwald Moll seized power. Thereafter, from 759 to c.808, when Eardwulf was restored, Northumbria had nine kings: six were deposed, one of them twice;[14] two were assassinated;[15] and there seem to have been several failed attempted usurpations. Only one king died peacefully.[16] Some stability seems to have been re-established thereafter: Eardwulf himself may have lasted only until 810, although the coinage may suggest that he survived until c.830.[17] In any case, he was succeeded by his son Eanred who died in 840/1. Unfortunately we have no evidence for Northumbria in this apparently peaceful period. Even so, the preceding instability of the eighth century, the outcome of continuing traditions of warrior-leadership, would in some way have impinged on how a reader of the eighth or early ninth century would have understood the Old English text of the runic inscription on the sides of the Ruthwell monument, with its 'powerful king' climbing the gallows, and its eager nobles. The killing of kings was a not uncommon occurrence.

As important as the bloodstained reality were the rather more stable Christian ideals of kingship, as set out by Bede and Alcuin.[18] These also appear on the Ruthwell monument, not least in the Latin phrase *iudex aequitatis*, 'Judge of justice'.[19] Yet while some of the ideas were stable, the Church of Bede's

lifetime differed greatly from that of Alcuin's, not least because of the elevation of York to the status of metropolitan, and because of the reforms initiated
by Archbishop Ecgbert,[20] which Bede himself had encouraged. More broadly
there is the matter of changing contacts with the continent. Northumbrians,
from the days of Wilfrid and Biscop in the second half of the seventh century,
had travelled abroad, and particularly to Rome.[21] They were followed in 690
by Willibrord, and in the eighth century by other northern missionaries.[22]
Contemporary with the later missionary contacts were Alcuin's own visits
to and permanent departure for the continent, as well as the papal Legatine
Mission, which visited Northumbria and Mercia in 786.[23] With Alcuin on the
continent, Northumbria and its Church came to be of particular interest to
Charlemagne, who noted the fate of its kings.[24] Alcuin, of course, also wrote
about the coming of the Vikings, and their impact on Lindisfarne.

In his discussion of the context of the Bewcastle and Ruthwell monuments
W. G. Collingwood put a good deal of emphasis on the late eighth-century
Church: 'The rivalry and the tragedies of the royal houses had little to do with
the people in general and still less to do with the church, which continued
to flourish under archbishop Ælberht (or Æthelbert, 767–780) the rebuilder
of York cathedral on a more magnificent scale. And the clergy were the real
rulers of Northumbria.'[25] Collingwood's notion of 'people in general' is less
than helpful: his point might be valid with regard to the servile classes working
on the land, but it would scarcely hold water for the military aristocracy. Nor
would many scholars any longer accept that Church and royal politics can
be so clearly separated – indeed Collingwood's own view of the clergy as
'the real rulers' of the kingdom undermines his assertion. Bede, based in
a royal monastery, overlooking a royal harbour and apparently within sight
of a royal palace,[26] wrote to advise King Ceolwulf and Bishop Ecgbert: the
latter worked hand-in-hand with his brother Eadberht (an indication that the
same classes and families were dominant in both spheres): Northumbria,
like Mercia, was addressed by the Legatine Missions of 786: Alcuin wrote
letters of advice to Kings Æthelred and Eardwulf. To separate Church and
State is clearly to ignore the realities – even if it is convenient to divide up
discussion of them for the sake of clarity.

In considering the importance of the Church for an understanding of
the Ruthwell and Bewcastle monuments there is not just a distinction to be
made between the beginning and end of the eighth century. Jarrow, a monastery closely associated with kings, was very different from York, dominated,
as it seems to have been, by its bishops.[27] Nor is the distinction only between
bishopric and monastery. It is equally important to distinguish between
individual monasteries: the culture and traditions of Jarrow were different
from those of Hexham under Wilfrid, Acca and his successors,[28] or even
from Lindisfarne, with which Jarrow had very close connections, to judge
from the manuscript evidence[29] and from Bede's association with the cult
of Cuthbert.[30] And just as the great ecclesiastical centres of Northumbria
each had their own distinctive culture, so too the communities at Ruthwell
and Bewcastle, which, as we will see, may well have been monastic, will also
have differed. When we look to other sites and documents of Northumbrian

history from which to construct 'contexts' for the production of the Bewcastle and Ruthwell monuments, we should always bear in mind that there will have been numerous differences between either of the two places and any other community proposed as a point of comparison. Indeed the uniqueness of each of the monuments should itself be a warning against trying to fit all our evidence into a straitjacket of a unified or coherent Northumbrian culture.

Bernicii and Deiri

At a more general political level it is important to remember that Northumbria was an amalgamation of smaller units, different territories, each associated with or defended by different groups of people, clans or families. An underlying political regionalism is a factor to be drawn into any discussion of the stone sculpture of Northumbria. Most obviously there is the distinction to be made between the two regions that scholarship refers to as 'Bernicia' and 'Deira', the one traditionally associated with Bamburgh, the other with York. In geopolitical terms these two units were supposedly fused as a result of the intermarriage of their two ruling dynasties, initially with the marriage of Acha, the sister of the Deiran king Edwin (616–633), to the Bernician Æthelfrith (592–616), and the subsequent accession of their son Oswald (634–642).[31] This union was consolidated when Oswald's brother Oswiu (642–670) married Edwin's daughter, Eanfled.[32] Thereafter, in so far as the distinction between Bernicia and Deira held any significance, it has been discussed largely in ecclesiastical terms. Indeed the high-medieval diocesan boundary between Hexham and York has been adduced as the key piece of evidence to show that the frontier between Bernicia and Deira lay on the Tees.[33]

Although it is perfectly possible that some diocesan boundaries of the twelfth century did conform to those of Bede's day, and although it is equally possible that Wilfrid's Hexham was regarded as belonging to the northern part of the Northumbrian kingdom, it is less clear that there was a fixed boundary between Bernicia and Deira. Indeed, it is less than clear that Anglo-Saxon Bernicia and Deira should be thought of in purely territorial terms. It is true that the names 'Deira' and 'Bernicia' appear to derive from British names, referring to natural features of the landscape. The *Historia Brittonum* states that 'Deira' and 'Bernicia' are the English forms of 'Deur' and 'Berneich'.[34] 'Deur' or 'Deifr' would seem to refer to oak trees and 'Berneich' to mountain passes: Kenneth Jackson translated the two names as 'The Land of the Oaks' and 'The Land of the High Passes'.[35] The British, then, thought of the two regions in geographical terms. In the pre-Viking sources, however, it is only in Welsh poetry and in the *Historia Brittonum*, originally composed at the court of King Merfyn of Gwynedd in the 820s,[36] that one finds recurrent reference to 'Bernicia' and 'Deira', as territorial units. It is far less clear that the Anglo-Saxons conceptualised them in that way. Bede does not use the words 'Deira' or 'Bernicia' (although translations of his work make frequent use of them), preferring instead to refer to peoples, the 'Deiri'[37] and the

'Bernicii',[38] and to their kingdom or province (*regnum/provincia Deirorum/ Berniciorum*). Similar terminology is to be found in the anonymous *Life of Gregory the Great*,[39] and in the *Vita Wilfridi* of Stephanus.[40] The implication would seem to be that Bede and his contemporaries thought in tribal, and not geographical, terms when considering the division of Northumbria into northern and southern parts. Thus, while the Britons envisaged the lands north of the Humber as geographical regions, the Anglo-Saxons thought in tribal terms: that is, for the latter the provinces of the Bernicians and Deirans were units held together by family, social and economic ties.

If we try to define the territories of the *Bernicii* and the *Deiri*, it soon becomes clear that boundaries are hard to fix. In some ways this is not surprising, and not just because the Anglo-Saxons were thinking in tribal rather than territorial terms. Although property or estate boundaries are likely to have been very precisely defined, features like rivers, which are often seen as providing ideal boundary lines, are also lines of communication and the central foci of economic zones. A people, tribe or even clan is likely to have tried to dominate the whole of such a zone. And it is the territory controlled by a tribe or people, or rather their leaders, not the individual estates defined by fixed geographical features, that concerns us.

The supposed descendents of Ida were the leading family of the *gens*, or people, of the *Bernicii*,[41] while those of Ælle were associated with Deira.[42] Oswine (642/3–651) is described by Bede as being of the *stirps*, descent-group, of Edwin (the son of Ælle), and also as ruling over the *provincia Derorum*.[43] According to the sixteenth-century antiquarian Leland, whose information came from the monks of Tynemouth, Oswine had been born in the neighbourhood of their monastery.[44] Such a late tradition might reasonably be taken with a pinch of salt, not least because Tynemouth also claimed to have Oswine's body.[45] Yet there is some reason for paying attention to the claim. Firstly, the monks of Tynemouth knew that Oswine had been born at a place called *Urfa*, but they did not know its exact whereabouts. Philologists, however, have noted that *Urfa* is a perfectly credible Saxon rendering of the Latin place-name *Arbeia*.[46] The Roman fort of *Arbeia* lies directly across the Tyne from Tynemouth, at South Shields. Further, recent re-examination of objects discovered during the nineteenth-century excavations of *Arbeia* has shown the site to have been a high-status centre in the seventh and eighth centuries.[47] This combination of fragmentary information, historical, philological and archaeological, is all the more significant in that monks of Tynemouth appear not to have understood the information that they passed on to Leland, who could do no more than repeat what he had heard. That is, they made no capital out of material that could have been useful to them. Since they cannot be accused of exploiting the information, they are unlikely to have made it up. It is likely, therefore, that Oswine, a member of the leading family of the *Deiri*, was indeed born on the banks of the Tyne, a river most historians would see as firmly inside Bernicia. This being the case, the tradition that the Bernician Oswiu, Oswine's enemy and nemesis, had him buried in Tynemouth also becomes suggestive. Oswiu would seem to have interred Oswine in sight of, if not actually in, territory that would have been appropriate for a ruler of the *Deiri*, but also at a place close enough to his own Bernician heartlands as to dampen the possibility that his enemy's tomb would become a focus of regional opposition.

The *Bernicii* and the Wall

The history of the frontier between the *Deiri* and the *Bernicii* does not impinge directly on Ruthwell and Bewcastle, but it is important to understand that the two places lie in the territory known to Bede as the *provincia Berniciorum*, the origins of which may have some significance for the interpretation of the site at Bewcastle.

Bede is remarkably silent about what modern historians term the ethnogenesis of the Bernician and Deiran peoples. He, of course, provides a general statement that the people of Northumbria were descended from the Angles, who, according to his *History*, were one of the three tribes that migrated to Britain from the lands of the Jutes and the Old Saxons and from *Angulus* (Angeln) in the fifth century.[48] He also paraphrases the British writer Gildas, who talks of the use of Saxon federates against the northern threat of the Picts,[49] and it is not impossible that this meant the deployment of troops from the continent in the area of Hadrian's Wall in the mid fifth century. But, Bede provides no specific origin legend for Northumbria and certainly no account of a migration from the continent to the territories of the Bernicians or the Deirans. Instead, we simply hear of the accession of king Ida 'from whom the royal family of the Northumbrians originated', in 547.[50] The *Historia Brittonum* adds little to this, except, perhaps rather surprisingly, to provide the ruling dynasties of what it does refer to territorially as *Berneich*/Bernicia and *Deur*/Deira with a genealogy stretching back to Woden, and to add the detail that a Deiran ruler Soemil first separated the two kingdoms.[51] Nor does the Anglo-Saxon Chronicle of the 890s have anything to add on the origins of the Bernician kingdom, although it provides origin legends for Kent, Wessex and Sussex. Given that genealogies stretching back to Woden are nothing other than ideological constructs developed for a variety of different political reasons, we are faced with the problem that the Anglian rulers of the *Bernicii* and the *Deiri* suddenly appear *ex nihilo*: they have no origin legend, and certainly they have no tradition of a past migration.

This negative point might once have been regarded as having no significance, even though archaeologists have long noted the paucity of early Anglo-Saxon material north of the Humber, and more particularly north of the Tyne.[52] That one should consider the implications of the near-absence of such finds, however, is suggested by stable isotope analysis of bones from the cemetery of West Heslerton, on the edge of the Yorkshire Wolds, near Malton, in the ancient province of the *Deiri*, a region generally accepted as having more incomers than the area further north. This indicated that only 'around one in six of the population were first generation immigrants from either eastern Continental Europe or, more likely Scandinavia'.[53] Equally important, 'a very high proportion of the buried population were first generation immigrants to the area from the west', which 'suggests a remarkably high degree of mobility with a considerable influx of people from previously settled areas of sub-Roman Britain and a smaller, but significant, proportion of continental immigrants'.[54] This is not proof that the dynasties of Ida and Ælle had been in Britain long before their emergence in the historical narrative. But it does mean that one should think carefully about the fact that those dynasties, and indeed the Northumbrian peoples in general, did not present themselves as incomers with origins on the continent.

The very fact that they called themselves *Deiri* and *Bernicii*, the people of the Celtic-named regions of *Deur* or *Deifr* and *Berneich* or *Brennych*,[55] might be an indication that the Northumbrians wished to think of or present themselves as indigenous. The people of Kent also adopted an older name, *Cantuarii* from *Cantia*, though in addition they traced the origins of their kingdom to the arrival of Hengest and Horsa. Unfortunately the terms *Deur* and *Berneich* give us no clue at to how the peoples of Northumbria looked on their past. They exist only as names, and names that, unlike *Cantia* (or *Cantium*), are only attested in the post-Roman world. They carry no history. They appear, apparently already in place as Anglo-Saxon territories, in the forms *Deifr* and *Brennych* in the early Welsh battle poem the *Gododdin*, where they are centres of opposition to the British warband that attacks *Catraeth*,[56] and in the poems of the Llywarch Hen Saga, where the men of *Brennych* are the opponents of King Urien of Rheged.[57] Because we hear of no British past for these regions, we do not know whether the name *Brennych* was old or new at the time of the establishment of the Anglo-Saxon *gens Berniciorum*. Nor do we know whether the name referred to a region that existed during the Roman period, or came into being only after what is conventionally thought of as 'the End of Roman Britain'. There are some indications of a revival of an older, pre-Roman, tribal geography after 410.[58] Yet we have no idea whether the emergence of the *Deiri* and *Bernicii* was part of that revival.[59]

It is perhaps more useful to consider the relation of the *Bernicii* to the geographical zone associated with Hadrian's Wall. In the seventh century the *Bernicii* controlled territory to the north and south of the Wall, ignoring the line it draws across northern England. It has, of course, long been known that the Wall itself did not mark an absolute boundary for the Romans.[60] There are important forts to the north of the Wall, among them Bewcastle. Effectively the Wall was part of a broad militarized zone. How, one might wonder, did this relate to the territory of *Berneich*? Were the *Bernicii* in some manner heirs to the Wall and the zone to the north and south of it?

Such questions are insoluble, but just as the Bernician context of Anglo-Saxon Bewcastle needs to be considered, so too does its relationship with the Roman past, and not just because Bewcastle was a major Roman fort. Some of its buildings must still have been standing at the time of the erection of the Anglo-Saxon monument, which seems deliberately to have been formed in the shape of a Roman obelisk, and to have been aligned to a Roman street, the *via principalis*.

One of the 'facts' most commonly asserted about 'the End of Roman Britain' is that in 406 (or perhaps 407)[61] the usurper Constantine III denuded Britain of its Roman troops, in his bid for the imperial throne. A sophisticated variant on the theme is that a considerable body of troops had already been withdrawn to the continent by Stilicho in the 390s.[62] It is, therefore, salutary to note the comment of Peter Salway:

> We have no evidence that any temporary depletion of the garrison of Britain to provide troops for the Continental invasion of 407 was not made up after the initial successes of Constantine's regime. In fact, the notion that Constantine removed the remaining garrison of Britain in 407 for a Continental adventure from which it was never to return is one of those apparently unshakeable ideas about Roman Britain for which there is no hard evidence either way.[63]

Moreover, there has been a suggestion of a post-Roman attempt to bring the Wall back into use.[64]

Even those who think that Constantine III took with him 'virtually all the sound regular troops still left in Britain in 407' acknowledge that 'regular frontier-army detachments' and 'federates', military units that were often of Germanic origin, are likely to have remained.[65] From the early fourth century onwards it is important to distinguish between Roman frontier troops, *limitanei*, and more crack troops, *comitatenses*, which were held in reserve.[66] Both types were used in the military zone of the Wall and its hinterland. Withdrawal of the *comitatenses* would have been easy: they were mobile units that could be deployed as needed. The *limitanei*, however, who were settled in the region they were expected to defend, would have been much harder to move. They were well entrenched. In addition to the forces themselves, there would have been many who had completed their military service, and had settled down to live with their wives or concubines. Since service in the Roman army was usually for twenty or twenty-four years, and since recruits were drawn from the age bracket of 19 to 35, many of these veterans would still have been physically fit.[67] They would doubtless have been able to organise themselves if necessary, and to train their own sons in the art of fighting. If it were only the *comitatenses* that were withdrawn to fight a civil war on the continent, there need have been no complete disruption of the Roman military or Roman military tradition on Hadrian's Wall in the fifth century.

Historians looking at the fate of the frontiers have often turned to an early sixth-century text describing the end of Roman Noricum, most of which lay in modern Austria.[68] According to Eugippius, in his *Vita Severini*, the military organisation of the Upper Danube region still survived, albeit in a demoralised fashion, after 476, when the last western Emperor was deposed. It was the disruption of the supply of pay that broke the morale of the frontier troops,[69] and even then some semblance of Roman life, military and civilian, survived until an official order for the abandonment of the province was issued in c.488.[70] In Britain pay certainly dried up, but there is no evidence for a withdrawal of the *limitanei*. The likelihood, and it can be no more, is that the frontier troops, the veterans and their immediate descendents, tried to keep the Roman lifestyle to which they were accustomed going in the zone of the Wall as best they could. One resource available for them would have been the material and ideological structures of the great forts of the region.

Until recently there was little archaeology to back up such a hypothesis. This had as much to do with early excavation methods as with what was actually in the soil. The discovery at Birdoswald of a sequence of rebuilding extending well into the fifth century, however, has provided evidence that seems to fit this model of continuity into the post-Roman period exactly.[71] Birdoswald was not, in fact, the first site where continuity through the fifth century was observed. Pride of place goes to the excavations at Wroxeter, on the Severn.[72] And the evidence for some continuity through the fifth century, and even into the sixth, if not the seventh and eighth, has been growing. Much of this material comes from sites on Hadrian's Wall, or associated with it. Writing in 1992 Ken Dark noted evidence from Benwell, Chesters, Housesteads, Chesterholm (*Vindolanda*), Carvoran, Birdoswald, Castlesteads, as well as Carlisle, Corbridge, South Shields and Binchester. Of these Housesteads and Chesterholm have produced evidence of sub-Roman refortification.[73] As Dark noted,

> It is ... remarkable that out of the twelve fourth-century Roman military sites in northern and western Britain to have produced convincingly datable structural, artefactual, or stratigraphic evidence of fifth- or sixth-century occupation, eleven were, almost certainly, part of the same Late Roman military command. Eight of these were probably within the same part of that command, and eight comprise a linear group (the only regional group) that stretches along the whole line of Hadrian's Wall from east to west. The two more substantial late fourth-century settlements adjacent to the Wall – Carlisle and Corbridge – have also produced fifth- or sixth-century evidence.[74]

Others have hypothesised continuing occupation at Netherby and Stanwix.[75] Whether or not there was an attempt to reuse the line of the Wall as a defensive unit, as Dark argued, it is surely clear that some forts were being deliberately utilised by what must increasingly have become a sub-Roman warrior aristocracy.

While it has become increasingly likely that there was survival of a sort into the sixth century, there is little evidence, as yet, to suggest further continuity into the Anglo-Saxon period. To date Birdoswald has produced a single Saxon pin (Fig. 12), though rather more has now been identified at South Shields – that is, Roman *Arbeia* and Saxon *Urfa*, the birthplace of Oswine. It has to be said, however, that it is unclear what evidence for the late sixth and early seventh centuries one might expect to find. New coins were not minted in that period, and seventh-century coins are rare. Importation of pottery from abroad largely dried up[76] and the native pottery industry collapsed, with the result that post-Roman society looks aceramic – although one might also guess that surviving pieces of Roman pottery came to be regarded as luxury items, and were thus treated with very much more care than had once been the case.

Since neither continuity nor discontinuity between the sub-Roman and Anglo-Saxon periods is likely to be proved or disproved archaeologically to everyone's satisfaction, it is perhaps worth asking a different question. Could the descendants of frontier troops on Hadrian's Wall have come to see themselves as members of the *gens Berniciorum* and subsequently as part

of the Anglian people of Northumbria? One factor that might have facilitated such a change in self-perception is the identity of the frontier troops
themselves. A number of the inscriptions put up by soldiers stationed on or
near the Wall in the second and third centuries were commissioned by men
who describe themselves as *Germani*, Germans, or as belonging to tribal
groups which would later be regarded as Germanic. There are examples, for
instance, from Chesters, and especially at Carrawburgh and Housesteads.[77]
Equally important, these men continued to worship their Germanic gods,
notably Mars Thincsus and various Germanic mother goddesses, the *Deae
Matres*, suggesting that they retained their own beliefs and traditions, even in
the service of Rome.[78] We recall the monumental relief sculpture of a 'Seated
Mother Goddess' (Fig. 10) that was found at Bewcastle in 1765. One particularly intriguing inscription is dedicated to a group of mother goddesses,
one of whom bears the name Beda![79] It is unfortunate that the fashion of
setting up inscribed monuments declined long before the fifth century: the
last dateable inscription comes from the year 307/8.[80] It is, thus, not possible
to prove that troops still stationed on the Wall in 407 shared a consciousness
of their Germanic past with those who set up such inscriptions. Nevertheless, it is clear that new troops of Germanic origin were sent to Britain in the
course of the third and fourth centuries.[81] Thus Burgundians and Vandals
are said to have been sent to Britain by the Emperor Probus (276–281),[82] and
a century later Valentinian I (364–375) transferred a detachment of Alamans
under their leader Froamar.[83] Although we cannot be sure where these
Germanic federates were stationed, the area of the Wall is not unlikely. Even
without these fourth-century additions we can be certain that the population
of the militarised zone surrounding the Wall was mongrel. Not everyone
would have seen himself or herself as Roman, Romano-British or British.
Already in the third and fourth centuries some might have been speaking a
Germanic language in their everyday exchanges with comrades – and this
may have been a factor in the subsequent emergence of Old English as the
dominant language in the region. When and why this took place is a mystery
made all the more puzzling by the indications that Germanic incomers of
the fifth and sixth centuries were not numerically the largest element in the
population of the region.

In short, for this society to redesignate itself as belonging to the *gens Berniciorum* and subsequently as Anglian would not have meant that its members
all abandoned a long-held Roman or British ethnic affiliation, for many may
have had none. The emergence of a province of the Bernicians in the region
that straddled Hadrian's Wall would have been something very much more
complex than the result of conquest or enslavement achieved in the sixth
century; although it might well have culminated in a family associated with
the fort of Bamburgh establishing dominance over the a large swathe of
territory – as implied by the recurrent emphasis in our sources on Ida's
succession and his building of a fort.[84] Such a model might be compared
with the reconstruction of the origins of the Frankish kingdoms suggested
already in the nineteenth century by Fustel de Coulanges, who emphasised
the settlement of Germanic troops within the province of Belgica by the

Romans from the early days of the Empire, and saw Merovingian leadership as emerging from those settlements, once Roman control had failed.[85] Fustel paid no attention to the origin legends of the Franks – and rightly so, since the migration story is clearly confused and is largely concerned to make ideological connections with Troy and with St Martin.[86] Since the *gens Berniciorum* lacks any such origin legend, there is no need to explain it away.

Some Roman elements have long been noted in the self-representation of early Anglo-Saxon rulers.[87] One should perhaps remember, in particular, the picture of the Deiran king Edwin, drawn by Bede. Edwin ensured that bowls were placed by springs, or perhaps fountains, along the roadside (*fontes lucidos iuxta puplicos viarum transitus*), and he had carried before him 'a banner called a *tufa* by the Romans and *thuuf* by the Anglians' (*illud genus vexilli, quod Romani tufam, Angli appellant thuuf*).[88] This would seem to suggest that what had been the northern provinces of Britannia retained some residual Roman notion of the symbols of power and continued to use them. The *provincia Berniciorum* would thus have had roots in the Roman past, which is something that should not be forgotten when considering the various Roman elements – some brought from abroad, but some already in Britain – which were used to produce the monuments at Ruthwell and Bewcastle.

Bewcastle and the Roman and Saxon past

It is against the background of a multicultural society that had evolved in the region of the Wall that one needs to set the production and first use of the monument at Bewcastle – as we shall see, the local context at Ruthwell is rather different, although culturally it was equally mixed. Unfortunately the excavations of Roman Bewcastle have so far not been as extensive or of the same quality as those carried out by Tony Wilmott at Birdoswald, although there is still much more to be dug. Because of the proximity and relationship between the two forts, *Fanum Cocidii* and *Banna*, linked by road and through the use of signal towers, one might well expect indications of continuity into the post-Roman period at Bewcastle as at Birdoswald. And the Bewcastle monument, aligned as it is with the *via principalis*, in any case, seems to imply a continuing regard for the Roman fabric.[89] On the other hand Bewcastle, even as a Roman site, differs in significant respects from Birdoswald. Although made to conform to the pattern of forts on the Wall, particularly in terms of size and of distance from its neighbour, it is also special, above all in its shape and in its association with the shrine of Cocidius, which may indeed have been its *raison d'être*. It is unique among the Wall forts in being named after a divinity. Was Roman Bewcastle built to control a cult-site of the Britons, which might otherwise have been a focus for independent regional sentiment? If it were, did the Northumbrian Church, or a pious Northumbrian king, put a Christian marker on an ancient, but still numinous religious site, and thus mark it out for the new religion?

That question raises the more general issue of the nature of Anglo-Saxon Bewcastle. Clearly it was a place of very high status. It may have been royal.

There are plenty of indications elsewhere of kings taking over Roman sites – though more often than not one discovers this to have been the case because of the alienation of land to the Church, as at Burgh Castle in present-day Suffolk.[90] As we shall see, most, if not all, land passed through the hands of the king. Roman forts, however, are likely to have been places of particular significance, not least because of their association with state power and ideology, and their strategic positioning. There is the case of *Arbeia*, which, as we have already seen, may well have been the birthplace of Oswine, and thus a royal palace. It was once thought that the runic inscription on the Bewcastle monument referred to Alcfrith, son of Oswiu,[91] who disappears suspiciously from history some time after the Synod of Whitby, perhaps as a result of rebelling against his father.[92] If Alcfrith were indeed interred at Bewcastle, one might wish to make a comparison with Oswine's burial at Tynemouth. Was this another instance of Oswiu choosing to bury a defeated rival at a place where his grave was unlikely to prove a focus for resentment? There might be a case for this, were Alcfrith to have been 'sub-king of Deira', as is frequently asserted, albeit without any evidential support.[93] Or, assuming Alcfrith to have been the son of Oswiu by his Rhegedian wife Rieinmellt (though there is no evidence to suggest that she was in fact the mother),[94] would a monument set up, as we shall see, on what was perhaps the border of Rheged, have been a concession to local feeling? Bewcastle looks out towards the eastern end of the Solway, which in some readings was Rheged's heartland, and in others its easternmost territory. Or could Bewcastle have been the site of Alcfrith's death?[95]

All these hypotheses are possibly, though not definitely, undermined by the redating of the monument at Bewcastle from the seventh to the eighth century, which means that Oswiu can have had no hand in it. And there is the simple fact that not enough of the inscription survives to be certain of what it actually commemorates.[96] Nevertheless, it would seem that there is a reference to an Alcfrith (only the 'lcfri' is legible), as well as to a woman called Kyniburg ('Kynibur*g').[97] Remarkably enough the only Cuniburga mentioned by Bede happens to be the daughter of Penda and wife of Alcfrith,[98] which may go some way to back up the identification of the man commemorated on the Bewcastle monument as Oswiu's son. There are, however, three Cuniburgs among the names of the queens and abbesses among the original entries of the *Liber vitae* of Durham – a manuscript begun in the mid ninth century containing a list of names to be commemorated liturgically at either Lindisfarne or Jarrow.[99] On the other hand, there is only one Alchfrith (*sic*) listed among the kings and *duces* of the *Liber vitae*. Coming in the left-hand column of the first page, under Edvini, Osvald, Osvio and Ecgfrith,[100] he is clearly Oswiu's son. If it were indeed he who was named on the monument, the memorial itself would seem to have been erected fifty or a hundred years after his death. Although at first this may appear unlikely, there are continental examples of funerary monuments being erected or renewed at some time after the death of the person commemorated,[101] and there are other possible Anglo-Saxon examples.[102] Moreover, the narratives of Bede and Stephanus show that Alcfrith's life was the subject of discussion in the early eighth century. Equally, the entry in the *Liber vitae* indicates that he was being remembered at the time that the manuscript was begun, perhaps in the 840s.[103]

It is also worth noting that towards the end of the original list of abbots there is the name Huaetred,[104] who might be identified with Hwætred, the one person other than Alcfrith and Kyniburg whose name is legible on the Bewcastle monument – and indeed the inscription names Hwætred as the man who had it erected.[105] Were this identification to be correct, then the *Liber vitae* would provide a remarkably late *terminus post quem non* for the erection of the monument. The fact that Huaetred's name occurs towards the end of the list of abbots might suggest that he had died not long before the *Liber vitae* was written, perhaps in the 820s or 830s. Any monument that he put up is likely to have been ninth-century, well over a hundred years after the death of Oswiu's son. It is, perhaps, more politic to make nothing of the names on the Bewcastle monument, other than to say that it commemorates a man with a name that is known to have been used in the Bernician royal dynasty.

The monument, taken together with what is known of other forts such as Burgh Castle, could be taken to indicate that Bewcastle was a royal place. But it is also a significant religious monument, boasting, apart from images of Christ presented as the lamb of God and as a figure adored by beasts, at least one inscription with the name 'Gessus Kristtus',[106] patterns of interlace which incorporate crosses, and also a sundial, which suggests interest in keeping the liturgical hours and in reckoning time. A likely implication of all these features is that the Bewcastle monument was erected by an ecclesiastical community of some sort: one might describe it as a monastery. Of course, Hwætred might have been its abbot.

Monasticism and land-tenure

Just as to say that Bewcastle is Northumbrian, so to identify Bewcastle as a monastery is not to say anything particularly precise.[107] We have already noted that there were significant differences between Wearmouth–Jarrow, Lindisfarne and Hexham. But this is only to list the best known of the Bernician monasteries mentioned in Bede's *Ecclesiastical History*. There were plenty more monastic communities, and they were all different. Indeed, it is not easy to offer a sharp definition of early Northumbrian monasticism. In all probability each followed its own monastic rule. Although the Rule of St Benedict had been set down in the sixth century, it had not, as yet, gained the status it was later to have. This is not to deny its significance in seventh- and eighth-century Anglo-Saxon England. Wilfrid claimed to be the first to introduce the Benedictine Rule to his homeland,[108] but the arrangements he made for his monasteries at his death were not Benedictine.[109] Wearmouth–Jarrow has been seen as an essentially Benedictine community, but, as Bede tells us, Benedict Biscop, the founder of Wearmouth, had examined the rules of seventeen continental monasteries, and extracted the best from them.[110] In Northumbria, as throughout western Europe, this was an age when the practices of a particular monastery were largely chosen by the abbot.[111] Where we have enough evidence, both in England and on the continent, we see that the abbot or abbess took what he or she wanted from the rules or traditions of other communities. Ecclesiastical historians nowadays refer to the period as the Age of the Mixed Rule, *regula mixta*. Moreover, while there was increasing influence from continental practice, Irish monastic tradition was also important. Although Lindisfarne seems to have severed its links with Iona after the Synod of Whitby,[112] there is nothing to suggest that there was any immediate change to its constitution. We might expect all communities to have performed a regular liturgy (albeit again one of the abbot's choosing) and, at least in theory, to have practised chastity. But because there was no single model for the monastic life, we can add little in the way of detail to this overall picture, except in the case of those few monasteries for which we have good hagiographical or historical evidence, either from Bede or from Stephanus. With the exception of Coldingham,[113] this means that we know only about the exemplary houses of Northumbria.

Fortunately we can go a little further, because of Bede's discussion of Northumbrian monasticism in his letter written in 734 to Bishop (soon to be Archbishop) Ecgbert of York.[114] Bede was concerned with the state of the Church in Northumbria, and above all with pastoral provision. He advised Ecgbert on the need for leadership[115] and preaching.[116] Because of the size of the diocese of York, he saw that Ecgbert needed the help of more preachers.[117] In looking at how to ensure better provision of pastoral care, he urged Ecgbert to collaborate with the king, Ceolwulf,[118] the man to whom he had just dedicated the *Ecclesiastical History*, a work which in many respects illustrates the ideals set out in the letter. In particular, he could see a way in which the king could help in the provision of more bishops. He argued that a number of monasteries might usefully be converted into the centres of new dioceses. This was not unlike the policy begun a generation earlier by Theodore, archbishop of Canterbury, who had tried, with partial success, to divide Wilfrid's enormous Northumbrian diocese into a number of smaller sees.[119] One of Theodore's successes was the foundation of the diocese of Hexham. Bede thought that the creation of other bishoprics within Northumbria would help justify the elevation of York to being a metropolitan see.[120]

In the course of arguing that some monasteries should become diocesan centres, Bede noted that there were a number of monastic foundations which might be handed over to endow new sees without any qualms, because they showed 'no trace of monastic life' (*nihil prorsus monasticae conversationis habentia*).[121] These monasteries were, in Bede's eyes, completely useless. It would have been better if the land had remained in secular hands, where it would have been liable to military service, and thus have contributed to the defence of the kingdom.[122] As a result Bede wanted Ecgbert to join Ceolwulf in tearing up the charters which originally transferred land to these useless monasteries. He then makes a number of points about the foundations themselves.[123] They had been set up by laymen, who had bought estates from the king, who, moreover, had granted hereditary rights over them, and these privileges had been confirmed by episcopal charter. The founders of these monasteries had then attracted monks expelled from other institutions, and they had also encouraged men of their own retinue to become monks – though this had not necessarily led to the end of conjugal relations. Bede does, however, admit that the monks 'sometimes rise from their beds to attend zealously to whatever ought to be done within the monastic enclosure' (*modo exsurgentes de cubilibus, quid intra septa monasterium geri debeat, sedula intentione pertractant*).[124] This may be an acknowledgement of some sort of religious life. The origins of this phase of monasticism Bede dates to the reign of Osred (705–716).[125] As for the founders themselves, he sees them as being local headmen and royal advisers. Indeed he comments that some claim to be both abbots and local governors at the same time.

Bede's denunciation of what are often referred to as 'bogus' monasteries is well known among social historians. It is central to an understanding of the issue of land-tenure in early Anglo-Saxon England.[126] It would appear from what Bede says that most, perhaps all, land had originally belonged to the king, who allocated it to followers in return for military service. When the warrior died, the land returned to the king, and was available to be granted to another. This pattern was inevitably broken by the Church, which could not survive on land granted for a lifetime. It needed grants of land in perpetuity. These it gained through the instrument of the charter. What Bede implies is that laymen soon saw the charter as an instrument by which they could gain land not just for themselves but also for their descendants: all they needed to do was found a monastery. Some, it would seem, made an attempt to attract trained monks to their foundations, others simply redesignated their own followers as monks.

The importance of Bede's analysis of land-tenure for any understanding of Anglo-Saxon society is enormous. It is just as great for any evaluation of Northumbrian monasticism. One implication is that most monasteries in Northumbria were not particularly reputable institutions, at least by Bede's standards. In other words, the monasteries which play a significant role in Bede's *History* and in his hagiography may not have been the norm. For every Lindisfarne, Melrose, Wearmouth, Jarrow, Hexham, Ripon and Whitby, there may have been a score of institutions that he regarded as disreputable. Not that all of the monasteries which appear in the *Ecclesiastical History* were beyond criticism: Coldingham is presented as having been deservedly consumed by fire. Its nuns had spent too much time asleep or eating, drinking and gossiping in their cells. They had also woven clothes to make themselves look more attractive and to gain the friendship of men from outside.[127] Coldingham, one might note, had been founded by Æbbe, aunt of King Ecgfrith, and it had been where his ex-wife, the saintly Æthelthryth, entered the religious life – a community of impeccable origins might go to the dogs.

Despite Bede's comments, how clear-cut was the distinction between a 'bogus' monastery and a house of which he approved? Here it is worth emphasising the fact that the depiction provided by the Letter to Ecgbert is polemical. It is meant to make certain foundations look as if they had no *raison d'être* other than the cupidity of aristocrats keen on ensuring that

they could pass property on to their descendants. But questions of property
and ownership were raised also with regard to foundations of which Bede
approved. Hereditary possession was an issue that dogged Wearmouth–
Jarrow. Bede presents Biscop as founding a near-perfect monastery: one
aspect of this is the founder's desire that family connection should play no
part in the appointment of his successors.[128] Yet Eosterwine, who acted as
abbot of Wearmouth in Biscop's lifetime, was his cousin.[129] Ceolfrith, the
first abbot of the combined monastery of Wearmouth–Jarrow, was also a
relative.[130] Moreover, even if one accepts that Eosterwine was indeed the best
man for the job, it is very clear that there were other members of Biscop's
family, perhaps even a brother, who were very keen to get their hands on
Wearmouth–Jarrow.[131] In terms of family interest, Biscop's foundation was
not so very different from those houses lampooned by Bede in the Letter
to Ecgbert. In its early years Wearmouth was dominated by a single family
– and while the early abbots were each determined to uphold a reputable
monastic tradition, there was at least one other relative on the sidelines, of
whom Biscop disapproved, waiting to take over. Indeed one might ask if the
savagery of Bede's attack on 'bogus' monasteries in the Letter to Ecgbert did
not owe something to a need to make Wearmouth–Jarrow look as different
from the majority of monasteries as possible. And one might note other
respects in which Wearmouth conforms to the pattern of foundations
denounced in the Letter to Ecgbert: just as Bede comments that the founders
of 'bogus' monasteries included local governors and royal advisers, so, one
should note, both Biscop and Eosterwine played significant roles at court,
and indeed the former continued to do so even after establishing himself
as abbot of Wearmouth.[132] In other words, although Wearmouth–Jarrow
was unquestionably a foundation of considerable religious stature, it could
also have been subject to the jibe that it was a family monastery, like those
denounced in the Letter to Ecgbert.

There is one other source which perhaps helps us to see that monasteries
founded for family or political reasons need not have been as lacking in
religious qualities as Bede implies. Æthelwulf's early ninth-century poem
De abbatibus tells of a monastery founded by *dux* Eanmund, who retired
from secular life because of King Osred's persecution of members of his
aristocracy (*multos persequitur*).[133] This places Eanmund's decision to found
a monastery firmly in the period which Bede saw as crucial for the foundation of 'bogus' houses. Although Osred was a mere eight years old at the
time of his accession,[134] his subsequent tyrannous behaviour was noted also
by Bede's contemporary Boniface: in this case what is specified is his viola-
tion of nuns.[135] Eanmund's initial conversion to the monastic life appears to
have been politically motivated: and the first monks seem to have been other
nobles intent on escaping Osred's clutches.[136] Æthelwulf suggests that it was
only after the monastery had been established that Eanmund sought advice
on how to live the monastic life.[137] As at Wearmouth–Jarrow, family connections played a considerable part in the subsequent history of the abbey: the
second and third abbots, Eorpwine and Aldwine, were brothers,[138] as were
the fourth and fifth, Sigbald and Sigwine.[139] Despite the pressure of politics

1 Bewcastle: Demesne Farm, Castle, Church, Monument, Rectory, and Shopford, July 1913, view from north-west

Moses Griffith. Del.   Comte. Sc.

2 Moses Griffith, Beu Castle (from Thomas Pennant, *A Tour from Downing to Alston-Moor*, 1801)

BEU CASTLE

3 Bewcastle
Roman
Fort and its
immediate
environs, aerial
view from
south

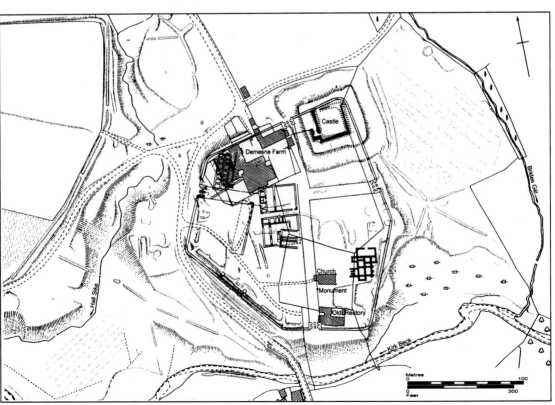

4 Bewcastle
Roman Fort

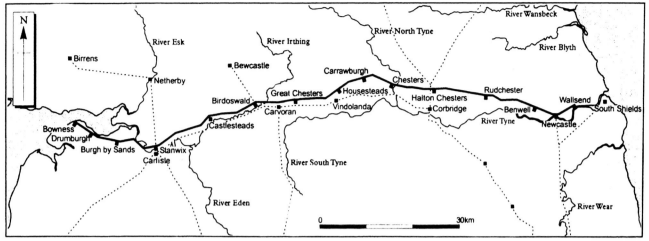

5 Hadrian's Wall, forts and major towns

6 Bewcastle: The Currick Long Cairn

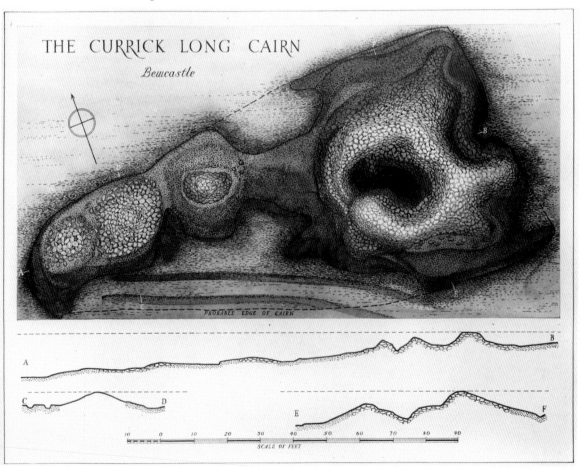

7 Silver plaques inscribed *Deo Cocidi*, from Bewcastle Roman Fort. Collection Tullie House Museum and Art Gallery, Carlisle

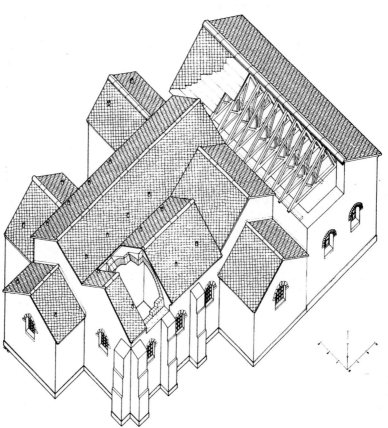

8 Suggested reconstruction of the bath-house, Bewcastle Roman Fort

9 'Gravestone showing a Lady with a Fan' (Murell Hill Tombstone). Collection Tullie House Museum and Art Gallery, Carlisle

10 'Seated Mother Goddess'. Collection Tullie House Museum and Art Gallery, Carlisle

11 'A Stone found lately at Bewcastle – in Cumberland – 1765'. Society of Antiquaries of London, Cumberland red folio, no. 3

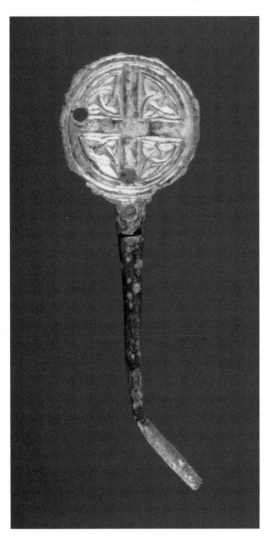

12 Anglo-Saxon disk-headed pin. Collection Tullie House Museum and Art Gallery, Carlisle

The *North and West Prospects of the famous Runic Obelisk at Bew-Castle in Cumberland. Taken by G. Smith.*

A perspective View Top, wherein the Cross was fixt, from an Elevation of the ocular Horizon.

The Prospects of the South and East Sides will be in our next.

On a Fillet on the North Side.

See the Runic Inscription on the West Side, p. 132.

The *Magna Britannia Antiqua & Nova*, speaking of this Obelisk, calls it "a Cross of one entire square Stone, about five Yards in Height, washed over with a white oily Cement. The Figure inclines to a square Pyramid, being two Foot broad at Bottom. On the West Side, among other Draughts, is a Picture of some holy Man in a sacerdotal Habit, with a Glory round his Head, and the Effigies of the blessed Virgin with a Babe in her Arms; on the North Side is a great deal of Chequer Work." This Book gives us but a very imperfect Account of the Inscriptions, and offers no other Representation than that here annexed.

If then this noble Monument has been hitherto so incorrectly described, what Defects may not be discovered in the other curious Remains of Antiquity, with which this County abounds more than any other in *Britain*? We believe, therefore, it will not be unsatisfactory to the Publick to be informed that the ingenious Gentleman who favoured us with this Draught, is at present compiling a full and accurate Description of this County. *Gentleman's Mag. vol. XII. 1742.*

13 G. Smith, 'The North and West Prospects of the famous Runic Obelisk at Bew-Castle in Cumberland' (from *Gentleman's Magazine*, 1742)

14 'Monument at Bewcastle'. Society of Antiquaries of London, Cumberland red folio, no. 3

15 Bewcastle monument, north and west sides

16 Bewcastle monument, south and east sides

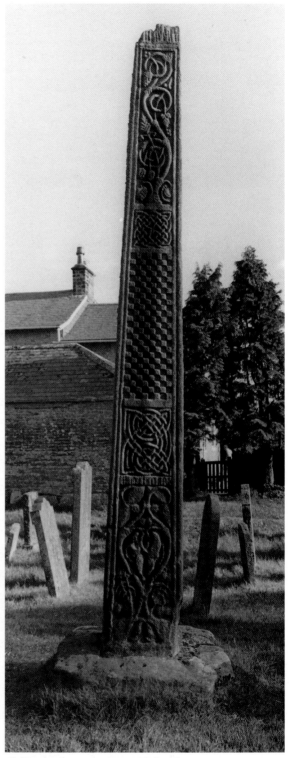

17 Bewcastle monument, west side   18 Bewcastle monument, north side

19 Bewcastle monument, east side

20 Bewcastle monument, south side

21 Bewcastle monument, west side: secular aristocrat

22 Bewcastle monument, west side: runic inscription

23 Bewcastle monument, west side: Christ on the Beasts

24 Bewcastle monument, west side: John the Baptist and runic inscription

25 Bewcastle monument, north side: medallion plant-scroll and runic inscription

26 Bewcastle monument, north side, detail: interlace and runic inscription

27 [*left*] Bewcastle monument, north side: chequer panel and interlace
28 [*right*] Bewcastle monument, north side: plant trail and runic inscription

29 Bewcastle monument, east side: inhabited plant-scroll

30 Bewcastle monument, east side: inhabited plant-scroll

31 Bewcastle monument, east side: inhabited plant-scroll

32 Bewcastle monument, south side: interlace and runic inscription

33 Bewcastle monument, south side: interlaced medallion scroll

34 Bewcastle monument, south side: interlace

35 Bewcastle monument, south side: sundial, plant trail and interlace

36 The Astronomer, detail mosaic pavement, Roman Villa, Brading, Isle of Wight

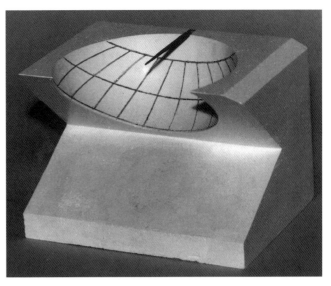

38 Allan A. Mills, Plaster hemicyclium for latitude 42° north. Collection Allan A. Mills

37 Roman hemicyclium from Città Lavinia. Collection British Museum

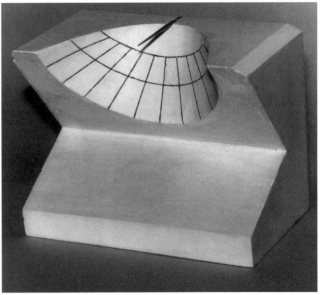

39 Conical dial found near Alexandria, at the base of Cleopatra's Needle. Collection British Museum

40 Allan A. Mills, Plaster conical dial for latitude 42° north. Collection Allan A. Mills

41 Fragment from ?Sun-dial, Housesteads. Collection John Clayton Collection, Chesters Museum

42 The Ruthwell monument, south (now west) and east (now south) sides

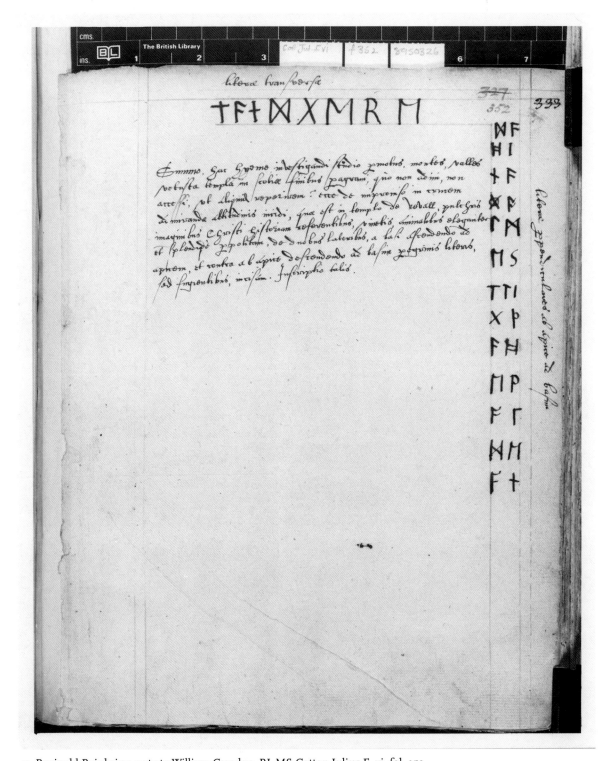

43 Reginald Bainbrigg, note to William Camden. BL MS Cotton Julius F. vi, fol. 352

44 *Monumentum Runicum* (from George Hickes, *Linguarum Veterum Septentrionalium Thesaurus*, 1703)

Plate 58

To the Hon.ble David Murray of Stormont Esq
This Plate is most humbly Inscrib'd.

45 Engraving of the top fragment of the upper stone, west (now north) and east (now south) sides (from Alexander Gordon, *Itinerarium Septentrionale*, 1726, Plate 58)

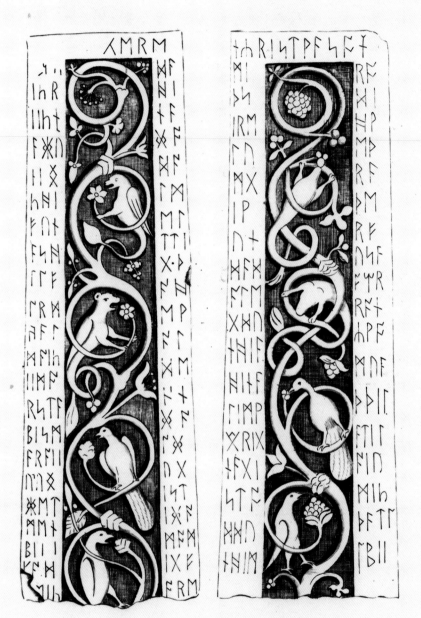

Plate 57

To the R.ᵗ Hon.ᵇˡᵉ Richard Earl of Burlington.

This **Plate** *is most humbly Inscrib'd*

46 Engraving of the top fragment of the upper stone, north (now east) and south (now west) sides (from Alexander Gordon, *Itinerarium Septentrionale*, 1726, Plate 57)

47 Engraving after Adam de Cardonnell, 'Stone at Ruthwell in Anandale' (from R. Gough, *Vetusta Monumenta*, Plate LIV, 1789)

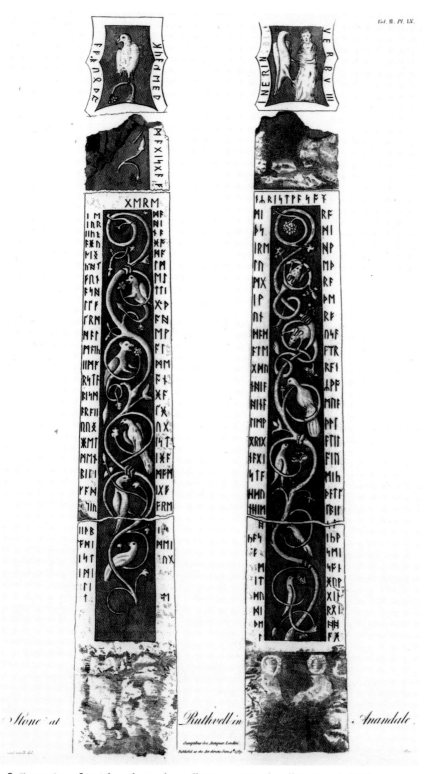

48 Engraving after Adam de Cardonnell, 'Stone at Ruthwell in Anandale' (from
Vetusta Monumenta, Plate LV, 1789)

49 [J. Rutherford], ['Runic Cross Ruthwell, 1887'], west (then south) side

50 J. R[utherford], 'Runic Cross Ruthwell, 1887', east (then north) side

RUNIC MONUMENT IN THE GARDEN BELONGING TO RUTHWELL MANSE.

51 Engraving by W. Penny after a drawing by Henry Duncan, 'Runic Monument in the Garden Belonging to Ruthwell Manse' (from *Archaeologia Scotica*, Plate XIII, 1833)

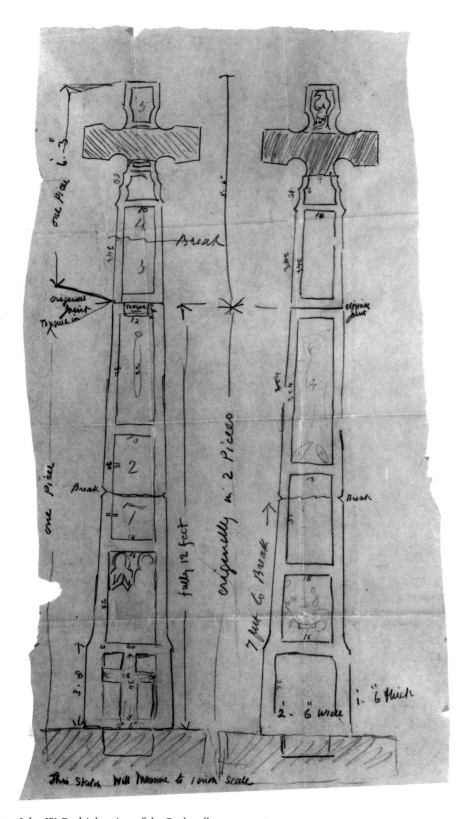

52 John W. Dods' drawing of the Ruthwell monument

53 The Ruthwell monument, west (now north) side, upper stone

54 The Ruthwell monument, west (now north) side, upper stone: John the Baptist or *Maiestas*

55 The Ruthwell monument, west (now north) side, lower stone: Christ on the Beasts

56 The Ruthwell monument, west (now north) side, lower stone: Sts Paul and Anthony Breaking Bread in the Desert

57 The Ruthwell monument, west (now north) side, lower stone: Flight into/out of Egypt

58 The Ruthwell monument, west (now north) side, lower stone: base stones: inhabited plant-scroll and runic inscriptions

59 The Ruthwell monument, north (now east) side, upper and lower stones: inhabited plant-scroll and runic inscriptions

60 The Ruthwell monument, north (now east) side, lower stone: inhabited plant-scroll and runic inscriptions

61 The Ruthwell monument, east (now south) side, upper stone

62 The Ruthwell monument, east (now south) side, lower stone: Christ and Mary Magdalen, Christ Healing the Blind Man

63 The Ruthwell monument, east (now south) side, lower stone: Christ and Mary Magdalen

64 The Ruthwell monument, east (now south) side, lower stone: Christ Healing the Blind Man

65 The Ruthwell monument, east (now south) side, lower stone: Annunciation

66 The Ruthwell monument, east (now south) side, lower stone: Crucifixion

67 The Ruthwell monument, south (now west) side, upper and lower stones: inhabited plant-scroll and runic inscriptions

68 The Ruthwell monument, south (now west) side, lower stone: inhabited plant-scroll and runic inscriptions

69 The Ruthwell monument, south (now west) side, lower stone: inhabited plant-scroll and runic inscriptions

70 The Ruthwell monument,
west side. Cast collection Durham
Cathedral Library

71 The Ruthwell monument, east side.
Cast collection Durham Cathedral
Library

72 Fragment: figure in profile, Ruthwell Church

73 Fragment: architectural sculpture

and family, the community founded by Eanmund was a centre of culture and piety. There was the scribe Ultan,[140] who has been associated in recent years (on slender grounds) with some of the great Northumbrian manuscripts.[141] And there is also the poet Æthelwulf himself. His vision, which provides a climax to the poem,[142] included a jewelled cross.

Æthelwulf was writing in the early ninth century, a hundred years after Bede. His poem is perhaps the last literary achievement of the so-called Northumbrian Renaissance, which had begun in the days of Wilfrid and Benedict Biscop. It shows that, despite the best part of a century of political uncertainty, cultural standards could still be high. There is no need to assign all the major Northumbrian artistic and intellectual works to the early eighth century just because of the achievements of Bede. Alcuin and Æthelwulf are reminders that Northumbria still had much to offer long after Bede's death. If the Bewcastle and Ruthwell monuments belong in the late eighth or early ninth century, Æthelwulf's work is a good deal closer to them chronologically than is Bede's.

For the moment, what is important is the combination of family, commemoration and monasticism to be found in the *De abbatibus*. No source tells us that Bewcastle was a monastery, but it is not difficult to see its monument as belonging to a community of the sort covered by the evidence we have just been discussing. We do not have to think of a monastery as intellectually or spiritually sophisticated as Wearmouth–Jarrow, although, as we shall see, the sundial implies scientific interest. Æthelwulf's *De abbatibus* and Bede's Letter to Ecgbert show how broad was the category of Northumbrian monasticism. The community that erected the Bewcastle monument, with its combination of commemorative runes, images of an aristocratic falconer and of Christ, and its sundial, could have been 'bogus' in Bede's terms, yet it could equally have been a model foundation. If Bewcastle were a monastic community, it could have been a royal house. Given what we know about land-tenure, at the very least it must have been built on property obtained from the king.

Ruthwell and Rheged

Some, but not all, of these factors are relevant for an understanding of Ruthwell and its stone sculpture. Scarcely any of them impinge in quite the same way as they do at Bewcastle. As we shall see, the iconography of the Ruthwell monument is of such a level of theological sophistication that it would be difficult not to assign it to a religious community – indeed it would seem to supply evidence as important as that of Æthelwulf's poem for the existence of a very highly developed Christian culture outside the known centres of Wearmouth–Jarrow, Lindisfarne, Whitby, Ripon, Hexham and York. To judge by the numbers of representations of women on the monument, it might even provide evidence for a female community, or at least a double monastery of women and men.[143] Given the importance of family for Northumbrian society and the Church, it is scarcely conceivable that there was no family interest in Ruthwell: but it is not obviously present on the monument, as it is on that at Bewcastle. Nor does the local Roman past obviously impinge: but it could have done. There was a Roman marching camp in the vicinity, but whoever set up the Ruthwell monument seems to have ignored it – although the present churchyard does straddle a Roman-Iron-Age circular enclosure, which may have been exploited by the religious community.[144] The fact that the Roman fort was ignored marks a difference with Bewcastle. Yet there is another more general difference, which is arguably more important for understanding the monument, and which takes us into a very different political landscape. We have already paused to consider the province of the *Bernicii*. It is necessary now to turn to another of the component parts of early Northumbria: the kingdom of Rheged.[145]

Here there is an immediate problem. Although Rheged is mentioned in a number of British sources, the name does not appear in Bede or even in the early ninth-century *Historia Brittonum*.[146] This latter history does, however, talk of a king Urien, his son Rhun, his grandson Royth and his great-grand-daughter Rieinmellt. Rhun is even credited with the conversion of Edwin,[147] while Rieinmellt is stated to have been one of the wives of Oswiu.[148] More important, an Urien, who is usually assumed to be the same as the father of Rhun, appears in poems attributed to Taliesin and in what has been identified as coming from the Saga of Llywarch Hen, in which he is presented as 'lord of Rheged'.[149] These poems, it should be noted, used to be accepted as genuine texts of the sixth century. Now a later date is thought more likely.[150] A date in the eighth or ninth century would, of course, bring their moment of production closer to that of the Ruthwell monument. Whatever their factual accuracy, they tell us something about how the Britons of North Wales writing in that period looked on the region of the upper Solway. They saw it as a region of desolation. As we shall see, some of the Britons who lived near the Solway coast might have agreed.

Since these early Welsh poems provide little historical precision, their exact date is scarcely central to any understanding of the history of Rheged. Even so, they are not likely to have invented the name of Urien's kingdom. Unfortunately, although they do provide some indication of Urien's sphere of military activity, which would appear to include Catterick and Wensley-dale,[151] they do not give any unquestionable indication of the location of the heartlands of his kingdom. Most scholars, however, have accepted the identification of Llwynfenydd, of which Urien is regularly said to be lord, as Lyvennet near Crosby Ravensworth,[152] between Shap and Appleby.

Crosby Ravensworth may have been central to Urien's power. It is unlikely, however, to have been Rheged's geographical centre, which surely lay further north, for a Welsh poem seems to describe the Solway as the sea of Rheged.[153] This description, however, allows more than one interpretation. It has often been assumed that Rheged was based on Carlisle. Yet, although the town and its hinterland have been well studied in recent years,[154] no one has produced firm evidence to show that it was central to Rheged. An alternative view is that Rheged was centred, at least initially, on Dunragit in Wigtonshire.[155] This view depends primarily on the place-name evidence: Dunragit meaning 'the Fortress of Rheged'. The interpretation of the name is plausible, and since the other indications of the whereabouts of the kingdom all point further east, it is certainly a reasonable hypothesis that Rheged expanded from Dunragit towards Carlisle and perhaps into the Pennine valleys. If this interpretation is correct, it should also be noted that, in the course of its expansion, the kingdom of Rheged would have taken in other Celtic groups present on the north coast of the Solway. The archaeological evidence has revealed the presence of Irish communities, notably on Ardwall Island, off Gatehouse of Fleet,[156] and Picts at Trusty's Hill.[157] In other words, the population of the Solway coastline would have been very different from that along the line of Hadrian's Wall, though each would have been polyethnic.

The location of Rheged is a matter of debate, and it cannot be said that any conclusion is as yet certain. Equally open is the question of the kingdom's importance. It has been seen both as powerful and as insignificant, depending largely on how much credence is given to the evidence of the Welsh poetry.[158] Praise poetry of the sort ascribed to Taliesin and Aneurin is notoriously difficult to use as historical evidence. On the other hand, the silence of Bede is not necessarily significant: he had no interest in the fate of the British. And just as the importance of Rheged is open to question, so too are the date of and reasons for its collapse. Even in Welsh tradition Urien is the one substantial ruler of the kingdom. Since his great-granddaughter was one of the wives of Oswiu, she is likely to have been born in the early seventh century. This would place Urien's *floruit* in the second half of the sixth century. How long Rheged survived thereafter is really a matter of guesswork. It has been argued that the Bernician Æthelfrith (592–616) was responsible for the collapse of the kingdom, and the fact that his successor, the Deiran Edwin (616–633), could attack the Isle of Man has been taken to show that he must have controlled the Solway.[159] Yet any interpretation of Edwin's actions needs to be set alongside the information provided by the *Historia Brittonum*, that he was baptised by 'Rhun son of Urien, that is Paulinus, archbishop of York'.[160] This extraordinary statement has inevitably prompted a score of theories, ranging from claims that Edwin really was baptised by Rhun, or that the latter stood sponsor at his baptism, to outright dismissal of what the source has to say. Since the author of the *Historia Brittonum* was writing in reaction to Bede's account,[161] one has to bear in mind that the statement is part of a battle over the reconstruction of the past. If Rhun were in any way associated with Edwin's baptism, one would assume that he was a figure of some influence: Rheged could thus have still been a kingdom of importance in the 620s. As open to differing interpretations is Rieinmellt's marriage to Oswiu.[162] This might indicate that the royal house of Rheged was a force to be reckoned with into the mid seventh century.[163] On the other hand, Rieinmellt might have been no more than the last survivor of a failing dynasty, and the marriage might be a factor in Oswiu's taking control of Rheged.[164] At least most historians agree that, when King Ecgfrith launched his attack on the Irish in 684, the Northumbrians really did have control of the waters of the Solway. Some, however, would see that control as having been achieved only during Ecgfrith's reign.[165] And since the chronology is problematic, it is scarcely surprising that the circumstances in which Rheged vanished are a mystery. Was the kingdom destroyed in battle, or did Oswiu's marriage mark a diplomatic takeover?[166] We have no means of telling.

Since Ecgfrith's reign provides the latest plausible date for the Anglian takeover of the Solway region, and since the Ruthwell monument is no longer thought to have been produced in the seventh century, there is no close connection to be drawn between political expansion and the erection of the sculptured column. Nevertheless, the pre-Anglian history of the Solway region should be taken into account when discussing the monument. For a start, it is important to recognise that the world of the Solway is radically different from that of Bewcastle and the lands to the east. Ruthwell is in a region which is likely to have regarded itself as British well into the seventh century. Nor is evidence for this Britishness restricted to the narrative and poetic sources. The place-names of present-day Dumfriesshire point very clearly to a significant British population. The adjacent parish to Ruthwell is Cummertrees, which means the community ('tref') of the Welsh (*Cymry*).[167] And this is not the only parish in the vicinity with a British name: there is Trailtrow, which also incorporates the 'tref' prefix, and Pennersax (British for 'the spur of the Saxons'). Not far away is Ecclefechan, a notable example of an 'eccles' place-name – and it would seem to imply the existence of a pre-Anglo-Saxon ecclesiastical community. Whether or not this region had been part of Rheged, on the basis of the place-names alone it was most certainly a region where there was still a significant British population in the early Middle Ages, and what is more important – since the genetic make-up of the region will not have been very different from that of much of North-umbria – it was a population that continued to distinguish itself from the incoming Anglians: the place-names indicate that the Cymry and the Saxons were coexisting but not integrating.

It is important to bear this in mind when considering Ruthwell and the inscriptions on its monument, especially the Old English runes, and their account of the crucifixion. A Briton, even a literate Briton who could cope with the Latin alphabet and language, is unlikely to have been able to read the runic script. The Old English language itself may well have been unintel-ligible. The presentation of Christ in terms of the warrior ethos of the Anglo-Saxons would have been intelligible, but may not have been welcome to the British peasantry confronted with the presence of dominant Anglian incomers. As we have seen, we do not know when or under what circum-stances the Anglians took control of the lands north of the Solway. The precise relationship between the indigenous population and the incomers will have depended on the nature of the takeover, and that relation will have changed over time. The Ruthwell monument may have been put up in a region that had long been under Anglian control, or that had been taken over only a mere generation earlier. This will have affected the extent to which, with its Old English inscriptions in runes, it was an affront to the local population. Yet whatever dates we give to the monument at Ruthwell, the presence of the British in the vicinity needs to be taken into account. The sculpted column was an Anglian monument, erected by a community of alien incomers, forcibly inserted into a predominantly British landscape. It was not merely an elegant depiction of Christian beliefs.

The ecclesiastical community at Ruthwell might usefully be considered in the light of evidence that we have for the expansion of the Anglian Church in other areas west of the Pennines. In the *Life of Wilfrid*, for instance, Stephanus records 'a list of the consecrated places in various parts which the British clergy had deserted when fleeing from the hostile sword wielded by the warriors of our own nation', and which had been given to Ripon.[168] Of course, from Stephanus's point of view the 'hostile sword of our own nation' was a good thing: the Britons would not have agreed. Stephanus goes on to specify lands *iuxta Rippel et Ingaedyne et in regione Dunutinga et Incaetlaevum*, which are usually identified as 'round Ribble and Yeadon and the region of Dent and Catlow'.[169] We do not know whether Ruthwell had once been in the hands of the British clergy, though Eric Mercer noted that 'an unshaped stone in the Whithorn manner with a plain cross upon it in a pecked technique has been found not far from the present church'.[170] In any case, it was not only ecclesiastical land that was transferred to Anglian churchmen. Equally well known is the later record of the grant of Cartmel, to the south of the Lake District, made to Cuthbert by Ecgfrith and, mysteriously, 'all the Britons with him' (*omnes Brittanni cum eo*), who, one assumes, were under duress.[171] What both these anecdotes make clear is the extent to which the Anglian Church, west of the Pennines, depended on property seized from the native Britons.

We have further indications of Lindisfarne's interests west of the Pennines in a story concerning the wanderings of the community of St Cuthbert during the Viking Age, related in varying detail in two late sources. According to these accounts, the monks of Lindisfarne thought to move themselves and their precious relics to Ireland, to avoid the threat posed to their monastery by the Vikings in the 870s or 880s.[172] They attempted to make the crossing of the Irish Sea from the mouth of the river Derwent, on the west side of the Lake District, but the conditions were too rough, and, after a manuscript of the Gospels was washed overboard, they were driven back to the shore. Subsequently – following a vision – they discovered the manuscript, which is usually identified as the Lindisfarne Gospels,[173] washed up on the beach. Rather surprisingly, by this time they are said to have been at Whithorn. It is unlikely that the places visited by the community of St Cuthbert were chosen at random. The majority were probably estates of the community or of friendly contacts. Ever since the days of Cuthbert himself Lindisfarne had contacts in the region of Carlisle and the Solway. The saint is known to have made at least one visit to Carlisle and rather more to St Herbert's Isle in Derwentwater.[174] We might guess that, as well as Cartmel to the south of the Cumbrian fells, the community of Cuthbert held property to the north of the Lake District. Unfortunately we have no detail on any land held to the north of the Solway.

The Church of the northern Solway

The pre-Viking sculpture of present-day Dumfriesshire presents us with our clearest evidence for the Anglian presence in the region. After Ruthwell, the most interesting place is Hoddom. Here there is evidence of a native site in the Roman period.[75] In later, twelfth-century, tradition, whose value is impossible to assess, Kentigern briefly established a bishopric at Hoddom, before transfering to Glasgow.[76] A substantial quantity of Anglian sculpture was found at Hoddom before 1939, but vanished during the 1939–1945 war, apparently used as hardcore by the Pioneer Corps.[77] A few surviving fragments, together with a photographic record, show that there was once very much more sculpture at Hoddom than is known from Ruthwell. At the same time there may have been nothing of comparable quality. Collingwood claimed, on the grounds of perceived similarities of style, that the monument at Ruthwell 'is Hoddom work, the first known example and the greatest effort'.[78] There is also some evidence that Roman material was taken to Hoddom from the nearby fort of Birrens in the Anglian period.[79] The quantity of sculpture from Hoddom, the archaeological evidence that it was a production centre of some importance, as well as the subsequent history and reputation of the site, implies that it differed from Ruthwell. It has been described as a minster,[180] although not everyone is agreed as to the meaning of the term. Less open to semantic debate is the description of Hoddom as a 'central church', with Ruthwell and a number of other churches as being dependent.[181] Yet this may not tell us about the relationship of Hoddom and Ruthwell in the eighth or early ninth centuries, when the latter could have been outside any local ecclesiastical jurisdiction. Ruthwell could have had some pastoral functions, as has been deduced from the iconography of the monument.[182] More certainly, the sculpture suggests that it was extremely well endowed, and that it housed a community which was theologically more sophisticated than that at Hoddom.

It is possible to broaden the focus and to look at developments as far west as Whitborn, and as far north as the Plain of Kyle. Even in the Roman period the lands north of the Solway had seen Roman occupation, despite the fact that they lay beyond Hadrian's Wall: there is good evidence for the existence of forts and other military outposts, as well as of routes west and north.[183] Ruthwell itself had been the site of a temporary camp. By comparison with other places in the region, however, its Roman past was insignificant. A major Roman road ran slightly to the north, passing Broadlee, Birrens, Burnswark, Ladyward, Murder Loch and on to Dalwinston, Barburgh Mill and Drumlanrig.[184] Presumably this route remained in use in the Anglian period. Certainly there is important Anglian sculpture along its path, not least at Thornhill and nearby, above a crossing of the river Nith, where a cross still stands, possibly where it has always stood.[185] Perhaps this was the route north taken by Eadbert in 750 or shortly after, when he seized the Plain of Kyle.[186]

Probably as important as the road system was the marine route down the Solway itself, which we have already seen was central to the oral history of

Ruthwell. This route led westwards to Galloway and ultimately to Ireland. The fleet which took Edwin's army to the Isle of Man may have sailed the length of the Solway.[187] So too, may that which transported Ecgfrith's army across to Ireland in 684.[188] This crossing, however, might equally well have been made from Portpatrick, in its original Celtic form, Port Righ, that is, the king's port.[189] The name *portus Ecgfridi*, by which the mudflats at Jarrow Slake on the lower Tyne were known,[190] suggest that Ecgfrith had a considerable interest in maritime power.[191]

If Dunragit really were the centre of the kingdom of Rheged, the maritime route would also have been central to the communications of that British kingdom, and to its expansion in the sixth century. By the time that the Ruthwell monument was being put up, Dunragit, like Rheged, was a place of the past. The same is not true of Whithorn, which may well have originated as the religious counterpart to Dunragit. Referring to the British bishop Nynian, Bede commented,

> His episcopal see is celebrated for its church, dedicated to St Martin where his [Nynian's] body rests, together with those of many other saints. The see is now under English rule (*iam nunc gens Anglorum obtinet*). This place which is in the province of the Bernicians (*ad provinciam Berniciorum*) is commonly called the White House (*Ad Candidam Casam*), because Ninian built a church of stone there, using a method unusual to the Britons.[192]

Bede's account has been bolstered by the remarkable finds made by Peter Hill in his excavations at Whithorn.[193] It is now clear that there was a substantial monastic town in the post-Roman and Anglian periods, although as yet Nynian's stone church, which seems to have lasted into the Anglo-Saxon period, has proved elusive.[194] The growing evidence for Whithorn sheds some light not only on Nynian and his episcopacy but also on a figure rather closer in time to the erection of the Ruthwell monument: Bishop Pecthelm.

Pecthelm is referred to by Bede as being Bishop of *Candida Casa* at the time of the composition of the *Ecclesiastical History*.[195] Writing of Whithorn, Bede says 'the number of believers has so increased that it had lately become an episcopal see with Pecthelm as its first bishop'.[196] This leaves much unexplained. Does the increase in the number of believers indicate that the Britons of the region had apostasised and only been rechristianised in Bede's day? Or does it imply a population growth for some unexplained reason?[197] And how recent was Pecthelm's appointment? It is often claimed that he was appointed only in 731, though the word *nuper* would allow that he had already been in post for a few years at the time of the composition of the *Ecclesiastical History*.[198] He was dead by 735, when his successor Frithuwold was consecrated.[199] The last known Anglian bishop of the see was Badwulf, who was still alive in 803.[200]

There is more to be said about Pecthelm. If Plummer was right, his name meant 'Helmet of the Picts',[201] implying not only that he was a northerner by birth but also that he had Celtic, and more precisely Pictish, connections. This may well have been a useful attribute for an Anglo-Saxon bishop of Whithorn. According to Bede, Nynian converted the southern Picts,[202] though he omits to tell us where they were settled. The symbol-stone from Trusty's Hill indicates that there had been Pictish presence in the Solway region. Bearing this in mind, it is also worth noting the fact that one of Pecthelm's successors, Pehtwine, had a name meaning 'Friend of the Picts'.[203] Pecthelm was, nevertheless, educated in the south, for he was a pupil of Aldhelm, that is at Malmesbury or Sherborne.[204] Perhaps it was through his West Saxon connections that Boniface came to know him, or of him. Clearly his reputation was considerable, for Boniface wrote to him on the question of whether it was canonical for a man to marry the mother of his godson.[205] We do not know what answer Pecthelm gave, but it is a remarkable testimony to his reputation as a theologian that Boniface should write to him from Germany. In addition, Bede reveals that he had an interest in penitential visions,[206] and miracle stories.[207] That a bishop of Whithorn had a reputation as a theologian is worth bearing in mind when it comes to consideration of the iconographic scheme of the Ruthwell monument: the north coast of the Solway could boast at least one intellectual of international status in the eighth century. Pecthelm or his pupils would have been perfectly capable of understanding, or even designing, a sophisticated work of theological art.

Although we know little else about Pecthelm or his successors, we do have one invaluable piece of information on the cult based at Whithorn, that of Nynian himself. The Latin *Miracula Nynie Episcopi* is a poem written by Alcuin's pupils, presumably in York, which they sent to him as a present after he had left for the continent.[208] It is, therefore, a work of the late eighth century, and takes us close in date to Æthelwulf and the *De abbatibus* – although one might wonder whether any part of it reflects the interests of Pecthelm, with his interest in the miraculous. The *Miracula Nynie* is a remarkable poem, not for its account of Nynian, which has little to offer on the British Church of the fifth century – and what information it does have on the matter is largely derived from Bede's *Ecclesiastical History*[209] – but for what it has to say about the flourishing of the saint's cult once Whithorn itself had been incorporated into the Northumbrian Church. It is useful also because it sheds light on how aware York was of some of the goings on in Galloway.

As Bede tells the story, Nynian was a Briton, who had been instructed in Rome, and then returned, preaching to the southern Picts, and founding in his episcopal see a church of St Martin, which was notable for being built in stone, 'a method unusual among the Picts'.[210] Nynian is thus presented as a figure conforming to continental, and not British, religious norms. This is a tale which would have fitted an Anglian reading of the saint, and could have prompted the reader to draw a comparison with the involvement of the Northumbrians, not to mention Bede and his abbot Ceolfrith, in bringing the northern Picts into a state of orthodoxy.[211]

The *Miracula Nynie* moves even further than does Bede to distance the saint from his background. His British origins are ignored, and he is presented first as travelling to Rome with no mention of his point of departure.[212] As a result, the reader sees him not as a Briton but as a Roman saint, wholly acceptable to an Anglo-Saxon audience. Having left Rome he comes to Britain, and sets out to evangelise the Picts.[213] Once in Britain, according to the *Miracula*, which here departs from Bede's narrative, Nynian was opposed by King Thuvahel.[214] Thus, when we do see the saint active in a British context, it is in opposition to the powers that be. What then follow are three standard miracles performed by the living saint.[215] More interesting are the following four miracles performed at or near his tomb,[216] two of which clearly involve Anglians – something which reinforces the representation of Nynian as a Northumbrian saint. The most striking of these last miracles, and indeed the story that provides the climax to the whole work, concerns the priest Plecgils, who regularly celebrated Mass at the shrine of Nynian.[217] He used to pray that he might see Christ in the flesh, and not just in the form of the host. Eventually his prayers were answered: Christ appeared on the patten, and Plecgils took him in his arms and kissed him. The story, which is an important one for the history of the Mass, spread beyond Alcuin's circle. It is repeated by Paschasius Radbertus in his *Liber de corpore et sanguine domini*.[218]

Although from the broader view of the history of religion the Plecgils story may well be the most important part of the *Miracula Nynie*, for an understanding of Ruthwell, the general presentation of Nynian is more thought-provoking. While the author of the *Miracula* could have protrayed Nynian as a major British saint, he decided to ignore his Britishness. Instead the British king Thuvahel is, momentarily, the villain of the piece. The *Miracula Nynie* is thus a work demonstrating the appropriation by the Anglians of the greatest British shrine in the Solway region. As such it needs to be set alongside the aggressively English aspects of the Ruthwell monument. Both are markers of the colonialising nature of Anglo-Saxon Christianity, and of the crushing of British tradition.

Pecthelm's reputation, the vision of Plecgils and the iconographic scheme of the Ruthwell monument are all indications of an Anglian cultural and theological sophistication on the north bank of the Solway in the eighth century. Unfortunately they are no more than indications. We lack Pecthelm's response to Boniface's letter, or any other work he might have written, except perhaps for a hymn to Nynian.[219] As for the iconography of the Ruthwell monument, it encourages us to look for an underlying theology, and, as we shall see, it is not difficult to hypothesise what that theology might have been. Yet no theological work survives from the Solway region. For Northumbrian theology we have to turn to the east coast of the kingdom, and particularly to Jarrow and to Bede. It is hardly surprising that commentators on the Ruthwell monument often have recourse to Bede and his works – and that links between Jarrow and Ruthwell have been suggested.[220] Yet although Bede was in contact with Pecthelm,[221] there is nothing to prove that Jarrow had direct connections with Ruthwell itself.

Ultimately for Ruthwell, as for Bewcastle, we lack the documentary evidence that makes Wearmouth–Jarrow, Hexham and Lindisfarne so much more accessible to the scholar. Exploration of a series of fragments, however, has allowed us to make some suggestions about the two sites, and to indicate some differences between them. While the evidence of Bede has meant that much of what we have considered relates to the late seventh and early eighth centuries, other fragments have allowed us to say something of the Roman and British pasts, as well as the late eighth and early ninth centuries. On the grounds of the iconography of their monuments, both Ruthwell and Bewcastle would seem to have been monastic, and to have been places of considerable religious culture, though on the surviving evidence Ruthwell was the more theologically sophisticated of the two. In neither case are we dealing with the dregs of Bede's 'bogus' monasteries, although Bewcastle may well have been a community dominated by family or political interest. More fundamental differences, however, might lie in their broader geographical and social settings. Close to Hadrian's Wall, Bewcastle belonged to a world which had long been ethnically mixed. Whether on not there was continuity from the Roman, through the sub-Roman past to the Anglian present, that past was physically very much in evidence, and the community at Bewcastle used it as a resource. Ruthwell looks very different. What Roman remains there were in the vicinity were ignored, and, while Romanness is certainly present in the sculpture on the monument, it does not relate to local resources. Equally, perhaps more, important, Ruthwell, like the neighbouring ecclesiastical centre at Hoddom, appears to be an Anglian intrusion in a still-British world. Such considerations of the 'history, dates and all' of Bewcastle and Ruthwell suggest that, despite any 'similarities' perceived in the iconography of the two monuments, the communities that erected them, and therefore the monuments themselves, were significantly different.

6

Reckoning time[1]

⌘

Observe, O clerk, how the sun advances point by point on the sundial; you may then wisely scrutinize those points that we speak of * * * (Byrhtferth, *Enchiridion*)[2]

I

On its west side (Fig. 17), the representation of an aristocratic layman with a hawk, a long commemorative inscription, Christ on the Beasts, 'iudex aequitatis' and 'salvator mundi', and John the Baptist with the Agnus Dei. The Bewcastle monument was produced to turn Anglo-Saxon minds from thoughts of the present to thoughts of the past, and from thoughts of the past and present to thoughts of the future. On the south side, a sundial (Fig. 20) reckons the passage of time. At Bewcastle, a concern with memory is represented alongside a concern with time. Whoever produced and first used the monument seems to have glimpsed the indispensable function of memory in all time calculation. Which is remarkable, for Books 11 and 12 of Augustine's *Confessions*, whose greatest originality lies in just that insistence and could have provided the resource for putting a concern with memory in a relation of association with time, seem to have been unknown in England until the eleventh or twelfth century.[3]

II

The sundial (Fig. 35) on the Bewcastle monument, probably our earliest surviving English instrument for calculating the passage of time, is no insignificant detail. Yet it has received scant attention from scholars of Anglo-Saxon stone sculpture, specifically, and scholars of Anglo-Saxon culture generally. Two of the most sustained discussions can be found in Éamonn Ó Carragáin's essay 'A Liturgical Interpretation of the Bewcastle Cross' and Rosemary Cramp's entry on the Bewcastle monument in *The Corpus of Anglo-Saxon Stone Sculpture*.[4] As we will show, Ó Carragáin is quite right to think that, though the sundial would have been of use to a community that recited the liturgical hours, it could not have been used to calculate the date of Easter or the spring equinox: 'Easter tables would have been less troublesome and more reliable'.[5] However, he is on less certain ground when he talks about the 'symbolic reasons' why the dial may have been included in the overall decorative scheme and to have interpreted it and the accompanying plant trail as metonymies of the inevitability of the signs that will announce the Lord coming in great power and glory as given in the parable of the fig tree, Luke 21.25–33.[6] While it is the case that the liturgical year links the conception of Christ and the birth of John the Baptist with the sun's course, and Christ on the Beasts at Bewcastle might connote the Second Coming, the sundial, an instrument that represents the sun's ordered progress, seems a strange device with which to represent the 'powers of heaven ... shaken', driven from their courses. As for the plant trail with its full foliage and ripened berry bunches, this seems an odd image with which to symbolise leaves beginning to appear from opening buds. Not that the sundial is devoid of theological significance. Given its frame of reference, that hardly seems likely.

In the *Corpus*, Rosemary Cramp points out that the Bewcastle sundial is the only dial to survive from the pre-Conquest period that is not set into the south wall of a church. It could, she thinks, be seen as part of a '"free standing" tradition' which would have included the solitary Welsh dial and the early Irish dials which 'are found on free standing pillars or slabs, as were also some Roman dials'[7] (Fig. 36). Cramp's mention of the Roman dials is especially interesting and useful for going on, for, while it seems that the Celtic dials must be regarded as distinct from the Anglo-Saxon dials, it is likely that both kinds of dial were adapted from knowledge of Roman dials. Unfortunately, Cramp is mistaken when she says, 'most horologists who have commented on the Bewcastle dial appear to believe that it is scientifically constructed in the tradition of Greek prime vertical dials'.[8] It would be more accurate to say that the Bewcastle dial is the earliest surviving prime-vertical sundial in Britain and, as we will show, that the competence and skill required to construct it had their beginnings in Graeco-Roman dialling. However, though it can be placed in relation to some Roman vertical plane dials, it is not 'scientifically constructed' along the same lines as Graeco-Roman dials. Cramp is also mistaken when, following Albert E. Waugh, she says that Bede 'provided tables for telling the time of day by noting and measuring the length of shadows and stepping them out with one's feet'.[9] These tables were available long before the eighth century and Bede did not devise those to which Waugh refers.[10]

III

Although the overall form of the Bewcastle sundial is not semicircular, the dial itself consists of the lower half of a circle with a radius of about 7¼ inches. It is divided into twelve divisions by thirteen lines that spread out from a central gnomon hole.[11] Three of these lines, unlike the others, are V-shaped in section, wide and deeply cut, and marked with cross-bars.[12] As it has survived, the gnomon hole is worn and damaged, enlarged and irregular, with the deepest part somewhat off centre. The holes on better preserved

pre- and post-Conquest medieval dials suggest that a rod-like gnomon was set into and projected from the hole at a right angle to the dial. The Bewcastle dial is, then, a vertical plane dial that was fitted with a gnomon set at 90° to it. Though the lines, like the gnomon hole, are damaged and weather-worn, it is clear that they were intended to divide the semicircle into equal divisions. They, more or less accurately, radiate at 15° from each other around the gnomon hole: the equal angles giving equidistant lines and equal areas. So, the dial is a protractor: a crude protractor; but, nevertheless, the product of basic geometry in a society that, though it was adept with the double-pointed divider compass and at dividing circles, may not have possessed the Roman compass nor, previously, had any need to measure angles in the form of a graduated semicircle.[13]

The Bewcastle sundial, as is the case with all pre- and post-Conquest medieval dials, does not mark equinoctial or equal hours. It would only do so if it were re sited on the equator. Nevertheless, it will, as will all dials of this kind in sunlight, mark local noon every day.

Presumably, for reasons that will become apparent, only the tip of the gnomon on the Bewcastle sundial was intended to mark the passage of time. Nowadays, a more or less accurate sundial must incorporate a sloping gnomon pointing at the pole star, the angular height of which is equal to the complement of the latitude on which it is to be used. At Bewcastle that is 35° (90° − 55° = 35°). The straight sloping edge or 'style' of the gnomon – or, more rarely, the tip of a gnomon set at 90° to the dial plane – throws a moving shadow cast by the apparent diurnal movement of the sun across the sky on to a horizontal or vertical plane. The radiating lines inscribed on that plane must also be laid out specific to the latitude of the site.[14]

This is what a south-facing, modern vertical plane dial that has been properly calibrated to work at Bewcastle looks like. You'll notice that, though the lines are arranged symmetrically across the vertical axis, they get closer

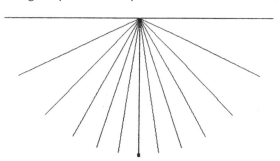

as they approach it from the horizontal. The angles narrow towards the vertical. These radiating lines are understood as hour lines. The edge of the sloping polar gnomon's shadow is always expected to take sixty minutes to move from one line to another on each day throughout the year. The dial has been designed to ensure that this will happen. This kind of properly calibrated dial with a sloping polar gnomon whose style height has also been properly calculated did not become possible in Europe until the end of the fifteenth century. Indeed, the earliest monumental sundial with a sloping polar gnomon dates from 1493.[15]

IIII

So what kind of time was the Bewcastle sundial intended to indicate? In the early Middle Ages, Northumbrian society was based on land, on agricultural production and landed property. Its consciousness of time would have been determined by the all-encompassing rhythms of nature: the movement of the earth and its moon in relation to the sun; the right time to sow and plant, and move herds; the tide coming in and going out; daylight and darkness, two very different phenomena, not a single unit. Night *and* day. Northumbrian time would have been mainly natural time. Without imaginary divisions of time. Without hours. The hour had almost no value in the economy of Anglo-Saxon Northumbria. 'Mainly' and 'almost' but not entirely, for some places in Northumbria in the late seventh and eighth centuries were responding to the need for another kind of time. This kind of time, social time, is based in and on the social structures and institutions that constitute it and are constituted by it. Social time is the time of calendars and clocks. The more man relates to these ways and means and systems of fixing the lengths and divisions of the year and the day, and so on, then the more time becomes removed from nature and the more it becomes *of* society.[16]

At its beginnings in Northumbria, as had been and would be the case elsewhere, monastic society was inaugurating social time. The churches of Rome, with their liturgical years and calendars, liturgical day and canonical hours, temporally regularised the year and the day in a precise and ordered manner. Monastic rules stipulated prayer three times during the hours of darkness (Compline, Nocturns or Vigils, and Matins or Lauds) and five times a day: during the first hour of daylight (*Prime*); half-way through the morning (*Terce*); midday (*Sext*); half-way through the afternoon (*None*); and at sunset (*Vespers*). The monastery was *the* place of sequestered, closed-off and closed-in situated action in place and time, of disciplined routine, of punctuated and punctual, synchronised and co-ordinated, timed social life.

V

But how did a monastery reckon the passage of time so that it could keep the moments of prayer at the correct times? We know that, in the ninth century, Alfred tried to develop the candle as an instrument for measuring the passage of time, six candles through the day, each burning for four hours in its wood and ox-horn lantern, but it would have been an expensive and unreliable way of measuring the hours and useless liturgically because it could not have coped with the summer and winter liturgy.[17] It seems unlikely that any monastery in England would have had a clepsydra or water clock before the tenth century and perhaps not before the eleventh or twelfth century.[18] The earliest known evidence for the use of the sand clock or hourglass dates to the fourteenth century, and its context of use was maritime not monastic.[19] Aside from chanting the stipulated monthly sequence of psalms to reckon the canonical hours at each season of the year, if a monastery wanted to keep the two stipulated moments of prayer in the hours of darkness, someone would have had to have kept awake with at least one eye on the course of the stars; whilst for the daylight moments of prayer he would have had to have followed the sun's course.[20]

At its beginnings, the artifice or factitiousness of social time was forced to correspond, wherever possible, to the observation of natural time. Hence, the Anglo-Saxon Church's appropriation of the idea of the sundial as a marker of the two moments of daytime prayer, Terce and None, that are not marked by natural phenomena as Sext is at local midday when the sun is at its highest elevation and a shadow is at its shortest length, as Prime is by daybreak, and Vespers by sunset.

So, the Bewcastle sundial, if only on a sunny day, might have been intended as an instrument for regulating that aspect of the life of a community which was concerned with the time of prayer. But how was the dial regulated? What controlled the number and arrangement of its divisions? To what requirements were they adapted and inscribed? The answers to these questions are by no means as obviously or solely related to regulating the liturgical day as one might think.

VI

That some pre- and post-Conquest sundials like the pre-Conquest dial on the church of St John at Escomb (which may have been produced close in

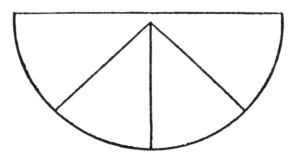

time to the Bewcastle dial) and the late-Saxon dial on St Gregory's Minister at Kirkdale (which must have been made between 1055 and 1064)[21] are inscribed with what at first seem a very strange number of lines. The dial at Escomb has three lines. The dial at Kirkdale has nine lines. These lines have been explained in terms of a system of time measurement that was peculiar to the Anglo-Saxons.

On a number of the dials, such as that at Bewcastle or Kirkdale, some

of the lines are distinguished by the addition of a cross-bar. Usually these correspond to the third, sixth and ninth hours of the day. But not always. The Kirkdale dial, for example, is further distinguished by a different kind of cross-piece. It has become established as a kind of conventional wisdom amongst antiquarians and horologists, and those medievalists whose study has touched on clocks and sundials, that the Anglo-Saxons reckoned time on a so-called 'octaval' system which divided the twenty-four hours of the day into eight parts or 'tides', each tide measuring three hours. The dial at Escomb might be taken as representing the octaval or 'tidal' system in its simplest form. It is for this reason, as the *Corpus* points out, that it has been suggested that the Bewcastle dial was originally inscribed with the octaval system and later subdivided to give it twelve hours.[22] While it is possible that the dial could have been subdivided later, it would have made little or no sense to have given it twelve equal angled lines after properly calibrated dials with sloping polar gnomons became relatively common from the sixteenth century onwards. More to the point, we see no reason why we should have much truck with the idea that the Anglo-Saxons measured time according to an octaval or tidal system that, at Bewcastle, had to be amended to the duodecimal system. As A. J. Turner, one of the more reliable historians of sundials, has made evident, the idea that the Anglo-Saxons used an octaval system entered published discourse only in 1879 when Reverend Daniel Henry Haigh came up with it in his essay on Yorkshire dials.[23] Haigh explained the octaval or tidal system with reference to, amongst other things, dubious similarities with dividing the day and night each into eight parts, which he found in nineteenth-century travellers' tales from Iceland, Hindustan and Burma, and with linguistic arguments intended to prove its Akkadian-Semitic origins and subsequent Aryan development. If in this matter we follow Bede, who makes no mention of the octaval or tidal system, then it is clear that those Anglo-Saxons who considered and calculated time divided the day into twenty-four hours: 'This *word* ["day"] is defined in two ways, that is, according to common parlance, and according to its proper [meaning]. On the whole, ordinary folk call the Sun's presence above the Earth "day". But properly speaking, a day comprises *XXIIII horis*, that is, a circuit of the Sun lighting up the entire globe.'[24] The Old English of Byrhtferth's *Enchiridion* is more useful here in illustration of this point than Bede's

Latin: 'It is the nature of the day to have twenty-four *tida* from the rising of the sun until it again displays its rising radiance.'[25] A 'tide' was the twenty-fourth part of a day or one hour. Or it was a canonical hour: 'Lo, archbishops with God's servants in orders rejoice the holy *tid* of tierce.'[26] The Bewcastle sundial seems to have been engraved with the idea of marking the progress of the sun at every seasonal hour *and* at the moments of daytime prayer. Though it did not mark the former with any precision, it would, as we'll see in a moment, function effectively as an instrument that marked the latter.

Anglo-Saxon sundials, no matter how many divisions they have or which hour lines are given special significance, seem always to have indicated the canonical hours of Terce, Sext and None. Sext, as you can imagine, would have been easily established with a plumb line against the gnomon's shadow. Thereafter, Terce and None would have been fixed with a divider compass bisecting the two right angles on either side of Sext; the four equal angles produced by this division thus establishing the necessary lines to give four equal divisions. Equal divisions; but not hours of equal length throughout the year. But did it matter? The Anglo-Saxons weren't living their lives by our standard hours; most of them were living and labouring to natural time. The point of the Anglo-Saxon dials is that on sunny days they would have worked sufficiently well to help regulate the hours of prayer.

Since the Bewcastle sundial seems to be the earliest surviving example in Anglo-Saxon England, from where did the idea of making it come? And if those persons who produced and first used the monument put the dial on it to help regulate the daylight social life of their community around Terce, Sext and None, then why did they inscribe it with *all* the hours between the first hour and the twelfth hour?

VII

As we have shown in previous chapters, those persons who produced and first used the Bewcastle monument probably imagined they were building or putting together a monument *iuxta morem Romanorum* and because of that probably needed a dial engraved, as Roman dials were engraved, like the Greek dials which brought the concept of hours to Rome, with twelve divisions each representing an equal part of daylight, sunrise to sunset. Over the last few years it's become increasingly apparent just how 'Roman' were some aspects of Anglo-Saxon Northumbria's material and visual culture. We should keep in mind that the Bewcastle monument was erected within the probably substantial remains of the Roman fort of *Fanum Cocidii*.

The Bewcastle sundial must be seen and understood as an aspect of the monument's Romanness. There can be little doubt that Anglo-Saxon tourists to Rome would have been familiar with Roman sundials and perhaps Graeco-Roman dials also. They may have come across them en route through Gaul or northern Italy, and they may have seen them in and around Rome.

What kinds of dial and what kind of knowledge of dialling were available to those persons who produced the Bewcastle monument? The majority of the surviving Greek and Roman dials are not planar dials, whether horizontal or vertical, but hemicyclia and conical dials. The hemicyclium (Fig. 37) is a hemisphere with the portion of the bowl that never received a shadow cut away; the conical dial (Fig. 38) is made of a cut cone (which would have been easier to carve). More conical dials seem to have survived than hemicyclia. Though in most cases these sundials have lost their gnomons, it seems from what survives that a bronze or iron gnomon was fixed horizontally in relation to the dial so that its apex would coincide with the geometric centre of the hollowed cut-sphere or cut-cone section beneath. Only the tip of the gnomon's shadow (Figs 39 and 40), not the full length of its edge, marks the time. Greek and Roman sundials were always intended to mark the twelve seasonal hours of daylight between sunrise and sunset. The hours were of equal length on a given day but varied during the year, being shortest at winter solstice and longest at summer solstice. With very few exceptions, Graeco-Roman dials are inscribed not only with the hour lines but also with lines marking the solstices and an equinoctial line. These ancient dials are calendars.

Much of the knowledge, competence and skill of the Greek diallers seems not to have been possessed by the Romans, who would have had no pressing need to perfect their dials after 46 BC when Julius Caesar introduced his civil calendar that fixed the changes of the seasons at 25 March, 24 June, 24 September and 25 December.[27] Though one still had to allow for the quarter-day error in the 365 day-year, with the introduction of the calendar anyone who needed to know when to move animals and plant crops – or when to begin a military campaign or wind one up – no longer had to watch the heavens. The astronomical successes that had enabled the production of the calendar negated one of the main reasons for theoretical and practical astronomy, for studying the movement of the heavens and for trying to make an accurate sundial.[28]

In *De architectura libri decem*, Vitruvius gave a list of thirteen types of sundial, many with the names of their inventors, and a description of the analemma, a figure that enabled celestial circles to be projected on to a plane surface, from 'which many different kinds of dials may be laid down and drawn'.[29] The former is intriguing but not very informative, while the latter would have been for the Romans difficult to grasp by the time it was drawn up some time shortly before 27 BC, because mathematical astronomy was becoming a lost knowledge. In the second century AD Claudius Ptolemy produced his three magisterial works of mathematical astronomy, the *Almagest*, the *Planetary Hypotheses* and the *Handy Tables*.[30] The *Almagest* contained his theories and methods of computing the positions of the stars, sun and moon and the other planets for any given time, the solstices and equinoxes, the lengths of the year, lunar month and seasons, his discussion of instruments for observing the position of the sun, and his introduction to trigonometry and spherical geometry. In the sixth century Cassiodorus, who considered Ptolemy the outstanding writer on astronomy among the Greeks, was able to make mention of these works, glimpsed their usefulness, but seems not to have known how to use them.[31] Ptolemy's work provided the foundation of mathematical astronomy in the Byzantine and Islamic worlds but in the Latin West, in company with Vitruvius's *Ten Books on Architecture*, it became lost knowledge. By the seventh century Ptolemy's name was confused with that of the Ptolemaic rulers of Egypt. It is hardly surprising that neither Vitruvius nor Claudius Ptolemy is mentioned in Bede's *De temporum ratione*.[32]

In what we take to be the best work on the relation of Roman sundials to Anglo-Saxon dials, Allan A. Mills explains, on the basis of what survives and with reference to reconstructions, how, as knowledge of the Greek achievements in mathematical astronomy and dialling became lost, the inscribed lines on Roman dials went out of kilter.[33] Mills shows how, when a properly calibrated dial is viewed from a position directly in line with its gnomon, 'to the eye, the hour lines appear to be fairly straight and meet at the base of the gnomon, although application of a ruler will show that in fact they converge in pairs towards an axis perpendicularly above it'.[34] The Romans were not as skillful diallers as were the Greeks (who invented and perfected these dials) and 'in practice many ancient dials not only have their hour lines converging on the base of the horizontal gnomon but are usually inscribed all the way up, although a shadow could never fall there. It appears that an oral tradition of a simplified incorrect construction evolved: twelve equal intervals along the equinoctial were ... joined to the base of the gnomon by straight lines'.[35] A vital clue to how to make a simple dial would have been obtained by looking into an incorrectly constructed conical dial, the most familiar type of dial in the Roman world, directly along its gnomon and assuming that it was inscribed with an equal-angle protractor. And such was the simplification involved that sometimes the equinoctial and solstice lines were omitted and the edge of the cut-sphere or cut-cone divided instead.[36] This misunderstanding might account for the development of certain vertical plane dials. One can imagine that

> three dimensional [hemicyclium and conical] dials were probably made in a few 'factories' by specialist masons following an oral tradition. Whatever the unperceived errors in the calibration, a stone carver of some skill would still be required to make them. A poor man could not afford to buy such a dial: a Roman officer in some distant outpost of the empire could not depend on the skill being available. Each would need a very simple dial which was easily described and made, by himself if necessary.[37]

Hence the type of late-Roman dial that seems to have been developed by taking the equal-angle protractor dial from the incorrectly calibrated dial and applying it to the vertical plane.[38]

We now need to qualify the observation made a moment ago that the most common Roman dials are conical dials. Though they are the most common, and some have been found in Roman Italy and Gaul, the majority have been found in eastern Mediterranean areas.[39] But planar dials are rarer. And amongst the vertical plane sundials, the equal-angle protractor sundials seem to be part of a distinct late tradition or, more probably, belated misunderstandings of the principles of a lapsed tradition.[40] The only Roman sundial to have been found in England (Fig. 41) is of this type. It was found at

Vercovicium (Housesteads) on Hadrian's Wall about sixteen miles away from Bewcastle (*Fanum Codicii*) via *Banna* (Birdoswald).[41]

VIII

There's no need of a lost prototype. The Bewcastle dial (Fig. 35) is best seen and understood as resourced by knowledge of Roman dials generally and perhaps by knowledge of vertical plane protractor-like dials specifically. *If* it were not resourced by knowledge of the latter then one can assume that it might have been designed by seeing the lines on a cut spherical or conical dial as an equal angle protractor and transferring them to the vertical plane.[42]

IX

Even so, there may be more to the Bewcastle sundial with its twelve hours than an intention to connote Romanness. Bede's interest in reckoning time and, it would seem, in sundials is well known. But here at Bewcastle, on the other side of the Pennines, there was someone who was interested in sundials and in reckoning time as well. We should take a look at Bede's interest in sundials because it will help us understand what is special about the Bewcastle dial and about its circumstances of production.

Rereading what Bede has to say about sundials, it seems that those who have attended to such matters, though never without registering a moment of doubt, have exaggerated his familiarity with actual sundials.[43] He may never have seen one or one that he himself had not made. And, of course, the knowledge of the astronomical mathematics that was necessary to make a more or less accurate dial was as lost to him as it was to everyone in the Latin West by the sixth or seventh century. If Ptolemy's work had been available to him, it would have been beyond the limits of his observation and arithmetic. Bede's main resource was Pliny's *Natural History*, especially Book 2, which is concerned with cosmology – the nature of the universe, the motion of the stars, sun, moon and other planets, the sphericity of the Earth – and Book 6, which is concerned with geographical issues – the size and shape of the Earth, the parallels of latitude, the changing duration of the longest day and the changing length of the noon shadow.[44] These books provided him with the rudiments of Greek cosmology and a basic understanding of the terminology and findings of Greek astronomy but not its mathematics.

X

The Bedan corpus, as it has come down to us, contains only nine references to sundials. They are all passing references and two of these are *duplicated*. Two references occur in quotations from Pliny's *Natural History* that he considered 'deserved a place' in *De temporum ratione*.[45] Another occurs in chapter 3 of *De temporum ratione*, the chapter on the smallest intervals of time, where he explains that the conventional division of an hour known as a *punctus* is so-called 'after the swift passage of the *punctus* on a sundial'. Earlier in the same chapter he says 'an hour has four *puncti* … and in some lunar calculations five *puncti*'. These references are puzzling because neither Graeco-Roman nor Anglo-Saxon dials divided the hours into quarters and because Bede refers to *puncti* as divisions not only of the solar hour but of the lunar hour also. Elsewhere, Bede *twice* made the point that the date of the spring equinox, as given by the Fathers, could be confirmed by consulting a sundial;[46] and, related to that, *twice* mentioned that the calculation of the leap year could be similarly confirmed.[47] Here Bede is referring to the sundial as an instrument that could be used to *confirm* the equinox not to determine its date. The last reference, which is exceptional in so far as it is not directly related to Bede's concern with the reckoning of time, can be found in the collection *In Regum librum XXX quaestiones* in his commentary on 2 Kings 20.1–11 and Isaiah 38.1–8, on how, at the prayer of Isaiah, the shadow on Ahaz's sundial moved back ten *lineas* as a sign that God would keep his promise to add fifteen years to the life of King Hezekiah.[48] Bede's commentary is unusual – though it is characteristic of his scientific curiosity – in so far as it is more concerned with trying to explain the miracle in terms of astronomy than by God's authority over nature.

Contrary to what some commentators have thought, Bede did not refer to sundials sufficiently often or so firmly that we can be certain he used them for observation and arithmetic. Bede's main concern was with Easter *computus* not sundials. In his discussions of the calculation of the date of the spring equinox or the length of a leap year, on the two occasions where he felt that what he was saying required empirical confirmation he deferred to his belief that *that* confirmation could be provided by reference to a sundial. Bede thought that a sundial could be used to confirm the date of the equinox. In this he was almost certainly mistaken. *If*, however, he could have consulted an accurately calibrated and constructed sundial on 21 March, it would not have provided the confirmation he so desired for by Bede's time the spring equinox had moved forward to around 17/18 March.[49]

It's easy to assume that Bede actually had a sundial, which he actually consulted. However, the various instruments that scholars have imagined that he could have had or could have made to get the necessary confirmation are either flawed with regard to construction and calibration or admittedly over-optimistic with regard to the weather and the user's powers of observational precision.[50] Bede could not have known how to make an accurate dial. This is not to say that he could not have attempted to do so. Given his inquiring mind, he almost certainly did. But no matter how its lines were laid out, it is a *horizontal* dial that Bede describes in *The Reckoning of Time* when he says that the spring equinox and the calculation of the leap year can be confirmed by consulting a *'horologii lineis interra'*.[51] If Bede used this kind of dial, a horizontal dial laid out on the ground, then it was, of course, not only inaccurate but also very unlike the dial at Bewcastle.[52] Whoever made the Bewcastle sundial was thinking about sundials, dialling and reckoning time in a different way from Bede.

XI

One wonders what the different individual members of the community at Bewcastle made of the sundial and its twelve hours. After all, the Anglo-Saxons were not living their lives, as we live ours, in small divisions of time, continually anticipating the conclusion of each fragment *as if* the whole point of activity lay in its end. And though some persons might have been living their lives according to monastic time there must have been others, perhaps many more, who were living, as it were, in a different time. It is easy to imagine that some of these, in whatever relationship they had with the monument, and perhaps puzzled or even mesmerised by the dial's novelty, must have wondered whether the dial controlled the movement of the sun rather than the sun the movement of the gnomon's shadow across the dial.

XII

An early medieval sundial needed to mark only Terce, Sext and None to help regulate monastic or burgeoning social time. Someone wanted the entire span of daylight, long and short, divided into twelve hours in the manner of ancient sundials *as if* the hours at Bewcastle would be defined as much by the artifice of the dial as by the daily round of monks or the natural times of sunrise and sunset. Artifice would bring monastic or burgeoning social time and natural time into an ordered relation. It's this division into twelve hours that makes the Bewcastle dial unique amongst pre-Conquest dials and with only three or four problematic exceptions all English and European post-Conquest medieval dials also.[53] Though whoever came up with the dial couldn't construct it as the Graeco-Roman dials were constructed, calibrated with the twelve seasonal hours of daylight that would be the same length during any given day but varied during the year, they could and did engrave it with twelve equal-angled equal divisions *as if* it did. That was the best that could be done at the time. They came up with a practical fiction that helped regulate an aspect of social time and represented what, at the time, would have been very esoteric knowledge indeed.

The sundial (along with the clepsydra) made by Boethius for King Theodoric at the insistence of Gundobad, lord of the Burgundians, and the dial (and clepsydra) that Cassiodorus made for his monastery at Vivarium are the last dials of the Graeco-Roman tradition for which we have evidence.[54] Given how little there was to work with in the early Middle Ages, the sundial on the Bewcastle monument, England's and probably Europe's earliest surviving post-Roman sundial, must be theorised, with whatever there is in the Bedan corpus, as having helped stall the decline of astronomy by preserving what knowledge there was to be preserved and pushing it as far as was possible. It represented the foreknowledge of what could be known and created the desire for more than was known. Over and above being made of a need to connote Romanness and to keep up with monastic times or the beginnings of social time, the Bewcastle sundial provides us with evidence of an attempt, or even for the beginnings of *the* attempt, to inaugurate the renewal of mathematical astronomy in western Europe, that is to say, it marks the re-emergence of science in the Latin West. It is to the point that this happened at Bewcastle, on a monument in the general view that is so concerned with memory and situates being-in-the-world between past and future, and that makes Bewcastle a very special place: whatever kind of place it was.

7

The Ruthwell runes and
The Dream of the Rood

⌘

We have been arguing for a history that refocuses critical attention on conceptions of the fragmentary, the particular and the local – the bits and pieces of Anglo-Saxon culture that form the basis of the evidence. To insist on these fragments *as* fragments offers ways to use some usual methodologies differently and to think through some different theoretical approaches or ways of seeing and understanding the various fragments of history that are our objects of study. In this chapter we first examine the vernacular runic texts inscribed on the narrow north and south (now east and west) sides of the Ruthwell monument (Figs 59, 60 and 67, 68, 69). The chapter begins, as it must, with the monument itself, with the lines of runic inscription and the problems or rather possibilities of their interpretation. Second, we consider, from a variety of critical perspectives, the well-known, oft celebrated relation of association between the runic texts and the later Anglo-Saxon poem *The Dream of the Rood*, written in 'stylish' minuscule (of an adapted Latin alphabet) in West Saxon and found in the Vercelli Book, an anthology of different kinds of texts – various homilies, verse texts and poems, including *Andreas* and *Elene* – all copied by the same scribe and, for palaeographic reasons, dated to the late tenth century.[1] This relation of association between the runic texts and *The Dream of the Rood* might be best characterised as one that is resistant to certain kinds of unifying historical analysis. Third, we consider the repetition of versions of the critical story about the relation of association between runic texts and manuscript poem that has been a consistent feature of Anglo-Saxon literary history and which, in as much as it determines a disciplinary matrix that puts pressures and limits on how our objects of study are to be approached, has become paradigmatic. Fourth, we turn the story around to acknowledge the distinctive character of the two artefacts – monument and manuscript poem – and, having turned it around, we note how the critical hermeneutic of the Ruthwell monument's fragmentary inscriptions changes.

A walk around a monument: motion as interpretation

Our book began with a consideration of the place of the Bewcastle monument. We also begin here with some words about place since part of the interpretative dilemma occasioned by the Ruthwell monument is that of place: where and what was its place; where and what was its being-in-the-world? Now reconstructed inside the church at Ruthwell (Fig. 42); before that, assembled in Reverend Henry Duncan's garden (Figs 49 and 50); and before that, in bits and pieces in Murray's Quire, a proprietary chapel that was not added to the church until some time between 1772 and 1790. Who knows where the monument was supposed to be? Or what? The episodes of movement, destruction, assemblage and description that punctuate the history of this monument are as central to the analysis of its various meanings in general as they are to the meanings of the runic texts inscribed on its narrow sides in particular.

No matter how many times the Ruthwell monument has been moved, taken down and made up, it is (and was at many moments in history) a three-dimensional stone sculpture *of* a particular place and time. The monument as a whole, runic inscriptions and inhabited plant-scrolls on its north and south sides, sculptural panels and Latin inscriptions on its west and east (now north and south) sides, invites a relationship with the beholder that is visual and tactile, kinetic and temporal. The inscriptions, English and Latin, are surely there to be seen and read, but the monument takes some time to see and 'read' and is marked by and incorporates various histories. We walk around the monument. We look at it, scrutinise it. Perhaps we touch it, or try to. There is, crucially, no definite place from which to begin or end this process.

Where should one begin reading the runes carved on the monument's narrow north and south sides (Figs 59, 60, 67, 68, 69)? Though an incipit + may once have been visible at the left of the border at the top of each side, and though the runes must have been laid out in linear relations of sequences of words so as to have made well-formed syntactical units or syntagms, it is by no means obvious what their lineaments are. Without knowing the arrangement that became accepted convention in the 1840s, which we'll look at in the next section of this chapter, the inscriptions might be seen as arranged in two columns to make a counter-intuitive border around the inhabited plant-scrolls and, thus arranged, to be read down the left column before the right. We might also see them as Reginald Bainbrigg, who in 1599 became the first person to take note of them, saw them (Fig. 43). Bainbrigg read those on the north side as beginning at the left of the top border (the + was still there when he came across the monument), down the right border, and from the bottom to top of the left border. Though, as we saw in Chapter 2, what might be seen as the same arrangement is found on the borders of some Greek icons and Italian panel paintings of the late sixth and seventh centuries, and does resemble some manuscript pages of the late Carolingian period, it is the reverse of what one might expect to find on the page of an early medieval manuscript where ornament usually frames text.

The recognition that the Ruthwell monument's runic texts are in English and are metrical as well as in stone and laid out as borders challenges other critical assumptions about Anglo-Saxon modes of textuality as well. To state the very obvious, an inscribed monument is not a manuscript page and the Ruthwell monument is unique in being inscribed with a text that is as 'poetic'[2] as this – we will consider its relation to Anglo-Saxon 'poetry' later. More usually, Anglo-Saxon poetry is located on the manuscript page, in a two-dimensional not a three-dimensional space. Vernacular poetry has a complex relation to the visual written codes and material dimensions of the manuscript page, certainly, and Anglo-Saxon habits of interpretation and composition are embodied, but we can be invited to walk around a poem only in a metaphorical sense.[3]

In many ways, the Ruthwell monument offers no secure place from which to begin or terminate our interpretive relationship, but it offers instead plenty of puzzles. Where do we start our looking, our reading? Where and when do we stop? How do the runic inscriptions engage the inhabited plant-scrolls within their margins and the figure panels and Latin inscriptions on the west and east sides? Questions about movement, perception and observation, seeing and telling are not inappropriate responses to the interpretive complexities of this monument.

How to see and read the runes? The challenge simultaneously simplifies and deepens when the inscriptions are transliterated and transcribed. Transliterated from their individual version of the runic furthorc into the Roman alphabet, edited, punctuated, lineated and represented according to modern typographic and editorial conventions, and finally translated into modern English, the runes are transformed into what is often known as the Ruthwell Crucifixion poem. This transliterated and translated reconstruction is necessarily an abstraction, a fragment materially and mentally removed from other fragments.[4]

Inscriptions	*Translation*
I (North side, now facing east, top and right border)	
[+ ond]gere dæ hinæ god almeʒttig þa he walde on galgu gistiga ʔodig fʔʔʔ ʔʔʔʔ men bug? ...	Almighty god unclothed himself when he wished to climb the gallows brave [before all] men [I dared not] bow...
II (North side, now facing east, left border)	
[ʔhof] ic riicnæ kyniŋc heafunæs hlafard hælda ic ni dorstæ	[I raised] up a powerful king, lord of heaven, I did not dare bend
ʔismærædu uʔket men ba ætgadʔʔ ʔʔʔ ʔiþ bʔodi bistʔmiʔ ʔiʔʔʔæ ...	Men mocked us both together, I [was] with blood drenched [poured]...

III (South side, now facing west, top
and right border)

[+] cris*t* wæs on   Christ was on the cross but eager ones
rodi hweþræ þer fusæ fearran   came from afar nobles to the one I
kwomu ?þilæ til anum ic þæt al   [beheld] it all
bi*h*??? sa?? ic w?s : miþ so?gu*m*   Sorely I was with sorrows troubled, [I]
gi*dr*œ??d h?a? ...   bowed ...

IV (South sde, now facing west, left
border)

miþ s?re*l*um giwundad alegdun hiæ   wounded with arrows
hinæ limwœrignæ gistoddu? him ??   They laid him down limb-spent, they
??? ???æs ??f??m ??ea?*du*? *hi*? þe? ...   placed themselves at the head of his
                                                                     body
                                                                     [they beheld there]...

We now know that the runes read horizontally left to right across the
margins. We also know that they are arranged to be read across the top border,
down the right border, and then top to bottom down the left border. As we
saw a moment ago, their most immediate relation of association is with the
inhabited plant-scrolls, with a formalised patterning of the natural world
(flora and fauna, the plant-scroll and the birds and animals that inhabit it),
and, in a more religious or theological register, with the Tree of Life.

Like the inhabited plant-scrolls, the runic inscriptions have their own
formalised patterns too. Some of this patterning is visual; the arrangement
of the inscriptions invites a meditation on how letters attract the eye and
signify.[5] Runes are very much sounds-as-letters made visible, especially on a
monument that makes use of the Roman and Greek alphabets as well. At the
same time, and more obviously, they signify to and for the ear. When read
aloud it becomes apparent that the texts are composed in Anglo-Saxon poetic
metre (although some lines seem a little heavy-handed when compared with
normative expectations and later examples of this metre). Alliteration, apposi-
tion, verbs in initial position – all used in these inscriptions – are examples
of strategies of poetic coherence, ways to bind language together, to create
thematic lines for the ear to follow, lines where silence features as strongly as
sound. Pause and effect.[6] This patterning of language, which is not obvious
unless the runes are read aloud (and thus formalised), seems to have some
relation of association with the structure of the inhabited plant-scroll, its
rhythm, the way it moves to the left and the right, and marks those moves
with different forms of flora and fauna. The use of visual and verbal, written
and aural signs on the narrow sides of the monument may be thought of as
related to the visual and textual signs on the other two sides: the programme
of religious and perhaps liturgically inflected visual scenes and Latin texts.
It is not our intention to puzzle this relation here, other than to reiterate
what was pointed out in an earlier chapter, specifically that it would be a
mistake to assume that the placing of the English inscriptions in the borders
on the narrow north and south sides of the monument was intended to

marginalise them and their meaning in relation to the Latin inscriptions. We might imagine instead that *that* was their appropriate place in a dynamic motional and emotive discourse that calls on any number of visual, verbal and emotional associations as we walk around the monument.

By critical consensus, the fragmentary, effaced and lost runic inscriptions are arranged into four groups, beginning on the north side and concluding on the south side. Efforts to read and to reconstruct them over the last 150 years or so appear to be confirmed by some seemingly corresponding lines in *The Dream of the Rood*. We will look at the problems presented by this correspondence for interpretation of the monument and the manuscript poem in due course. Here we point out that only those persons who had the power of literacy in two languages would have been able to read the Latin and the runic inscriptions, to think about their different scripts, and to bring them into a meaningful relationship with each other and the meanings of the sculptural panels. But the runes do not need not to be read for something of their meaning and value to signify. It is plausible, following our considera-tion of 'Northumbria' and of Ruthwell's place in the once British kingdom of Rheged, that the Anglian runes would have been unreadable and incom-prehensible to the native British subject people round about: they would have been regarded as a vivid aspect of the monument's intrusive silhouette, one that communicated in a Northumbrian dialect. They would have been truly mysterious. The vague suggestion of some secret knowledge concealed within these mysterious runes, however, would have resonated equally well, though differently, with lay, Christian, more or less unlettered Northum-brians as well as with secular aristocratic and clerical, more or less monastic audiences. These various possible audiences, readers and views offer us co-ordinates on a map of faith, class and power. Clearly, the runic inscriptions are there to be seen and read, or recited and heard, and thus their content made manifest if difficult to grasp. Hypotheses about who might have seen, read or heard them are important, but so too is the fact that the inscriptions seem to point more generally to a set of relations between seeing, reading, speaking, hearing and moving – not only across and down the lines of an individual inscription but from one side of the monument to another.

At this level of general description, the significance of the monument's narrow sides conforms well with its overall dynamic, which is that of a powerful, deliberately complicated visual and verbal, multi-linguistic state-ment about the reach of Christianity into the *temporal* world and an *eternal* linguistic domain of the Word.

The idea of a multivalent or polysemic and probably multi-functional monument can be pressed further. Though we now arrange the inscriptions in four groups, stanzas or *sententiae*,[7] as an orderly though not necessarily unified sequence of poetic statements, beginning on the north side and concluding on the south, there is no need to do so. The use of stanzas is rare in Old English poetry: there is no obvious reason, other than their relation to the later poem, *The Dream of the Rood*, and convention, for assuming that the lines must be arranged in four linked groups to be read in a particular sequence – as a poem on the Crucifixion, for example. It is also plausible (and, in terms of the argument of this book, more probable) that the inscriptions represent a series of fragments, which may or may not be of a larger whole, or *sententiae* to be read in any sequence or combination. It can be argued, then, that like the rest of the monument, the runes move across functions and registers. They can be read as stanza-like metrical units, according to modern ideas of what constitutes 'quotation', or as several continuous sentences. Because they are inscribed and sculptural, they can be related to those much shorter memorial metrical inscriptions common throughout the period. Because of their language, length, metre and thematic resonances, they can be related to Anglo-Saxon poetry generally, as well as, more particularly, to *The Dream of the Rood*. And because of their location on this particular monument, as we remarked a moment ago, they can be related to inhabited plant-scrolls and to the programme of figure sculptures and Latin inscriptions on its west and east sides. The design on the monument's narrow north and south sides could have had much to do with the disposition of the runic inscriptions to begin with.

The runes fill the areas available and those areas are material, sculptural in three dimensions, visual and tactile, and textual in two dimensions, visual and auditory. The reading and reciting of the runes, however, must be left to the beholder. The monument cannot read, but the runes do encode the implied voice of an 'I' and the implied voices of 'men' who mock. The monument can be said in a certain manner to speak.

The question of voice presents itself immediately. Reading the runes according to established convention, the first group of lines establishes the style as third person and the tense as past: in them, an almighty God is reported to have prepared himself to climb on to the gallows, brave before all men, and is contrasted with an 'I' (now partly illegible) that did not dare bow. In the second group of lines, an 'I', now seemingly *of* the gallows and certainly subject of the verb, lifted up ('ahof') a powerful King, Lord of Heaven and did not allow itself (or did not dare, as the verb, 'dorstæ', also implies) to bend. 'I' and King are mocked together by men and an 'I' is drenched with blood that pours ... (this latter phrase is almost illegible). The third group of lines begins in the same manner as the first group, again with a reported statement: Christ was on the Cross. The Cross is here identified and named for the first time – 'rod' – in a scene that attracted from afar eager ones and nobles to the One ('til anum'). The 'I' is reported to have observed this; then, distressed and sorrowful, it bowed. The fourth and final group of lines begins with a fragmentary statement about being wounded with arrows. 'They' take down the limb-spent body, and those persons who take him down dispose themselves at the head of his corpse and observe ... The runes, as we have them today, end with this act of observation, of beholding, though this is not necessarily where they once ended.

There is no explicit verb of speaking in these inscriptions. Who tells this story? Who speaks its 'I'? Whose voice has, as it were, become lost in the act of inscription?[8] The 'I' of the texts on the north side seems to be that of the '*galgu*/gallows'. On the south side it seems to be that of the '*rod*/cross'.[9] The verbs on the north side of the monument drive us through acts of removing

clothes, wishing to climb, daring not to bow, raising up and daring not to bend, mocking and being drenched with blood. Now at the south side, we begin with a remarkable stasis, a moment of contemplation, focus on a subject rather than movement: 'krist wæs on rodi / Christ was on cross'. The verb is about *being* not *doing* – not only the being of Christ but implicitly the being of the 'rod' for, if the narrating 'I' *is* 'rod', Christ *was* on it, which is to say on 'me'. And then, having thought about these words and grasped their significance, we're off again: travelling; observing; beholding; bowing; depositing; arranging; and, once again, observing. Death is the main theme of the runic inscriptions on the Ruthwell monument: death embraced and death perceived, observed and witnessed. Seeing, understanding and telling: that's another theme; though, interestingly, there are but two statements of seeing, both using the same verb, only one of which attaches to the 'I', and none whatsoever of telling. A final theme – it's the one that drives us, as readers, through these fragments – is movement, action as opposed to stasis.

Whether taken together or read separately, the runic inscriptions explore the idea of willing sacrifice so central to Christian faith, and so evident in the Mass, by way of vernacular metaphors of kingship that speak of a relationship between a king and a loyal subject who is party to the king's death – the notion of loyalty unto death is exploited by these metaphors even as it is distorted almost beyond recognition.[10] Throughout, the language addresses a volitional, violent, transgressive and embodied sacrifice: the body spent; the cross wounded. Class and gender (more precisely, masculinity) are implied via these conceptions of kingship and obedience as well as violence and death. What is clear, however, is that there is no ostensive mention of death overcoming life, defeat turning into victory, suffering becoming triumph, the temporality of a human turning into the transcendent eternity of a deity.

Seeing and speaking: a 'galga' and 'rod' that seems to speak, certainly moves and also sees and observes, inscribed on a stone monument. The prosopopoeia is clear, this gallows or cross has a face and a voice. It calls attention to itself as a person though the extent to which it calls attention to itself as a gendered entity is moot.[11] The personified object, gallows/cross, is a subject who speaks of itself as privileged participant in the Crucifixion. One that sees and tells. This is a richly complicated subject position: that of an unwilling but loyal party to the death of a king; that of an intimate participant who tells the crucifixion like it is. Whether gallows, cross or 'Cross', the inscriptions elicit a series of complex relationships that leave us hanging, criss-crossing between gallows and cross, cross and Cross, king and Crucified, Crucified and God, subjected and Subject, ignoble and noble, not eager and eager. These associations of identity demonstrate how expansive the category of cross or Cross must be, whether or not the monument actually took the form of a cross at the moment of its production and first use. Indeed, these various relations of identity are indications that the subjectification of the cross to Cross is only one dimension of the experience and meaning of the Crucifixion. And the Crucifixion, with one of its referents as the Mass, is in turn one of the most overdetermined events in Christianity. The Ruthwell runes thereby enact and make possible a sophisticated series of enunciations explored throughout and around the monument.

The 'I' of the inscriptions is personified in the manner of a riddle. It presents us with a question: What does it mean that an 'I' seems to refer to itself as 'galgu' and 'rod', gallows, cross and Cross? This riddle thematises not only the symbolization and onto-theology of the Cross – how gallows and cross becomes Cross – but also problematises the act of seeing: perceiving, observing and attesting to what has been perceived and observed. In what sense does a cross see? Who is looking at what, and what's seen. Who are the nobles and 'they' who undergo the action of the verb 'to observe, behold'? And how are we to theorise the relationship between the beholder who may or may not be able to read the runes or understand the monument but who is, nevertheless, necessarily affected by both? What is the riddle of seeing and reading, speaking and hearing, movement and being moved that is posed by the runes?

Runes and ruins, history and poetry

How to read the runes? One answer to that question is offered by the history of their perceived 'similarity' with the *Dream of the Rood*. Like *Beowulf* and the Sutton Hoo burial, the monument inscriptions and manuscript poem make a rather 'odd couple' and, like *Beowulf* and the Sutton Hoo burial, their pairing is one that historians, art historians and literary critics are loath to split asunder.[12] For some, the sleeping partner is the manuscript poem; for others, it is the monument inscriptions; and for a third group, the less scrupulous perhaps, monument inscriptions and manuscript poem are one and the same.[13] Least common, though now gaining some ground within critical practice, is the position that steadfastly refuses to acknowledge any form of association.[14] As with a refusal to acknowledge that the monument inscriptions and manuscript poem are different or, if different, with a 'clear thematic continuity',[15] critical preference for the manuscript poem (over the monument inscriptions) or for the monument inscriptions (over the manuscript poem), or for seeing them as thematically continuous, is usually a consequence of different interests and competences, discipline and convenience, and academic turf-battles.

By putting the runic inscriptions in relation to the manuscript poem, *as if* the relation was constant or continuous, it seems to be possible to connect the first and last great moments of Anglo-Saxon culture, to connect the beginnings of the so-called 'Golden Age of Northumbria' with the achievements in art and literature of the second half of the tenth century, the period known as the Benedictine reforms or revivals. The connection promises a unified narrative of Anglo-Saxon art and poetry that begins with the longest surviving runic inscription in the British Isles on one of the largest and most complete survivals of monumental sculpture from the period (the 'origins' of the high stone cross, no less) and ends with the first English dream vision poem[16] in the Vercelli Book (one of the four major codices of Old English poetry, all of which date from that period of the first flourishing of vernacular

literacy in England between 975 to 1025, give or take a few years).[17] The story
that establishes this connection is one that hints of centuries of continuity
throughout the Anglo-Saxon period.

From runic texts inscribed on a monumental stone sculpture to *The
Dream of the Rood* or from the inauguration of English poetry to its canonical
moment in the Anglo-Saxon period, this is a narrative destined to attract. But
as with the conjoining of *Beowulf* and the Sutton Hoo burial this conjoining
of two different material and textual forms, which seem to have something
in common, frustrates as much as it entices. The rigorous interdisciplinary methodology that would secure and make it thoroughly satisfying has
proved very hard to achieve. By contrast, the story of this seeming connection
is attractive and most commentators on Anglo-Saxon art and literature have
found it, or some version of it, more or less irresistible.

There are, of course, understandable reasons both for the almost irresistible urge to retell the story of the monument inscriptions and manuscript
poem as well as for that story's inevitably vague gestures toward historicity.
The intervening years between the first half of the eighth and late tenth
century, between the production and first use of the northern monument
and the production and first use of the southern manuscript,[18] cannot be
accounted for by direct reference to either or both. There is no direct causal
chain of textual or other evidence with which to recover a narrative constella-
tion of causes that would link the runic inscriptions carved on the Ruthwell
monument to the poem written in insular minuscules in the Vercelli Book
other than the perceived similarity between parts of the one to parts of the
other. It is this that makes the narrative so attractive and, at the same time, so
difficult to explore. Without any evidentiary basis for the apparent relation of
association, other than the apparently textual relationship itself, it's a matter
of 'the closer you try to approach the facts through history, the deeper you
sink into fiction'.[19] There is nothing new here. Writing literary history, or any
kind of history of the early medieval period, is largely an art of the possible,
the probable and the plausible. Yet no other seeming coincidence of bits of
different material and textual objects so challenges or resists its interpreters
to the extent that the relation between this particular monument and this
particular manuscript poem does.

The argument that *The Dream of the Rood* is above all a poem with little or
no direct connection to the runic inscriptions on the Ruthwell monument
is counter-intuitive, however. Even the most cursory glance at the critical
archive reveals just how frequently these two objects have been put together.
There *is* a relation of association and the historicity of that relationship has
been assumed to be 'fact'. But what kind of fact is it?

Apart from a brief resurfacing around 1100 in Italy, and a tentative identification in a catalogue of the fifteenth century, the historical record has
nothing to say about the Vercelli Book before the mid eighteenth century.
The Dream of the Rood enters written history, comes to cultural consciousness as it were, with modernity and in the nineteenth century between 1822
and 1833,[20] at more or less the same moment that the Ruthwell monument,
in the garden of the manse at Ruthwell, gains its cross-head in 1823 and is

published in *Archaeologia Scotica*, 1833.[21] The account of this double entry into modernity, one of the great tales of Anglo-Saxon scholarship, is often rehearsed. In the 1830s and 1840s John Mitchell Kemble, one of those whose name is rightly synonymous with the formation of modern Anglo-Saxon studies,[22] was engaged in the process of deciphering the runic inscriptions on the Ruthwell monument, working from the illustrations in George Hickes's *Linguarum Veterum Septentrionalium Thesaurus Grammatico-Criticus et Archaeologicus* (1703–1705) (Fig. 44), *Alexander Gordon's Itinerarium Septentrionale: Or, a journey thro' most of the counties of Scotland and those in the North of England* (1726) (Fig. 46) and Henry Duncan's 'An Account of the Remarkable Monument in the shape of a Cross, inscribed with Roman and Runic Letters, preserved in the Garden of Ruthwell Manse, Dumfriesshire', in *Archaeologia Scotica*. In his 'Anglo-Saxon Runes' of 1840, Kemble identified that the runic texts inscribed on the Ruthwell monument were in a Northumbrian dialect and established the basis of a more or less accurate transcription and transliteration of them in half-lines. He also made a good stab at giving the texts a date (eighth and ninth centuries) and identified them as poetic verses related to the sculpted images on 'the glorification of Christ through his Passion'.[23] Shortly after the publication of this article, however, Kemble got hold of a copy of Benjamin Thorpe's privately printed 1836 edition of the recently rediscovered Vercelli Book, which included what was then known as *The Dream of the Holy Rood*. Kemble saw a resemblance between the manuscript poem and the Northumbrian runic inscriptions on the Ruthwell monument, and used it to help confirm and correct his earlier efforts. This he published in 1844 as 'Additional Observations on the Runic Obelisk at Ruthwell, the poem of The Dream of the Holy Rood, and a Runic Copper Dish found at Chertsey', which includes the poem, lineated in the half-lines of 1840, together with a brief account of its literary critical importance.[24] Oddly, Kemble didn't supply the full, corrected text for the runic inscriptions, though this is rarely pointed out in critical retellings of the story. This interweaving of runic inscriptions and manuscript text is characteristic of his 1844 article.[25]

Kemble's reconstruction of the Ruthwell monument's runic inscriptions on the basis of the tenth-century manuscript poem occurred long after Reginald Bainbrigg had first noted its 'peregrinis literis, sed fugientibus' (foreign, but fluent letters) in 1599. As discussed in Chapter 2, the seventeenth-century history of the Ruthwell monument is one characterised by iconoclasm, ruin and subsequent intermittent antiquarian interest. Kemble's moment, by contrast, belongs to that phase of optimistic (though often vituperative) recovery of the Anglo-Saxon cultural record by gentleman scholars of the late eighteenth and early nineteenth centuries.[26] The occasion that appears to have prompted him to read the runes, and to which he refers in 1840, was – we mentioned it a moment ago – the publication of Duncan's 1833 'An Account of a Remarkable Monument in the shape of a Cross, inscribed with Roman and Runic Letters', together with, in particular, Finn Magnusen's and Thorleif Godmundson Repp's notoriously fanciful reading of them.[27]

The connections between the runes in ruins at Ruthwell that sparked the imagination of some early modern travellers and antiquarians,[28] the monument assembled in the manse garden between 1802 and 1823, published in 1833, and reconstructed in the church at Ruthwell in 1887, the discovery of the manuscript poem in Italy in 1822, its transcription in 1833 and 1836, and Kemble's decoding of the monument inscriptions and manuscript poem in 1844 are informed by, and formative of, issues of discipline and period that are not trivial. The 'cultural revolution' of the sixteenth century together with the 'political revolution' of the seventeenth, James Simpson has recently argued, gave 'forceful, violent, and enduring definition' to the medieval period as idolatrous and, henceforth, ruined. It is iconoclasm, the physical destruction of the medieval, which creates 'the very concept of the medieval as a site of ruin'.[29] The ruined monument at Ruthwell embodies, testifies to, and condenses this idea of the medieval past.[30] Ruins call on contradictory, ambivalent impulses. On the one hand, 'In the ruin history has physically merged into setting. And in this guise history does not assume the form of the process of an eternal life so much as that of irresistible decay.'[31] On the other hand, 'In the ruins of great buildings the idea of the plan speaks more impressively than in lesser buildings, however well preserved they are.'[32] The desire to recover, rescue and reconstruct the past from the ruin strives with and against the recognition that in the ruin '"history" stands written on the countenance of nature in characters of transience'.[33] It was certainly the indecipherable 'foreign, but fluent letters' in the ruins that attracted those antiquarians who like William Nicolson in 1697 made a 'progress in Scotland' to see the monument.[34] Like the monument itself, the apparent 'fact' of a relation of association between the monument and the manuscript poem is haunted by the idea of a ruined past, which appeals to and resists our attempts at reconstruction.

The accounts of the efforts of the early runologists, such as Kemble's avatars, Magnusen and Repp, to read the runic inscriptions on the Ruthwell monument offer a related view of the past as foreign, alien and governed by issues of illegibility and incompleteness. The Ruthwell ruins attract because they are ruins, set apart, though not altogether severed, from the present. Like the fragmentary runes on the fragmentary monument, the past is figured as a fragmentary text waiting to be deciphered, with all its attendant fantasies of completion and fulfillment. This view takes only a slightly modified form among modern runologists who, like their prede-cessors, are exercised by problems of legibility, incompleteness and partial knowledge. The modern scholar of runic texts, however, resists interpreting and explaining their meaning. Take, for example, R. I. Page who, like David Howlett, transcribes and transliterates Ruthwell's vernacular runic inscrip-tions, but baulks at interpreting and explaining their meaning – *as if* descrip-tion can be kept apart from discussion or *as if* transcription and transliteration are not, of themselves, an act of interpretation and explanation.[35] Like the ruined monument, on which these ruined runes appear, for runologists the medieval era is, to paraphrase Simpson, a self-enclosed age defined by a cataclysmic break with the past and marked by loss.[36]

If the association between runes and ruins helps us understand the efforts to read and interpret the inscriptions on the Ruthwell monument, so too does it have a part to play in the story of the discovery of the Vercelli Book poem and its relation to those inscriptions. In the 1840s, Kemble was clearly motivated by an intention to claim the disciplines of runology, philology and Anglo-Saxon studies for English, as opposed to Scandinavian, national scholarship.[37] At the same time, his reconstruction of the runes on the Ruthwell monument is a response in part to his outrage at the 'sacrilegious fury of the Presbyterian iconoclasts', which had caused the destruction of the monument in the first instance.[38] Scandalised by the sacrilege of iconoclasm and standing at the threshold of modern scholarship, Kemble set out on the task of reconstruction, confident in his methods and, at the same time, aware that there are limits to what can be done. (We might compare this with Duncan's efforts to reconstruct the monument.) For this reason, perhaps, the recovery of any precise connection between monument inscriptions and manuscript poem is ranked rather low in Kemble's quest for an accurate national methodology for the recovery of its own past. The past has given up some of its secrets in the form of a new Old English poem in a recently discovered Anglo-Saxon manuscript in the library of an Italian cathedral but it remains unclear how this new poem can be related to the fragmentary inscriptions on the ruined monument at Ruthwell in Scotland. For Kemble, this is a matter of methodology and evidence. 'The relation of the poem to the inscription', he argues, 'is perhaps not a matter of much interest, except in so far as the collation of the one proves the accuracy of the system by which the other was deciphered.'[39] The tone here is self-congratulatory and rightly so, however pompous and nationalistic the tenor of much of his work. In this particular instance, Kemble had been well on the way to reading the runes *without* the help of the newly discovered, recently entitled *The Dream of the Holy Rood*. This is a crucial point. It is, and was, possible to read the runic texts inscribed on the Ruthwell monument *independently* of the manuscript poem.

It is in this same 1844 article, 'Additional Observations on the Runic Obelisk at Ruthwell', that Kemble argues that the runic inscriptions on the monument either quote from a longer poem subsequently still available in later centuries or that a later poet used the monument inscriptions when he composed his longer poem. 'Let us suppose', he argues, 'that the poet attributed to his ear what was in fact the work of his eyes, and the address delivered to him by the cross, becomes an inscription upon one – the very inscription, in short, whose fragments are yet found upon the Ruthwell pillar.'[40] This brief speculation on eye and ear, seeing and hearing, predicts with uncanny accuracy the trajectory of more or less all discourse (including our own) as it pertains to the relation of association between the monument inscriptions and the manuscript poem for the next century and a half; so it's worth pausing here to consider what it means. Kemble conflates in the idea of 'the poet', the narrator of the Vercelli Book poem *and* the author of that poem (a familiar nineteenth-century critical move, but one that persists in some quarters even now). This poet-narrator thinks he's *hearing* a poem, when in fact he is *seeing* one. This vision-that-becomes-a poem is delivered to the poet-narrator by a speaking cross. This then 'becomes an inscription' (that is to say, is written) on a cross. And that inscription, or written 'poem' can be seen inscribed in fragments on the Ruthwell 'pillar'. What to make of this? Kemble has condensed two moments of production and first use – that of the Ruthwell monument and that of *The Dream of the Rood* – and whatever, if any, associative chains might connect them, into the sole idea of the poet-narrator. The genre of the Vercelli Book poem as a dream vision confirms the moment of production of the Ruthwell monument and its inscriptions (which is understood to be produced as a result of a visionary spoken poem). That moment in the history of the production of the Ruthwell monument is taken to be identical to the moment of production of the manuscript poem. At the same time, Kemble has put together two different, though connected, modes of communication or signification – the one, textual (the manuscript poem) and the other, sculptural (the Ruthwell monument). A dream vision poem, spoken by a personified cross to a dream narrator, has become a poem on a cross (or pillar), which was composed by that same dream narrator. Shades here of Cædmon's *Hymn*. Critics might *hear* the Vercelli Book poem but all too often, it seems, they *see* the Ruthwell monument.

Kemble's efforts to read the Ruthwell runes in the light of his understanding of the Vercelli Book poem provide the narrative framework for all subsequent stories about the relationship between this particular 'odd couple' of monument inscriptions and manuscript poem. From now on, there develops an often-unacknowledged critical tendency to see the manuscript poem *as if* it were the monument inscriptions and to treat the monument inscriptions *as if* they were part of the manuscript poem. The conflation of the two has its critical satisfactions. As far as Kemble was concerned, for example, the poet who composed this by now unified poem and single artefact is better than the Beowulf-poet or Cædmon in terms of the 'poet's own subjectivity'.[41] The comparison with poems known or alleged to be early in date is significant since it provides supplementary evidence that the date of the composition of the Vercelli Book poem must be similarly early. And, as an instance of a particular genre, the poem even turns out to be a good one, at least in comparison with 'the dull, commonplace manner which is so often the case with Anglo-Saxon religious verses'.[42] The character of Anglo-Saxon poetry is as much at stake in Kemble's work as the emergence of a national philology.

English poetry and Northumbrian runic inscriptions. No matter how we want to read the relation indicated by the copula 'and' in the title to this chapter, whichever element (monument inscription or manuscript poem) we want to emphasise, and however uneven that emphasis, from Kemble on, the two are bound, anxiously (though not inevitably) together.

Remembering and repeating

More than one hundred and sixty or so years after Kemble, critics are still pondering the relation of association between the runic texts inscribed on the Ruthwell monument and *The Dream of the Rood* in the Vercelli Book. By now, however, Kemble's work, so instrumental in establishing the relation in the first instance, is no longer significant and infrequently recalled. The critical questions that dominate the mid twentieth century and later are about transmission and chronology and continue to assume a close relation of association between the monument inscriptions and manuscript poem. In the mid twentieth century, critical discourse that addressed the Ruthwell monument's runic texts was informed by debates about Anglo-Saxon poetry and its manuscript evidence, although questions about the monument's relation to time and place continue to be important today. How might a poem travel? Might a poem remember its ancestors? How might *The Dream of the Rood* recall the runic texts inscribed on the Ruthwell monument?

Rethinking the evidence in the 1950s, for example, Kenneth Sisam remarked, 'the history that connects' the runic texts on the Ruthwell monument, *The Dream of the Rood* and two lines of Old English text on the Brussels Cross, 'must be one of movement and change that stretches the imagination'.[43] This idea conveniently introduces us, somewhat belatedly, to the Brussels Cross, an early eleventh-century reliquary, covered with sheet silver and once adorned with jewels, which had secreted within it a material reminder or *memento* of the historical Crucifixion: a fragment of the True Cross.[44] There are three inscriptions on this reliquary cross. On the back, across the cross-arm is arranged the text:

+ DRAHMAL ME WORHTE

+ Drahmal made me

Round the edges is a deeply engraved inscription in two parts. The first consists of two lines of alliterative verse:

+ ROD IS MIN NAMA GEO IC RICNE CYNING BÆR
BYFIGYNDE BLODE BESTEMED

+ Cross is my name; trembling, drenched with blood, I bore up the powerful king

The second is a dedicatory text:

ÞAS RODE HET ÆÞLMÆR WYRICAN AÐELLWOLD HYS
BEROÞO[R] CRISTE TO LOFE FOR ÆLFRICES SAVLE HYRA BEROÞOR

Æthelmær and his brother Æthelwold ordered this cross to be made for the glory of Christ [and] for the soul of Ælfric their brother

The inscription that Sisam refers to is, of course, the one that has the two lines of alliterating verse: 'Rod is min nama; geo ic ricne cyning bær byfigynde, blode bestemed.' It was to become a familiar piece of evidence in mid-twentieth-century debates about the runic inscriptions on the Ruthwell monument and the Vercelli Book poem, and we will consider its textuality in due course. For the moment we stay with Sisam's points about 'history' and 'movement and change': they are a major critical issue not only for understanding the Ruthwell monument but also for putting its runic texts in a relation of association with *The Dream of the Rood*.

What concerned Sisam in the 1950s was Old English poetic language and the extent to which evidence for it, and hence for the 'authority' of the poetic text itself, was reliable: no matter whether the evidence for that poetic text was carved on a monument or penned by a scribe or scribes in a manuscript or engraved in metal on the side of a reliquary made by Drahmal and commissioned by Æthelmær and Æthelwold to commemorate their brother Ælfric. Multiple copies of a given passage of Old English poetry offer the possibility of assessing textual and linguistic affinities and of posing the question of whether it is possible or desirable to recover a single authoritative originary text from which the copies were made.[45] Debates about the dating and transmission of Old English poetry, about how to assign dates for composition when the evidence suggests – not proves – a considerable 'history' of 'movement and change' across place and time, have long had a compelling force for Anglo-Saxonists. In the case of the early Northumbrian runic texts on the Ruthwell monument and *The Dream of the Rood*, Sisam was ambivalent. The uncanny resemblance of the Northumbrian runic text to the later West Saxon written poem and the text on the Brussels Cross reliquary pointed to a couple of hundred years of movement and change, transmission and adaptation, but where was the evidence? In an earlier celebrated article published in 1946, 'The Authority of Old English Poetical Manuscripts', Sisam was sceptical about the possibility of reconstructing this history, arguing that a comparison 'could not favour the hypothesis of accurate transmission' and that the variations between the two versions of the (assumed to be) single poem had much to do with the 'conditions of recording' – conditions which we might now want to think of as different historically and culturally specific moments and means of production.[46] This consideration of 'recording' – of setting down or preserving something in writing – of forming and of form, remains an important insight into the Ruthwell runes.

Sisam returned to these questions of variation in his later general inquiry into the evidence for Northumbrian/Anglian poetry, on the one hand, and the much larger and later evidence for West Saxon poetry, on the other.[47] The text inscribed on the Ruthwell monument points to a Northumbrian 'origin' and the text of the Vercelli poem to a West Saxon southern reworking: these two pieces of evidence helped Sisam build a case for a general 'stock' of Anglo-Saxon poetry, written in a specific, trans-temporal, trans-regional poetic dialect. There was, Sisam pointed out, no good reason why a poem composed in the south might not travel to the north, 'assume an Anglian dress or coloring' and return to the South.[48] The argument rested heavily on analogy. The Northumbrian Mailcoat riddle, a close translation of Aldhelm's Latin *Lorica* riddle, appended to the end of a ninth-century manuscript at Leiden in which the Latin riddle also appears, turns up as the later West Saxon Riddle 35 in the tenth-century Exeter Book anthology of Old English poetry.[49] Strikingly, the Exeter Book version bears very little trace or acknowledgement of the earlier Northumbrian version, which would seem to confirm Sisam's point. Poems don't much remember their ancestors, it seems. If riddles, such as the Northumbrian Mailcoat riddle, travel – or rather if people take riddles with them when they travel – why not other kinds of text, such as runic texts inscribed on the Ruthwell monument? Texts travel lightly and relatively safely if they're kept in the head. The case of the Leiden Riddle is also compelling as an analogy for the transmission of the Ruthwell text because of a second, implied, analogy – this time of genre. Both the runic inscriptions on the Ruthwell monument and *The Dream of the Rood* have long been associated with riddles and with riddling.[50] The problem with this sort of reasoning, as Sisam knew, was, and is, that there are no very good reasons why any particular text, riddle or otherwise, should travel across time and place, and be given a different material form and function (stone monument, anthologised manuscript poem, silver and jewelled reliquary). That Anglo-Saxon society was one predominantly of transitional orality might help here, since we are still dealing with a history of transmission, movement and change between two written texts that were intended to be read and spoken – monument inscriptions and manuscript poem, very distant in time and place. This mixed form, visual and oral, becomes problematic, however, if we continue to assume that both texts are versions of a single originary poem.[51]

Problems of reasoning, hypothesis, probability and evidence bedevil other examples of an apparently lengthy history of movement and change across time and place in the Old English poetic corpus. This group has occasioned some very speculative (and notorious) debates, for example about the various dates adduced for the composition and transmission of *Beowulf*, as well as those more secure in terms of evidence and transmission (though not composition), like Cædmon's *Hymn*, and perhaps too Bede's so-called *Death Song*.[52] In fact, Cædmon's *Hymn* and Bede's *Death Song* have been regularly cited as supporting evidence for the transmission of the runic texts inscribed on the Ruthwell monument to *The Dream of the Rood*.[53] Texts travel, certainly, as do books and objects throughout the medieval period, but neither the *Hymn* nor the *Death Song* travels from stone monument to manuscript or from manuscript to stone monument, let alone from stone monument and/or manuscript poem on to reliquary cross. These examples serve only to highlight the forceful specificity of the runic texts on the Ruthwell monument, the Vercelli Book poem and the Brussels Cross reliquary.

Notwithstanding that, the critical compulsion to repeat and rework the story of the relation of association between the runic inscriptions on the Ruthwell monument and *The Dream of the Rood* in the Vercelli Book persists. Michael Swanton followed Sisam's idea of the relationship between monument inscriptions and manuscript poem in his edition of the Vercelli Book poem in 1970, as have most other commentators.[54] Critical discourse frames this story as a debate, but Jonathan Wilcox's recent summary demonstrates the extent to which matters have failed to move on over the centuries. Repeating, apparently without knowing it, the essence of Kemble's hypothesis, Wilcox states that 'it is conceivable that the poet of the Vercelli Book version saw the poetic utterance upon the cross and used this as the kernel for his longer poem, but more likely that the creator of the cross abstracted out the most pertinent part of the poem for his programme'.[55] *Either* the person or persons responsible for coming up with runic texts inscribed on the narrow north and south sides of the Ruthwell monument quoted from a complete poem, now best represented by the much later West Saxon *The Dream of the Rood*, *or* the poet responsible for an originary poem, later preserved in that West Saxon text, composed his poem seeing or knowing about the Ruthwell monument and using it as a motivating intention and resource. At which point, all interpretative movement stops, held instead in an oscillating stasis or critical aporia between manuscript poem and monument inscriptions. Even so, note that questions of seeing and seeing ... as, explored in other chapters of this book as ways of thinking about the relation between the Ruthwell and Bewcastle monuments, prove useful to understanding literary criticism's accounts of the runes and the manuscript poem.

This compulsion to return repeatedly to the question of the relation of association between the monument inscriptions and the manuscript poem merits a little more analysis. For the compulsion to repeat, which is at the centre of Freud's *Beyond the Pleasure Principle*, symptomatises the most general character of the instincts, namely, their conservatism.[56] Lacking precise details with which to fill out a story about the relation between the runic texts inscribed on the Ruthwell monument and *The Dream of the Rood* in the Vercelli Book, literary history and literary criticism settles for repeating the bare bones of what is known without recalling the 'prototype' *as if* it is dealing with matter of the moment. Scholarship has not changed its story significantly since Kemble established the prototype in the 1840s. Repeating and forgetting are intimately linked. As Freud reminds us: we repeat what we cannot remember. What is it that we cannot recall or repress or decide to forget? Is it that, without more texts being brought to practical consciousness from the historical unconscious, the relation of association between the Ruthwell monument's runic texts and *The Dream of the Rood* in the Vercelli Book may never be recollected, articulated and discharged?

Matters of text

Remembering and repeating. One way that criticism works to try to make the Ruthwell monument's runic inscriptions (more) meaningful is by repeating the seeming affinities between the words carved on the stone monument and the words written on the manuscript page. It is time to turn to these seeming affinities, to matters of text. And to consideration of text needs to be added that of 'context'. A context can sometimes supplement and enrich understanding of texts but, because any 'context' is necessarily a 'connection' of several 'texts', it always adds an additional layer of complexity to the process of interpretation and explanation. Critical work on the text of the manuscript poem and of the text of the monument inscriptions has been characteristically contextual, drawing on local knowledge – ecclesiastical, devotional, liturgical, monastic practice and so on – which is itself textual. However, all too often, the construction of a context ignores the historical and cultural specificities that define different times and places, the different circumstances of production and use of each text, the conditions of their connection, and so on. It puts aside, and even obscures, questions of transmission, history, movement and change, chronology, time and place, material and forming, form and function. At the heart of this effort to understand the text of the Ruthwell runes resides the assumption that the monument inscriptions and manuscript poem are really one and the same, that there is an almost immediately meaningful relationship between them. Whatever history is to be located in this constructed context is generally relegated to noises off in the background. Textual scholars of the early medieval period are rarely indulged in their desire to have multiple versions of any given text to compare, contrast, resolve and correct, as Sisam knew;[57] it would be hard indeed to give up the perceived relation of association between a text inscribed on a stone monument made in the eighth century and a text in a manuscript put together in the tenth century.

Yet, what are the affinities between the two texts? The text inscribed on the Ruthwell monument corresponds only to lines, parts of lines, and even bits of parts of lines 39–42, 44–45, 48–49, 56–59 and 62–64 of Swanton's edition of *The Dream of the Rood*. This correspondence can be tabulated:[58]

Ruthwell inscriptions	*Vercelli Book Dream of the Rood*
[+ ond]geredæ hinæ god almeʒttig þa he walde on galgu gistiga	Ongyrede hine þa geong hæleð, (þæt wæs God ælmihtig) (line 39)
	Strang ond stiðmod; gestah he on gealgan heanne, (line 40)
ʔodig f??? ???? men	modig on manigra gesyhðe, þa he wolde mancyn lysan (line 41)
*b*ug? ...	Bifode ic þa me se beorn ymbclypte; ne dorste ic hwæðre bugan to eorðan (line 42)
[ʔhof] ic riicnæ kyniŋc	Rod wæs ic aræred. Ahof ic ricne Cyning, (line 44)
heafunæs hlafard *h*ælda i*c* ni dorstæ	heofona Hlaford; hyldan me ne dorste. (line 45)
ʔismæræ*d*u uʔket men ba æ*t*gad?? ??? ʔiþ bʔodi bistʔmʔ ʔiʔ??æ	Bysmeredon hie unc butu ætgædere. Eall ic wæs mid blod bestemed, (line 48) begoten of þæs guman sidan, siððan he hæfde his gaste onsended (line 49)
[+] cris*t* wæs on rodi	cwiðdon Cyninges fyll. Crist wæs on rode. (line 56)
hweþræ þer fusæ fearran kwomu ʔþilæ til anum ic þæt al bi*h*??? sa?? ic wʔs miþ soʔgu*m* gi*dr*œ??d hʔaʔ ...	Hwæðere þær fuse feorran cwoman (line 57) to þam æðelinge. Ic þæt eall beheold (line 58) Sare ic wæs mid [sorgum] gedrefed, hnag ic hwæðre þam secgum to handa (line 59)
miþ sʔre*l*um giwundad alegdun hiæ hinæ limwœrignæ gistoddu? him ?? ??? ???æs ??fʔʔm ??eaʔduʔ hiʔ þeʔ ...	standan steame bedrifenne; eall ic wæs mid strælum forwundod (line 62) Aledon hie ðær limwerigne, gestodon him æt his lices heafdum (line 63) beheoldon hie ðær heofenes Dryhten, ond he hine ðær hwile reste, (line 64)

Despite the damaged state of the monument inscriptions, and allowing for differences in dialect and date of language and epigraphy, several points emerge from this comparative exercise. First, the text inscribed on the monument relates only to that section of the later poem that deals most explicitly with the Crucifixion, largely voiced by the Cross, although, as we have seen, there is no explicit reference to a speaking cross on the Ruthwell monument. Second, the relationship between some of the lines in the text inscribed on the monument and in the manuscript poem seems to be one of 'paraphrase' (line 41 perhaps, lines 45, 48, 57 and 63), 'variation' (perhaps lines 39, 41, 44) and, possibly, 'quotation' (lines 39, 44, 56 and perhaps 62, which correspond in each case to the first line of each of the four groups of inscriptions or *sententia* on the monument). *If so*, which text is paraphrasing or quoting from which or *what* is moot. Third, some of the lines of the text on the monument are apparently deliberately metrically incomplete, at least according to later, normative standards of metre for Old English poetry (lines 41, 56, 62 and perhaps 42); others appear to be more conventional (whether half or full) metrically (lines 39, 45, 57, 58). Finally, there is a high proportion of hypermetrical lines in this section of the manuscript poem and, apparently, in the runic text inscribed on the monument (lines 48, 59, 63, perhaps 49 and 64). There are, then, some similarities between monument inscriptions and manuscript poem. But, there are also differences. And, similarities from one point of view will turn out to be differences from another.

This kind of compare-and-contrast analysis, which we suspect that all students of Anglo-Saxon poetry have conducted at one time or another, highlights the need to consider some larger theoretical issues, especially those that pertain to 'similarity'. In Chapter 3 we showed, with reference to Nelson Goodman's strictures on similarity, how problematic it is to take similarity as offering empirical evidence for the description, discrimination, and classification of style in Anglo-Saxon stone sculpture, generally, and, specifically, the relation of association in art history between the Ruthwell and Bewcastle monuments. Goodman's strictures should also give pause for thought to those by whom compare-and-contrast exercises are seen as useful tools for the analysis and interpretation, history and criticism of literary texts.

> Similarity does not pick out inscriptions that are 'tokens of a common type', or replicas of each other.[59]

> Similarity does not provide the grounds for accounting two occurrences performances of the same work, or repetitions of the same behaviour or experiment.[60]

> Similarity between particulars does not suffice to define qualities.[61]

> Similarity cannot be equated with, or measured in terms of, possession of common characteristics.[62]

Similarity has its place and uses but is only really useful in relation to difference. On what basis do we compare a now fragmentary eighth-century Northumbrian stone sculpture that has on two of its four sides fragmentary runic inscriptions that collect a series of vernacular poetic statements of some of what seem to have originally been 16 lines about the Crucifixion, arranged around two inhabited plant-scrolls, with parts of a late tenth-century manuscript poem of southern provenance, of some 156 lines, in the genre of a dream vision, in a West Saxon poetic *koiné*, in a modified Romanised script, penned in minuscules? Literary history and criticism undertake this particular compare-and-contrast exercise because of their compulsion to repeat a principle of discrimination that was established long ago by Kemble. So, not surprisingly, the judgements reached always affirm those types of relationships that are unconsciously *of* the prototype (that is, they always echo Kemble's view of these relationships). Even then, in order for two entities to be compared-and-contrasted, the text inscribed on the monument and parts of the manuscript poem, and thus found to be the same, there must be a third entity that stands in some relation of association to both, which forms the ground or basis of the comparison. For our table of inscribed text and written poem to have any analytic worth – to have any sense – something has to be supplied.

If the runic texts inscribed on the Ruthwell monument and the *The Dream of the Rood* in the Vercelli Book are to be seen as similar we must be able to point to some aspect of context, language, theme or genre that they both evidence and which has the same meaning and value. We need to consider each of these, if only briefly.

Firstly, context. When thinking about a context that might have produced and used the runic texts inscribed on the Ruthwell monument and *The Dream of the Rood* in the Vercelli Book it's usual to refer to what we know about monasticism or liturgical practice in the early Middle Ages. This seems to place the monument inscriptions and manuscript poem into the same frame of reference: the liturgy, the sacrament of baptism, the cult of the Cross, the veneration of Mary, and so on and so forth. But can the two texts be accommodated within this same frame of reference? It seems not. For example, though there is a moment in *The Dream of the Rood* wherein the tree sees itself as *exalted* above all other trees as Mary was *raised up* above all other women (lines 90–94), there is no such reference in the runic texts inscribed on the Ruthwell monument. One should come as close to the text as one can but not add to it. At least one commentator has read a reference to Mary *as if* it were there, implied or inferred, but to read it that way one must read into the runic texts what one has first read in the manuscript poem.[63] There is nothing ostensive in the runic text that invites one to compare the honour given to the cross with the honour accorded Mary. Nevertheless, there are at least two images of Mary in the sculptural programme on the monument's west and east sides. The veneration of Mary was developing in England in the eighth century, initially as an aspect of feasts of Christ, but the four Marian feasts, as they would become, seem to have been introduced gradually, sporadically, with some confusion[64] and to have met with some resistance.[65] A developed cult of the Virgin in the liturgy did not become established until the eleventh century.[66] One might construct a Marian frame of reference for the production of both texts but it would be different in each instance. Moreover, the construction of a liturgical context that would establish an immediate connection across some two hundred or so years would lack much, if any, analytical clarity. Why? Because it would have to assume that the liturgy was a stable and universal determining frame of reference across time and place. Which, as we will see in the next chapter when we consider the idea of the 'Northumbrian' cross, it clearly was not.

Next, matters of language. Leaving aside the obvious difference that the texts at Ruthwell are inscribed in runic letters and that the *The Dream of the Rood* is in minuscules, the language of the two texts and the principles governing the ways their words are combined and organised are different. As we've noticed, the words of the runic texts are in a form of Anglian, Northumbrian dialect, though this may not amount to much given that the monument inscription is the most significant evidence we have for the study of this dialect. The manuscript poem is in a particular form of later West Saxon. As Sisam understood, the language of Anglo-Saxon poetry is a *koiné*, which is very difficult to date. Nevertheless, because language changes across place and time, the two texts may provide evidence for a diachronic analysis; they may also provide evidence for a synchronic analysis of the system of language use at a particular time. We might also consider the way the words are combined into phrases, clauses and *sententiae* to convey ideas that are taken to be similar. A study of early medieval manuscript culture might help here, especially with regard to the principles of trans-formation and variation or *mouvance*.[67] A stretch of discourse changes, in accordance with different rules of transformation, and produces variation (of morphology, phonology, syntax, graphology etc.). We would expect to find variation also because of adaptation and editing in the process of inscription. Since there is no conception of a fixed and stable text in this period, we would expect to find, in other words, the kinds of transformation and variation that the text inscribed on the monument and the text in the manuscript seems to evidence. For this reason alone, every version of any given text must be *read* and understood *as* unique. Bluntly, we are not dealing with one text in two versions but with two very different texts. To interrupt this discussion of the language of the two texts and the principles governing the ways their words are combined and organised, to which we'll return in due course, let's recall another telling comparison between fragments of two texts that could be read as similar: namely Borges's comparison of Cervantes's and Pierre Menard's *Don Quixote*, to which we referred in our discussion of the idea of style, constant form and similarity. Even if the runic text on the Ruthwell monument and *The Dream of the Rood* were word for word and *sententia* for *sententia* the same, we would still be considering two very different texts.

Now, the texts' images and themes. We touched on these matters a moment ago, when we made reference to the absence and presence of Mary. Here it's useful to bring back the two lines of alliterative verse engraved on the Brussels Cross reliquary in their relation of association with the Ruthwell runic inscriptions and the Vercelli Book *The Dream of the Rood*: 'Rod is min nama; geo in ricne cyning bær byfigynde, blode bestemed'.

Each text has a cross that seems to speak or does speak (though only the Ruthwell and Vercelli Book texts have a cross that seems to refer to itself as 'I'), moves in some way (all of them bow, though only in the Brussels and Vercelli texts does the cross tremble), and is drenched with blood (though only in the monument inscriptions and the Vercelli text is it said that the cross is wounded).

As the tabulated correspondences between the texts inscribed on the

Ruthwell monument and parts of the text in *The Dream of the Rood* show, there is sometimes a marked affinity in the actual words that encode and communicate these ideas. There are also several such affinities between the text on the Brussels Cross reliquary and the other texts.

The affinity between the shorter text on the Brussels Cross –

Rod is min nama; geo in ricne cyning bær byfigynde, blode bestemed

Cross is my name; trembling, drenched with blood, I bore the powerful king

– and parts of lines 44 and 48 of *The Dream of the Rood* seems compelling, though the act of naming of the Cross and the use of form (metre, alliteration) is more prosaic in the Brussels text than in the manuscript poem:

Rod wæs ic aræred; ahof *ic ricne Cyning* (44)

As a cross was I raised; I held up the noble king

Bysmeredon hie unc butu ætgædere. Eall ic wæs mid *blode bestemed.*(48)

They mocked us both together. I was made wet with blood …

There is also a less compelling affinity with the second *sententia* on the north side of the Ruthwell monument:

[ʔhof] ic riicnæ kyniŋc heafunæs hlafard hælda ic ni dorstæ ʔismæradu uʔket men ba ætgadʔʔ ʔʔʔ ʔiþ bʔodi bistʔmiʔ ʔiʔʔʔæ …

[I raised] up a powerful king, lord of heaven, I did not dare bend
Men mocked us both together, I [was] with blood drenched
[poured] …

Presumably, the Brussels Cross has 'beran' not 'ahebban' in conformity with the alliteration – what we might call the linguistics of literariness – of the rest of its text, which might account too for the different emphasis of this initial phrase – not 'Cross was I raised' as Vercelli puts it, but 'Cross is my name'. Are these affinities of imagery and thematics *and* words to be understood as allusions, indirect or passing recollections or as intentional directly intertextual references? Should we see them as unintended similarities or as intended similarities? Or, with Goodman's strictures on similarity in mind, should we see them as differences?

With these matters in mind, let us return to the relation of association between the text inscribed on the Ruthwell monument and *The Dream of the Rood* with regard to aspects that might be understood as generic. The text on the monument might be read as sharing affinities of genre with *The Dream of the Rood*, but the latter signals its genre more obviously than does the former. Its first word indicates clearly and dramatically that it is a poem: 'Hwæt'. And despite its not concluding with 'Amen', as do a number of other religious poems of the period, it does move to a formal closure that utilises the so be it of an entry in to Heaven: 'ælmihtig God, Þær his eðel wæs / Almighty God, where his homeland was' (Swanton, *The Dream of the Rood*, line 156). *The Dream of the Rood* begins and ends according to conventional expectations of Old English poetry. The texts inscribed on the

Ruthwell monument seem not to mark beginnings and endings formally: '[+ ond]geredæ hinæ god almeʒttig / Almighty god unclothed himself' and, as we have it today, '??eaʔduʔ *hiʔ* þe ... / [they beheld there] ...' – none of the recent reconstructions of the missing runes, probably correctly, puts an 'Amen' to it.[68] *The Dream of the Rood*, in other words, makes obvious that it is a poem. The *sententiae* inscribed on the Ruthwell monument, by contrast, do not announce that they are structured in the form of a poem or as parts of a poem; although the texts are so early in date that any comment about its genre may be risky. The runic texts might be best understood as a hybrid genre. We also note that *if* the texts on the Ruthwell monument are to be judged by the later norms of Old English poetry then alliteration and metre are occasionally unconventional. As we have seen already, there are a number of hypermetric lines (possibly four) and a number of short, apparent half-lines (possibly one or two in each group of lines). Compared with the text of *The Dream of the Rood*, alliteration is sometimes a little clumsy and sometimes non-existent – 'crist wæs on rodi' being the most obvious example – and the runic texts do not utilise the language of poetic literariness – figuration, dream vision, frame narratives and so on – to the extent that the later poem does. That's why we've been describing the runic inscriptions as 'poetic', not as 'poetry'.

However we might want to assess the various perceived similarities between the monument inscriptions and the manuscript poem, it is worth restating that they account for only a small portion of the latter. On the one hand, there's a runic text that is poetic rather than poetry, which frames two sculptured panels of inhabited plant-scroll and is related to a complex programme of figure sculptures on the monument's other sides, each individual sculpture accompanied by a Latin inscription. On the other hand, there's a poem written in a familiar, conventional late Anglo-Saxon style, included in an anthology that shows no sustained use of runes,[69] has no formal programme of images (and precious little by way of textual decoration in the form of initials and so forth), and has as its immediate frame of reference a book produced by a complex process of bringing together a mixture of Anglo-Saxon religious prose works and English poems. *The Dream of the Rood*'s immediate 'context' is, indeed, other 'texts' – texts that are very different from those contextualising the runic inscription of the Ruthwell monument.[70]

How to account for the affinities between these texts on artefacts so different in form and function? These artefacts, each produced at a different time and place, seem to have been intended to represent something of the mystery of the cross and Cross, though that was not their only function. The thoroughly textual *The Dream of the Rood* needed to include within it descriptions of the cross and Cross that were so vivid that its reader would see those objects in his or her mind's eye. The Ruthwell monument and the Brussels Cross needed to supplement their different material forms with text. It seems to us that the most likely and most straightforward explanation of the affinities between the text inscribed on the eighth-century monument at Ruthwell, the text contained within *The Dream of the Rood* in the late tenth-century Vercelli Book and the text engraved in alliterative metrical verse on the eleventh-century Brussels Cross reliquary is that each makes use of a conventional, probably primarily spoken topos that was widely available as a resource in Anglo-Saxon culture for some considerable time, one that was subject of and to the whole process of history, movement and change, which determined its form, function and context of use.

Perception as interpretation: seeing runes, reading, speaking, hearing, and seeing ... as

The runic texts inscribed on the narrow north and south sides of the Ruthwell monument, which tell of the Crucifixion in the implied voice of the Cross, offer in another form – textual, runic, poetic, non-iconic – something of the mysteries of Christian belief that are represented by the sculptural panels and Latin inscriptions on its west and east sides. Because they are poetic, they participate not only in the historically and culturally specific circumstances of the monument's production and first use but also in the conditions of Anglo-Saxon culture and poetry generally. What is it, then, that a study of vernacular poetry tells us about the Ruthwell monument? For poetry, in its most general sense, is crucial to any understanding of the Ruthwell monument and its vernacular inscriptions.

Anglo-Saxon ideas about belief (the mystery that is the Mass, for example) can be connected with the mystery of the runes and with the poetic puzzle, or riddle, of interpretation itself. There is, for example, an evident homology between letters as visible signs (perhaps especially runic letters), riddles and the Mass in Anglo-Saxon culture. Each of these, on their different levels of writing, genre and belief, is structured as an enigma. For the late Anglo-Saxon homilist Ælfric, in his Easter Sunday sermon (Second Series), for example, the Mass is a 'gerynu' (a rune or mystery or enigma) of faith and understanding, whereby one thing is seen and another meant. Runes, riddles, and mysteries are profoundly related, as indicated by the word 'ryne'.[71] And letters, runic or otherwise, are visible signs. Letters introduce words by way of the eye and the ear: 'Verba enim per oculos non per aures introducunt'.[72] Is it a tree, a cross, a sword, a gallows, asks the Old English Exeter Book Riddle 55: 'wordum secgan hu se wudu hatte / say in words what this wood is called' (lines 15–16).[73] Letters transform sound into sight. The Anglo-Saxon reader learns to read by looking at the letters, perhaps also by pointing to them with an 'æstel', and by sounding them out – thus bringing ideas to practical consciousness: ideas and concepts, mental intercourse as it exists for the reader and for others. Indeed, representations of reading are primarily visual, as the celebrated example of Asser's account of Alfred's attraction to the letters of his mother's book of Anglo-Saxon poetry indicates. Alfred learns to read by looking at poetry.[74] Reading is also etymologically connected with riddling in Anglo-Saxon culture. 'Rædan': to read (by seeing); to counsel or advise (by speaking).[75] Both concepts, reading and riddling, encode structures of sight, sound, hearing, and counsel brought to understanding.

It is to the point that the Anglo-Saxons were familiar with the idea of the

Five Senses and that, amongst them, they seem to have privileged Sight. We're reminded that the late ninth-century Fuller Brooch, in the collection of the British Museum, is decorated with representations of human figures representing the five senses and that the largest of these – it's in the lozenge or cross at the centre of the brooch, dominating its design – is a three-quarter, full frontal personification of Sight.[76] The identity of the enamelled figure on the Alfred Jewel, in the collection of the Ashmolean Museum, Oxford, which could be the handle of an 'æstel', has been interpreted as a personification of Sight, which would be an apt subject with which to have decorated such an object.[77]

The oral and aural features of Anglo-Saxon riddles are well known, but they also engage with visual codes. Riddles draw on structures of seeing ... as much as they do on those of speaking. Though primarily a genre of voice, many vernacular riddles deploy a rhetoric of sight. What appears to be mere convention, the formula, 'I saw', 'Ic seah', which begins so many riddles in the Exeter Book,[78] is a way of signifying that seeing, reading and saying open the mind to the structure of signification itself. All riddles explore the process of identifying and naming or naming and identifying.

Identifying and naming. Naming and identifying. Seeing, speaking and hearing. It seems that, as far as the Anglo-Saxons were concerned, these three individual faculties of perception were key to reading and writing, to acquiring literacy and being literate, and to understanding the mysteries or counsel secreted in texts both profane and, signally, sacred. And along with seeing, hearing, movement was also involved and the sense of touch. The *æstel* moves across the page, follows the letters and perhaps touches them, as did the pen that wrote them. Our eyes move across and we move around the Ruthwell monument and perhaps we touch the runes as the Anglo-Saxons may have done. The author of *Vita Samsonis*, written between the seventh and ninth centuries, claims to have touched the cross inscribed by the saint on a pagan standing stone.[79] The antiquarians and runologists of the nineteenth century certainly approached the task of reading the runes by touching them.[80] Body and mind, sense and cognition, perception and observation, seeing and seeing ... as are thoroughly and *movingly* engaged when it comes to making sense of the Ruthwell monument.

The Ruthwell monument is a catalyst for and participant in the processes of making and puzzling meaning in and through time, for both Anglo-Saxon and modern interpreters. How to read the runes? When is a poem not a poem? What does it mean for an 'I' to implicitly refer to itself as gallows, cross, Cross? Earlier, when we first considered the question of voice, we asked, 'Who speaks this "I"?' We now realise that the answer to that last question must be, most properly, whoever had and has the skills and competences to read and speak the texts inscribed on the monument. And what did and do those persons *read*, *speak* and *hear*, it *as*? What did they, and what do we, *see* the runic texts inscribed on the monument, and the monument itself, *as*?

The vernacular runic inscriptions on the narrow north and south sides of the Ruthwell monument may well play off against the likelihood that, at the moment it was produced and first used, the monument did not have the shape of a cross; or they may be explored in relation to changing ideas about crosses and the idea of Cross in the Anglo-Saxon period and later. Interpretation and explanation of the runes as a riddle about crosses may be useful also for understanding the meanings of the Ruthwell monument much later in its history when, for example, it was in fragments or, now, as the remarkable monument in the shape of a cross that was first assembled by Henry Duncan between 1802 and 1823. Despite the monument being set in cement when it was moved into the church in 1887 (Fig. 42), its meaning remains as uncertain and unstable as when it first attracted the attention of the antiquarians in the late sixteenth and seventeenth century. The runic texts inscribed on its north and south sides can be read as a riddle that would have us meditate on the meaning of 'rod' as much on the Crucifixion and onto-theology of 'Cross', but any interpretation and explanation of them and of the monument itself will be partial and provisional, however historically informed.

To read the runic texts only as a riddle (a single riddle or even a riddle of singularity) is to offer only one example of the ways they might be read. Their meaning, like the meaning of the monument itself, *is always in process* – in the process of being made. To insist otherwise, and certainly to insist on one explanation only or above all others *as if* it were *the* explanation, would be to reify that one explanation and close down the very process of making sense of things that the monument embodies. It would be to remove the Ruthwell monument from the very kinetic and kinaesthetic processes, the different levels of movement, interaction of body and mind, sense and cognition that it was almost certainly made to effect in its first place.

8

The Northumbrian cross: evidence and silence

⌘

Oswald's cross

From the eighth century onwards the stone cross was a relatively common monument in some regions of Anglo-Saxon England.[1] From the ninth century at the latest, Ireland and Scotland could also boast numerous examples.[2] In addition there is good literary evidence for crosses on the continent, beginning as early as the fifth century, although there are no known examples surviving from that date, and it is unclear, in any case, how many were made of timber rather than stone.[3] Yet, despite the widespread distribution in the early medieval West, and indeed beyond, of crosses at least some of which were stone, such monuments seem to have been particularly numerous and to have had a special significance in Northumbria,[4] and it is worth asking why. As we shall see, no single explanation seems adequate, but the convergence in the Northumbrian region of a number of factors may provide an answer.

One much-cited prototype is the wooden cross erected by Oswald before the battle of Heavenfield, the story of which is told by Bede.[5] The newly established Bernician king was facing the army of the Briton Cadwallon, who had destroyed his three predecessors, Edwin, Osric and Eanfrid. The battle was to take place just to the south of Hadrian's Wall, the *vallum* of which would have presented one or other party with a significant defensive position. In gathering his army there Oswald may have benefited from the Stanegate, the Roman road which ran to the south of the Wall, and from the Roman bridge at nearby *Cilurnum* (Chesters): though those same lines of communication could also have aided Cadwallon's mobility. With the Wall behind him, Oswald was also towards the southern limits of his own Bernician heartland. According to Bede:

> The place is still shown today and is held in great veneration where Oswald, when he was about to engage in battle, set up the sign of the holy cross and, on bended knees, prayed God to send heavenly aid to His worshippers in their dire need. In fact it is related that when a cross had been hastily made and the

hole dug in which it was to stand, he seized the cross himself in the ardour of his faith, and held it upright with both hands until the soldiers had heaped up the earth and fixed it in position.[6]

This is, of course, only a story, and it first appears in the *Historia ecclesiastica*, although Bede is likely to have derived it from the monks of Hexham, for he goes on to relate that they made it

> their custom to come every year, on the day before that on which King Oswald was killed, to keep vigil there for the benefit of his soul, to sing many psalms of praise, and, next morning, to offer up the holy sacrifice and oblation on his behalf. And since that good custom has spread, a church has lately been built there so that the place has become yet more sacred and worthy of honour in the eyes of all.[7]

Perhaps surprisingly it is a church, and not a cross, that they set up there. The date of the pilgrimage is also interesting: it was held not on the anniversary of the victory at Heavenfield, but on that of Oswald's death at Maserfelth, traditionally Oswestry, on the Welsh border, in 642 – in other words it was linked to commemoration of the dead king, 'for the benefit of his soul', rather than the celebration of the victory over Cadwallon.

Yet although Bede was able to draw on Hexham tradition when he set down his account of Heavenfield in the 730s, that does not mean that the story was accurate. Hexham was not founded until 672, nearly forty years after the battle. Moreover, there are certain aspects of Bede's account which are distinctly suspect. Thus, in emphasising the erection of the cross, Bede portrays Oswald and his army as Christian, while the opposing British army, led by Cadwallon, is presented, by implication, as pagan. Cadwallon acts impiously, *impia manu*: he is a savage tyrant, *tyrannus saeviens*: he is a wicked leader of the Britons, *infandus Brettonum dux*.[8] There is no acknowledgement here that Cadwallon was a Christian ruler: that his British subjects had long been Christian, nor that the Northumbrians, having only recently been christianised, had apostasised after Edwin's death. Oswald, indeed, might have been one of the few Christians in the Northumbrian army. It is true that Bede does go on to admit that Christianity among the Bernicians was in its infancy: 'as far as we know, no symbol of the Christian faith, no church, and no altar had been erected among the whole Bernician population before that new leader of the host, inspired by his devotion to the faith, set up the standard of the holy cross when he was about to fight his most savage enemy'.[9] Yet this statement is also problematic. It is not very easy to square with Bede's own evidence for missions within Northumbria during the reign of Edwin.[10] It is as if the achievements of the Bernician Oswald are being deliberately extolled at the expense of those of the Deiran Edwin. Clearly Bede's presentation of the battle of Heavenfield has more to do with the creation of a myth of Christian origins and of Oswald's sanctity than with the accurate recording of events. We can do no more than say that the story, as Bede tells it, was current in Northumbrian discourse from the time of the composition of the *Ecclesiastical History*. We may even guess that what Bede presents as longstanding Hexham tradition may actually have been relatively new: he certainly admits that the foundation of a church on the site of Heavenfield was recent, and the same would seem to have been true of the cult of Oswald.[11]

Bede's account of Heavenfield, therefore, should not be taken as proof that the origins of the Northumbrian predilection for stone crosses lay in Oswald's actions immediately before the battle. Rather, the account should be seen as relating to a growing interest in the cult of the cross in early eighth-century Northumbria, and should be set alongside the stone crosses themselves, as well as the cruciform images with which many of the Insular Gospel books are illuminated. The story of Oswald at Heavenfield is thus an illustration of a burgeoning Northumbrian interest in the idea of the cross, rather than an explanation of that interest. It may also have played a role in promoting the cross as a key sign for the Northumbrians. Alcuin retells the account, as he does most of Bede's *Ecclesiastical History*, in his *Versus de patribus, regibus et sanctis Euboricensis ecclesiae*.[12] In addition he repeats Bede's account of a miracle effected by soil from the place where Oswald's bones had been washed.[13] This, however, prompts an outburst which is entirely Alcuin's:

> Of you, too, shall I sing, holy, powerful, venerable cross,
> famed for many miracles, even though my verse is unworthy
> to praise you. You bestowed what was lost in the past;
> now, once again, by you victory was granted to king Oswald,
> as my poor verse has told. From that moment,
> your glory shone forth in wondrous miracles,
> and all Britain, acclaimed for her faith, thronged to you,
> seeking a cure for her various ills ...[14]

Constantine and Helena: visionary and discovered crosses

A second story, which also requires consideration, is that of the vision of the Emperor Constantine. The story of Oswald at Heavenfield might even be seen as a Bernician response to traditions associated with the emperor, whose vision of a symbol, which came to be interpreted as a cross,[15] was certainly known in northern England.[16] Constantine, after all, was elected emperor in 306 at *Eburacum*, or York, the Roman provincial capital, which lay in what was to become the heartland of the Deirans by the seventh century.

An inscription on a stone slab from Jarrow has been reconstructed as stating *In hoc singulari signo vita redditur mundi*: 'In this unique sign was life restored to the world.'[17] The sign itself is clearly the cross, which is also carved on the slab – though the slab itself is not cross-shaped. Scholars have long been aware that the quotation derives from Rufinus's version of Constantine's vision before the battle of the Milvian Bridge in 312.[18] Rufinus's *History* was known by Bede, who used it as a resource on several occasions. That there is an allusion to it on a stone slab from Jarrow is, therefore, no surprise. A further Bernician reference to the story might also be present on the Bewcastle monument, which apparently made reference to 'this token of victory', or 'victory cross' or 'victory memorial'.[19]

There is perhaps one further hint that the story of Constantine's vision was well known in Northumbria. A number of *sceattas*, or silver pennies, of series G, type 3a, which have been assigned to York, have a profile bust, arguably of an emperor, looking upwards, with a cross directly in front of him. It has been suggested that the figure is Constantine, and that the image is intended to depict his vision.[20] If the identification of the image and of the place of issue for series G is correct – and both are certainly plausible – we have evidence for a clear association of York, the city of Constantine's elevation, with traditions relating to his conversion. The story of the vision before the Milvian Bridge, one might say, was part of the loose change of the kingdom.

There is, then, evidence, some strong and some intriguing and plausible, to suggest that the story of Constantine's vision was in circulation in Northumbria, and that it may have played a part in the development of the cult of the cross in the region. It is, however, necessary to register a few caveats. Although the tale of the emperor's vision was known, less is made of it in our sources than might have been expected, given its importance in the narrative of the christianisation of the Roman Empire. Neither Bede nor Alcuin, in his versification of Bede, relates it, even though both of them knew Rufinus's *History*.[21] The existence of the Jarrow inscription makes Bede's silence particularly surprising. Nor does either Bede or Alcuin pause to comment on the fact that Constantine was elevated as emperor at *Eburacum*, following his father's death in the city – and this despite Alcuin's own association with York. Although Bede mentions Constantine, he does so with a certain amount of circumspection. In all probability this is because Jerome's portrayal of the emperor is a good deal less than complimentary: he emphasises Constantine's murder of his son, and states that he died a heretic.[22] Jerome's account may well have problematised Constantine for Bede and Alcuin, just as it did for the Gallo-Roman historian Gregory of Tours.[23] These are but the first of a number of problematic silences that we need to register in considering the idea of Northumbrian cross.

Despite these silences, the story of Constantine's vision should certainly be seen as having considerable currency within Anglo-Saxon England. If one looks beyond Northumbria, there is the evidence of a number of Old English versions of a narrative known as the *Finding of the True Cross*,[24] most notably Cynewulf's poem *Elene*.[25]

Elene tells of Constantine's conversion to Christianity, although it transforms his conflict with Maxentius into a war against the Huns.[26] Faced with a numerically superior enemy, the emperor was consoled by a celestial messenger, who directed him to look for a sign of victory in the sky. Looking up, he saw 'a beautiful tree of glory in the vault of the skies. The shining tree was brilliantly and radiantly inscribed with letters: "With this emblem you will overpower the enemy in the perilous offensive; you will halt hostile armies."'[27] Constantine then 'commanded a symbol in the likeness of Christ's cross – just as he, battle-leader of armies, saw that emblem that was lately revealed to him in the heavens – to be made with great urgency'.[28] With this as his standard he defeated the barbarians, and on discovering the Christian meaning of the cross he underwent baptism. At this point Cynewulf switches his attention from Constantine to the emperor's mother, Helena, who is sent by her son to the Holy Land to find the True Cross. She interrogates members of the Jewish community, and as a result discovers the three crosses, which had been buried on Calvary. The True Cross on which Christ died is then identified as a result of the raising of a dead man. The narrative of the poem continues with an account of the empress's encasement of the fragments of the Cross in a jewelled reliquary, followed by the conversion of Judas, the Jew who revealed the relics, and who, having changed his name to Cyriacus, was appointed bishop of Jerusalem. Although the poem concludes with a meditation on the End of the World by the author, the narrative effectively closes with Helena having the nails from the Cross turned into a bridle for Constantine's horse. With the help of these relics, the emperor would 'overpower every enemy in combat'.[29] The images of the Cross and the relics associated with it are presented as symbols of war and victory for a military aristocracy.

Unfortunately, although we know the name of the author, his date and therefore that of the poem is uncertain. Scholars, however, do not regard the *Elene* as being early in the Old English canon. Moreover, Cynewulf himself is generally thought to have been Mercian. In other words, although the *Elene* has rightly been drawn into discussions of the idea of the jewelled cross, the *crux gemmata*, in Anglo-Saxon art,[30] it can be seen only as illustrating the presence of the idea, not as originating or spreading it. In any case, the story of the finding of the True Cross is not confined to Cynewulf's poem. There were at least three Latin versions of the narrative known as the Finding of the Holy Cross, the *Inventio Sanctae Crucis*,[31] in circulation in the early medieval West, one of them as early as c.500,[32] and there is one version in Old English prose.[33] Cynewulf's poem is largely a versification of one of the Latin accounts – a point which proves that a Latin *Inventio Sanctae Crucis* was circulating in Anglo-Saxon England before the date of the composition of the *Elene*. The story could therefore have been in circulation in Northumbria by the eighth century.

Taking all these indicators together, while the evidence is suggestive rather than clear-cut, the story of Constantine's vision of the Cross might have served as a resource for Bede's narrative of Oswald at Heavenfield, and both stories may have had special significance in Northumbria: that of Constantine because he was made emperor in York (though the currency of this information is uncertain), and that of Oswald, because it concerned a Northumbrian king, and his defeat of the Briton Cadwallon. Both stories may have contributed to the popularity of the cross as a symbol in Northumbria. It is also important to remember the military aspects of the sign of the cross in these stories. As we have seen, the Ruthwell monument must have been an intrusive and commanding silhouette of Northumbrian power in a region with a significant British population, for whose ancestors Cadwallon might have been a hero.

The holy places

The tale of Helena's role in the finding of the True Cross and in the enshrining of the relics of the Passion, while not directly relevant to Northumbrian history, or the telling of it, had considerable cultural significance for Christians in the north of England. Unlike Constantine's vision, the Finding of the Cross was an 'event' referred to by Bede. It was recounted in the context of descriptions of the Holy Land. The *Ecclesiastical History* includes a number of passages taken from Adomnan's *De locis sanctis*, or rather from Bede's own version of it, which includes a description of the church set up on Golgotha by Constantine, on the site where his mother had discovered the True Cross.[34] Even in the eighth century, after the Arab capture of Jerusalem, a cross marked the supposed site of the crucifixion.[35] It had been erected by the patriarch Modestus, c.614, apparently during the Persian occupation of the city,[36] and was made of silver, or more likely was encased in silver. This would seem to be the monument that is described by Adomnan, in his account of Arculf's pilgrimage to the Holy Land.[37] Like Bede,[38] who does little more than edit him, Adomnan implies that the cross was inside the Golgotha church. From these accounts the cross does not seem to have been a bejewelled cross, nor was it radiant like that of Constantine's supposed vision. All this indicates that the actual cross set up by Modestus cannot have provided the model for the *crux gemmata*. It is impossible to say how long the monument set up by Modestus survived. In the 720s, when the Anglo-Saxon Willibald went on pilgrimage to Jerusalem, he saw 'three wooden crosses standing there outside the church ... beneath a pent roof'. Inside, a cross stood above the sepulchre itself, but no comment is made on the material of which it was made.[39]

What preceded the cross set up by Modestus is unclear: according to the ninth-century author Theophanes, the Emperor Theodosius II (408–450) sent a gold cross, decorated with gems, to be installed on Golgotha, but, if this were the case, it is surprising that no earlier account mentions it.[40] Indeed, the absence of any clear statement about the monuments on Golgotha prior to the seventh century suggests that there was no monumental *crux gemmata*.[41]

Representations of a bejewelled cross, like that to be found in the early fifth-century apse mosaic of Santa Pudenziana in Rome, are not depictions of any actual cross known to have been set up on Golgotha. On the other hand, the reliquary of the True Cross, which had been kept in Jerusalem until the Persian wars of 614,[42] and which was moved to Constantinople in 636,[43] was bejewelled. The various versions of the *Inventio Sanctae Crucis* ascribe the commissioning of a jewelled case for the relics, rightly or wrongly, to Helena. Up until the Persian wars, this reliquary was displayed in Jerusalem on Good Friday and Encaenia (the feast of the restoration of the Temple, which coincided with that of the discovery of the True Cross on 14 September).[44] Exactly what it looked like is unknown, but it was of a size for the bishop to hold it down. The fourth-century pilgrim Egeria described the ritual as follows:

A table is placed before [the bishop] with a cloth on it, the deacons stand round, and there is brought to him a gold and silver box containing the holy Wood of the Cross. It is opened, and the Wood of the Cross and the Title are taken out and placed on the table. As long as the holy Wood is on the table, the bishop sits with his hands resting on either end of it and holds it down, and deacons round him keep watch over it.

The reason for this was that some over-zealous pilgrim had once bitten off a piece of the relic. 'Thus all the people go past one by one. They stoop down, touch the holy Wood, first with their forehead and then with their eyes, and then kiss it, but no one puts out his hand to touch it'.[45] The relic of the True Cross itself, then, was a sizeable, but not enormous, piece of wood. Jewelled crosses, such as that sent to the Pope by the Emperor Justin II (565–578) and Empress Sophia, may have been intended to call to mind its reliquary case. Perhaps some westerners conflated the commemorative cross erected on Golgotha with the bejewelled reliquary of the fragments of the True Cross.[46] It would be wrong, however, to see the *crux gemmata* as being solely derived from such a conflation. The jewelled cross is a common image in late Antiquity and the early Middle Ages, and was surely imagined independently by numerous scholars and craftsman.

Constantine's vision, the reliquary of the True Cross, the monuments of Golgotha and Oswald's actions at Heavenfield all may have played a part as resources for the imagining and imaging of the Cross in early eighth-century Northumbria. Whatever the factual basis behind the vision of the cross, the discovery by Helena[47] and the story of Oswald's battle, every one of these narratives was in circulation to a greater or lesser extent in Bede's day, when the geography of the Holy Places was under discussion, not least because of Adomnan's account of Arculf's visit to the Holy Places, and Bede's reworking of that text.

Pope Sergius and the rediscovery of a relic of the true cross

It is possible that interest in the cult of the Cross in England was enhanced by a discovery made by Pope Sergius (687–701) in Rome. The story is told in full in the official history of the popes, the *Liber pontificalis*:[48]

In the shrine of St Peter the apostle this blessed man [i.e. Sergius] discovered, by God's revelation, a silver casket lying in a very dark corner; because of tarnishing during the years that had gone by, it was not even clear whether it was silver. So after praying he removed the seal impressed on it. He opened the reliquary and inside he found placed on top a feather cushion made all of silk, which is called *stauracis*. He took this away and lower down he saw a cross, very ornate with various precious stones. From it he removed the four plates in which the jewels were embedded, and he found placed inside a wonderfully large and indescribable portion of the saving wood of the Lord's Cross. From that day, for the salvation of the human race, this is kissed and worshipped by all Christian people on the day of the Exaltation of the Holy Cross in the basilica of the Saviour called Constantinian.

We can be sure that this episode was known about in Northumbria. Travellers to Rome, including Hwaetbert, the future abbot of Wearmouth–Jarrow, could have brought back news of Sergius's find.[49] Bede not only knew the *Liber pontificalis* but he even transcribed the account of the discovery of the reliquary into the chronicle, which forms chapter 66 of the *De temporum ratione*.[50] Clearly Sergius's discovery had an impact.[51] One should not, however, confuse Sergius's discovery with the institution of the Feast of the Exaltation of the Holy Cross. The feast was not new. It had long been celebrated in Byzantium on 14 September, and would appear to have been celebrated in Rome since at least the pontificate of Pope Honorius (625–638).[52] Sergius was merely adding the veneration of a rediscovered relic to a feast already celebrated in some parts of the Christian world.

Crosses in use

The various traditions relating to Helena, Constantine, Oswald and Sergius may help us to understand the vogue for stone crosses in eighth-century Northumbria, but they do little to explain the function of those crosses. Here the direct evidence is remarkably unhelpful. The Reverend John Dinwiddie assumed that the Ruthwell monument was a preaching cross, where the sacraments could be celebrated.[53] This, however, is the hypothesis of a nineteenth-century presbyterian minister, and not the evidence of an early medieval source. Unfortunately, there seems to be no early evidence to show stone crosses being used in this way. Certainly our information is too sparse for us to draw any conclusions from silence. Yet it is useful to begin with what early medieval sources do tell us about the use of crosses, stone and wood.[54]

We have already noted the problems presented by Bede's account of the wooden cross set up by Oswald at Heavenfield.[55] Another cross is mentioned in the *Life of Cuthbert*, where Bede talks of that set up by the saint on Farne. Cuthbert asked the monks of Lindisfarne to bury him to the east of it, but they preferred to take his body back to the monastery.[56] Unfortunately Bede tells us nothing about Cuthbert's cross, or the material of which it was made. In the *Vita Wilfridi* Stephanus talks of a wooden cross erected at Oundle, on the spot where Wilfrid's body was washed, after his death.[57] A further Northumbrian text of the early ninth century, Æthelwulf's *De abbatibus*, talks of altar crosses seen in a vision,[58] as well as a tall cross, set up by abbot Sigwine, who was buried next to it.[59] Another pre-Viking source, the *Hodoeporicon of St Willibald*, provides the fullest statement on the use of a cross in Anglo-Saxon England. The *Hodoeporicon*, or 'Traveller's Book', is an account of Willibald's journeys, above all to the Holy Land. The authoress of the account, Hugeburg, wrote on the continent, but like Willibald, who may have been a relative, she probably came from Wessex. According to Hugeburg, when Willibald was still a child, he fell desperately ill.

> When his parents, in great anxiety of mind, were still uncertain about the fate of their son, they took him and offered him up before the holy Cross of our Lord and Saviour. And they did this not in the church but at the foot of the Cross, for on the estates of the nobles and good men of the Saxon race it is a custom to have a cross, which is dedicated to our Lord and held in great

reverence, erected on some prominent spot for the convenience of those who wish to pray daily before it. There before the cross they laid him.[60]

They promised 'to dedicate him to the service of Christ under the discipline of monastic life'. And the child recovered. This account provides our longest single statement as to how crosses were used in Anglo-Saxon England, and in it they appear as foci for private devotion on secular estates.

This haul of early references to crosses in Anglo-Saxon England can be supplemented with the evidence of later historical sources, notably by Symeon of Durham (d. c.1128) who wrote both about the cross of Bishop Æthelwald of Lindisfarne, which the monks took with them on their journeys round the north of England before settling in Durham,[61] and of those set up at Acca's tomb at Hexham: 'two stone crosses, decorated with wonderful carving, one at the head and the other at the foot of the grave'.[62] Symeon's reference to the Hexham monuments has come to have particular significance in the historiography of Northumbrian sculpture, because it has been thought to date the so-called Acca's cross and thus to provide a much-needed chronological anchor – though this depends both on the accuracy of Symeon's information and on the monument having been correctly identified. In many respects, however, Symeon's comments on the cross commissioned by Bishop Æthelwald for the community on Lindisfarne are more interesting, because of their precision.

> He [Æthelwald] had had embellished by the work of craftsmen a stone cross, and in memory of the saint he had his name inscribed on it. Much later the heathens broke the top of this cross when they sacked the church of Lindisfarne, but afterwards with the ingenuity of a craftsman the broken part was joined again to the remainder by means of pouring in lead. Always afterwards it was the custom to carry this cross round with the body of St Cuthbert, and for it to be held in honour by the people of Northumbria on account of both saints. Down to the present day it stands loftily in the cemetery of this church (that is the church of Durham), and it exhibits to onlookers a monument to both bishops.[63]

Æthelwald, it should be remembered, was supposedly responsible for the binding of the Lindisfarne Gospels,[64] which like several other insular Gospel Books of the period contain elaborate cruciform images.

If we turn from the Anglo-Saxons to the Britons, there is little early evidence, but the *Life of Samson of Dol*, written on the continent at some point between the seventh and ninth centuries, has one relevant story set in Cornwall. The saint, en route from Wales to Francia, stopped at an idol, and carved a cross on it, as the hagiographer himself could witness: 'On this hill I myself have been and have adored and with my hand have traced the sign of the cross which St. Samson with his own hand carved by means of an iron instrument on a standing stone.'[65] The story shows both the christianisation of an idol and also the subsequent reverence shown to the stone by the hagiographer, who touched the incised cross himself.

The Irish Saint's Lives relating to the pre-Viking period boast numerous references to crosses.[66] If one limits oneself to the texts that are accepted as being early in date, there are references to crosses as boundary markers.[67] There were also wayside crosses, some of which marked burials.[68] Perhaps more striking is the use of crosses to mark events in the lives of saints, or at least the hagiographical association of crosses with such events. This is attested both in the *Life of Columba* by Adomnan,[69] and also in Muirchu's *Life of Patrick*.[70] Muirchu relates that a cross was later erected to mark the spot from which Patrick saw the place where he had been held as a slave. Adomnan, who lived on Iona for much of his life, tells of crosses being set up where Columba's uncle Ernán died, and where the saint rested on his last walk from the barn to the monastery.

In contrast to Britain and Ireland, the continent does not boast surviving carved crosses of unquestionably early date. That there were crosses is, however, clear from the written evidence, although this does not state whether or not they were carved or decorated. Perhaps there are early stone crosses or fragments of them which have yet to be correctly dated. Like the English and Irish material, the continental evidence from the pre-Viking period also shows crosses marking points in the lives of saints. The spot where Audoin experienced a vision was marked by a wooden cross.[71] More commonly, crosses marked the routes taken by saints, or along which their corpses were carried. The places where Germanus stopped to pray on his final journey to Ravenna, around the year 440, were marked by oratories and crosses, *signa crucis elata*, according to the fifth-century hagiographer Constantius.[72] Crosses marked both the route of the funeral procession of Ansbert of Rouen in the seventh century,[73] and the stations where the body of Bonitus rested, when it was translated from Lyons to his episcopal city of Clermont in the early eighth.[74] As with the information given in Irish sources, it is rare to find a comment on the material out of which a cross was made, although Sigebert of Gembloux, writing around 1100, states explicitly in his *Life of Lambert* that there was a stone one at Stablo, between the oratory and the dormitory: *Haec crux lapidea erat inter oratorium et dormitorium*.[75] Unfortunately this detail is not present in the earliest, ninth-century, version of Lambert's *Life*, which does, nevertheless, record the saint's penitential devotion before the cross.[76] In mid-winter, when the other monks rushed from the church to their living quarters to warm up, Lambert used to stand by a cross with his arms stretched out, reciting psalms. As Bruno Krusch noted, this was penitential practice prescribed in the eighth-century Rule for Canons of Chrodegang of Metz.[77] Other references to crosses in monasteries can be found in material relating to Columbanus and his foundations. In the regulations for his monks, Columbanus makes it clear that they were expected to approach the cross, after having received a blessing.[78]

More graphic is the account of the last hours of Athala, the Burgundian who succeeded Columbanus as abbot of his Italian foundation of Bobbio. Shortly before his death Athala had himself carried out of his cell:

> Seeing the cross which he had ordered to be set up there, so that leaving and entering the cell he might protect his forehead by touching it, he became sad and began to cry and remember the trophy of the cross. 'Hail sweet cross,'

he said, 'you who have carried the ransom of the world, and who bears the eternal standard; you bore the salve of our wounds, you were anointed with his blood, who came from heaven to this vale of tears to save the human race, who spread out in you the stain of a first Adam a while ago and now a second Adam washes away the blot.'[79]

The idea of the bloodstained cross is a recurrent one, and, of course, can be found in the runic inscriptions on the Ruthwell monument.

Moving south from Bobbio, one comes to the evidence, or lack of it, for Rome itself. Bede and his contemporaries may have thought of stone crosses as a type of Roman monument, just as he thought that building in stone was a Roman trait.[80] Yet if one turns to the pilgrim guide known as the *Einsiedeln Itinerary*, one finds no references to crosses among the monuments to be visited in the city of Rome itself, but, as has been mentioned in Chapter 3, the visitor is directed to various Roman obelisks and 'pyramids'.[81] Nor are crosses mentioned in the passages on Rome to be found in Vienna MS 795. The pilgrim to the Holy Land was, of course, better served, with the silver cross erected on Golgotha,[82] and the wooden cross to be found in the Jordan, at the site of Christ's baptism.[83]

As has often been remarked, there is nothing in the written record to indicate that there were 'preaching' or 'market' crosses in the middle-Saxon period. Clearly, some crosses were foci for private devotion and for acts of penitence. Otherwise those that we have been discussing appear first and foremost as markers of events: of Christ's baptism and crucifixion, of moments in the lives of saints, and of places of rest on long journeys. There is also a strong association with death, translation and burial. The cross on Golgotha could fit into this last category, and so very clearly do those marking the resting places of Bonitus and Ansbert in Francia, and the washing of Wilfrid's body at Oundle in England. Cuthbert wished to be buried next to his cross on Farne. According to Æthelwulf's *De abbatibus*, Sigwine was buried next to the cross he erected. Although the monument at Bewcastle may not have had a cross-head at the moment of its production and first use, the inscription, with its apparent reference to 'this token of victory' and its list of names, together with what may have been an adjoining burial, would seem to suggest some commemorative or funerary function, and to relate it to the 'pyramids' recorded at Glastonbury, Canterbury and elsewhere in the eleventh century. Taken together, the written evidence reveals the stone or wooden cross to be a remarkably fluid symbol, often marking stages of bodily or spiritual movement, progression, or liminal experience,[84] which also extends, particularly in the case of the cross on Golgotha, to being a focus of pilgrimage, which may have been yet another of the intersecting features which underpinned the popularity of the cross in Northumbria.

Ruthwell: the evidence of images

Some of these references to crosses in the written record may help in understanding the function of the monument at Bewcastle, while some may illuminate that at Ruthwell. For the monument at Ruthwell, however, our best evidence is the iconography of the monument itself, and what can be deduced of its meaning. Although the images illustrate various narratives, it is clear that the designer wished them to be considered in ways that were not merely illustrative of those narratives. Points of unnecessary detail are stripped out: the scene of the hermits Paul and Anthony has no raven (Fig. 56): it is far from clear that Joseph was ever portrayed in the Flight into or out of Egypt (Fig. 57), although he would appear to have been mentioned in the surrounding inscription. The implication would seem to be that the beholder is being asked to consider the inner meanings of the scenes, rather than their narrative content. In recent years more than one reading of the Ruthwell monument's sequence of images have been given, and it is perfectly possible, even likely, that more than one reading was intended. Indeed the monument would seem to be polysemous, deliberately open to different interpretations in different circumstances, at different times of the year. It could also have been reinterpreted by succeeding generations, as liturgical practices changed. It is, therefore, possible to offer more than one reading – and also to insist that yet other readings are likely. First, however, it is necessary to provide a brief description of the scenes on the main faces of the monument. The description considers the pinkish-grey lower stone first, moving from the ground upwards, before turning to the pale red upper stone. If the viewer were expected to bow before a cross, as is likely, he or she would naturally read it from bottom to top.

At the very bottom of the monument, on what is regarded as having originally been its east side, is a much worn image of the Crucifixion (Fig. 66). Above the arms of its cross are symbols of the sun and moon, while on either side of Christ two figures, possibly Stephaton and Longinus, can be made out. Stylistically the image would seem to be later than the others on the stone, and it is now regarded as being an addition. When it was added is a matter of guesswork.[85] Above the Crucifixion there is a depiction of the Annunciation (Fig. 65), in which Gabriel, with one hand raised, approaches the Virgin. The inscription, or *titulus*, surrounding the image is badly damaged. On the top the letters

... INGRESSVSANG*EL*??

are legible, while down the left side it is possible to read:

TEC??B*E* ...

The reference is clearly to Luke 1.28: 'And after he had gone up to her, the angel said: "Hail, full of grace; the Lord is with you; blessed are you among women."' *Et ingressus angelus ad eam dixit: ave gratia pleta: Dominus tecum: benedicta tu in mulieribus.*[86]

Above the Annunciation Christ is represented healing the blind man (Fig. 64). The scene has considerable energy as Christ leans forward. It is just possible to make out the remains of a rod with which he touches the blind man's eyes. Iconographically this looks back to a long tradition in which Christ was portrayed as a magician.[87] There is an extraordinary blank space in the bottom third of the panel, which has never been satisfactorily explained.

Is it unfinished? Or was something painted on to it? What remains of the surrounding inscription begins on the left:

+ETPRAETERIENS?VIDI...

It continues on the right:

ANATIBITATE?ETSA...

This seems to be derived from John 9.1: 'And passing by, he saw a man who had been blind from birth.' *Et praeteriens Iesus vidit hominem caecum a nativitate.*

The panel at the top of the lower stone represents Christ with the penitent woman, who is usually identified with Mary Magdalen (Fig. 63). Christ is portrayed frontally, with his right hand in a gesture of blessing, while in his covered left hand he holds a book (doubtless a Gospel book). Below is the Magdalen. We see only her upper body: head, right arm and hand. It is unclear whether she is kneeling at Christ's feet, or whether she is standing and he is raised high above her. She dries his feet with her long hair. The carving of Christ seems to be very much more finished than that of the Magdalen, whose arms and hair in particular are represented simply and boldly, some would say crudely. Is the image of the sinner deliberately portrayed as being less perfect than that of Christ? Or is the carving of the Magdalen unfinished? One should perhaps compare the blank space at the bottom of the panel of Christ and the Blind Man. Like the blank space in that scene, the apparently inchoate representation of the penitent occupies a third of the panel. Do we have an indication that the carvers worked from the top of each scene downwards? Were these particular scenes conceived sectionally and divided into thirds? In each of them Christ's head and arms are represented in the top third, while the middle is filled with the folds of garments. The inscription on the scene of the Magdalen begins at the top:

+ATTVL????ABA

it continues down the right side:

STRVM·VNGVENTI·&STANSRETROSECUSPEDES

then on the left:

EIVSLACRIMIS·COEPITRIGARE·PEDESEIVS?&CAPILLIS.

and concludes at the bottom:

CAPITISSVITERGEBA

The quotation is derived from Luke 7.37–8: a woman who was a sinner 'brought an alabaster box of ointment, and stood at His feet behind Him weeping and began to wash His feet with her tears, and wiped them with the hair of her head' *Et ecce mulier, quae erat in civitate peccatrix, ut cognovit quod accubuisset in domo pharisaei, attulit alabastrum unguenti; et stans retro secus pedes eius, lacrymis coepit rigare pedes eius, et capillis capitis sui tergebat.*

The bottom scene of the opposite, west, side shows Mary, sitting on a donkey (Fig. 57). As in numerous Byzantine images, she was probably presented sidesaddle, facing the onlooker, and holding Christ. In front of the donkey there is a bulge in the stone, which may be the remains of a representation of Joseph, although it is easier to see it as a tree. The damaged *titulus*, however, would seem to have referred to Joseph. Along the top of the scene it is possible to make out:

+MARIA·ETIO ...

and along the left side:

·TV ...

The words have been reconstructed to mean 'Mary and Joseph retreated to Egypt by way of the desert', or 'Mary and Joseph left Egypt by way of the desert', which may include an allusion to either Matthew 2.13–14 or Matthew 2.19. Scholars have debated whether the panel represents the Flight into, or out of, Egypt, on the grounds of the direction in which the donkey is facing.[88] In the *Libri Carolini*, written between 790 and 793, Theodulf of Orleans commented that 'the same blessed Virgin, is portrayed, as she travelled down to Egypt, or as she returned from Egypt to the land of Israel, borne on an ass, carrying a child in her arms, with Joseph in front'.[89] He noted that the image was to be found not only in basilicas but also on plates and in cups, on silk clothes and even on blankets.

Immediately above is a non-Biblical panel, showing two figures breaking bread (Fig. 56). Iconographically the image would seem to have been derived from that of the so-called *Concordia Apostolorum*, a representation of saints Peter and Paul.[90] The *titulus*, however, shows that another Paul is intended. As Theodulf also pointed out in the *Libri Carolini*, words could be crucial for the identification of a scene.[91] The inscription begins at the top:

+SCS·PAVLVS.

It continues on the right:

ET·A ...

and concludes on the left:

FREGER V?T·PANEMINDESERTO

The sentence has been reconstructed as saying: 'Saint Paul and Anthony, two hermits, broke bread in the desert.'[92] The scene, then, represents a moment in Jerome's *Life of St Paul, the First Hermit*, when Anthony visited him, and the two broke bread together.

The top panel of this side, which we have already analysed in some detail in Chapter 4, shows Christ standing on the snouts of two animals whose paws cross (Fig. 55). He is represented frontally, again with his right hand raised in blessing, but with his left hand clutching a scroll or perhaps even a *mappa* – the object used to start the consular games. Indeed, it is possible that a consular diptych has been used as a resource in the construction of the image.[93] The scene is often likened to its equivalent on Bewcastle, although it differs in many points of detail, not least the drapery of Christ's garments. The beasts are also different from their counterparts on Bewcastle, where much less of their bodies is portrayed. Again, the Ruthwell panel (though not that at Bewcastle) can be split up into thirds, with Christ's head and arms occupying the top, his garments the middle, and his feet and the beasts the lower section. As on the panel of the Magdalen, the bottom third seems less finished than does the image of Christ, although here we may be dealing with wear on the stone. The *titulus*, while Biblical in phraseology, seems not to come from any particular verse of the Bible. It is also strangely laid out, with its text shifting from the right-hand border to the left hand and back again, in the middle of a word. Starting at the top, it reads:

IHSXPS

it continues on the right side:

IVDEX:AEQVITATIS·

and then on the left:

BESTIAE·ET·DRACONES·COGNOUERVNT·INDE

before returning to the right:

SERTO·SALVAꝐOREM·MVNDI·

Fortunately the inscription is more or less complete. It is, therefore, possible to translate it: 'Jesus Christ, Judge of justice. Beasts and dragons acknowledged in the desert the Saviour of the world.' Clearly neither the image nor the *titulus* refers to the Lord trampling on the asp and the basilisk, the lion and the serpent, as in Psalm 90.13 (*Super aspidem et basiliscum ambulabis, et conculcabis leonem et draconem*), of which there are numerous representations.[94] There is no hint that the beasts are being trampled on, nor are they evil. Their function is to recognise the Lord: *cognoverunt*. Mark 1.13 may be relevant: 'And he was there in the wilderness forty days, tempted of Satan; and was with the wild beasts.' *Et erat in deserto quadraginta diebus, et quadraginta noctibus: et tentabatur a Satana: eratque cum bestiis.* Again, however, there is no hint that the animals recognised Christ. The echoes of the Canticle of Habbakuk may be stronger (3.2: in the pre-Vulgate version of the Latin Bible, the *Vetus Latina*): 'Between two living beings you will become known.' *In medio duorum animalium innotesceris.*[95] It is also possible that an onlooker would have recalled to mind a passage in the *Life of Cuthbert*: after the saint had walked into the sea, and then returned to pray on the shore, 'immediately there followed in his footsteps two little sea animals, humbly prostrating themselves on the earth; and licking his feet, they rolled upon him, wiping him with their skins and warming them with their breath'.[96] In Bede's version they are explicitly called otters, *lutraeae*.[97]

We turn now to the pale red upper stone. The main panel on one side shows two figures embracing (Fig. 61). Iconographically this image has a long history, which includes the sculptures from around 300 of Diocletian and his imperial colleagues, known as the Porphyry Tetrarchs, once in

Constantinople and now in Venice, as well as much more humdrum mass-produced terracottas of an embracing couple.[98] In Christian iconography the image is normally associated with the Visitation: the meeting of the Virgin and Elizabeth, after the Annunciation. Both women were pregnant, Mary with Christ, and Elizabeth with John the Baptist, who 'leaped' in his mother's womb (Luke 1.41). As in the case of the image of Paul and Anthony, however, the *titulus* indicates that a different scene is being represented. And here Theodulf's words are all the more telling:

> When man sees an image of a beautiful women with a little boy in her arms, if no inscription was ever carved or, having been carved, if it had been destroyed for some reason or other, how can we tell whether it is Sara holding Isaac, Rebecca bearing Jacob, Bathsheba showing off Solomon, Elizabeth carrying John, or some other woman with her child? And if we turn to pagan myths, which we often find portrayed, how can we know whether it is Venus holding Aeneas, Alcmena carrying Hercules or Andromache with Astyanax.[99]

Elsewhere in his argument Theodulf also raises the question of what a man should do when faced with an image which has lost its inscription. Should he destroy it as being Venus, or preserve it as being Mary?[100] Fortunately something does survive of the Ruthwell inscription relating to the panel which represents two women greeting. It is in a mixture of runic and Roman letters, and reads, on the right side:

+dominnæc

on the left:

marþa

and on the top:

mari?m?

There have been various attempts to interpret these letters. The two names, however, are clearly those of Mary and Martha. It is intriguing that here Mary and Martha are named, while the iconography suggests Mary and Elizabeth, just as on the image of the hermits Paul and Anthony are named, although the iconography is that of Peter and Paul. The designer or designers would seem to have used name-association in their search for images appropriate to their subjects. Thus Mary and Elizabeth are changed for (a different) Mary and Martha, while Peter and Paul are changed for (a different) Paul and Anthony.[101]

On the other side there is a scene which is now generally understood as John the Baptist holding the Lamb of God (Fig. 54), although it has also been plausibly interpreted as an apocalyptic *Maiestas*.[102] Like that of Christ on the Beasts, it is also found on the Bewcastle monument. The *titulus* is very badly damaged, but on the left side the letters:

... DORAMVS

and on the bottom:

VTNONCVM

can be made out. These have been radically expanded to mean: 'We worship the Lamb of God, and not him alone but the whole Trinity.'[103] So much of this is hypothetical that it is dangerous to extrapolate from it.

As for the cross-head, on one side – above Mary and Martha – it boasts an image of an archer (Fig. 61), which can also be found on the coinage of the period.[104] The middle of the cross and the arms are substitutes commissioned by the Reverend Henry Duncan. At the top, above the archer, was an image of an eagle (Fig. 53), although the uppermost stone, as now reconstructed, is back-to-front. What currently appears above the archer is an image of a man and a bird, obviously intended to represent St John and his symbol. This image properly belongs directly above that of two figures, representing St Matthew and his symbol. In other words, we can be sure that on one side the arms of the cross-head carried representations of the other two Evangelists: Luke with his bull, and Mark with his lion. What went on the cross arms above the archer is unknown.

It has been noted that it is possible to give a very straightforward reading of the cross as an illustration of the Christian and monastic life, *ecclesia* and *vita monastica*.[105] There is much to be said for being straightforward. Taking the imagery of the pinkish-grey lower stone first, and leaving on one side the Crucifixion as a later addition (albeit one that is not incompatible with the overall scheme), it can be read thus: the Annunication, with its *titulus* derived from Luke 1.28, marks the introduction of the Word of God; the Healing of the Blind Man, with an inscription alluding to John 9.1, indicates understanding of the Word; the scene of the Magdalen, with its accompanying words referring to Luke 7.37–38, then shows ensuing penitence.[106] All these images thus mark a growing commitment to Christianity: they have plausibly been seen as representing the Church, *ecclesia*.

On the opposite side there is the Flight into, or out of, Egypt. Above that there is the meeting of the hermits Paul and Anthony, and their breaking of bread together. Higher still is an image of Christ adored by beasts. As both Saxl and Schapiro observed in the 1940s, an obvious unifying feature of all these panels is the desert,[107] and indeed the word *desertum* appears in the left-hand border of the images of Paul and Anthony and Christ on the Beasts, where the designer has even gone to the trouble of breaking the order of words to achieve the desired effect. Perhaps the word *desertum* was also to be found in the left-hand border of the Flight into/out of Egypt, which is now illegible: the two Biblical passages which have been adduced as possible resources for the *titulus* both include it. Since the desert can easily be understood as representing the monastic life, this second side can be seen as constituting a statement of the *vita monastica*.

This reading can be extended to the top stone, even though there has also been debate as to which way round it was originally placed.[108] In the traditional reconstruction the image above the scene of Christ and the Magdalen has two female figures facing each other. As we have seen, the iconography is unquestionably that of Visitation, but the fragmentary inscription clearly names Mary and Martha rather than the Virgin and Elizabeth.[109] It may well be that an allusion to the Visitation was intended, and indeed a scriptural passage relating to Mary and Martha was read at the Feast of the Dormition of the Virgin.[110] None the less, the importance of inscriptions in the identification of images is clear from Theodulf's comments in the *Libri Carolini*, and, since the inscription directs the reader to understand the image as Mary and Martha, this must be the prior (if less sophisticated) reading.[111] In any case, Mary and Martha standing for the two classic types of Christian Life, contemplative and active,[112] provide a satisfying conclusion to the sequence of images illustrating entry into the Church, and at the same time serve to direct the viewer to the other side, the monastic face of the monument. The panel on the side opposite that of Mary and Martha is usually thought to represent John the Baptist. Associated as he is with the wilderness, John makes a fitting addition to the desert iconography of the monastic face of the monument. The alternative reading of the scene as a *Maiestas* does not fit so neatly with a monastic interpretation, although it could be understood as a culmination of the whole programme.

Above the image of Mary and Martha, at the base of the cross-head, there is the image of an archer (Fig. 61), while at the very apex of the Cross is an image of an eagle (Fig. 53), which is probably to be read as an image of Christ.[113] The archer has caused a good deal of bewilderment, for typologically the image could refer either to a preacher or to the devil.[114] It has even been seen as a secular figure, analogous to the falconer on Bewcastle.[115] There are obvious attractions in seeing the image as referring to the preacher: would one really put a representation of evil so close to the boss of the cross? On the other hand, it may be that discussion has been too limited. The archer could be taken to refer to one of the Old English inscriptions in the borders of one of the monument's narrow sides. There we find that the Cross was 'wounded with arrows'. Arrows, of course, are unbiblical, with regard to the Crucifixion: although his side was pierced by a spear, no one shot Christ on the Cross. We may wish to see the word as an elaborate metonym for nails. Whoever was responsible for designing the upper stone, may, however, have decided to take the image literally: and arrows presuppose an archer.[116] The presence of the archer could, therefore, be a very sophisticated means of drawing not only the upper and lower stones together, but also of integrating the sides, with their inhabited plant-scrolls and runic inscriptions, to the faces with the figure panels. If one sees the archer in this light, one might go further and suggest that he is shooting upwards, over the cross, and by implication directing the viewer to the other side. Equivalent visual signposting may be present on another work of Northumbrian provenance, the Franks Casket, where a bird seems to direct the viewer from the image of the Virgin and Child on the front of the box anticlockwise to the left-hand end. One might also wonder if it is mere coincidence that an archer is shooting his arrow straight into what was once the handle of the casket's lid.

It is, then, perfectly easy to find a programme which unites the two stones of the Ruthwell monument. Mary and Martha on the one side and the Baptist on the other can be seen as completing the sequence of images on the lower stone, while the archer can be seen as further holding the programme together. If the monument were placed within a church one might go further and hypothesise that the side presenting *ecclesia* was set facing the laity, while that presenting *vita monastica* was visible to clergy or religious. Not only is there a thematic coherence. There is a recurrence of certain intellectual tricks. We have noted that, just as iconography usually associated with Peter and Paul is applied to Paul and Anthony, so too that of Mary and Elizabeth in the Visitation is re-employed for Mary and Martha. It is, thus, quite possible that one designer conceived the whole scheme. However, there are some indications that the upper stone was carved later, and these are not only to do with the technical differences between the carvings of the two stones discussed in Chapter 4. In particular, the *titulus* relating to Mary and Martha, unlike all the other *tituli*, is in a mixture of Roman and runic letters. If the suggestion that some panels on the lower stone are unfinished is accepted, it may be that we have evidence for interruption in the production of the monument. The upper stone might have been carved when work was resumed. How long that interruption might have lasted can only be guessed at. It might not have been long before the programme was resumed: it might have been a generation or more. There is no way of telling.

On the other hand, it is possible to argue not only that production on the lower stone was interrupted but also that the upper stone, when it was added, marked an extension to what was originally conceived of as a decorated column. It is, perhaps significant that the two main scenes on the top stone have both posed problems of identification, whereas on the lower stone only the images of Paul and Anthony and of Christ on the Beasts would have been hard to identify without their *tituli* – and both those images are to be found on the more spiritually advanced monastic face of the monument. As we have already noted, the image of Christ on the Beasts and that of the Baptist (or *Maiestas*) also appear at Bewcastle. Indeed the scenes are placed in the same relationship one to another, with the Baptist above Christ on the Beasts. This raises the issue of which monument was produced first and whether the one served as a resource for the other. There is no way of knowing, but, if the upper stone on the Ruthwell monument were an addition to the lower, one might argue that the arrangement at Bewcastle was deliberately being replicated. Originally the Ruthwell monument had one of the scenes which was represented on the monument at Bewcastle: subsequently a second was added. Whether or not the lower stone at Ruthwell was earlier than the monument at Bewcastle, the upper stone would then be later. According to this reading, as one of a number of possible chronological hypotheses, one could envisage the lower stone being carved during the lifetime of Bede or Alcuin: the Bewcastle monument being set up in the early ninth century (if Hwætred is the abbot named in the *Liber vitae* of Durham), and the Ruthwell monument being completed only a few decades before the Viking takeover of York in 867. One might also note that the addition of Mary and Martha significantly alters the proportion of women represented on the monument, and that this might point to a change in the type of community at Ruthwell.[117] Was Ruthwell transformed from being a male to being a female house?

There are examples of such changes in the history of Northumbrian monasticism.[118] These hypotheses deserve an airing, though it would be wrong to use them as the basis for any further argument.

Ruthwell and the theological debates of the seventh and eighth centuries

The straightforward categorisation of the iconography as indicating the Christian Church and the desert is only a beginning when it comes to reading the Ruthwell monument. There are clearly more, and more complex, ways of understanding the iconography.[119] The *tituli* invite theological reading, and indeed they have often been understood in the light of Bede's biblical commentaries.[120] Some of the interpretations offered by modern scholars relate to theological debates that had specific importance in the late seventh and eighth centuries. The *Agnus Dei* panel has been linked to the fact that the so-called Quinisext Council, held in Constantinople in 692, condemned the representation of Christ as a lamb. In reaction Pope Sergius refused to comply with imperial legislation.[121] He may have restored images in which Christ was represented as the lamb,[122] and he instituted the singing of the *Agnus Dei* antiphon at the moment of the breaking of the host in the Mass.[123] That the representation of the *Agnus Dei* at Ruthwell and at Bewcastle in some way reflects the liturgical innovation made by Pope Sergius is possible, though the iconography of the lamb was much older than the seventh century: indeed it is common on late Roman sarcophagi and in the fifth- and sixth-century mosaics of Ravenna and Rome.[124] The image, therefore, is no proof of a direct link between Sergius's introduction of the chant into the Mass and the iconography of the monuments at Ruthwell and Bewcastle. And even if the presence of the *Agnus Dei* in the iconographic programmes were inspired by the inclusion of the chant in the Mass, that is no reason to think that the sculptors of either monument were responding to a recent papal initiative.

Equally problematic is the suggestion that the runic account of Christ's ascent of the Cross – 'Almighty God unclothed himself when he wished to climb the gallows' – should be understood in the context of the debate over monotheletism in the late seventh and early eighth centuries.[125] Monotheletism, the doctrine that Christ only had one, divine, will, was issued in 638 by the Emperor Heraclius, as an attempt to solve the theological divisions afflicting the Byzantine Empire at the time of the Arab invasions of Syria and Palestine. It was rejected, in the West notably by Maximus Confessor and Pope Martin, not least because it suggested that Christ had no independent human will. The debate continued through the seventh century and into the eighth. It impinged most directly on the Anglo-Saxon Church in 679 when the issue was considered at the Council of Hatfield, where Pope Agatho was seeking support for his own anti-monothelete stance, prior to the sixth ecumenical council in 680–681. The visit to England of John the Roman Archcantor, who was to teach singing and the liturgy at Wearmouth, was primarily concerned with gaining support for the papal position at the time of the council of Hatfield.[126] Moreover, while John was at Wearmouth, a copy

of the anti-monothelete canons of Pope Martin was made for the monastery.[127] We can, therefore, reckon that the Northumbrian Church was well
aware of the monothelete heresy and the problems it posed.

The images of the Ruthwell monument can certainly be read as presenting
Christ both as God and incarnate as a human being, but this scarcely amounts
to an anti-monothelete statement: rather it reflects Chalcedonian orthodoxy,
that Christ had two natures. The vernacular runic inscriptions, however, only
draw attention to one and not two wills, in the phrase 'he wished to climb the
gallows'. Since Christ is explicitly described as Almighty God, only his divine
will is in question: his human will is not being considered. Indeed, Éamonn
Ó Carragáin has rightly remarked that the inscription comes close to the
heresy of patripassianism – the heresy which saw God himself as suffering
on the cross.[128] The runic inscriptions actually come nearer to presenting a
monothelete statement than a contradiction of the heresy. We can probably
conclude that the monothelete debate had no significant bearing on the
iconography of Ruthwell.

Ruthwell and the rites of the church

Interpreters of the Ruthwell monument have turned not only to theology
but also to the related evidence of the liturgy. Certain ritual themes are
immediately suggested by the images. The Healing of the Blind Man, while
representing an initial understanding of Christianity, can also be seen more
specifically as referring to the ceremony of the *Apertio Aurium*, literally the
'Opening of the Ears', a rite of doctrinal explanation undergone by catechu-
mens in the Lenten period before they received baptism.[129] The Magdalen
can easily be read as alluding to penitential practice.[130] Much of the desert
imagery, above all the breaking of the bread by Paul and Anthony and, as we
have seen, the Baptist's presentation of the Lamb of God can be read as being
Eucharistic.[131] So too, can the image of Christ recognised by the beasts, if its
titulus is understood to refer to the Canticle of Habbakuk, for the Canticle was
sung on days associated with the crucifixion and death of Christ.[132] A Eucharistic reading is especially helpful in drawing the sides of the monument into
a relationship with the figure panels. The True Vine, which is surely what is
represented by the inhabited plant-scrolls on Ruthwell, is an obvious reference to the wine of communion, while the animals devouring the grapes
might be seen as representing the elect.[133] When we add the runic inscriptions, with their description of the Crucifixion, we have a programme that is
easily read in terms of Carolingian theology: 'A large amount of the ninth-
century literature that dwells on the crucified Christ's torments or sacrifice
ties them to penance, the mass, or the eucharist.'[134]

Ruthwell and the Roman liturgy

Much less clear is the extent to which a liturgical reading of the Ruthwell
monument should make reference to papal changes made to the Roman
liturgy in the course of the seventh century. That some of these innovations
were known about in Northumbria is certain. John the Archcantor, who

accompanied Benedict Biscop back from Rome to England in 679, primarily in order to attend the Council of Hatfield, also stayed on to teach chant
and liturgical practice to the monks of Wearmouth.[135] A third member of the
party was Ceolfrith, who would be the first abbot of Jarrow, which had yet
to be founded. Since John was in charge of the liturgical arrangements at
St Peter's, he could well have introduced the community of Wearmouth to
any new developments in the various papal or presbyteral liturgies in Rome.
Bede, indeed, says that

> he taught the cantors of the monastery the order and manner of singing
> and reading aloud and also committed to writing all things necessary for
> the celebration of festal days throughout the whole year; these writings have
> been preserved to this day in the monastery and copies have now been made
> by many others elsewhere. Not only did John instruct the brothers in this
> monastery, but all who had any skill in singing flocked in from almost all the
> monasteries in the kingdom to hear him, and he had many invitations to teach
> elsewhere.[136]

Certainly, then, the opportunity existed for any liturgical innovations made
by the papacy prior to 679 to be introduced into Wearmouth, and indeed into
any Northumbrian monastery.

John, arriving in 679, cannot have been a conduit for the liturgical
reforms of Pope Sergius (687–701). These not only specified that the *Agnus
Dei* should be sung during the Mass but also made special provision for
four established feasts, the Presentation in the Temple, the Annunciation,
the Dormition and the Nativity of the Virgin, which were later regarded as
Marian,[137] in addition to introducing veneration of the rediscovered the relic
of the True Cross into the Feast of the Elevation of the Cross.[138] Since all
these innovations are mentioned in the *Liber pontificalis*, we can be sure
that there was knowledge of them in Northumbria. As we have already
noted, the iconography of the Ruthwell and Bewcastle monuments could
suggest an awareness of the introduction of the *Agnus Dei* chant into the
Mass, although it does not have to. Marian devotion has been noted in the
Lindisfarne Gospels.[139] Scholars have drawn attention to a number of indications that the eighth-century Anglo-Saxon Church celebrated the so-called
Marian feasts.[140] Although there is very little to suggest that many communities celebrated the full set of feasts in pre-Viking England,[141] the Metrical
Calendar of York does include the Purification, Annunciation, Assumption
and Nativity of the Virgin.[142] Four Marian feasts are also mentioned in the *De
abbatibus* of Æthelwulf, although there is some debate as to which four were
intended.[143] Perhaps more important, Æthelwulf suggests that Abbot Sigbald
(d. 771), who introduced the feasts in the third quarter of the eighth century
had some difficulties in persuading the monks to accept them.

The iconography of the Ruthwell monument has been read as reflecting
special reverence for the Virgin. There is good evidence to show that 25 March
was regarded as the date at which the Annunciation and the Crucifixion took
place,[144] and it is likely that an educated onlooker could have connected the
Annunciation panel with the overall idea of the cross. He or she might also
have recognised in the iconography of the Visitation, used in the scene of

Mary and Martha, a reference to the conception of John the Baptist, which itself links to the conception of Christ. In addition, since the account of Mary and Martha in Luke 10.38–42 was a possible lection for the Feast of the Dormition, a viewer well versed in liturgy could have made a connection with the cult of the Virgin.[145] The iconography, however, does not prove that the images were chosen because of the cult: it merely shows that awareness of the cult would give them a specific meaning.

We should be careful to distinguish between clear evidence that the Roman liturgy had been used as a resource, and the possibility of interpreting iconographic or ecclesiastical evidence retrospectively in the light of Roman liturgical texts. Unfortunately our evidence for the performance of specific liturgical practices in Northumbria is both fragmentary and diffuse. There is little in the way of liturgical books.[146] Something may be deduced from the evidence relating to Northumbrians, such as Willibrord, on the continent.[147] Otherwise our information is largely made up of details of design and annotations in Gospel books. We do have the evidence of the Burchard Gospels, a '6th-century Italian Gospel book with late 7th or 8th-century Wearmouth–Jarrow annotations',[148] which reveals an awareness in Bede's monastery of readings used in the course of the Roman stational liturgy.[149] This is scarcely surprising: Wearmouth–Jarrow was the very place which preserved liturgical material in its archives from John the Archcantor. Yet, while there is also some evidence that a Roman lectionary of a type in use between the pontificates of Gregory I and Gregory II was consulted by the Wearmouth–Jarrow annotators, the basic liturgical calendar which can be reconstructed from the Burchard Gospels is not Roman but Neapolitan.[150] Bede's homilies also indicate that it was a Neapolitan pericope that was used at Wearmouth–Jarrow.[151] These points, and other indications in Bede's martyrology, might suggest that the liturgy at Bede's monastery was influenced above all by Archbishop Theodore (668–690) and Hadrian, who accompanied him to England to become abbot of Saints Peter and Paul, Canterbury.[152] Hadrian had been an abbot in the Naples region.[153] Benedict Biscop set out with the two of them on their journey from Rome to England in 668–669,[154] six years before the foundation of Wearmouth. Biscop might well have followed Neapolitan practice having learnt it from Hadrian. The impression that Bede and others give of Rome as the fount of liturgical practice is likely to be the result of 'the rhetoric of Roman unity and liturgical community'.[155]

The feasts of the Cross in Northumbria

Taken together, the indications that we have for liturgical practice in eighth-century Northumbria suggest considerable diversity.[156] The various liturgies in use in Rome provided one set of resources, but so too did those in use elsewhere in Italy, in Francia and indeed in other parts of England. As Bede tells us, John was by no means the only expert in chant to spend time in Northumbria. 'With the exception of James (the Deacon) ... the first singing master in the Northumbrian churches was Æddi surnamed Stephen, who was invited from Kent by the most worthy Wilfrid.'[157] Stephanus mentions Eona as another singer brought back by Wilfrid to Northumbria.[158] Bede also relates that Acca, who was himself a 'musician of great experience', 'invited a famous singer, Maban, who had been instructed in methods of singing by the successors of the disciples of St. Gregory in Kent, to teach him and his people; he kept him for twelve years teaching them such church music as they did not know, while the music which they once knew and which had begun to deteriorate by long use or by neglect was restored to its original form'.[159]

If we turn specifically to the cult of the Cross, we find evidence once again of numerous liturgical resources, some of which were Roman, but others not. Two feasts of the Cross were celebrated in the West. Pope Sergius had his recently found relic of the Cross displayed on the Feast of the *Exaltatio*. A Feast of the Discovery of the Cross (*Inventio*) was celebrated in the seventh-century Gallican liturgy, on 3 May, as required by the legend of the *Inventio Sanctae Crucis*.[160] This second feast would appear to be a Merovingian innovation, since it appears in the Bobbio Missal:[161] it was certainly not a Roman feast in origin, and does not appear in the so-called *Hadrianum*, the Roman Gregorian Sacramentary sent to Charlemagne.[162] A celebration in May is also indicated in Cynewulf's *Elene*.[163] There was, therefore, more than one feast of the Cross, and it is clear that the Frankish feast of the *Inventio* was celebrated in pre-Viking England: the *Exaltatio* is less in evidence. Cynewulf's poem might, however, be no more than evidence that the ninth-century Mercian Church knew of the Gallican Feast of the Invention of the Cross. How widespread either the *Inventio* or the *Exaltatio* was in eighth-century Northumbria, however, is a moot point. Although a Feast of the Cross is listed in the Burchard Gospels, it is again the Frankish *Inventio Crucis* (presumably the feast of 3 May), and not the *Exaltatio*.[164] So too, the Calendar of Willibrord – admittedly not a manuscript written in Northumbria, but certainly associated with a Northumbrian – lists only the *Inventio*.[165] Michael Lapidge's recent reconstruction of a Latin *Vorlage* of the Old English Martyrology, which he ascribes to Acca of Hexham, also includes the *Inventio* but not the *Exaltatio*.[166] Yet when Charles Jones tried to establish a text for Bede's *Kalendarium*, he could find no reason to include either of the feasts of the Cross,[167] and his scepticism is supported by the absence of any appropriate Bedan homily.[168] Nor does MS Sangallensis 451, which Henri Quentin thought the best surviving witness to Bede's *Martyrology* ('le plus précieux exemplaire qui nous reste de l'œuvre de Bède'),[169] include the feast of the *Inventio* among the entries in its martyrology.[170] Unfortunately the text of the Sangallensis breaks off on 25 July (VIII Kl Aug): it therefore does not cover September, and the Feast of the Elevation.[171] The best one can say is that, if, as is likely, the *Inventio* was celebrated at Wearmouth–Jarrow in the early eighth century, the model behind the celebration is unlikely to have been Roman: indeed the inspiration was almost certainly Frankish. The Roman liturgy was probably not the most significant resource for the cult of the Cross in England: the evidence for Frankish influence is stronger.

If we turn from the evidence of Bede at Wearmouth–Jarrow to that of Alcuin at York, we find yet more silence. Unfortunately what may prove to be the key text, Alcuin's *De laude Dei*, has yet to be published in full.[172] Among the texts from the single manuscript of the work that have been published are a collection of antiphons, which the editor has suggested were those introduced to Wearmouth–Jarrow by John the Archcantor.[173] None of the chants is for either the *Inventio* or the *Elevatio* of the Cross. Alcuin did compose a *Missa de Sancta Cruce*, though apparently this was not intended for the Feast of either the Invention or the Exaltation.[174] It would seem to have been written for the *Adoratio Crucis* on Good Friday.[175] For his Mass, moreover, while he did draw on a liturgy of the *Exaltatio*, it was not that of Sergius, but one drawn from an earlier Mass set.[176] Of course, Alcuin is likely to have composed his Mass at Tours rather than in York: his *Missa de Sancta Croce* may not have been celebrated in Northumbria. Tours itself had once been a place of liturgical innovation. It has even been seen as a source for liturgical development in Rome.[177] No feast of the Cross is included in the Metrical Calendar of York, which has been seen as the work of one of Alcuin's successors as master of the school.[178] Although Bede's accounts of John the Archcantor and Pope Sergius may lead us to expect to find strong evidence for Roman influence underlying the cult of the Cross in late seventh- and eighth-century Northumbria, that evidence does not seem to be forthcoming. Indeed, it is not clear that either of the feasts of the Cross was generally celebrated in the northern kingdom.

There is no evidence for the liturgical cult of the Cross from eighth-century England to compare with that of the Sacramentary of Gellone, an eighth-century Gelasian sacramentary (that is, a Frankish sacramentary of a type devised for the Frankish Church later in the reign of Pippin III (751–768),[179] written probably at Meaux in Francia, between 790 and 804.[180] The manuscript boasts a remarkable representation of the crucified Christ, with quantities of blood streaming from his side.[181] Also, the initial for the liturgy of the *Inventio Crucis* on 3 May marks out the feast with a representation of the Jew Judas-Cyriacus digging for the three crosses on Golgotha.[182]

Reading silence

Of course, evidence for eighth- and early ninth-century Northumbria is fragmentary and incomplete. A historian may choose either to ignore the gaps, as if they are not there, or to draw attention to them. If one takes the second course, the conflict between Bede's interest in John and Sergius, and the absence of material to prove that the papal liturgy was used as a resource for particular ceremonies at Wearmouth–Jarrow, becomes a point of significance, implying that pope and archcantor had less influence than Bede wished to imply, and that they never really challenged the variety that was a hallmark of pre-Carolingian liturgy and cult.[183] Indeed, the disjunction becomes one more indication of a slippage between actual liturgical practice and 'a created tradition, which validated the customs of the Anglo-Saxon Church by claiming their Roman descent'.[184]

This negative reading is of some importance in assessing the development of the cult of the Cross in Northumbria. Just as the popularity of the form of the Cross in the region cannot be adequately accounted for by the story of Oswald at Heavenfield, or by tales of Constantine, so too it cannot be ascribed to the impact of papal activity. All three factors are likely to have played a part, as may accounts of visits to the Holy Land, such as that set down by Adomnan, whose importance is clear from the fact that it was reworked by Bede. Indeed, one may suspect that there was a considerable wish to recreate within the liturgy of individual monasteries and churches the sites of Christ's life for those who could never go on pilgrimage. But again, our sources allow us to do no more than hypothesise.

The absence of any clearly dominant factor explaining the Northumbrian cross may, however, itself be important. Various forces contributed to the popularity of crosses, or of monuments which were intended to be seen and understood as crosses, even if they were incised slabs or obelisks. We have noted a number of likely factors. One might add the existence of crosses in other media: the silver cross carried by Augustine as he went to meet Æthelberht, which Bede thought fit to record,[185] or the images of crosses in Insular, especially Northumbrian, Gospel books, which are certainly another example of the increasing significance of the cross as symbol. Perhaps most important, all these influences seem to have been in play in the early eighth century, at precisely the time that art historians are now inclined to place the initial development of the stone cross, on grounds of style.

At this point one should also return to certain aspects of the frames of reference which have already been discussed in Chapter 5: monasticism, and land-tenure, because they too are likely to have contributed to the flourishing of stone-carving, and in particular, the Northumbrian cross. Indeed, we are dealing with a period when a whole set of social and economic factors intersected to determine the production of Anglo-Saxon stone sculpture. Although not all of the surviving Anglian sculpture of the pre-Viking period should be associated with monasteries,[186] and indeed our fullest description, that of the *Hodoeporicon*, shows that crosses could be found on secular estates,[187] it is likely that a good proportion of the material was monastic in origin. Known monastic sites boast some of the most important collections of pre-Viking sculpture. Other sites which are not known from the written record to have been monastic may be argued to have been monasteries because their monuments boast certain iconographic or liturgical features. The sundial on the Bewcastle monument, and the complexity of the iconography on the Ruthwell monument, as well as its desert imagery, would seem to identify both sites as monastic, although as we have seen in Chapter 5 the term 'monastery' in the early eighth century might cover a wide range of institutions.

Exactly how a community of monks or nuns, or both, might have used the monument at Ruthwell is a matter of guesswork. The literary sources we have already examined suggest that crosses were foci for prayer,[188] and this could easily have been the case at Ruthwell. To prayer one might add a more general practice of contemplation, which the iconography of the monument would certainly have facilitated.[189] Indeed, the theological sophistication of the

Ruthwell monument demands thought. As we have already seen, the image of the Magdalen might indicate that it was a focus for penitence, whether private or institutional, just as the cross at Stablo was the site of Lambert's penances.[190] The monument at Ruthwell is rather less likely to have provided a focus for any regular outdoor celebration of the Mass. First, no one has yet pointed to evidence which proves that crosses were so intended or used (although a priest with a portable altar might easily have chosen to celebrate before a cross).[191] Second, the remaining fragment of Anglian architectural sculpture (Fig. 73) on display in Ruthwell parish church suggests that there was a stone building in the vicinity by the ninth or tenth century.[192] Since there are no indications of its foundations in aerial photographs, one must assume that it lay on the same spot as the current church[193] (which was largely rebuilt by Reverend Henry Duncan in the nineteenth century), or nearby in the cemetery. At Ruthwell, after the original church had been built[194] there would have been no need to celebrate the Mass in front of the monument, unless, that is, the cross is to be seen as part of the internal decoration of the church itself, in which case the celebrant could have stood before it, just as priests stood before the mosaic images of crosses which adorn the apses of such Roman churches as Santa Pudenziana and Santo Stephano Rotondo. The positioning of a cross between the lay and monastic congregation may be attested by the ninth-century Plan of St Gall.[195]

In considering the Ruthwell and other monuments as likely to have been monastic, there is a more general point to be made. The development and increase of monasticism in Northumbria in the late seventh and eighth centuries can itself be seen as a cause of the growing popularity of the idea of the Cross and of the production of stone crosses. Certainly the earliest monasteries, notably Lindisfarne, go back to the first half of the seventh century, and the foundations of Wilfrid and Biscop in the 670s and 680s show a growing enthusiasm for monastic foundation. The real escalation in the founding of monasteries, however, seems to have come slightly later. Or, at least, Bede saw the numbers of new monastic foundations as constituting a problem only after the beginning of the eighth century. In condemning the institution of 'bogus' monasteries, whereby families obtained land in perpetuity, supposedly to found religious houses, Bede dates the beginnings of the practice to the reign of Osred (706–716). By implication, the early eighth century saw a major increase in monastic foundation. While condemning the family monasteries of this period, Bede does, however, seem to acknowledge that they did celebrate the liturgy. Many of them, then, must have been properly functioning monasteries, with churches, and not merely secular scams which had no purpose other than the acquisition of land. But the erection of a stone monument, especially one with an inscription, is a comparatively durable way of marking one's claim, and that of one's family, to land.[196] It may be that some of these family monasteries had stone monuments, and that one should set the drive towards monastic foundation alongside the other factors that we have already seen as contributing to the popularity of the Northumbrian cross.

The desire to gain land for one's family to hold in perpetuity, which, as far as Bede was concerned, was the more disreputable aspect of the increase in monastic foundation, may have wider ramifications. A monastery, intended to be a permanent institution, would have played a major role in fixing and preserving family memory. Monks would have been expected to commemorate the founder of their house. At the same time, commemoration is an attested function of some early stone monuments. The Bewcastle monument, in particular, with its long commemorative inscription, needs to be seen in this frame of reference. Even if it lacked a cross-head at its moment of production, as a self-proclaimed 'token of victory' it presented itself as a cross, and could have been seen and used as such. Liturgical commemoration, of course, was not new, and in certain respects the commemorative inscription on the Bewcastle monument might be seen as having the same function as a diptych of names, or a *Liber vitae*.[197] Diptyches are attested in written sources from a much earlier date, and the Barberini diptych of the sixth century would seem to show evidence of having been used liturgically around the year 600.[198] So too, *Libri vitae*, which could be placed on the altar, are attested for earlier centuries, but it is worth emphasising that our earliest surviving examples are of the eighth century.[199] An interest in commemoration seems to have escalated in the same period as the stone cross came to the fore.

But the acquisition of land for the purpose of founding monasteries implies something more: the availability of wealth and resources. In short, the circumstances of production changed. Warriors were being given the chance to acquire property for their families in perpetuity. Land was the prime source of power and wealth. Wealth, obtained in order to found a monastery, gave the founder the wherewithal to build churches and to commission monuments – some of them commemorating members of the family. Economic and social change is as important as any spiritual or religious factor in the development of the Northumbrian Cross. It was this that made possible the flourishing of stone sculpture in Northumbria. The presence of stonemasons, whether brought in from the continent or trained in Northumbria, meant that wealth could be directed towards the commissioning of objects in stone, and the stories of Oswald and Constantine, as well as Sergius, may have ensured that the preferred form of monument was a cross, or something that could be so identified. This particular convergence of factors, which was not replicated elsewhere, would seem to provide the best answer to the question with which this chapter began, of why the stone cross seems to have become an especially common monument in eighth-century Northumbria.

Spiritual things/material things

⌘

Your holiness should, together with the most pious king, tear up the irreligious and wicked deeds and documents of earlier rulers of our people, and should provide in our land those things which are useful either to God or to lay society, lest in our times either religion come to an end, together with the love and fear of Him who sees within us, or with the diminishing of our military forces those who should defend our borders against barbarian incursions disappear. It is shocking to say how many places that go by the name of monasteries have been taken under the control of men who have no knowledge of true monastic life, with the result that there is nowhere that the sons of the nobles or retired soldiers can take possession of.

Bede, *Epistola ad Ecgbertum*[1]

At a certain stage of their development, the material productive forces of society come into conflict with the existing relations of production or – this merely expresses the same thing in legal terms – with the property relations within the framework of which they have operated hitherto. From forms of development of the productive forces these relations turn into their fetters. Then begins an era of social revolution. The changes in the economic foundation lead sooner or later to the transformation of the whole immense superstructure. In studying such transformations it is always necessary to distinguish between the material trans-formation of the economic conditions of production, which can be determined with the precision of natural science, and the legal, political, religious, artistic or philosophic – in short, ideological forms in which men become conscious of this conflict and fight it out.

Karl Marx, 'Preface', *A Contribution to the Critique of Political Economy*[2]

Our book, which began with 'place' and is based in and made of 'fragments', ends with that most fundamental difference of number and kind: class, the fragmentation of interest and places in society bound up with particular historical phases in the development of production. Until recently scholars considered that the surviving corpus of pre-Viking Anglo-Saxon stone sculpture, because it seems to have been produced at sites associated with 'religious communities', was best characterised as 'in some sense monastic' or as a 'monastic art',[3] but that view has to be modified by what we have come to understand about the character of Anglo-Saxon monasticism and by what we know about crosses sited in locations that were not in the strict sense monastic.

We know from Bede's letter to Ecgbert, which we considered in Chapter 5, that there were some monasteries which, as far as he was concerned, 'only in the most foolish way deserve the name of monastery, having absolutely nothing of real monastic life about them'.[4] He considered that these places were 'useless to God and man' because they 'neither serve God by following a regular monastic life nor provide soldiers and helpers for the secular powers'.[5] Bede was troubled. Nobles who had bought land from the king on the pretext of building monasteries, having obtained this land, with hereditary right by charters confirmed in writing, and freed from both military and divine service, whether tonsured or not, called themselves 'abbots' and served as laymen in charge of monks.[6] As far as he was concerned, the monks in these 'monasteries' were not genuine monks but monks who had been expelled from proper monasteries, camp followers and hangers on, 'cohorts of the deformed' who were occupied with their wives and children.[7] To make matters worse, some noblemen also obtained land for their wives to build monasteries who then authorised themselves 'spiritual guides to the handmaids of Christ'.[8] It is clear that Bede considered these monasteries bogus. He wanted them 'confined by the discipline of regular monastic life and expelled far beyond the borders of the holy Church by joint episcopal and conciliar authority', but saw little likelihood of this happening. The bishops themselves supported this way of establishing monasteries because they were driven by 'that same love of wealth that impelled the purchasers to buy such monasteries'.[9]

Bede was worried about the effect that the spread of monasticism was having on the numbers of warriors committed to military service. He'd registered his concern some three years before, towards the end of his *Historia ecclesiastica*. There, he went only so far as to comment that only the future would show what would be the result.[10] In his letter to Ecgbert he was more forthcoming about his anxieties. Increasing numbers of aristocrats were evading their military duties. In point of fact, so many young men were entering the regular, irregular and bogus monasteries that Bede feared the land north of the Humber would not be able to defend itself or its church against invasion by barbarians.[11] Also, the land pool had diminished to such an extent that there was insufficient land with which to reward veteran soldiers and gift the sons of warriors. They were leaving the kingdom travelling in search of, or to, more generous and congenial lords.[12] Though warriors must always have travelled outside their native kingdoms, some of them travelling abroad,[13] this migration must have been happening in larger numbers than usual for Bede to be worried about it.

The class that produced and first used Anglo-Saxon stone sculpture was the aristocracy. In Northumbria, in the late seventh century and eighth century that class, as it was in the rest of England, was developing into two blocs, factions and fractions within those factions: the military aristocracy, which it always had been, and a growing church aristocracy of bishops, abbots, priests and so on; each defining itself, making itself intelligible in relation to the other; each asserting its independence while at the same time acknowledging itself as the condition of the other's existence. It would be a mistake, however, to take the ways a class defines itself as nothing more than ideas, for ideas are but the consequences of material contradictions, specifically the different ways in which the material and mental productive forces within the aristocracy were coming into conflict with the existing relations and reproduction of the relations of production. As the new church aristocracy came to own more and more land, so the military aristocracy would have wanted more and more land to maintain the status quo. The church and military aristocracies both gained land but some of the latter held it under rights of tenure that applied to the former. The king lost land, the basis of everything, to both factions within the aristocracy. Whether or not the conversion to Christianity enlightened the Northumbrian darkness, it effected a change in the its economic basis and social relations of production, law and ideology. Bede's remarks in his letter to Ecgbert and in the *Ecclesiastical History* afford us a glimpse of the ways that, in eighth-century Northumbria, the burgeoning division between residual material and emergent mental forces of production within the aristocracy, both dependent on each other but somewhat different with regard to landed property, the labour force and the labour process, the extraction of surplus and what to do with it, have to be seen as antagonistic.

Bede's letter to Ecgbert indicates an exacerbated conflict within the church aristocracy, conflict within the military aristocracy, and conflict between the church and military aristocracies. He must be alluding to these conflicts at the end of the *Ecclesiastical History* when he writes that 'the outset and the course' of Ceowulf's reign has been 'filled with so many grave disturbances'.[4]

Unless the force of class intervenes so obviously in the process of history as it did with the plunder and settlement of England by the Vikings and then by the Normans, scholars of Anglo-Saxon stone sculpture usually overlook that their objects of study are the survivals of a particular class. The corpus of Anglo-Saxon stone sculpture was produced and first used by the class that owned or possessed the means of production, land and the productive force of peasants and slaves, that exploited the labour process and extracted surplus from it, a surplus that could also be taken by plunder and settlement: the aristocracy.

Bede's letter vividly records one aspect of the complexity of class: that there is never only one means of production in any society for individuals to possess or be denied. Any social formation will be a palimpsest of old and new modes of production, and hybrids born of their commingling: the military aristocracy and the church aristocracy, and the various comminglings of the two. One of these hybrid social formations seems to have been that which manifested itself in the foundation of what, putting a positive gloss on what Bede tells us, are probably best thought of as familial or hereditary monasteries – properties that would have been more or less indistinguishable from the estates of the properly military aristocracy, especially the estates of those nobles who had built churches on them. We know that some of the monasteries of which Bede approved, some of which were built *iuxta morem Romanorum* and some not, erected stone monuments on their properties. And, as we have seen, though the evidence is slight, we know that nobles on secular estates erected crosses, though it is not known whether they were stone crosses. Did the familial or hereditary monasteries produce stone monuments? There's no reason why they should not have done so.

It seems to us that the surviving corpus of pre-Viking Anglo-Saxon stone sculpture, which was once understood as *of* ecclesiastical production and use (a 'monastic art' of 'religious communities'), now has to be seen and understood somewhat differently. Of course, many of the survivals will have to be seen and understood as *of* ecclesiastical production and use (of the institution of the Church). But some will have to be seen and understood as *of* predominantly secular production and use (of the institution of the family, tribe or clan), and others as *of* both secular production and use (of the family, tribe or clan) *and of* ecclesiastical production and use (with theological content but not of the institution of the Church). We take it that any monument will represent and refashion the ideas and beliefs of the aristocracy according to the class factional or fractional and institutional place of the persons who produced and first used it. The obvious encompassing richness and complexity of the Ruthwell monument's theological content is usually taken as evidence for seeing and understanding it as having been produced and used by an ecclesiastical institution, most probably a monastery, to function in relation to some, thus far, unknown liturgy. We see no reason to challenge that view but keep in mind the complexity of what constituted monasticism. That the Bewcastle monument was erected to the memory of [Al]cfri[th] and, on its west side, rises from the representation of a military aristocrat might suggest that it was of secular production but given that, on the surface, it seems to support some of the theology that is represented on the Ruthwell monument, we keep in mind the complexity of what constituted the idea of a theologically informed devout secularity. So, we recognise the differences within the aristocracy and see them as implying a difference that would have determined the production and first use of any specific monument. This difference could account for the intention and function, form and content of the monuments at Ruthwell and Bewcastle.

At the end of our book, we hang on to the givens that are built deep into the form of each monument: the difference between the church and secular aristocracy and the ideas and beliefs that they held in common but also contested. These ideas are expressed in other surviving fragments of history, not only Bede's *Ecclesiastical History* and letter to Ecgbert. For example, they punctuate Stephanus's *Vita Wilfridi* and begin the story of the monastery that is the subject of Æthelwulf's *De abbatibus*.[15] This encourages us to say something about 'ideology' – or, more accurately, 'ideologies' for ideology, like *mentalités*, must always be plural – and the way the two monuments seem to represent, refashion and ritualise ideology.

Ideologies are those systems of ideas and beliefs, images, values and techniques of representation, each with its own structures of closure and disclosure, its own horizons, its own ways of allowing certain perceptions and rendering others impossible, by which particular social classes or factions and fractions within a class, in conflict with each other, attempt to naturalise their own special place in history.[16] Every ideology tries to give a quality of inevitability to what is a specific and disputable connection with the forces and relations of production. It represents its interests, for example, with regard to property, to what it is to be a man or a woman, to ways of living and dying, as coherent, natural, eternal. It takes as its material the real substance, the constraints and contradictions of a given historical place and time, of Northumbria between about 700 and around 750, and, in the way it represents them, imagines and images those contradictions solved, imagines and images a particular order of things as validated; makes clear or obscures the difference between Northumbria as a past-part of the historical ancient Roman Empire and as an integral present-part of a burgeoning ecclesiastical Republic of St Peter centred on Rome; makes clear or obscures the difference between an internally politically conflicted Northumbria contained within its own frontiers and a Northumbria confirmed in the idea of an eternal kingdom that transcended the frontiers of all kingdoms; makes clear or obscures the differences between two ways of seeing the world and two spoken and written languages for bringing it to practical consciousness, and two ways of materialising that consciousness as sculptural form; makes clear or obscures the difference between two sexes, at least two concepts of nobility, at least two kinds of property, and at least two factions within a class. The Ruthwell and Bewcastle monuments: two different material forms and thematics, each one determined in its complex way by its basis in a different class faction or fraction, produced by and producing social life. Two different material constructs made for use in some activity. The monuments exercise cognitive functions, and those functions would have been related to the objectives, ideas and beliefs of a social group. Each monument would have subjected those persons who used it to some ritualized behaviour, for example, of explaining, recognizing and accepting Christ and coming to terms with the Christian doctrine and the monastic ideal, of making sense of place, of reckoning time, of remembering, and so on; and, in the performance of these rituals, it would have situated whoever used it in a particular relation to it and to themselves, affecting and effecting their awareness, knowledge and feelings, of what and who they were, and where they were in the order of things. Such is the materiality of ideology that it has an unavoidable presence even as one tries to avoid it, resists rejection even as it is rejected. The Bewcastle and Ruthwell monuments, each one an object to which, after interacting with it, after being subjected by the regulatory practices of its context of use, taking note of its ideas, beliefs, images, values, ways of seeing and understanding the world, and so on, its beholders were expected to assent to a particular idea of being-in-the world: 'Amen'.[17]

Class. Ownership and possession of land. Rights with regard to the productive forces and the relations of production. Secular and ecclesiastical societies and institutions. Different ideas and beliefs. Different material forms and the constituent parts, distinctive attributes and characteristics of form and facture. Different intentions and functions. *If* the Ruthwell and Bewcastle monuments, two of the most refined and spiritual survivals of Anglo-Saxon stone sculpture, are to be explained without resorting to the idea of style, formalism, formalisation or intuitive analogies of form and content, without falling back on the kinds of conjectured similarities that never hold up under detailed critical study, they have to be *seen* and understood *as* two material forms or fragments of ideology, each determined by its place in the complexity of class affiliations and divisions, and the differences and conflicts between them, that were, in the eighth century, affecting and effecting the idea of 'Northumbria'. To have that as our conclusion is not to reduce our explanation of the monuments to their places in the 'class struggle' or to the conflicts between status groups. Rather, it is to remind ourselves that no refined and spiritual things, like the Bewcastle and Ruthwell monuments, could exist were it not for the struggle for the crude and material things,[18] which, whatever the disagreements amongst historians about the nature and significance of social conflict in the Middle Ages, is the class struggle by any other name.

Notes

⌘

Exordia

1 Said, *Beginnings: Intention and Method*, p. 3.
2 Brown, 'Report on the Ruthwell Cross. With some references to that at Bewcastle in Cumberland', pp. 224–225.
3 Bailey and Cramp, *The British Academy Corpus of Anglo-Saxon Stone Sculpture*, Vol. II, *Cumberland, Westmorland and Lancashire North-of-the Sands*, pp. 19–21, 61–72.
4 Haigh, 'The Saxon Cross at Bewcastle', pp. 167–176.
5 Brown, 'Report on the Ruthwell Cross', p. 219.
6 Saxl, 'The Ruthwell Cross', pp. 1–19; Schapiro, 'The Religious Meaning of the Ruthwell Cross', pp. 232–245.
7 Wherever we refer to the Latin inscriptions on the Ruthwell monument we usually follow the transcriptions, given after computer-enhanced digital photographs, in McKinnell, 'Ruthwell Cross, § 2', pp. 626–629. Doubtful forms are given in italics, and each present but illegible character is represented by a question mark. Three dots represent an uncertain number of lost characters.
8 Schapiro, 'The Religious Meaning of the Ruthwell Cross', pp. 234–235.
9 Schapiro, 'The Religious Meaning of the Ruthwell Cross', p. 236.
10 Saxl, 'The Ruthwell Cross', pp. 3–4.
11 Schapiro, 'The Religious Meaning of the Ruthwell Cross', pp. 238, 235. Saxl, 'The Ruthwell Cross', p. 4.
12 Schapiro, 'The Religious Meaning of the Ruthwell Cross', p. 237.
13 Saxl, 'The Ruthwell Cross', p. 2.
14 Saxl, 'The Ruthwell Cross', pp. 6–7, Saxl thought that 'the Cross was erected in the brief space of Roman might in Britain between Whitby and Bede'.
15 Schapiro, 'The Religious Meaning of the Ruthwell Cross', pp. 239–240.
16 Schapiro, 'The Religious Meaning of the Ruthwell Cross', pp. 241–242.
17 Bede, *Historia ecclesiastica gentis anglorum*, III 25 (henceforward *HE*); Stephanus, *Vita Wilfridi*, 10.
18 Ó Carragáin, 'Liturgical Innovations Associated with Pope Sergius and the Iconography of the Ruthwell and Bewcastle Crosses', pp. 131–147.
19 Schapiro, 'The Religious Meaning of the Ruthwell Cross', p. 240.
20 Saxl, 'The Ruthwell Cross', p. 7.
21 Saxl, 'The Ruthwell Cross', p. 7.
22 Saxl, 'The Ruthwell Cross', p. 8.
23 Saxl, 'The Ruthwell Cross', p. 8.
24 Saxl, 'The Ruthwell Cross', p. 8.

25 Saxl, 'The Ruthwell Cross', p. 10.
26 Saxl, 'The Ruthwell Cross', p. 10.
27 Saxl, 'The Ruthwell Cross', p. 10.
28 Saxl, 'The Ruthwell Cross', p. 10.
29 Saxl, 'The Ruthwell Cross', pp. 12–13.
30 Saxl, 'The Ruthwell Cross', p. 13.
31 Saxl, 'The Ruthwell Cross', p. 13.
32 Saxl, 'The Ruthwell Cross', p. 13.
33 Saxl, 'The Ruthwell Cross', p. 18.
34 Society of Antiquaries of London, Cumberland red folio, no. 3. This sculpture was, until 1885, given as recorded at Netherby, where it was, rather than at Bewcastle from whence it was removed, see for example: Hutchinson, *The History of the County of Cumberland Vol. II*, after p. 534 see no. 13; Lysons and Lysons, *Magna Britannia, Vol. 4, Cumberland*, p. clvi no. 72; and Bruce, *Lapidarium Septentrionale*, p. 403, no. 785. Its removal was first noted by Ferguson, 'The *Lapidarium Septentrionale* &', p. 144, no. 784.
35 Schapiro, 'The Religious Meaning of the Ruthwell Cross', p. 240; Brown, *The Arts in Early England*, Vol. V, *The Ruthwell and Bewcastle Crosses*, pp. 219–286.
36 Schapiro, 'The Religious Meaning of the Ruthwell Cross', p. 244.
37 Schapiro, 'The Religious Meaning of the Ruthwell Cross', pp. 241, 242 n. 76, 241.
38 Schapiro, 'The Religious Meaning of the Ruthwell Cross', p. 241.
39 Schapiro, 'The Religious Meaning of the Ruthwell Cross', p. 243.
40 Schapiro, 'The Religious Meaning of the Ruthwell Cross', p. 243.
41 Schapiro, 'The Religious Meaning of the Ruthwell Cross', p. 243.
42 Schapiro, 'The Religious Meaning of the Ruthwell Cross', p. 243.
43 Schapiro, 'The Religious Meaning of the Ruthwell Cross', p. 243.
44 Schapiro, 'The Religious Meaning of the Ruthwell Cross', pp. 245, 243.
45 Schapiro, 'The Religious Meaning of the Ruthwell Cross', p. 243.
46 *Corpus*, Vol. II, p. 71.
47 Bede, *HE*, IV 26.
48 See for example Kirby, 'Strathclyde and Cumbria: A Survey of Historical Development to 1092'. We remember how stimulating we found the discussion of Rheged in Smyth, *Warlords and Holy Men: Scotland AD 80–1000*, pp. 20–27.
49 As far as we know, Mercer, 'The Ruthwell and Bewcastle Crosses', pp. 268–276, was the first to bring Rheged into the published discourse of the Ruthwell and Bewcastle monuments.
50 Schapiro, 'The Religious Meaning of the Ruthwell Cross', pp. 241, 242.
51 Cramp, 'The Anglian Sculptured Crosses of Dumfriesshire', pp. 9–20.
52 Cramp, *Early Northumbrian Sculpture*, 1965.
53 Cramp, 'The Anglian Sculptured Crosses of Dumfriesshire', pp. 12, 13.
54 Wormald, 'Bede, "Beowulf" and the Conversion of the Anglo-Saxon Aristocracy'; Marx and Engels, *The German Ideology*; Marx, 1859 'Preface' to *A Contribution to the Critique of Political Economy*; Engels, 'The Origin of the Family, Private Property and the State'; Wittgenstein, *Philosophical Investigations*; Hanson, *Patterns of Discovery: An Inquiry into the Conceptual Foundations of Science*; Goodman, *Problems and Projects*; Barthes, *Mythologies*; Barthes, *Image/Music/Text*; Barthes, *The Rustle of Language*; Foucault, *The Archaeology of Knowledge*; Kuhn, *The Structure of Scientific Revolutions*; Barnes, *Interests and the Growth of Knowledge*.

Chapter 1: Place

1 Preliminary versions of this chapter were presented in Fred Orton, 'A Sense of Place: Building Dwelling Thinking at Bewcastle', *A Place to Believe In: Medieval Monasticism in the Landscape*, Wake Forest University/King's College London, July 2003, and Fred Orton, 'The Bewcastle Monument: A place where castles stood and grandeur died', *Object-Excavation-Intervention: Dialogues between Sculpture and Archaeology*, Henry Moore Institute Leeds, June 2004.

2 Basso, *Wisdom Sits in Places: Landscape and Language among the Western Apache*, p. 3.

3 Bailey and Cramp, *The British Academy Corpus of Anglo-Saxon Stone Sculpture*, Vol. II, *Cumberland, Westmorland and Lancashire North-of-the Sands*, 'Bewcastle 1. Cross-shaft and –base', p. 71.

4 Brown, *The Arts in Early England*, Vol. V, *The Ruthwell and Bewcastle Crosses*, p. 17.

5 Haigh, 'The Saxon Cross at Bewcastle', p. 152, who brought it into published discourse as a secular aristocrat or, as he put it, 'the king whose name is mentioned in the inscription above it'. See also: Kitzinger, 'Interlace and Icons: Form and Function in Early Insular Art', pp. 10–12; Bailey, *England's Earliest Sculptors*, pp. 66–67; and Karkov, 'The Bewcastle Cross: Some Iconographic Problems', pp. 11–20.

6 Our use of the terms 'place' and 'region' derives mainly from Heidegger, *Being and Time*. The vocabulary of 'being' – 'being-in-the-world', 'being-alongside', 'being-with', and so on – and 'present-to-hand', 'ready-to-hand' and 'close-to-hand' also derives, in the first instance, from *Being and Time*. 'Mere things' and 'equipment' are there in *Being and Time* but we had most in mind the way they're used in 'The Origin of the Work of Art', pp. 143–203. 'Building', 'dwelling', and 'thinking', of course, come mainly from Heidegger, 'Building Dwelling Thinking'.

7 Marx and Engels, *The German Ideology*, p. 7.

8 Day, Land, Price, Mills, and others, *Geology of the Country around Bewcastle*, pp. 9–14.

9 Day, et al., *Geology of the Country around Bewcastle*, pp. 1–2.

10 Day, et al., *Geology of the Country around Bewcastle*, p. 2.

11 Day, et al., *Geology of the Country around Bewcastle*, p. 255.

12 Day, et al., *Geology of the Country around Bewcastle*, pp. 93–94, 123–124.

13 Day, et al., *Geology of the Country around Bewcastle*, pp. 261–262. Grey, 'The Landscape of Bewcastle and Its Rocky Foundations', p. 9.

14 Day, et al., *Geology of the Country around Bewcastle*, pp. 6, Plate XV, 262–263.

15 Day, et al., *Geology of the Country around Bewcastle*, p. 262; Grey, 'The Landscape of Bewcastle and its Rocky Foundations', p. 9.

16 Day, et al., *Geology of the Country around Bewcastle*, pp. 232, 262; Grey, 'The Landscape of Bewcastle and its Rocky Foundations', p. 10.

17 Grey, 'The Landscape of Bewcastle and its Rocky Foundations', p. 10.

18 Grey, 'The Landscape of Bewcastle and its Rocky Foundations', p. 10.

19 Day, et al., *Geology of the Country around Bewcastle*, Plate XV, pp. 252, 255–256.

20 Maughan, 'The Maiden Way, Section II – The Branch Way and Roman Station at Bewcastle', p. 126. He describes the bog as 'a sort of quicksand'. See also Maughan, *A Memoir of the Roman Station and Runic Cross at Bewcastle with an Appendix on the Roman Inscription on Caeme Craig, and the Runic Inscription in Carlisle Cathedral*, p. 4.

21 See De la Bédoyère, *Hadrian's Wall: History & Guide*, p. 101. See also Bidwell, ed., *Hadrian's Wall 1989–1999: A Summary of Recent Excavations and Research Prepared for the Twelfth Pilgrimage of Hadrian's wall, 14–21 August 1999*, p. 145. It is likely that the same forest conditions pertained around Bewcastle also.

22 On the pollen evidence for hazel, willow and oak around Bewcastle, see Raistrick, 'Report upon Earth-Samples from Bewcastle', pp. 235–236, and Raistrick, 'Report upon Earth-Samples from Shield Knowe', pp. 160–161.

23 See Wilmott, 'A Possible Prehistoric Cist at Birdoswald, Cumbria', pp. 27–29.

24 For a useful survey of sites, see Jackson, 'Earliest Bewcastle', pp. 15–16, with location map. For the most complete survey, see the Cumbria Sites and Monuments Record, County Offices, Kendal. Like Jackson's, our discussion of sites, except for the reference to the hut circles at Woodhead, stays within the boundary of the Parish of Bewcastle. Several important Bronze Age sites, such as those around Woodhead and High Grains, are located a short distance from Bewcastle in the Parish of Askerton. It is also worth noting that a partly polished axe of 'dark green volcanic tuff' was found close to Shopford in a sike near Whitebeck (also in the Parish of Askerton), see Cumbria SMR no. 19213.

25 Hodgson, 'Some Notes on the Prehistoric Remains of the Border District', pp. 168–170.

26 Henshall, *The Chambered Tombs of Scotland*, Vol. 2, p. 160 and note 3 – the others are

Samson's Bratful at Ennerdale, South Cumberland, and Cow Green at Crosby Raven-worth, Westmorland. We should, perhaps, situate the Currick most closely in some relation of association with Stiddrig, an unchambered, trapezoidal long cairn 5 miles south-west of Moffat, towards the head of Annandale, and Windy Edge, a chambered long cairn, less than ten miles to the north-west of Bewcastle, a thousand feet up on Bruntshiel Hill just above Liddel Water. Windy Edge, which was originally about 140 feet long and 33 feet wide, and the larger of the two, can itself be regarded as an outlier of a group of long cairns 60 miles to the west at Cairnholy, above the eastern shore of Wigtown Bay, Kirkcudbrightshire. On Stiddrig and Windy Edge see Henshall, *The Chambered Tombs of Scotland*, pp. 419–420 and 420–422, respectively; see also the entries in The Royal Commission on the Ancient and Historical Monuments of Scotland, *Eastern Dumfriesshire: An Archaeological Landscape*, pp. 19, 59, 102, 294, no. 432 and pp. 100, 102–104, 294, no. 433, respectively.

27 Maughan, 'The Maiden Way, Section III – Survey of the Maiden Way through the Parish of Bewcastle', p. 233. Maughan refers to it by its local name, the 'Curragh'.

28 Maughan, 'The Maiden Way, Section III – Survey of the Maiden Way through the Parish of Bewcastle', pp. 216–235 at 233.

29 Hodgson, 'Some Notes on the Prehistoric Remains of the Border District', pp. 168–170. See also Royal Commission on Historical Monuments (England), *Monuments Threatened or Destroyed. A Select List: 1956–1962*, p. 13 and illus. p. 10.

30 Here we follow Burgess and Shennan, 'The Beaker Phenomenon: Some Suggestions', see especially Burgess, 'Part I: General Comments on the British Evidence', pp. 309–323.

31 Hodgson, 'Some Excavations in the Bewcastle District: II. A Hut-Circle Near Woodhead', pp. 164, 165.

32 Hodgson, 'Some Excavations in the Bewcastle District: I. A Bronze Age Tumulus on the Shield Knowe', pp. 154–160. See also Maughan, 'The Maiden Way, Section III – Survey of the Maiden Way through the Parish of Bewcastle', p. 225.

33 Hodgson, 'Some Excavations in the Bewcastle District: I. A Bronze Age Tumulus on the Shield Knowe', pp. 156, 158–159.

34 Hodgson, 'Some Excavations in the Bewcastle District: I. A Bronze Age Tumulus on the Shield Knowe', see the appended Alex Low, 'Report on the Bones from the Shield Knowe Tumulus', p. 160.

35 Maughan, 'The Maiden Way, Section III – Survey of the Maiden Way through the Parish of Bewcastle', p. 230. Maughan, ibid., pp. 230–231 and illus., also records that in the late 1840s to early 1850s a bronze spearhead was found in the peat near Camp Graves.

36 Maughan, 'The Maiden Way, Section III – Survey of the Maiden Way through the Parish of Bewcastle', pp. 230–231. This place was ploughed over, and attempts to locate it have proved unsuccessful.

37 Davenport, 'The Bewcastle Cauldron', pp. 228–230.

38 Davenport, 'The Bewcastle Cauldron', p. 228.

39 Although there is evidence that deforestation in the immediate area around Birdoswald occurred during the late Iron Age, which would suggest a local population, no associated settlements have yet been found – see Wilmott, 'A Possible Prehistoric Cist at Birdos-wald', pp. 27–29. The stone walled hill fort at Carby Hill on Liddel Water, some eight miles away to the north-east, about half a mile from the northern boundary of the parish of Bewcastle, in Roxburghshire, Scotland, was probably built a hundred years or so after the Roman occupation of the region began – see Royal Commission on the Ancient Monuments of Scotland, *Roxburghshire*, Vol. I, pp. 32, 90.

40 Hoaen and Loney, 'Bronze and Iron Age Connections: Memory and Persistence in Matterdale, Cumbria', p. 52.

41 The three food vessels that came to light when Shield Knowe was excavated are all 'Yorkshire Vases' of the 'Abercromby type' – see Hodgson, 'Some Excavations in the Bewcastle District: I. A Bronze Age Tumulus on the Shield Knowe', p. 159.

42 On the history of the fort, we generally follow Austen, *Bewcastle and Old Penrith: A Roman*

Outpost Fort and a Frontier Vicus, 'Part I: Excavations in the Roman Fort at Bewcastle, 1977–78', pp. 41–50.

43 We've taken Breeze and Dobson, *Hadrian's Wall,* as our guide to the general history of the Wall, occasionally supplemented by Bidwell, ed., *Hadrian's Wall 1989–1999* and De la Bédoyère, *Hadrian's Wall: History & Guide.*

44 Breeze and Dobson, *Hadrian's Wall,* pp. 26, 33.

45 Breeze and Dobson, *Hadrian's Wall,* p. 46.

46 This in answer to the questions posed by 'Table 2' in Bidwell, *Hadrian's Wall 1989–1999,* p. 15.

47 The first-century fort at High Rochester (*Bremenium*), close to the line of Dere Street, the eastern trunk road north and the principal invasion route into Scotland, was abandoned until the building of the Antonine Wall whence it became an outpost fort for Hadrian's Wall, see De la Bédoyère, *Hadrian's Wall: History & Guide,* p. 121, and Bidwell, *Hadrian's Wall 1998–1999,* p. 188. Little is known of the fort at Risingham (*Habitancum*): it may have come into being in the first century; if so, like High Rochester, it was probably rebuilt in the AD 140s as an outpost fort for the Wall, see De la Bédoyère, *Hadrian's Wall: History & Guide,* p. 121.

48 Breeze and Dobson, *Hadrian's Wall,* p. 46.

49 Breeze and Dobson, *Hadrian's Wall,* pp. 40, 46, 58; see also Simpson, Richmond and St Joseph, 'The Turf-Wall Milecastle at High House', pp. 220–232.

50 Breeze and Dobson, *Hadrian's Wall,* p. 46.

51 For excavation reports or fieldwork see Collingwood, 'The Roman Fort at Bewcastle'; Richmond, Hodgson, and St Joseph, 'The Roman Fort at Bewcastle'; Gillam, 'Recent Excavations at Bewcastle'; Gillam, 'The Roman Bath-house at Bewcastle'; Sainsbury and Welfare, 'The Roman Fort at Bewcastle: An Analytical Field Survey'; Gillam, Jobey, Welsby, et al., *The Roman Bath-house at Bewcastle*; and Austen, *Bewcastle and Old Penrith.*

52 See Sainsbury and Welfare, 'The Roman Fort at Bewcastle: An Analytical Field Survey', p. 140, fig. I; Austen, *Bewcastle and Old Penrith,* p. 43.

53 On the organisation of the Roman army see Breeze and Dobson, *Hadrian's Wall,* pp. 159–162. On these kinds of units being stationed at Bewcastle see notes 57 and 58 below.

54 For Chesters, Birdoswald and Stanwix see Breeze and Dobson, *Hadrian's Wall,* p. 70 (but note Taylor, *The Forts on Hadrian's Wall: A Comparative Analysis of the Form and Construction of Some Buildings,* p. 123, measures Stanwix about 609 feet by 700 feet on the basis of excavations of 1984); for Burgh-by-Sands, see Taylor, *The Forts on Hadrian's Wall,* p. 124; for Bowness-on-Solway, see Austen, 'How Big was the Second Largest Fort on Hadrian's Wall at Bowness on Solway?', p. 7.

55 Austen, *Bewcastle and Old Penrith,* p. 5, fig. 2. Our reconstruction of the ground plan, see above Fig. 4, moderates the size but not substantially. (Measuring Roman forts from the traces that survive is something of an imprecise science.) This plan brings together information provided by Richmond, 'The Roman Fort at Bewcastle', p. 196, fig. 1; Austen, *Bewcastle and Old Penrith,* p. 5, fig. 2; the RCHM's map of the fort's earthworks in Sainsbury and Welfare, 'The Roman Fort at Bewcastle: An Analytical Field Survey', p. 140, fig. I; and the geophysical survey of part of the fort and the area around it that was carried out in June 2000 and September 2002 by J. A. Biggins and D. J. A. Taylor (TimeScape Research Surveys). We are grateful to Biggins and Taylor for access to the interim statement of their unpublished report.

56 For the sizes of the forts on the Wall, see Breeze and Dobson, *Hadrian's Wall,* table 3, p. 54, and Taylor, *The Forts on Hadrian's Wall,* appendix, table 1, p. 140. Note, however, that it has now been established that Bowness, once estimated as covering 7 acres, actually covers an area of 5.88 acres, see Austen, 'How Big was the Second Largest Fort on Hadrian's Wall at Bowness on Solway?'

57 On the *cohors milliaria peditata* see Breeze and Dobson, *Hadrian's Wall,* pp. 159–162, and on the *cohors I Dacorum* being stationed at Bewcastle see Austen, *Bewcastle and Old Penrith,* pp. 44, 50.

58 On the *cohors milliaria equitata* see Breeze and Dobson, *Hadrian's Wall,* pp. 159–162, and

on the *cohors I Nervana Germanorum milliaria equitata* being stationed at Bewcastle see Austen, *Bewcastle and Old Penrith*, pp. 46–47, 50.

59 Following Austen, *Bewcastle and Old Penrith*, pp. 41–50.

60 See Austen, *Bewcastle and Old Penrith*, p. 42, numismatic evidence suggests that the fort was abandoned c. AD 312. But note ibid., p. 32, on the Cambreck parchment ware and Huntcliff type of cooking pot found at Bewcastle, which may indicate that the fort was occupied as late as c. AD 370; see also Gillam, Jobey, Welsby, *The Roman Bath-house at Bewcastle*, p. 23.

61 Sainsbury and Welfare, 'The Roman Fort at Bewcastle: an Analytical Field Survey', p. 143, referencing John Hodgson, *History of Northumberland*, Pt II, Vol. III, Newcastle-upon-Tyne, 1840, p. 206, and Maughan, *A Memoir of the Roman Station and Runic Cross at Bewcastle*, pp. 4, 7.

62 Sainsbury and Welfare, 'The Roman fort at Bewcastle: An Analytical Field Survey', p. 139.

63 Bruce, *The Roman Wall: A Historical, Topographical, and Descriptive Account of the Barrier of the Lower Isthmus, Extending from the Tyne to the Solway*, p. 344.

64 Haldane, *The Drove Roads of Scotland*, pp. 6–19.

65 We're aware, of course, that bogs were the depositories of votive offerings from the Bronze Age through Romano-British times into the medieval period. Perhaps the bog at Bewcastle hasn't received the attention from historians and archaeologists that it deserves.

66 Lewis, *Temples in Roman Britain*, pp. 104, 123, and Breeze and Dobson, *Hadrian's Wall*, p. 282. On Cocidius see Fairless, 'Three Religious Cults from the Northern Frontier Region', pp. 224–242 at 228–235.

67 Fairless, 'Three Religious Cults from the Northern Frontier Region', p. 228. See also for the inscriptions on altars Collingwood and Wright, *The Roman Inscriptions of Britain*, Nos 985, 988, 989, 993 and 966 (there is no record of the discovery of this altar which was recorded in 1772 at Netherby but is now thought to have come from Bewcastle) and for the two silver embossed votive plaques see Nos 986 and 987.

68 Fairless, 'Three Religious Cults from the Northern Frontier Region', p. 229.

69 Fairless, 'Three Religious Cults from the Northern Frontier Region', p. 234, citing Richmond and Crawford, 'The British Section of the Ravenna Cosmography', p. 34.

70 See Collingwood and Wright, *The Roman Inscriptions of Britain*, nos 966, 988–989.

71 Fairless, 'Three Religious Cults from the Northern Frontier Region', pp. 228–229. Richmond and Crawford, 'The British Section of the Ravenna Cosmography', p. 34, suggested that the shrine of Cocidius was situated somewhere in the area between Stanwix, Netherby and Bewcastle. Birley, *Research on Hadrian's Wall*, p. 233, suggested Bewcastle was the site of the shrine.

72 Birley, *Research on Hadrian's Wall*, p. 233, thought that the 'easiest explanation' of the 'special place' that Cocidius had 'acquired in the religion of the garrison' was that 'the fort had been planted on a pre-existing shrine ... and the god had been taken over by the Roman army together with his shrine'. For some recent thinking along these lines see Martin Henig, '*Murum civitatis, et fontem in ea a Romanis mire olim constructum*', pp. 1–18, espec. p. 12.

73 Sainsbury and Welfare, 'The Roman Fort at Bewcastle: an Analytical Field Survey', p. 143. Biggins's and Taylor's unpub. geophysical survey found traces of buildings to the north and west of the fort some of which could have been post-Roman and possibly medieval.

74 See Breeze and Dobson, *Hadrian's Wall*, p. 51, who explain why and how the original plan was varied, see table 2, p. 50, for the actual distances between the forts.

75 On the road as it leaves Birdoswald, see Wilmott, *Birdoswald. Excavations of a Roman Fort on Hadrian's Wall and Its Successor: 1987–92*, 'Appendix 1: The Maiden Way North of Birdoswald', p. 411. The road is marked on the most recent Ordnance Survey map to within half a mile of High House, 2½ miles south-south-east of the fort. Today, it is difficult to discern and, because of the terrain and restrictions, practically impossible to walk.

Maughan surveyed it in March 1854, see Maughan, 'The Maiden Way. Survey of the

Maiden Way from Birdoswald, the Station of Amboglanna, on the Roman Wall, North-ward into Scotland; with a Short Description of Some Remarkable Objects in the District. Section I – Survey of the Maiden Way through the Parish of Lanercost', pp. 1–22.

76 See Day, et al., *Geology of the Country around Bewcastle*, pp. 266–267, which is of the opinion that the fort was built with stone that 'probably came from ancient quarries in the Earthwork and Parkhead sandstones near Grossgreens. Some larger blocks may possibly have been brought from the great crags of the Long Bar on Whitelyne Common'. The crags of the Long Bar are said to have provided the stone for the monument also. See the 'Rough-out of cross-shaft(?)' on Long Bar that the *Corpus*, Vol. II, p. 162 and illus. 621, describes as 'a tapering rectangle of stone cut out of the outcrop on three sides but still attached at the base'. We should note, however, the discussion in *Geology of the Country around Bewcastle*, p. 94: 'At outcrop this sandstone has a system of rectangular joints so that on weathering it tends to break into roughly rectangular blocks, some of which are pockmarked in a fashion resembling artificial working by chisels. It thus seems unlikely that a similarly pockmarked rectangular block, locally reputed to be the "brother" of the stone which now forms the monument, was in reality quarried'.

77 Some time between Spring 1852 and early 1854 Maughan, 'The Maiden Way, Section I', p. 19, fig. III and p. 22, traced the road to its river crossing at a ruin called the 'Dollerline', now identified as the earthworks and buried remains of a medieval dispersed settlement about 700 yards east of the fort, Cumbria SMR no. 68. Three years later he refers to it again and records that across from it, on the north side of the beck, there is a small embankment or raised road leading to the eastern gate of the Station, see Maughan, *A Memoir on the Roman Station and Runic Cross at Bewcastle*, p. 4.

Collingwood, 'The Roman Fort at Bewcastle', pp. 178–182, was able to follow the road from Birdoswald to just beyond Spadeadam, then could not find it until about half a mile from Bewcastle where he thought it was 'represented by the straight length of the modern road for about 700 yards S. of Shopford'. He reckoned that it 'forded Kirk Beck where the modern bridge stands, and approached the fort as it does now'.

In June 1923, W. G. Collingwood, R. G. Collingwood's son, tried to find the line from High House to the fort, see W. G. Collingwood, 'The End of the Maiden Way', pp. 110–116. He tracked the road cutting north-west from 'about 500 yards S.S.E. of High House' to Kirk Beck, 50 yards east of Byer Cottage.

Richmond, 'The Roman Fort at Bewcastle', p. 196, fig. 1 and p. 199, fig. 3, favoured a point closer to Byer Cottage.

The end of the road was most recently traced by Biggins's and Taylor's 2000 and 2002 geophysical survey of part of the fort and its immediate area. The line of the road was seen as a well-defined agger close to the river and as an anomaly on the magnetometry image. Though the probable route differs from that put forward by Collingwood (1924), and Richmond (1938), it seems that the road crosses Kirk Beck more or less where Collingwood thought it did, about 50 yards east of Byer Cottage, and enters and exits the *porta praetoria* at a slight angle to the *via praetoria*.

78 Gillalees Beacon was first identified by Maughan, see 'The Maiden Way, Section I', p. 9, fig. II, and p. 10; see also Richmond, 'The Tower at Gillalees Beacon, called Robin Hood's Butt', pp. 241–245. On Barron's Pike see Topping, 'A "New" Signal Station in Cumbria', pp. 298–300, and Jones and Wooliscroft, *Hadrian's Wall from the Air*, pp. 135, 141, fig. 89.

79 Ferris and Jones, 'Transforming an Elite: Reinterpreting Late Roman Binchester', p. 1.

80 Henig, '*Murum civitatis, et fontem in ea a Romanis mire olim constructum*', p. 2.

81 Convenient summaries of work in progress or overviews of work done can be found in Wilmott and Wilson, eds, *The Late Roman Transition in the North. Papers from the Roman Archaeology Conference, Durham 1999*, see especially Wilmott, 'The Late Roman Transition at Birdoswald and on Hadrian's Wall', pp. 13–23, and Ferris and Jones, 'Transforming an Elite: Reinterpreting Late Roman Binchester', pp. 1–11. But see also Dark, 'The Late Roman Transition in the North: A Discussion', pp. 81–88, and Simon Esmonde Cleary, 'Summing Up', pp. 89–94.

82 Wilmott, 'The Late Roman Transition at Birdoswald and on Hadrian's Wall', pp. 13–23, and Wilmott, *Birdoswald Roman Fort: 1800 Years on Hadrian's Wall*, pp. 113–126. On the pin, see Cramp, 'An Anglo-Saxon Pin from Birdoswald', pp. 90–93.

83 Bidwell, *Hadrian's Wall*, pp. 80, 82.

84 Ferris and Jones, 'Transforming an Elite: Reinterpreting Late Roman Binchester', pp. 1–2, 3.

85 See Campbell, *The Anglo-Saxons*, p. 40, fig. 40.

86 Campbell, *The Anglo-Saxons*, p. 38.

87 Thomas, *Christianity in Roman Britain to AD 500*, pp. 310–314, reading the *Confessio*, Part I.1, lines 1–8, has suggested that St Patrick, the Apostle of Ireland, who was abducted from his father's estate near the *vicus Bannaven Taberniae* and whose father was a *diaconum*, a member of the provincial-Roman governing class, and whose family had possessed Latin names for at least three generations, came from the region. Thomas placed the estate somewhere in the area around *Banna* (Birdoswald). *If* Patrick did come from somewhere near Birdoswald, this would further suggest the persistence of a sub-Roman world at the western end of the Wall in the general area of Bewcastle.

88 For traces of activity at the fort and in the town until at least the fifth century see McCarthy, *Roman Carlisle*, pp. 134–140. A brief summary of the archaeological evidence for *Lugubalium* and its Anglian successor settlement is provided by McCarthy, 'Carlisle and St Cuthbert'.

89 Bede, *HE*, IV 29. See also Bede, *Vita Sancti Cuthberti*, XXVII.

90 Anon., *Vita Sancti Cuthberti*, ch. VIII, and Bede, *Vita Sancti Cuthberti*, XXVII. For further discussion of these passages to supplement what follows see McCarthy, *Roman Carlisle*, pp. 152–153. Cuthbert visited Carlisle again, shortly before his death, in AD 687, see *HE*, IV 29.

91 Bidwell, *Hadrian's Wall 1989–1999*, p. 175.

92 Bidwell, *Hadrian's Wall 1989–1999*, p. 175.

93 McCarthy, *Roman Carlisle*, p. 85.

94 McCarthy, *Roman Carlisle*, pp. 83, 134.

95 William of Malmesbury, *Gesta Pontificum*, 99. McCarthy, *Roman Carlisle*, pp. 83, 134, thinks that Malmesbury's '*triclineum*' might have been either a temple dedicated to Mars and Victory or the *principia*.

96 McCarthy, *Roman Carlisle*, pp. 134, 136.

97 Henig, '*Murum civitatis, et fontem in ea a Romanis mire olim constructum*', p. 3.

98 Most *civitas* capitals had intramural wells, but, though the town at Carlisle had at least one aqueduct and baths, thus far a well has not come to light – see Burgers, *The Water Supplies and Related Structures of Roman Britain*, p. 61. On drainage and water management at Carlisle, especially within the area of the fort, see McCarthy, *Roman Carlisle*, p. 85.

99 Burgers, *The Water Supplies and Related Structures of Roman Britain*, p. 23.

100 See Dore, *Corbridge Roman Site*, pp. 7–8, and p. 9 for a photograph of the remains as they are today and a reconstruction drawing.

101 Anon., *Vita Sancti Cuthberti*, ch. III, see also Bede, *Vita Sancti Cuthberti*, XVIII, which turns the anonymous author's '*statim fontem aquae vive*' (definitely a fountainhead, a spouting or spurting of water) away from its Mosaic connotations into a '*foveam quam in crastinum emanante ab internis unda repletam invenerunt*' (something more like a well).

102 William of Malmesbury, *Gesta Pontificum*, 99. William's reference to the Roman walls and buildings at Carlisle comes in the context of some general remarks about what he saw in *Nordanimbrorum*.

103 Collingwood, 'The Bewcastle Cross', p. 14.

104 Following Austen, *Bewcastle and Old Penrith: A Roman Outpost Fort and a Frontier Vicus*, pp. 7–16, 48–49.

105 Taylor, *The Forts on Hadrian's Wall*, pp. 13–26, provides a very useful introduction to the techniques of Roman building construction, which unfortunately does not discuss the construction of bath-houses.

106 Gillam, Jobey, Welsby, et al., *The Roman Bath-house at Bewcastle*, pp. 10–11, 13–14, 20–22.

107 Gillam, Jobey, Welsby, et al., *The Roman Bath-house at Bewcastle*, pp. 11, 14.

108 See Gillam, Jobey, Welsby, et al., *The Roman Bath-house at Bewcastle*, p. 14. 'Tufa voussoirs were found in abundance', though 'there were rather more to the north-west, north and east of the heated suite than within the debris overlying it'.

    'Tufa' is the name given to a rather cavernous sponge-textured rock usually composed principally of the mineral calcite ($CaCO_3$), and then often referred to as 'calcareous tufa'. It is typically deposited as a precipitate from springs with water carrying a high proportion of calcium carbonate. Small accumulations of tufa are comparatively common around springs in the limestone country of northern England, though the deposits produced are usually measurable in a few cubic metres; larger deposits are known, but rather unusual. Though frost and rain could break it down if used out of doors, Roman architects and builders in Britain seem to have valued it because it could be easily cut to shape and, when used indoors, in the construction of bath-houses, would resist heat and fire.

    On the calcareous tufa voussoirs found in the bath-house at Chesters and Parker Brewis's brilliant interpretation of how they formed the arched ribs supporting the vault above the *caldarium* see MacDonald, 'The Bath-house at the Fort of Chesters (*Cilurnum*)', pp. 278–282.

    Mindful that Roman builders used local stones wherever possible, most probably the material for the voussoirs used in the construction of the bath-house at Bewcastle, like the rest of the stone, was quarried not far from the fort. Day, et al., *Geology of the Country around Bewcastle*, p. 263, note that an area of calcareous tufa, extending over about one acre, is located less than 2 miles south-west of the fort near Bogside Farm. Once extensively burrowed by rabbits and now 'sett' about by badgers, this area of tufa is several feet thick. We thank Ann and Tony Burford for allowing us access to this most interesting and unusual feature on their land.

109 Gillam, Jobey, Welsby, et al., *The Roman Bath-House at Bewcastle, Cumbria*, p. 14.

110 Birley, *Vindolanda's Military Bath Houses. The Excavations of 1970 and 2000*, p. 27.

111 On the castle see Jackson, 'The History of Bewcastle Castle', pp. 32–35.

112 In 1271 the parson, Robert de Scardeburgh, was granted eight oaks from the Forest of Inglewood 'to build his church at Bewcastle' – see Jackson, 'Religious History of Bewcastle', pp. 28–31 at 28. In 1792 a faculty was granted for 'the taking down six yards and a half in length of the west end' and to increase the height of the walls by 'one yard or more'; the tower at the west end was added at this time – see Curwen, 'St Cuthbert's Church, Bewcastle', pp. 246, 247. The church fabric was extensively altered again in 1901. Thomas Pennant visited Bewcastle in 1773 along with his draughtsman Moses Griffith. Griffiths's drawing was used to make the engraving that illustrated the entry under 'Beu Castle' in Pennant's *A Tour from Downing to Alston-Moor*, 1801, pp. 180–182, opp. 180 (Fig. 2). Drawn before the alterations, it shows a monument several feet away from the towerless and porch-less west end, and away from the entrance, which, if it were the only one, seems to have been on the north side of the church.

113 Much depends on how one explains what the 1954 and 1956 excavations of Gillam and Jobey did and did not bring to light. Gillam's report remained unpublished until 1993.

    Given that there is nothing to suggest that the bath-house was demolished at the time the fort was once supposed to have been abandoned 'in the face of an enemy offensive', it seems that what we're given in the report suggests that the bath-house was more or less carefully dismantled and the stone used elsewhere.

    We note: (1) that though some *tegulae* (flat roof tiles that were laid lengthways, overlapping one another following the pitch of the roof) and *imbrices* (curved watertight roof tiles that covered the junction between two *tegulae*), broken stones, and some complete individual but seemingly not large stones were found in the area of the *apodyterium*, no debris from the stone walls was found there; (2) that nothing deemed significant, and certainly no material from the vault or the walls, was found on the floor of the vestibule; (3) that nothing is made of the complete disappearance of the flags from the raised floors of the *caldarium* and *tepidaria* and the more or less complete absence of substantial pieces of debris between the *pilae* that would have supported them; and (4) that evidence for the total collapse or careless demolition of the whole building comes only from the *sudatorium*, *frigidarium* and cold bath, which contained stone that seems to have been dumped in it – mainly facing stones from walls, calcareous tufa voussoirs from the vaulting in the hot suites, and 'stone flags' that were 'thin as from roofs', which could have been bits of the raised floor in the *caldarium* and the *tepidaria*.

All this seems to suggest that the roof superstructure, the masonry vaulting and the walls were removed before the floors, which would have been the last things to have been taken away from the site; and this, in turn, seems to suggest that – perhaps after the building had been partly demolished by the Romans (when it went out of use as a bath-house) or after a partial collapse (for as we've seen it seems doubtful that the whole building would have collapsed as a result of decay after the garrison had quit the fort), or perhaps even before it had begun to collapse – the bath-house was demolished in a more or less orderly fashion and its stones used elsewhere. That 'elsewhere' could have been only the church or the castle.

114 Henig, '*Murum civitatis, et fontem in ea a Romanis mire olim constructum*', p. 12.
115 It's worth noting what Heidegger has to say about Marx and Marxism in his 'Letter on Humanism', written in Dec. 1946 and first pub. 1947, only four or five years before 'Building Dwelling Thinking'. See 'Letter on Humanism', p. 243, where Heidegger credits Marx for seeing history in terms of alienation and, because of that, acknowledges Marxist history as 'superior to that of other historical accounts' with regard to the history of Being. He goes on to point out that neither phenomenology nor existentialism has entered into a productive dialogue with Marxism, a dialogue that is 'certainly also necessary to free oneself from naive notions about materialism, as well as from the cheap refutations that are supposed to counter it'.
116 Heidegger, 'Building Dwelling Thinking', p. 350.
117 Heidegger, 'Building Dwelling Thinking', pp. 350, 348–349.
118 Heidegger, 'Building Dwelling Thinking', p. 362.
119 Heidegger, 'Building Dwelling Thinking', pp. 351–352.
120 Heidegger, 'Building Dwelling Thinking', p. 353.

Chapter 2: Fragments

1 This chapter is a revised and expanded form of Orton, 'Rethinking the Ruthwell Monument: Fragments and Critique; Tradition and History; Tongues and Sockets'.
2 *The Acts of the General Assemblies of the Church of Scotland, from the Year 1638 to the Year 1649. Inclusive. Printed in the year 1882. To which are now added the index of the unprinted Acts of these Assemblies; and the Acts of the General Assembly 1690*, pp. 92–93.
3 The title of this act is taken from the *Index of the principal Acts of the Assembly holden at St Andrews, 27 July, 1642, not Printed*, appended to *The Acts of the General Assemblies of the Church of Scotland, from the Year 1638 to the Year 1649*, p. 4. For the text of the act see Minutes of the General Assembly of the Church of Scotland, 30/7/1642, National Archives of Scotland, CH 1/1/9, p. 15 – located and first published by Okasha, *Hand-List of Anglo-Saxon Non-Runic Inscriptions*, p. 108 n. 6, who mistranscribes 'Ruthwall' for Ruthwell.
4 Stephen, *History of the Scottish Church*, Vol. II, p. 282 n. 2.
5 Duncan, 'An Account of the Remarkable Monument in the shape of a Cross, inscribed with Roman and Runic Letters, preserved in the Garden of Ruthwell Manse, Dumfriesshire', p. 317.
6 Craig, 'Parish of Ruthwell', p. 447.
7 Craig, 'Parish of Ruthwell', p. 455.
8 Cockayne, *Complete Baronetage*, Vol. II, 1625–1649, p. 292.
9 See Cockayne, *The Complete Peerage or A History of the House of Lords and All Its Members From The Earliest Times*, Vol. XXII, *Skelmersdale to Towton*, p. 288, and Cockayne, *The Complete Peerage of England, Scotland, Ireland, Great Britain and the United Kingdom Extinct or Dormant*, Vol. I, *AB-Adam to Basing*, p. 165.

10 Cockayne, *The Complete Peerage of England*, Vol. I, p. 165.

11 Quoted by Cockayne, *The Complete Peerage of England, Scotland, Ireland, Great Britain and the United Kingdom Extinct or Dormant*, Vol. I, p. 165.

12 Craig, 'Parish of Ruthwell', p. 455, notes that John Murray acquired estates not only in Scotland and Ireland but also in England.

13 See 'Donegal Studies-History of Donegal-Landlords of Donegal', http://www.donegal-library.ie/memory/landlords.htm.

14 Cockayne, *The Complete Peerage*, Vol. I, p. 165.

15 Cockayne, *The Complete Peerage*, Vol. I, p. 165; for more detail of the entail see Cockayne, *The Complete Peerage or A History of the House of Lords and All Its Members From The Earliest Times*, Vol. XXII, pp. 288–289.

16 Cockayne, *The Complete Peerage*, Vol. I, p. 165.

17 See Wishart, *The Memoirs of James Marquis of Montrose 1639–1650*, p. 129 notes 8–9, 12–14. See also Stephen, *History of the Scottish Church*, pp. 302–303.

18 Cockayne, *The Complete Peerage*, Vol. I, p. 165.

19 Cockayne, *The Complete Peerage*, Vol. XXII, pp. 292, 294.

20 Cockayne, *The Complete Peerage*, Vol. XXII, p. 294.

21 Cockayne, *The Complete Peerage*, Vol. XXII, p. 295.

22 Cockayne, *The Complete Peerage*, Vol. VIII, pp. 387–390.

23 Cockayne, *The Complete Peerage*, Vol. VIII, pp. 390–392.

24 Duncan, 'An Account of the Remarkable Monument in the shape of a Cross', p. 371.

25 Dinwiddie, 'The Ruthwell Cross and the Story It Has to Tell' (1910), p. 110. This essay was amended and extended and republished as *The Ruthwell Cross and Its Story: A Handbook for Tourists and Students* (1927), and revised as *The Ruthwell Cross and the Ruthwell Savings Bank: A Handbook for Tourists and Students* (1933).

26 Dinwiddie, *The Ruthwell Cross and Its Story: A Handbook for Tourists and Students*, pp. 89, 91 – compare with Dinwiddie, 'The Ruthwell Cross and the Story It Has to Tell', p. 110.

27 Dinwiddie, *The Ruthwell Cross and Its Story: A Handbook for Tourists and Students*, pp. 80–81 – here Dinwiddie takes his own earlier interpretation and attributes it to Gavin Young; compare with Dinwiddie, 'The Ruthwell Cross and the Story It Has to Tell', pp. 111–112.

28 Dinwiddie, *The Ruthwell Cross and Its Story: A Handbook for Tourists and Students*, p. 81.

29 See Dinwiddie, 'The Ruthwell Cross and the Story It Has to Tell', p. 110 – Dinwiddie chose not to carry forward this observation into the later versions of his story.

30 Pennant, *A Tour in Scotland and Voyage to the Hebrides 1772*, pp. 85–86.

31 Dinwiddie, *The Ruthwell Cross and Its Story: A Handbook for Tourists and Students*, p. 92.

32 Dinwiddie, *The Ruthwell Cross and Its Story: A Handbook for Tourists and Students*, pp. 89, 91.

33 William Nicolson, 'Bishop Nicolson's Diaries: Part II', p. 196.

34 Dinwiddie, *The Ruthwell Cross and Its Story: A Handbook for Tourists and Students*, p. 98. These alterations were undertaken during the lifetime of David Murray (1727–1796), Sixth Viscount of Stormont, Lord Scone and Lord Balvaird, and, on the death of his uncle William in 1776, Second Earl of Mansfield.

35 See Duncan, 'Parish of Ruthwell', p. 235 – the earliest burials within 30 feet of the east end of the church date to 1803 and 1810.

36 Special thanks are due to Richard K. Morris for taking a look at the fabric of Murray's Quire, and to Ellen Shortell for measuring it and the rest of the church.

37 *The Royal Commission on the Ancient and Historical Monuments and Constructions of Scotland, Seventh Report with Inventory of Monuments and Constructions in the County of Dumfries*, p. 188, No. 539, 'Heraldic Panel. Ruthwell Church'.

38 RCAHMCS, *Dumfries*, pp. 187–188 n. 539.

39 In 1927 Dinwiddie, *The Ruthwell Cross and Its Story: A Handbook for Tourists and Students*, p. 96, has this coat of arms 'over the entrance to the burial vault'.

40 On the architecture of the 'burial-aisle' see Colvin, *The Architecture of the After-Life*, pp. 296–306, and for an interesting discussion of lairs and burial-aisles and the ways they

served to emphasise the status of the families that used them see Spicer, '"Defyle not Christ's kirk with your carrion": Burial and the Development of Burial Aisles in post-Reformation Scotland'.

41 Craig, 'Parish of Ruthwell', p. 456.

42 John Murray was buried on 17 October 1640 at Hoddom – see Cockayne, *The Complete Peerage of England*, Vol. I, p. 165.

43 Duncan, 'An Account of the Remarkable Monument in the shape of a Cross', p. 316.

44 Brown, 'Report on the Ruthwell Cross', pp. 224–225.

45 Duncan, 'An Account of the Remarkable Monument in the shape of a Cross', pp. 313–326.

46 Duncan, 'An Account of the Remarkable Monument in the shape of a Cross', p. 315.

47 Duncan, 'An Account of the Remarkable Monument in the shape of a Cross', p. 315.

48 Duncan, 'An Account of the Remarkable Monument in the shape of a Cross', p. 316. Duncan also saw them as 'considerably broader' and 'cut-deeper and more sharply, than those below, of which they appear to be an imitation'.

49 Duncan, 'An Account of the Remarkable Monument in the shape of a Cross', p. 315.

50 Brown, 'Report on the Ruthwell Cross', p. 223.

51 Brown, 'Report on the Ruthwell Cross', pp. 223–224.

52 Brown, 'Report on the Ruthwell Cross', p. 224, where he acknowledges a 'private communication' from 'Mr. Postlethwaite, the well-known authority on Cumbrian geology'. However, Brown's geology and petrology derived mainly from Barbour, 'Regarding the Origin of the Ruthwell Cross', pp. 28–31, who thought that 'rock fulfilling the required conditions is obtainable in the immediate vicinity'. Barbour thought that it could have come from 'a quarry at a place about 300 yards north of the Ruthwell Station'. Hewison, *The Runic Roods of Ruthwell and Bewcastle with a Short History of the Cross and Crucifix in Scotland*, p. 40, with Barbour again cited as authority, is of the opinion that it was here, in this quarry, that 'the Dream of the Rood become realised upon stone'. If stone was ever quarried at this location it was of the Silurian age, probably greywacke. For more on these matters see Orton, 'Rethinking the Ruthwell Cross; Fragments and Critique; Tradition and History; Tongues and Sockets', pp. 78, 97 n. 8.

53 Brown, 'Report on the Ruthwell Cross', p. 223.

54 Duncan, 'Parish of Ruthwell', p. 219. See also the entry by Reverend George Gillespie, 'Parish of Cummertrees', p. 246, which borders Ruthwell at the east, noting limestone and sandstone 'along the south of the parish [that] is of very soft quality, and lies generally below a covering of sand, gravel, or moss; towards the middle of the parish it becomes harder, and lies under, or parallel with, limestone. In the north of the parish, the sandstone rises to the surface, and is so hard a quality that it is very difficult to wrought.' Murray, 'Parish of Mouswald', p. 443, to the north, records that the 'chief rocks are greywacke' with 'a blue limestone ... on a farm at Bucklerhole'. Thomson, 'Parish of Dalton', p. 371, to the north-east, records 'greywacke, which sometimes alternates with greywacke slate' and, in the south-east of the parish, greyish-white sandstone with limestone of inferior quality.

For a useful and accessible introduction to the geology of the region see Greig with Goodlet, Lumsden, and Tulloch, *British Regional Geology: The South of Scotland*.

55 Dinwiddie, *The Ruthwell Cross and Its Story: A Handbook for Tourists and Students*, p. 94, observed that 'The stone is of a hard gritty freestone and not of a more soft and laminated structure, like the red freestone which has been, and is still, quarried in the same district for building purposes'. Wherever it came from, Dinwiddie thought that it must have been 'conveyed a distance of at least four miles'. He was at a loss to explain how 'it was quarried and transported that distance in those far distant times and without the aid of modern mechanical appliances'.

56 What follows is taken from Andrew A. McMillan, British Geological Survey, Edinburgh, Report EE04/0651, 'Examination of Stone in the Ruthwell Monument, 2. Observations from Site Visit, 19 August 2004: 'Lower stone – All the characteristics observed point the two stones being of the same origin and likely to have been a single block from the

same bed. It is a quartz-rich sandstone, medium-grained with subrounded to subangular quartz with a small proportion (<5%) of weathered white feldspar. It is of uniform appearance, pale pinkish grey (Munsell Rock-color Chart, The Geological Society of America, 1991, 5YR 8/1), moderately well sorted and is non-micaceous. The stone is massive and no obvious bedding was detected.

Upper stone – two stones … of reddish hue with original carving separated and supported by additional masonry blocks. On the south side of the monument the lower stone with carved feet is enclosed by newer masonry.

From an examination of the south side, the lower stone, enclosed by newer masonry, is a quartz-rich sandstone, subrounded to subangular quartz, with Fe oxide coatings, medium grained, moderately well sorted, pale red (5R 6/2). The upper original stone is almost identical although there are additionally lenses of coarse-grained subrounded quartz with granules up to 3 mm across. Neither stone is obviously laminated.

On the north side of the monument, two blocks of pale red sandstone on which a single figure is carved have been pieced together. The two blocks have identical characteristics to those on the south side.

Provenance – Pale pinkish grey lower stone. It is highly likely that the two blocks are from the same bed. The macroscopic characteristics of this sandstone are similar to those observed in sandstones from the Carboniferous of the Solway basin. Thick beds of sandstone, which could have yielded suitable block for both building and carving, are present within the Lower Carboniferous of Annandale and Langholm districts. However it should be noted that similar sandstones occur throughout the Northumberland–Solway basins and that a 'far travelled' (e.g. >10 miles) source of the stone cannot be categorically excluded on geological grounds.

Provenance – Pale red upper stone. It is highly likely that the two carved stones on the south side are from the same bed. The reddened nature of these stones might point to a source from the New Red Sandstone (Permian or Triassic) of the neighbouring districts of Dumfries (Permian), Lochmaben (Permian) or Annan-Gretna (mainly Triassic) (D. C. Greig, *British Regional Geology. The South of Scotland*, 3rd Edition, Edinburgh, HMSO, 1971). Of these the Permian desert sandstones of Dumfries and Lochmaben basins may be ruled out. The Annan-Gretna sandstones, belonging to the St Bees Sandstone Formation, are generally finer grained than the original carved stones in the monument. Typically, the St Bees Sandstone exhibit a fine lamination, again not present in the carved stones. On balance it is concluded that the upper carved stones are also of Carboniferous provenance but from a bed of secondarily reddened sandstone. Such beds are commonly known from the Carboniferous strata of the district. It is not impossible for the stones of both the lower and upper sections of the monument to have been taken from different beds in the same excavation.

Note. No samples were taken for petrographic analysis. Should this be permitted, a more definite statement may be made.'

57 Greig, Goodlet, Lumsden, and Tulloch, *British Regional Geology: The South of Scotland*, Ch. 6, 'Carboniferous', pp. 61–85.

58 In 1824 blocks of New Red Triassic Sandstone quarried at Gallowbank (now Galabank), one mile above where they would be used in construction of the bridge across the River Annan at Annan, were floated downstream on specially built barges – see Hawkins, *The Sandstone Heritage of Dumfriesshire*, p. 4.

59 For example, the fragment of the tenth-century cross-shaft in St Luke, Great Clifton, Cumbria: see Bailey and Cramp, *Corpus of Anglo-Saxon Stone Sculpture*, Vol. II, *Cumberland, Westmorland and Lancashire North-of-the-Sands*, pp. 110–111, and the fragment of the tenth to eleventh century cross-shaft at Kirkby Stephen, also in Cumbria, see ibid., Kirkby Stephen 4, p. 123.

60 Bailey, *England's Earliest Sculptors*, pp. 6–7, records that gesso can still be seen on the surface of some fragments of seventh-century carvings of animals at Hexham and the modelled busts on a fragment of an eighth-century shaft at Otley, the earliest survival of gesso on Anglian sculpture in Northumbria. Bailey, *Viking Age Sculpture in Northern*

England, p. 25, also points out that eighth- and ninth-century sculptures at Monkwear-mouth and Ilkley still carry traces of a red colouring. He thinks it likely that, as well as serving a decorative purpose and adding to the meaning of the sculpture, the gesso or red paint was there to seal and waterproof the stone. For more on these matters see Lang, 'The Painting of Pre-Conquest Sculpture in Northumbria', and most recently Bailey, 'Anglo-Saxon Sculptures at Deerhurst', p. 2.

It is worth noting that *most* of the evidence for Anglo-Saxon stone sculpture being painted polychrome comes from survivals of the Viking Age – see Lang, *Corpus of Anglo-Saxon Stone Sculpture*, Vol. III, *York and Eastern Yorkshire*, Middleton 3, St Mary Castlegate York 3, York Minster 6, Clifford Street York 1, and Newgate 1; and Lang, *Corpus of Anglo-Saxon Stone Sculpture*, Vol. VI, *Northern Yorkshire*, Catterick 1, Croft on Tees 1, Kirklevington 1, and Melsonby 1. It could be that most pre-Viking stone sculpture was not dressed with red haematite paint or painted polychrome. We guess that the whiteness of gesso, rather than red haematite paint or polychrome, may have been more appealing to what one might call the Anglo-Saxon aesthetic of the pre-Viking Age – see Cramp, 'Beowulf and Archaeology', p. 63, and Alexander, 'Some Aesthetic Principles in the Use of Colour in Anglo-Saxon Art', p. 146. The pre-Viking Germanic Anglo-Saxons seem to have taken pleasure in techniques of decoration and ornament that produced vivid effects of light and dark, shiny and dull or matt more than contrasts of hue. We note that this delight in light and dark, which may seem antipathetic to the classical Mediterranean aesthetic of the Roman world that informs the Ruthwell monument and so much Anglo-Saxon stone sculpture, including of course the Bewcastle monument, is compatible with it. One only has to bring to mind what St Augustine, with at least one eye on Roman architecture, has to say about the interplay of form and interval, solid and void, light and dark, in achieving a unified whole or balanced totality – see St Augustine, *De civitate Dei*, Bk XI, Ch. XXIII. The interplay of light and dark *is* colour in the late Antique world.

61 See for example, the 'Roman Merchant's Stone' found at Bowness-on-Solway in 1790, Tullie House Museum and Art Gallery, Carlisle, recorded in Collingwood and Wright, *The Roman Inscriptions of Britain*, 2059: '[To the Mother Goddesses] I, Antonianus, dedicate this shrine. But do ye grant that the increase in my venture may confirm my prayers, and soon will I hallow this poem with golden letters one by one.'

62 Farrell, 'Reflections on the Iconography of the Ruthwell and Bewcastle Crosses', pp. 365 and 368, and, thereafter, in Farrell with Karkov, 'The Construction, Deconstruction, and Reconstruction of the Ruthwell Cross: Some Caveats', pp. 43–44. Farrell's observations prompted further puzzling about this fragment by Meyvaert, 'A New Perspective on the Ruthwell Cross: *Ecclesia* and *Vita Monastica*', pp. 100–102, Bailey, 'The Ruthwell Cross: A Non-Problem', pp. 141–148, and Orton, 'Rethinking the Ruthwell Cross: Fragments and Critique; Tradition and History; Tongues and Sockets', pp. 79–80, 98–100 ns 13–17. Although Bailey convincingly demonstrated that the 'incongruous fragment' was once an integral part of the pale red upper stone or cross, Farrell's point that it may not have been 'part of the single cross we now have in Ruthwell church' remains moot.

63 See also the illustrations in Stuart, *The Sculptured Stones of Scotland*, Vol. II, Plates XIX–XX, and Stephens, *The Old-Northern Runic Monuments of Scandinavia and England now first collected and deciphered by George Stephens, Esq., F.S.A.*, Vol. 1, facing p. 405, which follow and add to Duncan's drawing. We note also that the illustration in Stephens's *The Old-Northern Runic Monuments of Scandinavia and England* transposes the narrow north and south sides of the monument. J. Basire's drawing, also after Duncan, in Kemble, 'On Anglo-Saxon Runes', fig. 17 facing p. 35, gives an even more radical misrepresentation of this part of the monument.

64 Howlett, 'Two Panels on the Ruthwell Cross', pp. 333–336, and Howlett, 'Inscriptions and Design on the Ruthwell Cross', pp. 71–76, 83. See also Meyvaert, 'An Apocalypse Panel on the Ruthwell Cross', pp. 11–14.

65 Kitzinger, 'Interlace and Icons: Form and Function in Early Insular Art', p. 9 and fig. 1.8. Kitzinger notes that the runic inscriptions in the borders on the monument's narrow

north and south sides are arranged in the same way. The painting, as it has survived, seems either to date to or to have been amended in the early eighth century, see Belting, *Likenes and Presence: A History of the Image before the Era of Art*, p. 126.

66 Fred Orton thanks Éamonn Ó Carragáin for drawing his attention to this then recently restored painting and its poem inscription during a trip to Rome in September 1999. It is illustrated in Ó Carragáin, *Ritual and the Rood: Liturgical Images and the Old English Poems of the* Dream of the Rood *Tradition*, Pl. 8.

67 Bede, *Historia abbatum*, 6. See Paul Meyvaert, 'Bede and the Church Paintings at Wearmouth-Jarrow', *Anglo-Saxon England* 8 (1979), pp. 63–77.

68 Page, *An Introduction to English Runes*, p. 150. On how the inscriptions may have been arranged to make them easier to read, see Ó Carragáin, 'The Ruthwell Crucifixion Poem in Its Iconographic Contexts', pp. 8–12. For some interesting observations on how the runes may have been arranged to function decoratively within the borders, see King, 'The Ruthwell Cross - A Linguistic Monument (Runes as Evidence for Old English)', pp. 68–69.

69 Okasha, *Hand-list of Anglo-Saxon Non-Runic Inscriptions*, p. 111; Ó Carragáin, 'Seeing, Reading, Singing the Ruthwell Cross: Vernacular Poetry, Old Roman Liturgy, Implied Audience', p. 95. Wherever we refer to the Latin inscriptions on the Ruthwell Cross we usually follow the transcriptions given after computer-enhanced digital photographs by McKinnell, 'Ruthwell Cross, § 2', pp. 626–629. Doubtful forms are given in italics, and each present but illegible character is represented by a question mark. Three dots represent an uncertain number of lost characters.

70 McKinnell, 'Ruthwell', pp. 626–627, who notes that Howlett, 'Inscriptions and Design on the Ruthwell Cross', p. 73, reads and reconstructs the inscription as 'marþa|maria mr|dominnæ' – see also Howlett, 'Two Panels on the Ruthwell Cross', p. 334. McKinnell's computer-enhanced digital photographs show a cross that is usually read as the right side of the 'r' of 'mr' at the end of the top inscription. He points out that this must be the beginning of the inscription and so rules out the reconstruction by Howlett.

71 Bearing in mind that McKinnell, 'Ruthwell', gives 'marþa|mar[?]m[?]', see Howlett, 'Two Panels on the Ruthwell Cross', p. 334 and 'Inscriptions and Design of the Ruthwell Cross', p. 73, conjecturing that what he saw as 'marþa|maria mr' could mean, according to whether one takes the uncharacteristically drastic abbreviation 'mr' as 'mater' or 'merentes', *either* 'Martha and Mary mother of the Lord' *or* 'Martha and Mary, meritorious ladies'. If so, the former mistakes the gender of the word for 'Lord' by giving 'dominnæ' for 'domini'.

72 McKinnell, 'Ruthwell', p. 627, and Hawkes and Ó Carragáin with Trench-Jellicoe, 'John the Baptist and the *Agnus Dei*: Ruthwell (and Bewcastle) Revisited', pp. 133, 134, 135.

73 First noticed by Meyvaert, 'An Apocalypse Panel on the Ruthwell Cross', pp. 11–12.

74 Howlett, 'Two Panels on the Ruthwell Cross', p. 333, and 'Inscriptions and Design on the Ruthwell Cross', p. 76, read the inscription as '[...]DORAMUS [E]T NON EUM', which he conjectured to completion as '+ADORAMUS ET NOT EUM SINGILLATIM TOTAM VERO TRINITATEM / We adore the Lamb of God, and not Him singly, but the whole Trinity.'

75 Duncan, 'An Account of the Remarkable Monument in the shape of a Cross', p. 321.

76 Ball, 'Inconsistencies in the Main Runic Inscriptions on the Ruthwell Cross', 2.1, p. 108, assuming that Duncan thought he was *reconstructing* something, was of the opinion that the Ruthwell Cross might be 'the result of a bungled reconstruction undertaken by Dr. Henry Duncan'.

77 Reginald Bainbrigg's note, British Library MS. Cotton Julius VI, fol. 352, was first published by Page, 'An Early Drawing of the Ruthwell Cross', pp. 285–288. Bainbrigg made two tours of the area around Hadrian's Wall, the first in 1599 and the second in 1601. It seems most likely that he visited Ruthwell on the first trip – see the detail and itinerary in Hepple, 'Sir Robert Cotton, Camden's *Britannia*, and the Early History of Roman Wall Studies', pp. 8–9. For something more on Bainbrigg see Haverfield, 'Cotton Julius F.VI. Notes on Reginald Bainbrigg of Appleby, on William Camden and on

Roman Inscriptions', pp. 344–349. See also Edwards, 'Reginald Bainbrigg, Westmorland Antiquary', pp. 119–125. On the idea of historical 'fact' as that which is 'worthy of memory, i.e. worthy to be *noted*', see Barthes, 'The Discourse of History', pp. 137–140.

78 'Ecce de improviso in crucem admirandae altitudinis incidi, quae est in templo de Revall, pulchris imaginibus Christi historiam referentibus, vinetis, animalibus eleganter et splendide p[er]politam, de duobus lateribus, a basi ascendendo ad apicem, et contra ab apice descendendo ad basim p[er]egrinis literis, sed fugientibus, incisam. Inscriptio talis.'

79 Another historical example of something that is seen as a cross that does not have the shape of a cross is provided by the so-called 'Acca's Cross' in the abbey at Hexham. This monument was put together from four fragments, which were found at different times and different locations. Even before they were put together, the fragments were referred to as 'Acca's Cross' for the cross that was described by Symeon of Durham as standing over the grave of Bishop Acca who died in 740 and was buried at Hexham. It is still cross-headless for a cross-head has not been found.

80 See McFarlan, *James McFarlan*, p. 83.

81 Nicolson, *Letters on Various Subjects, Literary, Political, and Ecclesiastical, to and from W. Nicolson*, Vol. I, No. 23, 24 May 1697. Edward Lhwyd was one of the first antiquarians to make the case for a sophisticated British civilisation on the basis of surviving artefacts. Nicolson asked Lhwyd that if he had 'any Danish gentlemen in the University (now that my friend [Ole] Worm has left it) who are skilled in their antient language, I should be ready and glad to communicate the whole to them, and my thoughts upon it.'

82 Hickes, *Linguarum Veterum Septentrionalium Thesaurus Grammatico-Criticus et Archaeologicus, Pars Tertia: seu Grammaticae Islandicae Rudimenta*, tab. IIII, between pp. 4–5.

83 'Bishop Nicolson's Diaries: Part II', p. 195.

84 'Bishop Nicolson's Diaries: Part II', 5 July 1704, p. 196.

85 'Bishop Nicolson's Diaries: Part II', p. 196.

86 *Camden's Britannia, Newly Translated into English with Large Additions and Improvements, by Edmund Gibson*, p. 910.

87 'Account of the Curiosities at Dumfries by Doctour Archibald', p. 187. See also MacDonald, 'Dr. Archibald's "Account of the Curiosities of Dumfries" and "Account Anent Galloway"', pp. 50–64.

88 MacDonald, 'Dr. Archibald's "Account of the Curiosities of Dumfries" and "Account Anent Galloway"', p. 51.

89 See 'A Broken Cross in Revel Church in Annandale, 18 May, 1699', in Mitchell and Clark, eds, *Geographical Collections Relating to Scotland made by Walter Macfarlane*, p. 255.

90 Gordon, *Itinerarium Septentrionale: Or, a Journey thro' most of the Counties of Scotland and Those in the North of England*, pp. 160–161 plates 57 and 58.

91 The illustration of the north and south sides is inscribed for the Right Honourable Richard Earl of Burlington, a well-known patron of antiquarian literature whose interest in the monument would not have been as vivid or as personal as David Murray's.

92 Pennant, *A Tour in Scotland and Voyage to the Hebrides*, pp. 84–85.

93 See Cassidy, 'The Later Life of the Ruthwell Cross: From the Seventeenth Century to the Present', pp. 9–10, and Orton, 'Rethinking the Ruthwell Cross', p. 100, n. 16.

94 Duncan, 'An Account of the Remarkable Monument in the shape of a Cross', pp. 318–319.

It is not known where or when the fragment (Fig. 72) exhibited in the Dinwiddie memorial surround was found. Baldwin Brown doesn't mention it in his 'Report on the Ruthwell Cross', 1920. Nor does Dinwiddie mention it in *The Ruthwell Cross and Its Story: A Handbook for Tourists and Students*, 1927. There have been few attempts to associate it or integrate it with the monument – for one attempt see Cramp, 'The Evangelist Symbols and Their Parallels in Anglo-Saxon Sculpture', pp. 118–120, 122.

95 Nicolson, 'Bishop Nicolson's Diaries: Part II', p. 196.

96 This discussion of 'objective history' takes from Roland Barthes, 'The Discourse of History', pp. 127–140, and 'The Reality Effect', pp. 141–148. Also in mind was Geary,

Phantoms of Remembrance: Memory and Oblivion at the End of the First Millennium, pp. 10–11, on how, in the modern epoch, a false dichotomy was established between 'collective memory' and 'history'; the former is oral, the latter is written; the latter begins where the former ends. The dichotomy holds that while 'collective memory' is 'the fluid, trans-formative and enveloping lived tradition of a social group', 'history' is 'analytic, critical, and rational, the product of the application of specialized scientific methodology'. These distinctions are very deceptive.

97 See, for some examples: Barbour, 'Regarding the Origin of the Ruthwell Cross', pp. 28–29; Brown, 'Report on the Ruthwell Cross', p. 223; and Cassidy, 'The Later Life of the Ruthwell Cross: From the Seventeenth Century to the Present', pp. 6–8.

98 See Fentress and Wickham, *Social Memory*, passim, for interesting and useful discus-sions of oral history, oral memory and oral tradition.

99 Barthes, 'The Discourse of History', p. 138. Greary, *Phantoms of Remembrance*, p. 12, makes a related point: 'If the writing of modern historians appears analytic, critical, and rational, the reason is that these are the rhetorical tools that promise the best chance of influencing the collective memory of our age'.

100 Nicolson, *Letters on Various Subjects, Literary, Political, and Ecclesiastical, to and from W. Nicolson*, Vol. I, p. 63, No. 24, 24 May 1697.

101 'Bishop Nicolson's Diaries: Part II', p. 196.

102 Pennant, *A Tour in Scotland, and a Voyage to the Hebrides*, p. 85.

103 Craig, 'Parish of Ruthwell', p. 456.

104 Duncan, 'An Account of a Remarkable Monument in the shape of a Cross', p. 317.

105 Barthes, 'The Death of the Author', p. 146.

106 Symeon, *Libellus de Exordio*, II.12, III.1, i.12.

107 Barthes, 'The Reality Effect', pp. 141–142.

108 'Bishop Nicolson's Diaries: Part II', pp. 195, 196–197. On the several fords across the Solway Firth see McIntire, 'The Fords of the Solway', pp. 152–170.

109 Laurie, 'Parish of Tinwald', p. 486.

110 McMillan, 'Parish of Torthorwald', p. 498.

111 McMillan, 'Parish of Torthorwald', p. 498. We also note what, in the sixteenth century, John Leland recorded concerning the Roman fort at Netherby on the River Esk, *The Itinerary of John Leland in or about the years 1535–1543*, Vol. 5, p. 51: 'Ther hath bene mervelus buyldinges, as appere by ruinus walles, and men alyve have sene rynges and staples yn the walles, as yt had bene stayes or holdes for shyppes ... The ruines be now a iii. myles at the lest from the flowyng water of Sulway sandes. The gresse groweth now on the ruines of the walles.'

112 McMillan, 'Parish of Torthorwald', pp. 498–499.

113 Gillespie, 'Parish of Cummertrees', p. 248. On salt making at Ruthwell see Pennant, *A Tour in Scotland, and Voyage to the Hebrides*, pp. 86–87.

114 Pennant, *A Tour in Scotland, and Voyage to the Hebrides*, p. 87.

115 Duncan, 'An Account of a Remarkable Monument in the shape of a Cross', p. 317.

116 The forts are, east–west: Annan Hill and Annanfoot, presumably controlling the estuary of the River Annan and the ford across the Solway Firth between Annan and Bowness over Bowness Wath; Ruthwell; Ward Law and Lantonside. For a useful discussion of the Roman occupation of the region see Wilson, 'Roman and Native in Dumfriesshire', pp. 103–160.

117 Crowe, 'Excavations at Ruthwell, Dumfries, 1980 and 1984', pp. 46–47.

118 Stevenson, 'Further Thoughts on Some Well Known Problems', pp. 21–22.

119 Stevenson, 'Further Thoughts on Some Well Known Problems', p. 21. Stevenson is drawing on E. Coatsworth, 'The Iconography of the Crucifixion in pre-Conquest Sculp-ture in England', unpub. Ph.D. Thesis, University of Durham, 1979.

120 Dods's letter to Hewison is to be found in an envelope interleaved in the National Museums of Scotland's copy of Hewison's *The Runic Roods of Ruthwell and Bewcastle with a Short History of the Cross and Crucifix in Scotland*, NMS Library Accession No. 7983, ATTIC CC 310 HEW. For previous references to it see: Stevenson, 'Further Thoughts on

Some Well Known Problems', p. 21; Farrell with Karkov, 'The Construction, Deconstruction, and Reconstruction of the Ruthwell Cross: Some Caveats', pp. 38–40, 42, which reproduces its first two pages; Mac Lean, 'Technique and Contact: Carpentry-Constructed Insular Stone Crosses', pp. 167–168; and Orton, 'Rethinking the Ruthwell Monument: Fragments and Critique; Tradition and History; Tongues and Sockets', where it is transcribed in full, pp. 89–92.

121 See note in Hewison's handwriting in *The Runic Roods of Ruthwell and Bewcastle*, p. viii.

122 'Bishop Nicolson's Diaries', p. 196, and Duncan, 'An Account of a Remarkable Monument in the shape of a Cross', p. 320.

123 McFarlan, *James McFarlan*, p. 83. The measurements provided by Duncan, McFarlan and Dods are cause for confusion. Those seeking clarification are directed to Orton, 'Rethinking the Ruthwell Monument: Fragments and Critique; Tradition and History; Tongues and Sockets', p. 105 n. 55.

124 Mitchell and Clark, *Geographical Collections Relating to Scotland, Made by Walter Macfarlane*, p. 255.

125 Pococke, *Tours in Scotland 1747, 1750, 1760 by Richard Pococke, Bishop of Meath, From the Original Ms. and Drawings in the British Museum, edited with a Biographical Sketch of the Author, by Daniel William Kemp*, 'Tour Through Scotland, 1760', p. 32.

126 Pennant, *A Tour in Scotland and Voyage to the Hebrides*, p. 85.

127 McFarlan, *James McFarlan*, pp. 88–89.

128 Wright (1840–1872), *The Ruthwell Cross and Other Remains of the Late Hannah Mary Wright*, pp. 20–21. She tells us that she made her visit during the incumbency of Duncan's successor, Reverend Alexander Stevenson (1844–1858).

129 See Cramp, *Corpus*, Vol. I, Pt 1, pp. 217–221, and ills 1210–1212, Rothbury 1a–c, 'Incomplete cross-shaft and -head in three fragments', which is dated to the first half of the ninth century. The round dowel-hole in the top of 1b, illus. 1211, is evidence for the way that it was joined to the cross-head. The square dowel-hole in the face of 1aB, illus. 1217, the surviving cross-arm, is taken to be a repair. See also Bailey and Cramp, *Corpus*, Vol. II, p. 118 and ills 371–376, Isel 1 'Upper part of cross-shaft', which is dated to the tenth century, and pp. 127–128 and ills 427 and 429, and Lowther 1a–b, 'Part of a cross-shaft in two pieces', which is dated late eighth to early ninth century, but note that it is not known whether this is a repair.

Chapter 3: Style, and seeing ... as

1 This chapter draws on two abbreviated attempts to think through similarity with regard to style by Orton: 'Rethinking the Ruthwell and Bewcastle Monuments: Some Strictures on Similarity: Some Questions of History', and 'Rethinking the Ruthwell and Bewcastle Monuments: Some Deprecation of Style: Some Consideration of Form and Ideology'. The reconsideration of the several pieces of antiquarian evidence for the shape of the form of the Bewcastle monument sticks fairly close to material presented in Orton, 'Evidence the Terminal Feature: More or Less on the Bewcastle Monument'.

2 Schapiro, 'Style', p. 287.

3 For some important and very useful different ways of seeing the Ruthwell and Bewcastle monuments in terms of style see: Brown, 'Report on the Ruthwell Cross. With some references to that at Bewcastle in Cumberland', and Brown, *The Arts in Early England*, Vol. V, *The Ruthwell and Bewcastle Crosses*; Collingwood, *Northumbrian Crosses of the Pre-Norman Age*; Saxl, 'The Ruthwell Cross'; and Cramp, 'The Anglian Sculptured Crosses of Dumfriesshire', and 'Early Northumbrian Sculpture'.

4 Schapiro, 'Style', pp. 287–312.

5 Schapiro, 'Style', p. 311.

6 Collingwood, *Northumbrian Crosses*, p. 9.

7 Collingwood, 'A Pedigree of Anglian Crosses', p. 114.

8 Collingwood, *Northumbrian Crosses*, p. 184.

9 Collingwood, *Northumbrian Crosses*, 'Preface', n.p.

10 Collingwood, *Northumbrian Crosses*, 'Preface', n.p., p. 24.

11 Collingwood, *Northumbrian Crosses*, 'Preface', n.p.

12 Collingwood, *Northumbrian Crosses*, 'Preface', n.p.

13 Collingwood, *Northumbrian Crosses*, p. 184.

14 Collingwood, *Northumbrian Crosses*, p. 39.

15 See Panofsky, 'Iconography and Iconology: An Introduction to the Study of Renaissance Art', pp. 51–58.

16 Fish, 'What Is Stylistics and Why Are They Saying Such Terrible Things About It?', pp. 69–71.

17 Hanson, *Patterns of Discovery: An Inquiry into the Conceptual Foundations of Science*, excerpted as 'Observation', in Harrison and Orton, eds, *Modernism, Criticism, Realism*, pp. 69–83 at 75.

18 See, for example, Cramp, *The British Academy Corpus of Anglo-Saxon Stone Sculpture*, Vol. I, Pt 1, *County Durham and Northumberland*, 'General Introduction to the Series', pp. ix–li, and subsequent volumes.

19 Schapiro, 'Style', see for example, pp. 306, 307.

20 Goodman, 'Seven Strictures on Similarity' in *Problems and Projects*, reprinted in Harrison and Orton, eds, *Modernism, Criticism, Realism*, pp. 85–92.

21 Goodman, 'Seven Strictures on Similarity', *Modernism, Criticism, Realism*, p. 91.

22 Goodman, 'Seven Strictures on Similarity', p. 87.

23 Goodman, 'Seven Strictures on Similarity', p. 88.

24 Goodman, 'Seven Strictures on Similarity', p. 89.

25 Goodman, 'Seven Strictures on Similarity', p. 90.

26 Goodman, 'Seven Strictures on Similarity', p. 90.

27 Goodman, 'Seven Strictures on Similarity', p. 90.

28 See Borges, 'Pierre Menard, Author of the *Quixote*', p. 69. Borges wryly comments that though Cervantes's text and Menard's are 'verbally identical', the second, while suffering from a 'certain affectation', is 'almost infinitely richer'. We also note that Borges considers the 'contrast in style ... vivid'.

29 Goodman, 'Seven Strictures on Similarity', p. 90.

30 Goodman, 'Seven Strictures on Similarity', p. 91.

31 Goodman, 'Seven Strictures on Similarity', p. 91.

32 Goodman, 'Seven Strictures on Similarity', p. 92.

33 See, for example, *Corpus*, Vol. II, p. 66, with regard to some types of interlace on the Bewcastle monument and some panels of interlace in the Lindisfarne Gospels.

34 Goodman, 'Seven Strictures on Similarity', p. 91.

35 Wittgenstein, *Philosophical Investigations*, Part IIxi, 193e–204e, at 202e, excerpted as 'Seeing and Seeing as', in Harrison and Orton, eds, *Modernism, Criticism, Realism*, pp. 57–68 at 66.

36 Wittgenstein, *Philosophical Investigations*, 193e, *Modernism, Criticism, Realism*, p. 59.

37 Wittgenstein, *Philosophical Investigations*, 200e, *Modernism, Criticism, Realism*, p. 64.

38 *Corpus*, Vol. II, Bewcastle 1, p. 61.

39 *Corpus*, Vol. II, Bewcastle 2, p. 72.

40 *Corpus*, Vol. II, appendix C, 'Lost Stones for which No Illustration Has Survived', Bewcastle 7, pp. 172–173.

41 Bailey, 'Innocent from the Great Offence', p. 99.

42 Bailey, 'Innocent from the Great Offence', p. 99.

43 Howard, 'Observations on Bridekirk Font and on the Runic Column at Bewcastle in Cumberland', pp. 113–118, extracted in Cook, *Some Accounts of the Bewcastle Cross between the Years 1607 and 1861*, 'IX. Henry Howard's Account, 1801', pp. 154–158. Howard recorded the socket in his letter of 16 April 1801, see his 'Observations on Bridekirk Font and on the Runic Column at Bewcastle', p. 117. Lysons and Lysons, *Magna Britannia, being a concise topographical account of the several counties of Great Britain*, Vol. IV, *Cumberland*, measured it as 8½ by 7½ inches – anthologised in Cook, *Some Accounts of the Bewcastle Cross*, 'X. Lysons' *Magna Britannia*, 1816', p. 159. This socket was filled with cement in 1890, see Ferguson, 'Report on Injury to the Bewcastle Obelisk', p. 54.

44 It's worth noting the following from Ferguson, 'Report on Injury to the Bewcastle Obelisk', p. 55: 'In the centre of the top [of the base-block] a socket, 1 ft. 11 in. square, is sunk to a depth of 11 in.; in this the obelisk fits and is secured by lead run in between it and the sides of the socket. Part of the south side of the socket has been broken off, probably by the action of frost, and is missing; it has been replaced by the loose stone mentioned before, which is a rough undressed piece of a different kind of stone from the rest of the socket. This piece had at some time or other been displaced, and reset on a slope so as to run water in under the obelisk. Mr. Baty [the master-mason and quarry worker who undertook the repairs and secured the monument in the socket in 1890] found that a large piece was broken off the part of the obelisk concealed in the socket, and is missing. This would point to the obelisk having had either an accidental injury, while it was first being elevated and placed in position, or a subsequent fall.' That the monument was secured in the base block with lead was first noticed by Haigh, 'The Saxon Cross at Bewcastle', p. 150.

45 See Haverfield, 'Cotton Julius F.VI: Notes on Reginald Bainbrigg of Appleby, on William Camden and Some Roman Inscriptions', p. 355: 'Crux quae est in caemiterio est viginti fere pedum, ex uno quadrato lapide graphice exciso cum hac inscriptione.'

46 Camden, *Britannia, sive, Florentissimorum regnorum Angliae, Scotiae, Hiberniae, et insularum ad iacentium ex intima antiquitate chorographica descriptio*, p. 644: 'In ecclesia quae quodammodo collapsa vice saxi sepulchralis iacet haec vetusta inscriptio aliunde translata

LEG II AVG
FECIT

In coemiterio Crux in viginti plùs minùs pedes ex uno quadrato saxo graphicè excisa surgit, & inscripta, sed literis ita sugientibus ut legi nequaquam possint. Quod autem ipsa Crux ita interstincta sit, ut clypeus gentilitius familae de *Vaulx*, eorum opus fuisse existimare licet.'

47 First pointed out by Page, *Corpus*, Vol. II, appendix C, 'Lost Stones for which No Illustration Has Survived', 7, Bewcastle, p. 173.

48 Prevost transcribed and ed., 'A trip into England for a few days in 1741 by Sir John Clerk', p. 260.

49 Hepple, 'Lord William Howard and the Naworth-Rokeby Collection of Inscribed Roman Stones', p. 88.

50 On Nicolas Roscarrock, his time at Naworth and his relations with William Howard, see Rowse, 'Nicholas Roscarrock and His Lives of the Saints', pp. 3–31. On Roscarrock and William Howard see also Howard S. Reinmuth Jr, 'Lord William Howard (1563–1640) and his Catholic Associations', *Recusant History* 12 (The Catholic Record Society, 1973–74), pp. 226–234.

51 Roscarrock, letter to William Camden, BL MS Cotton Julius C.V. fol. 77, extract anthologised in Cook, *Some Accounts of the Bewcastle Cross*, p. 131. See also Page, 'The Bewcastle Cross', in Page, *Runes and Runic Inscriptions: Collected Essays on Anglo-Saxon and Viking Runes*, p. 60, who transcribes Roscarrock's letter somewhat differently. The other escape, 'the one in Cornwall', was that Camden had turned St Columb, a female saint, into St Columbanus – see Rowse, 'Nicholas Roscarrock and His Lives of the Saints', p. 15.

52 All four notes and their copies of the inscription are discussed in Cook, *Some Accounts of the Bewcastle Cross*, pp. 262–267, and Page, 'The Bewcastle Cross' (1960), in Page, *Runes and Runic Inscriptions*, pp. 66–68 – see also Page, *Corpus*, Vol. II, appendix C, 'Lost Stones for which No Illustration Has Survived', Bewcastle 7, pp. 172–173. Our account of these notes makes a different narrative and comes to a different conclusion.

53 Page, 'The Bewcastle Cross', p. 68.

54 Page, 'The Bewcastle Cross', p. 67.

55 Page, 'The Bewcastle Cross', p. 68.

56 Page, 'The Bewcastle Cross', pp. 67–68.

57 See Page, *Corpus*, Vol. II, p. 173.

58 See, for example, Brown, *The Arts in Early England*, Vol. V, *The Ruthwell and Bewcastle Crosses*, p. 117, fig. 10, and Collingwood, *Northumbrian Crosses of the Pre-Norman Age*, p. 85, fig. 102.

59 Page, 'The Bewcastle Cross', pp. 66–67.

60 See Page, *Corpus*, Vol. II, p. 173.

61 See the discussion of these 'inessentials' in Page, 'The Bewcastle Cross', p. 67.

62 Worm, *Danicorum monumentorum libri sex: e spissis antiquitatum tenebris et in Dania ac Norvegia extantibus ruderibus eruti*, p. 161: 'Sculpta fuit haec Inscriptio Epistylio crucis lapidae, Beucastri partibus Angliae borealibus (ubi Dani plurimum versabantur) Camdenoq; & mihi simul exhibita Anno Domini 1618, ab Antiqvitatum inter proceres Angliae pertissimo Domino Guilielmo Howard novissimi Duci Norfolciae filio.' Page, 'The Bewcastle Cross', p. 67, gives the text of a manuscript version, possibly a draft, that survives in MS Gl. Kgl. Sml. 2370 4°, Royal Library, Copenhagen. Page, 'The Bewcastle Cross', pp. 66–68, and *Corpus*, Vol. II, p. 173, is of the opinion that 'the drawings, skilfully reproduced by men unacquainted with English runes, make it amply clear that the text read ... ricæs dr[y]htnæs (translation: "of the powerful king" or "of the king's power")'.

63 Nicolson, 'A Letter ... Concerning a Runic Inscription at Beaucastle', pp. 1287–1291, taken from Cook, *Some Accounts of the Bewcastle Cross*, 'III. Nicolson's Letter to Obadiah Walker, 1685', p. 133.

64 'Nicolson's Letter to Obadiah Walker, 1685', p. 134.

65 'Nicolson's Letter to Obadiah Walker, 1685', p. 134.

66 'Nicolson's Letter to Obadiah Walker, 1685', p. 134.

67 Hutchinson, *The History of the County of Cumberland*, Vol. I, pp. 81–83. The engraving that illustrates the 'Bewcastle Monument', opp. p. 85, is the only one to show the remains of a tongue; we should ignore it.

68 Cox, ed., *Magna Britannia et Hibernia, antiqua & nova: or, A New Survey of Great Britain, wherein, to the topographical account given by Mr. Camden, and the late editors of his Britannia is added a more large history*, Vol. I, p. 388.

69 See Smith, [Letter], *Gentleman's Magazine*, Vol. 12, June 1742, pp. 318–319 at 318, July 1742, pp. 368–369, and October 1742, p. 529 – extracted in Cook, *Some Accounts of the Bewcastle Cross*, 'VI. Smith's Letter to the *Gentleman's Magazine*, 1742', pp. 142–146, which does not include the text on p. 318 and so omits Smith's version of the illustration in *Magna Britannia* that so offended him. For something on Smith see Gordon Maley, 'George Smith the Geographer and His Ascent of Crossfell', pp. 135–144.

70 Smith, [Letter], *Gentleman's Magazine*, July 1742, p. 368.

71 The most convenient introduction to this matter is still Spence, 'The Pacification of the Borders, 1593–1628', pp. 59–160.

72 Spence, 'The Pacification of the Borders', p. 123, citing a letter from Sir William Hutton to the Earl of Cumberland, December 1611.

73 Spence, 'The Pacification of the Borders', p. 122, and Curwen, 'Bewcastle', p. 196.

74 Spence, 'The Pacification of the Borders', p. 122 n. 188, 135.

75 Spence, 'The Pacification of the Borders', pp. 102, 123, 136.

76 Spence, 'The Pacification of the Borders', pp. 146–147.

77 Spence, 'The Pacification of the Borders', p. 150.

78 Armstrong, 'An Account of a curious OBELISK, of one Stone, standing in the Church Yard of Bewcastle, in the North East Part of Cumberland, about 16 Miles from Carlisle', p. 388, see Cook, *Some Accounts of the Bewcastle Cross*, 'VII. Armstrong's Plate, 1775,' pp. 147–149 at 147. For something on Armstrong see Hutchinson, *The History of the County of Cumberland*, Vol. I, p. 80.

79 *Corpus*, Vol. II, illus. 117, 118.

80 Library of the Society of Antiquaries of London, Cumberland red folio, no. 3.

81 A search of the Society of Antiquaries of London Minutes Book for the period 1765–1768 turned up no reference to these drawings. We thank Bernard Nurse, Librarian, for his help with this matter. Also in the portfolio is what seems to be an impressed drawing of the large runic inscription on the west side of the Bewcastle monument subsequently

used to make the engraved illustration in Howard, 'Observations on Bridekirk Font and on the Runic Column at Bewcastle in Cumberland', pp. 113–118.

82 Lyttelton, 'An Account of a Remarkable Monument in Penrith Church Yard, Cumberland', Pl. IV facing p. 48.

83 Whilst levelling the ground for the house, Graham recovered a large quantity of Roman remains and went about acquiring Roman inscribed stones and sculptures from other sites and other collections. On Graham's collecting activities see Birley, 'The Roman Fort at Netherby', pp. 18–19 and 27. Ferguson, 'The *Lapidarium Septentrionale*, &', p. 144, No. 784, first noticed that the 'Seated Mother Goddess' came from Bewcastle: 'This was found at Bewcastle. In an album belonging to the Society of Antiquaries is a drawing of it with the legend: "Drawing of a stone found recently at Bewcastle and removed to Netherby 1765." [*sic*]'.

84 Collingwood and Wright, *The Roman Inscriptions of Britain*, Vol. I, *Inscriptions on Stone*, p. 322, No. 966.

85 See Birley, 'The Roman Fort at Netherby', p. 27.

86 Thomas Pennant, *A Tour in Scotland and A Voyage to the Hebrides*, p. 80.

87 Pennant, *Tour from Downing to Alston-Moor*, pp. 180–182.

88 *Corpus*, Vol. II, pp. 72–73.

89 *Corpus*, Vol. II, p. 72.

90 *Corpus*, Vol. II, p. 72.

91 *Corpus*, Vol. II, pp. 115–117 and illus. 355, 357, 359, 361.

92 Hawkes, '*Iuxta Morem Romanorum*: Stone and Sculpture in Anglo-Saxon England', pp. 78–79, 95 n. 26.

93 Hawkes, '*Iuxta Morem Romanorum*: Stone and Sculpture in Anglo-Saxon England', p. 79.

94 See Nash, *Pictorial Dictionary of Ancient Rome*, Vol. I, pp. 283–286 and 276–279 respectively.

95 *Einsiedeln Itinerary*, for the column of Antoninus Pius see Route 2, pp. 168–172.

96 See Nash, *Pictorial Dictionary of Ancient Rome*, Vol. I, pp. 270–275, 282, and 280–281 respectively.

97 Bede, *HE*, II 4.

98 The basilica of Sta Agnese fuori le Mura, which was founded by the emperor Constantine's daughter Constantia in AD 342, features in the *Einsiedeln Itinerary*, see Route 2, pp. 168–169.

99 *Einsiedeln Itinerary*, for the column of Augustus see Route 2, pp. 168–172, Route 4, pp. 175–178 and for the obelisk on the Collis Hortorum see Route 2. See also, for a useful historical guide to the fourteen known ancient obelisks of Rome, with bibliography, Nash, *Pictorial Dictionary of Ancient Rome*, Vol. II, pp. 130–161; for the obelisk of Augustus see pp. 134–136, and for the obelisk that stood on the Collis Hortorum see pp. 144–147.

100 See Nash, *Pictorial Dictionary of Ancient Rome*, Vol. II, pp. 161–162.

101 Dodwell, *Anglo-Saxon Art: A New Perspective*, pp. 113–118, devoted several paragraphs to puzzling what the Anglo-Saxons meant by 'pyramid'. What follows agrees with Dodwell with regard to the function but not the form of pyramids, which seems to us, reading the sources he cites, a more complex matter.

102 See Taylor, 'The Anglo-Saxon Church at Canterbury', pp. 101–130, espec. 127, 11(c), where he cites Eadmer, *De reliquiis Sancti Audoeni*: 'Tumba super eum in modum pyramidis grandi sublimique constructa habente ad caput sancti altare matutinale'.

103 Taylor, 'The Anglo-Saxon Church at Canterbury', p. 126, 10, citing Osbern's *Vita Sancti Dunstani*: 'quae ad australem partem altaris in modum pyramidis exstructa fuit'.

104 William of Malmesbury, *Gesta pontificum*, 148. It is not clear from William's description whether the wooden cover projecting out over Wulfstan's grave was suspended from the arch above or rested on top of the tomb.

105 Here we have followed the advice of Scott, ed. and trans., *De antiquitate Glastonie ecclesie*, p. 196, n. 75, and used the version given in William of Malmesbury, *De gestis regum*, ed. Stubbs, Vol. I, Bk I, 21. See *De antiquitate Glastonie ecclesie*, 31, where what seems to be a

thirteenth-century interpolation tells us that 'Arturo, inclito rege Britonum, in cimiterio monachoruum inter duas pyramides cum sua coniuge tumulato'. On William's skepticism with regard to Arthur see ibid., pp. 21, 24, 28, 31, 31 and 35.

106 According to Cramp, 'The Pre-Conquest Sculptures of Glastonbury Monastery', pp. 148–161 and ns 7, 9, 10 and 11, this relation was first discussed in Clapham, *English Romanesque Architecture before the Conquest*, pp. 163–189. Cramp herself referred to William of Malmesbury's 'pyramids' in relation to the Bewcastle and Ruthwell monuments in her Jarrow Lecture, *Early Northumbrian Sculpture*, p. 8. We note that by the eighteenth century the pyramids at Glastonbury were being set in relation to the Bewcastle monument, if not the Ruthwell monument, see Hutchinson, *The History of the County of Cumberland*, Vol. I, pp. 85–86. It is also worth noting that Dodwell, *Anglo-Saxon Art: A New Perspective*, pp. 113, 279–280, n. 123, points out that Nicolson and Burn, *The History of the Antiquities of the Counties of Westmorland and Cumberland*, Vol. 2, p. 410, refers to the two fragments of 'Giant's Grave' at St Andrew's, Penrith, Cumbria (see Bailey and Cramp, *Corpus*, Vol. II, 'Penrith 4 Cross-shaft and part of –head', pp. 136–137, and 'Penrith 5 Cross-shaft and part of –head', pp. 137–138) as 'pyramidal'. The monument at Penrith brings to mind the interpolated mention in William of Malmesbury, *De antiquitate Glastonie ecclesie*, Ch. 31, p. 82, to Arthur being buried between the two pyramids at Glastonbury, see note 105 above.

107 Nash, *Pictorial Dictionary of Ancient Rome*, Vol. II, pp. 59–60, see also Middleton, *The Remains of Ancient Rome*, Vol. II, p. 287.

108 Nash, *Pictorial Dictionary of Ancient Rome*, Vol. II, pp. 321–323, Middleton, *The Remains of Ancient Rome*, Vol. II, pp. 284–287.

109 Middleton, *The Remains of Ancient Rome*, Vol. II, p. 287.

110 Rushforth, '*Magister Gregorius De Mirabilibus Urbis Romae*: A New Description of Rome in the Twelfth Century', pp. 45–58, see p. 56: 27–28 '*De piramidibus sepulcris potentum*' and '*De piramide Augusti [Meta C. Cestii]*'.

111 Rushforth, '*Magister Gregorius De Mirabilibus Urbis Romae*', pp. 56–57: 29. Gregorius devotes some time to describing what is now the Vatican obelisk, which he associates with Julius Caesar because the gilt bronze globe fixed to its pyramidion was thought to contain Caesar's ashes.

112 For the obelisk of the Collis Hortorum see the *Einsiedeln Itinerary*, Route 2, pp. 168–169, 172; it's the '*piramidem*' next to the Thermae Sallustianae. The Meta Romuli was near the start of four routes: Route 1, pp. 162–167; Route 2, pp. 168–172; Route 8, pp. 189–196; and Route 12, pp. 205–211.

113 Before leaving this discussion of Anglo-Saxon pyramids, we need to note Lantfred's mention of a *pyramidis* at Winchester in his prefatory letter to the monks of the Old Minster at Winchester, which Dodwell, *Anglo-Saxon Art: A New Perspective*, p. 113, interprets as slender column, flat at the top. But see Lapidge, *The Cult of St Swithun, Winchester Studies 4.ii, The Anglo-Saxon Minsters of Winchester*, pp. 282, 283, espec. p. 282, n. 149, interprets it as a four-sided pyramid or pyramidal spire on the top of St Martin's tower.

114 Hutchinson, *The History of the County of Cumberland*, Vol. I, pp. 86–87.

115 See Kjølby-Biddle, 'Iron-bound Coffins and Coffin-fittings from the Pre-Norman Cemetery', pp. 489–521.

116 Taken from Page, *Corpus*, Vol. II, pp. 61 and 65.

Chapter 4: Forms of difference

1 The drift of this chapter was established by Orton, 'Rethinking the Ruthwell and Bewcastle Monuments: Some Strictures on Similarity: Some Questions of History'; Orton, 'Rethinking the Ruthwell and Bewcastle Monuments: Some Deprecation of Style: Some Consideration of Form and Ideology'; and Orton, 'Northumbrian Identity in the Eighth Century: Style, Classification, Class and the Form of Ideology'.

2 Hume, *A Treatise of Human Nature*, Bk I, Pt I, Section V.

3 Cramp, 'The Anglian Sculptured Crosses of Dumfriesshire', pp. 12, 13.

4 Haigh, 'The Saxon Cross at Bewcastle', pp. 167, 169, 175–176, 180, was, as far as we're

aware, the first person to bring the Ruthwell and Bewcastle monuments into a close relation of association. He saw both monuments as 'the work of the same artist or artists'. He noted some of the differences but did not labour them – certainly not with regard to different intentions and functions. He thought that both monuments – 'all these ancient crosses' – were 'sepulchral monuments'. Moreover, he conjectured that the Ruthwell and Bewcastle monuments 'once formed the same monument, one at the head and the other at the foot of the grave'.

5 Bailey and Cramp, *The British Academy Corpus of Anglo-Saxon Stone Sculpture*, Vol. II, *Cumberland, Westmorland and Lancashire North-of-the Sands*, p. 69. These specific differences were pointed out in Brown, *The Arts in Early England*, Vol. V, *The Ruthwell and Bewcastle Crosses*, pp. 128–129, and subsequently in his 'Report on the Ruthwell Cross with some references to that at Bewcastle', *The Royal Commission on the Ancient and Historical Monuments of Scotland*, Vol. V, *County of Dumfries*, pp. 226–227. Baldwin Brown seems to elide the question of whether the inner forelimbs of the beasts on the Bewcastle monument cross or not. Though the limbs have been eroded away by weathering, they must once have been visible and probably crossed – for an interesting exchange of views on this matter see Bailey, 'Innocent from the Great Offence', p. 101, and Orton, 'Rethinking the Ruthwell and Bewcastle Monuments: Some Strictures on Similarity; Some Questions of History', pp. 72–73 n. 22. Another difference noted by Brown, *The Arts in Early England*, pp. 130–131, and 'The Ruthwell Cross', p. 227, but not noted by the *Corpus*, is that, while one cannot see a moustache on the Christ at Bewcastle, 'the Christ of the Ruthwell Cross possesses a well-marked moustache seen most conspicuously as it lies over the right cheek running back towards the angle of the jaw'.

6 Saxl, 'The Ruthwell Cross', pp. 7–8, 10.

7 Saxl, 'The Ruthwell Cross', p. 10.

8 See for example Saxl, 'The Ruthwell Cross', pp. 8–11, and Kitzinger, 'The Coffin Reliquary', pp. 292–299. For a neat summary of this material see *Corpus*, Vol. II, pp. 70–71.

9 For a stimulating discussion of these matters see Mathews, *The Clash of Gods: A Reinterpretation of Early Christian Art*. Mathews is developing the work of Grabar, *Christian Iconography: A Study of Its Origins*, and Kitzinger, *Byzantine Art in the Making*. We have drawn on all three in what follows.

10 Grabar, *Christian Iconography: A Study of Its Origins*, p. 43.

11 Riegl, *Spätrömisch Kunstindustrie*, p. 26. See also, for what follows, Riegl, 'The Main Characteristics of the Late Roman *Kunstwollen*', pp. 87–103.

12 *Corpus*, Vol. II, p. 63.

13 Æthelwulf, *De abbatibus*, XIV ll. 445–446, XX ll. 623–633, for two descriptions of how the interior of an early medieval church was illuminated to dramatic effect.

14 *Corpus*, Vol. II, p. 69.

15 For some other Roman resources – Jupiter columns, sculptural panels on triumphal and honorific arches, and sculptural reliefs that survived from the forts around Hadrian's Wall – and how they might have been appropriated to the idea of making a stone cross, see Mitchell, 'The High Cross and Monastic Strategies in Eighth-Century Northumbria', pp. 90–91, 94.

16 Bede, *HE*, I 2.

17 For a stimulating discussion of these matters see Howe, 'Rome: Capital of Anglo-Saxon England', pp. 147–172.

18 Hawkes, '*Iuxta Morem Romanorum*: Stone Sculpture in Anglo-Saxon England', pp. 69–99.

19 *Corpus*, Vol. II, p. 61, measures it 22¼ by 21¼ inches at the bottom and 16 by 11 inches at the top. William Nicolson saw it as inclining to a 'square pyramid; each side whereof is near two foot broad at bottom, but upwards more tapering', see Nicolson, 'A letter ... concerning a runic inscription at Beaucastle', pp. 1287–1291, taken from Cook, *Some Accounts of the Bewcastle Cross between the Years 1607 and 1861*, p. 134.

20 See Haigh, 'The Saxon Cross at Bewcastle', p. 152, who brought this figure into published discourse as a secular aristocrat or, as he put it, 'the king whose name is mentioned in

the inscription above it'. See also: Kitzinger, 'Interlace and Icons: Form and Function in Early Insular Art', pp. 10–12; Bailey, *England's Earliest Sculptors*, pp. 66–67; and Karkov, 'The Bewcastle Cross: Some Iconographic Problems', pp. 11–20.

21 See Cramp on interlace in the *Corpus of Anglo-Saxon Stone Sculpture, General Introduction*, pp. xxviii–xlv, drawing on G. Adcock, *A Study of the Types of Interlace on Northumbrian Sculpture*, unpub. M.Phil. Thesis, University of Durham, 1974. For two very useful discussions of the multiplication of crosses, negative and positive crosses, and interlace see Stevenson, 'Aspects of Ambiguity in Crosses and Interlace', pp. 1–27, and Hawkes, 'Symbolic Lives: The Visual Evidence', pp. 328–334.

22 Hawkes, 'Symbolic Lives: The Visual Evidence', p. 329.

23 Hawkes, 'Symbolic Lives: The Visual Evidence', p. 332.

24 Hawkes, 'Symbolic Lives: The Visual Evidence', p. 333.

25 See for example *Beowulf* 1447–1454 and 1519–1534.

26 See Kitzinger, 'Interlace and Icons: Form and Function in Early Insular Art', pp. 3–4, who, with regard to the idea of the apotropaic, points out that more or less everything depends on the context of use.

27 See Page, *Corpus*, Vol. II, pp. 61–62, 65.

28 Page, 'The Use of Double Runes in Old English Inscriptions', p. 102.

29 Page, 'The Use of Double Runes in Old English Inscriptions', p. 102.

30 Higgitt, 'The Stone-Cutter and the Scriptorium: Early Medieval Inscriptions in Britain and Ireland', p. 156.

31 These terms come from Geary, *Phantoms of Remembrance: Memory and Oblivion at the End of the First Millennium*, Ch. 2, 'Men, Women, and Family Memory'.

32 Howlett, 'Inscriptions and Design of the Ruthwell Cross', pp. 86, 87, 88, with one eye on *The Dream of the Rood*, conjectures that 'dryhten' was in line 15: biheaꝥduꝥ hiꝥþeꝥ ('heafunæs dryctin) / they beheld there Heaven's Lord').

33 On the social construction of gender, mainly in later medieval monasticism, and the north side of a building as proper to the positioning of women see Gilchrist, *Gender and Material Culture: The Archaeology of Religious Women*, esp. Ch. 5, 'The Meanings of Nunnery Architecture', pp. 128–149.

34 See Geary, *Phantoms of Remembrance*, Ch. 2, 'Men, Women, and Family Memory'.

35 See, for example, the detail and discussions in Gilchrist, *Gender and Material Culture*, and Hollis, *Anglo-Saxon Women and the Church: Sharing a Common Fate*.

36 Wood, 'Ruthwell: Contextual Searches', p. 113.

37 See the discussion in *Corpus, General Introduction*, Ch. 5, 'Dating Methods', pp. xlvii–xlviii.

38 *Corpus, General Introduction*, Ch. 5, 'Dating Methods', p. xlvii.

39 Mac Lean, 'The Date of the Ruthwell Cross', p. 70.

40 Goodman, 'Seven Strictures on Similarity', p. 92.

41 *Corpus, General Introduction*, Ch. 5, 'Dating Methods', p. xlvii.

42 A useful overview and critical discussion of this issue is provided by LaCapra, *Rethinking Intellectual History: Texts, Contexts, Language*, Ch. 1, 'Rethinking Intellectual History and Reading Texts', pp. 23–71. For a consideration directly related to medieval studies, see Spiegel, 'History, Historicism, and the Social Logic of the Text', pp. 59–86, espec. 75–78.

43 See Clark, *Image of the People: Gustave Courbet and the 1848 Revolution*, pp. 12–13.

44 Clark, *Image of the People*, p. 13.

Chapter 5: Fragments of Northumbria

1 To a large extent this chapter is a reconsideration and expansion of ideas expressed in Wood, 'Ruthwell: Contextual Searches'.

2 The two most recent surveys are Higham, *The Kingdom of Northumbria AD 350–1100*, and Rollason, *Northumbria 500–1100: Creation and Destruction of a Kingdom*.

3 Bailey, *England's Earliest Sculptors*, pp. 42–43.

4 Bailey, *England's Earliest Sculptors*, p. 43. Ó Carragáin, *Ritual and the Rood*, p. 213, suggests 730–760. The breakthrough in terms of 'typological' dating was, of course, made by

Collingwood, *Northumbrian Crosses of the Pre-Norman Age*, pp. 111–119: though it should be added that Collingwood was careful to supply a sketch of the history of eighth-century Northumbria.

5 Page, 'Language and Dating in Old English Inscriptions', p. 36; 'The Bewcastle Cross', p. 69: 'The most likely date – on linguistic grounds alone – for Great Urswick and Ruthwell is 750–850, while the third Thornhill stone seems to be rather later. The language of the Bewcastle inscriptions, as far as it survives, is at a similar stage to that of Great Urswick and Ruthwell, and a date 750–850 is therefore a possible one for the Bewcastle Cross.'

6 The period is covered concisely by Wormald, 'The Age of Offa and Alcuin', pp. 114–115. For fuller coverage see Higham, *The Kingdom of Northumbria*, pp. 141–172: Rollason, *Northumbria*, pp. 192–5.

7 Lapidge, 'Acca of Hexham and the Origin of the Old English Martyrology', p. 68, has noted that Bede, *Continuatio*, s.a. 731, ed. Colgrave and Mynors, *Bede's Ecclesiastical History of the English People*, which argues that the passage on the deposition is wrongly translated by Colgrave, who translates *remissus* as 'restored to his kingdom', when the word should mean 'removed'. A subsequent abdication by Ceolwulf is, however, recorded in the *Continuatio*, s.a. 737.

8 Alcuin, *Versus de patribus, regibus et sanctis Euboricensis ecclesiae*, ll. 128–172.

9 Symeon of Durham, *Libellus de exordio atque procursu istius hoc est Dunhelmensis ecclesie*, II 3.

10 Bede, *Continuatio*, s.a. 750. For the date, Kirby, 'Strathclyde and Cumbria: A Survey of Historical Development to 1092', pp. 83–84. The date given in the *Historia regum*, ed. Arnold, pp. 40–41, is 756. For the southern frontier of Northumbria in the eighth and early ninth centuries, Sawyer, *From Roman Britain to Norman England*, pp. 106–107.

11 Rollason, *Northumbria*, pp. 176–177.

12 Alcuin, *Versus de patribus, regibus et sanctis Euboricensis ecclesiae*, ll. 1249–1287.

13 The letter of Pope Paul to Eadbert, ed. Haddan and Stubbs, *Councils and Ecclesiastical Documents relating to Great Britain and Ireland*, Vol. III, *The English Church 595–1066*, pp. 394–396, may suggest that the policy was not exactly what Bede would have wanted.

14 Dates for the following reigns are taken from *The Blackwell Encyclopaedia of Anglo-Saxon England*, ed. Lapidge, Blair, Keynes and Scragg, p. 504: Æthelwald Moll (759–765), Alhred (765–774), Æthelred I (774–778/9, 790–796), Osred II (788–790), Osbald (796), Eardwulf (796–806?, restored 808?).

15 Ælfwald I (778/9–788), Æthelred I (774–778/9, 790–796).

16 Ælfwald II (806?–808?).

17 Rollason, *Northumbria*, p. 196.

18 Wallace-Hadrill, *Early Germanic Kingship in England and on the Continent*, pp. 72–123.

19 The translation is that of McKinnell, 'Ruthwell Cross, § 2', p. 627.

20 The evidence for Ecgbert's work comes largely from Alcuin's *Versus de patribus regibus et sanctis Euboricensis ecclesiae*, ll. 1248–1288.

21 Crawford, *Anglo-Saxon Influence on Western Christendom 600–800*; Levison, *England and the Continent in the Eighth Century*; Wood, *The Missionary Life. Saints and the Evangelisation of Europe 400–1050*.

22 Wood, 'York and the Anglo-Saxon Missions to the Continent'.

23 Wormald, 'In Search of Offa's "Law-Code"'; Cubitt, *Anglo-Saxon Church Councils c.650–c.850*, pp. 153–190; Story, *Carolingian Connections. Anglo-Saxon England and Carolingian Francia, c.750–870*, pp. 55–92.

24 Alcuin, *Epistolae*, 101. Story, *Carolingian Connections*, pp. 93–211.

25 Collingwood, *Northumbrian Crosses of the Pre-Norman Age*, p. 115.

26 See Wood, 'Bede's Jarrow': Ó Carragáin's image of Bede in 'contemplative tranquillity at Wearmouth-Jarrow', *Ritual and the Rood*, p. 284, scarcely tallies with modern readings of Biscop's monasteries.

27 Rollason, *Northumbria*, pp. 202–207.

28 On Acca, Lapidge, 'Acca of Hexham and the Origin of the Old English Martyrology', esp. pp. 65–69.

29 Brown, *The Lindisfarne Gospels: Society, Spirituality and the Scribe.*

30 Most obvious from Bede's rewriting of the anonymous *Life of Cuthbert*: Colgrave, *Two Lives of Saint Cuthbert.*

31 Bede, *HE*, III 6.

32 Bede, *HE*, III 15.

33 Hunter Blair, 'The Boundary between Bernicia and Deira'.

34 *Historia Brittonum*, 61.

35 Jackson, *Language and History in Early Britain*, pp. 70–75.

36 Higham, *King Arthur: Myth-making and History*, pp. 119–124.

37 *Deiri*, Bede, *HE*, II 1; *Regnum Deirorum, HE*, III 1; *Provincia Deirorum, HE*, II 14, III 6, 14, 24, IV 12; *Partes Derorum, HE*, III 23.

38 *Gens Berniciorum*, Bede, *HE*, III 2; *Regnum Berniciorum, HE*, III 1; *Provincia Berniciorum, HE*, II 14, III 4, 6, 14, 24, IV 12, V 14.

39 *Vita Gregorii*, 9, where *Deire* is a tribal name.

40 Stephanus, *Vita Wilfridi*, 15, 20, 54: *rex De(γ)rorum et Berniciorum.*

41 *Historia Brittonum*, 57.

42 *Historia Brittonum*, 62.

43 Bede, *HE*, III 14.

44 Leland, *De Rebus Britannicis Collectanea*, p. 43: 'E regione Tinemutha fuit urbs vastata a Danis Urfa nomine, ubi natus erat Oswinus rex'.

45 The material is gathered by Plummer, *Bedae opera historica*, vol. 2, p. 164.

46 Breeze, 'The British-Latin Place-names *Arbeia, Corstopitum, Dictim*, and *Morbium*'.

47 Wood, 'Bede's Jarrow'.

48 Bede, *HE*, I 15.

49 Gildas, *De excidio Britonum*, 23.

50 Bede, *HE*, V 24.

51 *Historia Brittonum*, 57, 61.

52 Higham, *The Kingdom of Northumbria*, pp. 70–71. See the distribution map in Lucy, *The Anglo-Saxon Way of Death*, p. 2. For the other side of the equation, Faull, 'British Survival in Anglo-Saxon Northumbria'.

53 Budd, et al., 'Investigating Population Movement by Stable Isotope Analysis: A Report from Britain', p. 135.

54 Budd, et al., 'Investigating Population Movement by Stable Isotope Analysis: A Report from Britain', p. 136.

55 *Historia Brittonum*, 61.

56 *Gododdin*, ll. 60, 88, 208, 498, ed. Jarman, *Aneirin, Y Gododdin. Britain's Oldest Heroic Poem.*

57 E.g. 'The Head of Urien', ed. and trans. Rowland, *Early Welsh Saga Poetry*, pp. 420–422 (text), 477–478 (translation).

58 Higham, *The Kingdom of Northumbria*, p. 90.

59 Koch, *The Gododdin of Aneirin. Text and Context from Dark-Age North Britain*, p. 216, discusses the possible relationship between the names *Berneich* and *Brigantes*, the latter being the dominant tribe at the time of the Roman invasion in the northern part of what became Roman Britain.

60 E.g. de la Bédoyère, *Hadrian's Wall. History & Guide*, pp. 25–26.

61 Kulikowski, 'Barbarians in Gaul, Usurpers in Britain'.

62 Most recently Kulikowski, 'Barbarians in Gaul, Usurpers in Britain'; Drinkwater, 'The Usurpers Constantine III (407–411) and Jovinus (411–413)'.

63 Salway, *Roman Britain*, p. 429.

64 Dark, 'A Sub-Roman Re-defence of Hadrian's Wall'.

65 Faulkner, *The Decline and Fall of Roman Britain*, p. 173. See also Bury, *History of the Later Roman Empire*, Vol. 1, pp. 188–189: Esmonde Cleary, *The Ending of Roman Britain*, p. 142: Burns, *Barbarians within the Gates of Rome*, p. 251: Drinkwater, 'The Usurpers Constantine III (407–411) and Jovinus (411–413)', p. 275, with n. 40.

66 Jones, *The Later Roman Empire (284–602)*, p. 608. On the *limitanei* in general, the discus-

sion by Fustel de Coulanges, *Histoire des institutions politiques de l'ancienne France*, Vol. 5, *Le bénéfice et le patronat pendant l'époque mérovingienne*, pp. 8–9, remains crucial.

67 Jones, *The Later Roman Empire*, p. 635.

68 Thompson, *Romans and Barbarians. The Decline of the Western Empire*, pp. 113–133: Heather, *The Fall of the Roman Empire. A New History*, pp. 407–415.

69 Eugippius, *Vita Severini*, 20

70 Eugippius, *Vita Severini*, 44.

71 Wilmott, *Birdoswald Roman Fort: 1800 Years on Hadrian's Wall*, pp. 122–126.

72 White and Barker, *Wroxeter: Life and Death of a Roman City*.

73 Dark, 'A Sub-Roman Re-defence of Hadrian's Wall?', pp. 111–112.

74 Dark, 'A Sub-Roman Re-defence of Hadrian's Wall?', p. 113. Note also Mercer, 'The Ruthwell and Bewcastle Crosses', p. 275, on Brampton, Carlisle and Cartmel.

75 McCarthy, 'Rheged: An Early Historic Kingdom near the Solway', pp. 366–367.

76 There is of course the evidence of Mediterranean amphorae from coastal sites in Cornwall, Wales, south-west Scotland and Ireland: Campbell, 'The Archaeological Evidence from External Contacts: Imports, Trade and Economy in Celtic Britain A.D. 400–800'.

77 Collingwood and Wright, *The Roman Inscriptions of Britain*, Vol. 1, *Inscriptions on Stone* (henceforth RIB), 1483, 1525, 1526, 1593, 1597. If one includes Batavians, Toxandrians, Frisians and *Tungri* the numbers increase significantly.

78 Mars Thincsus RIB 1593: for Matres, see RIB indices: Collingwood and Wright, *The Roman Inscriptions of Britain*, 1, *Inscriptions on Stone, Epigraphic Indices*, compiled by Goodburn and Waugh, p. 70.

79 RIB 1593.

80 RIB indices 1, p. 33.

81 Wood, 'The Crocus Conundrum', p. 80.

82 Zosimus, *Historia nova*, I, 68, 1–3.

83 Ammianus Marcellinus, XXIX, 4, 7.

84 *Historia Brittonum*, 56, 57, 61: *Anglo-Saxon Chronicle*, s.a. 547, trans. Whitelock.

85 Fustel de Coulanges, *Histoire des institutions politiques de l'ancienne France*, Vol. 2, *L'invasion Germanique et la fin de l'empire*, pp. 460–488.

86 Wood, 'Defining the Franks'.

87 Deanesly, 'Roman Traditionalist Influence among the Anglo-Saxons'. Although much of the detail of Deanesly's argument has been superseded, the case nevertheless deserves consideration.

88 Bede, *HE*, II 16. See the comments of Wallace-Hadrill, *Bede's Ecclesiastical History of the English People. A Historical Commentary*, pp. 80–81.

89 See above, Chapter 1.

90 Bede, *HE*, III 19.

91 Page, 'The Bewcastle Cross', p. 48, lists the leading proponents of the idea. Mac Lean, 'The Date of the Ruthwell Cross', pp. 55–9, revisits the discussion.

92 It should be noted that our evidence for Alcfrith is less than satisfactory. He appears six times in Bede's *History*. In the first reference (III 14) Bede alludes to his rebellion, though he provides no detail. In the second reference (III 21) we hear of his involvement in the conversion of Peada of the Mercians. Then (III 24) Bede talks of his fighting alongside his father at the Battle of the Winwæd. In the following chapter (III 25) Bede relates his support for Wilfrid in the run up to the Synod of Whitby. In III 28 he sends Wilfrid to Francia for consecration. His friendship with Wilfrid is mentioned in V 19. Stephanus, our other source for Alcfrith, mentions him exclusively for his support for Wilfrid: *Vita Wilfridi*, 7, 8, 9, 10. Bede's presentation of Alcfrith is curious. One might guess that he wished to dissociate the image of Alcfrith the rebel from that of Alcfrith the supporter of Wilfrid, and that this determines what appears to be the unchronological reference to his rebellion. The result, however, is that strictly speaking we do not know at what point in his career Alcfrith rebelled, nor whether his rebellion ended in his death.

93 Alcfrith is often stated in modern scholarship (e.g. by Keynes in *The Blackwell Encyclo-*

paedia of Anglo-Saxon England, p. 503), to have been 'sub-king of Deira'. There is nothing in Bede, or any early source to support this. Bede calls Alcfrith *rex* in *HE*, III 28 and V 9. Stephanus, *Vita Wilfridi*, 7, 8, 9, also refers to him as *rex*, and in *Vita Wilfridi*, 7, 10, he talks of the joint rule of Oswiu and Alcfrith. The fact that he gave Ripon to Wilfrid shows that he had Deiran interests, but it does not prove that he was sub-king of Deira. Nor does one need to place him in the south of Northumbria to understand his friendship with Penda's son Peada: Alcfrith himself was married to Penda's daughter, *HE*, III 21. Plummer, *Baedae opera historica*, Vol. 2, p. 120, infers that he was sub-king of Deira from a reference to his brother Ecgfrith in the twelfth-century *Liber Eliensis*. The early evidence does not allow us to attribute to him a sub-kingship, nor does it prove that he was solely associated with the Deiran kingdom.

94 *Historia Brittonum*, 57. The connection is made, however, in Cramp, *Whithorn and the Northumbrian Expansion Westwards*, p. 13, and McCarthy, 'Rheged: An Early Historic Kingdom near the Solway', p. 370.

95 There would then be a comparison to be made with Gilling, the site of Oswine's murder: Bede, *HE*, III 14.

96 Page, 'The Bewcastle Cross'. Perhaps more information will be gleaned from the images recently scanned by Archaeoptics Ltd: see http://minotaur.archaeoptics.co.uk/index. php/200-cross-runic-inscri. Ray Page has also drawn our attention to a previously unpublished drawing of the inscription in a letter sent by William Nicolson to Ralph Thoresby on 9 September 1691, to be found in Yorkshire Archaeological Society MS 6, Thoresby Correspondence, Miscellaneous Letters, not printed, vol. 1. The accompanying letter (but not Nicolson's drawing) can be found in W. T. Lancaster, ed., *A General Selection of the Letters addressed to Ralph Thoresby*, Thoresby Society, Vol. 21 (Leeds, 1921), pp. 22–23. As yet, however, there is nothing to suggest that this new evidence will radically affect our understanding of the inscription.

97 Page, entry on Bewcastle 1, in Bailey and Cramp, *Corpus of Anglo-Saxon Stone Sculpture*, Vol. II, p. 63: also Page, 'The Bewcastle Cross', p. 52.

98 Bede, *HE*, III 21. Plummer, *Baedae opera historica*, Vol. 2, p. 142, also notes Cuneburg, an abbess in contact with Lull (Boniface, ep. 49) and a twelfth-century reference to a Cyniburga, supposed daughter of Cynegils and wife of Oswald, which he reckons is likely to have been a confused reference to the wife of Alcfrith.

99 *Liber vitae ecclesiae Dunelmensis*, ed. Stevenson, pp. 3–4, fol. 13r, cols 2 and 3: see also the facsimile, ed. Hamilton Thompson.

100 *Liber vitae ecclesiase Dunelmensis*, p. 1, fol. 12r, col. 1.

101 For the shrine of Chrodoara at Amay see Wood, 'Genealogy Defined by Women: The Case of the Pippinids', pp. 248–250.

102 Collingwood, *Northumbrian Crosses of the pre-Norman Age*, p. 116.

103 The date is given by Brown, *The Lindisfarne Gospels*, p. 85.

104 *Liber vitae ecclesiase Dunelmensis*, p. 9, fol. 17v, col. 2.

105 Page, entry on Bewcastle 1, in Bailey and Cramp, *Corpus of Anglo-Saxon Stone Sculpture*, Vol. II, p. 65.

106 Page, 'The Bewcastle Cross', pp. 49, 51–52.

107 See now Blair, *The Church in Anglo-Saxon Society*, pp. 112–113.

108 Stephanus, *Vita Wilfridi*, 14, 47.

109 The division of property in *Vita Wilfridi*, 63, is not Benedictine.

110 Bede, *Historia abbatum*, 11, ed. Plummer, *Baedae opera historica*.

111 Wormald, 'Bede and Benedict Biscop'.

112 Smyth, *Warlords and Holy Men: Scotland AD 80–1000*, pp. 116–140.

113 Bede, *HE*, IV 25.

114 Blair, *The Church in Anglo-Saxon Society*, pp. 108–112.

115 Bede, *Epistola ad Ecgbertum Episcopum* (henceforth Ep.) 2.

116 Bede, *Ep.* 4.

117 Bede, *Ep.* 5.

118 Bede, *Ep.* 9.

119 Blair, *The Church in Anglo-Saxon Society*, pp. 95–96.
120 Bede, *Ep.* 10.
121 Bede, *Ep.* 10.
122 Bede, *Ep.* 11.
123 Bede, *Ep.* 12.
124 Bede, *Ep.* 12.
125 Bede, *Ep.* 13.
126 John, *Land Tenure in Early England*; Charles-Edwards, 'The Distinction between Land and Moveable Wealth in Anglo-Saxon England'; Abels, *Lordship and Military Obligation in Anglo-Saxon England*, pp. 43–57; Wood, 'Land Tenure and Military Obligations in the Anglo-Saxon and Merovingian Kingdoms: The Evidence of Bede and Boniface in Context'.
127 Bede, *HE*, IV 25.
128 Bede, *Historia abbatum*, 11.
129 Bede, *Historia abbatum*, 8.
130 Bede, *Historia abbatum*, 13.
131 Bede, *Historia abbatum*, 11.
132 Bede, *Historia abbatum*, 8.
133 Æthelwulf, *De abbatibus*, II.
134 Bede, *HE*, V 18.
135 Boniface, *Ep.* 73.
136 Æthelwulf, *De abbatibus*, IV.
137 Æthelwulf, *De abbatibus*, V–VII.
138 Æthelwulf, *De abbatibus*, XIII.
139 Æthelwulf, *De abbatibus*, XIV–XV.
140 Æthelwulf, *De abbatibus*, VIII.
141 Henderson, *From Durrow to Kells. The Insular Gospel Books 650–800*, pp. 40, 118, 126, 129.
142 Æthelwulf, *De abbatibus*, XXII.
143 Farr, 'Worthy Women on the Ruthwell Cross: Women as a Sign in Early Anglo-Saxon Monasticism'; Karkov, 'Naming and Renaming: the inscription of gender in Anglo-Saxon stone sculpture'; Wood, 'Ruthwell: Contextual Searches', pp. 112–113.
144 Crowe, 'Excavations at Ruthwell, Dumfries, 1980 and 1984'.
145 For an early argument that Rheged was relevant to Bewcastle and Ruthwell, Mercer, 'The Ruthwell and Bewcastle Crosses', pp. 274–276. The most recent statement of the case is Mac Lean, 'The Date of the Ruthwell Cross', pp. 59–64.
146 Rollason, *Northumbria*, p. 87.
147 *Historia Brittonum*, 63.
148 *Historia Brittonum*, 57. On the marriage, Smyth, *Warlords and Holy Men: Scotland AD 80–1000*, pp. 22–24; Stancliffe, 'Oswald, "Most Holy and Most Victorious King of the Northumbrians"', p. 57; McCarthy, 'Rheged: An Early Historic Kingdom near the Solway', p. 370; Rollason, *Northumbria*, p. 88, especially for the discussion of her appearance as Raegnmaeld in the *Liber vitae* of Durham.
149 Rowland, *Early Welsh Saga Poetry*, pp. 75–119.
150 Rowland, *Early Welsh Saga Poetry*, pp. 388–389.
151 Rollason, *Northumbria*, p. 87.
152 Kirby, 'Strathclyde and Cumbria', pp. 79–80: McCarthy, 'Rheged: An Early Historic Kingdom near the Solway', pp. 359, 369. On the problems of identification of the place in the Llywarch Hen cycle, however, see Rowland, *Early Welsh Saga Poetry*, p. 551.
153 McCarthy, *Roman Carlisle and the Lands of the Solway*, p. 147.
154 McCarthy, *Roman Carlisle and the Lands of the Solway*; Phythian-Adams, *The Land of the Cumbrians: A Study in British Provincial Origins, AD 400–1200*; Higham, *The Kingdom of Northumbria*, pp. 82–83, opts for a similar geographical situation.
155 McCarthy, 'Rheged: An Early Historic Kingdom near the Solway', pp. 357–381.
156 Thomas, 'Ardwall Island: The Excavation of an Early Christian Site of Irish Type, 1964–5';

'An Early Christian Cemetery and chapel on Ardwall Isle, Kirkcudbright', which includes a full discussion of Irish presence in the territory north of the Solway.

157 Thomas, 'Excavations at Trusty's Hill, Anworth, Kirkcudbrightshire, 1960'; Mac Lean, 'The Date of the Ruthwell Cross', pp. 64–65; more controversial, but not without interest, is Cummins, *The Picts and Their Symbols*, pp. 69–81.

158 Rollason, *Northumbria*, p. 87.

159 On Æthelfrith, Bede, *HE*, I 34: on Edwin and Man, *HE*, II 5: Kirby, 'Strathclyde and Cumbria', p. 80.

160 *Historia Brittonum*, 63.

161 Higham, *King Arthur: Myth-making and History*, pp. 119–124

162 *Historia Brittonum*, 57.

163 Mac Lean, 'The Date of the Ruthwell Cross', p. 63.

164 Rollason, *Northumbria*, p. 88. Here one might note Bede, *HE*, IV 3, on Wilfrid's ecclesiastical authority within Oswiu's kingdom, also *HE*, III 24.

165 Mac Lean, 'The Date of the Ruthwell Cross', pp. 63–64, argues for a late date.

166 Smyth, *Warlords and Holy Men: Scotland AD 80–1000*, pp. 23–26 argues for conquest: he is supported by Stancliffe, 'Oswald, "Most Holy and Most Victorious King of the Northumbrians"', p. 57 n. 116.

167 Crowe, 'Early Medieval Parish Formation in Dumfries and Galloway', p. 204. For the place-name Ruthwell, see Chinnock, 'Etymology of the Word Ruthwell'.

168 Stephanus, *Vita Wilfridi*, 17, trans, Colgrave.

169 For an alternative view of the identification of *Ingaedyne* see Faull and Moorhouse, *West Yorkshire: An Archaeological Survey to A.D. 1500*, p. 183.

170 Radford, 'An Early Cross at Ruthwell'; Mercer, 'The Ruthwell and Bewcastle Crosses', p. 273.

171 *Historia de Sancto Cuthberto*, 6. On Cartmel, note Mercer, 'The Ruthwell and Bewcastle Crosses', p. 275, citing Simpson and Richmond, *TC&WA&AS*, n.s. 36 (1936), p. 182.

172 *Historia de Sancto Cuthberto*, 20: Symeon, *Libellus de exordio atque procursu istius hoc est Dunelmensis ecclesie*, II 11–12.

173 Brown, *The Lindisfarne Gospels*, pp. 87–88.

174 Anon. *Vita Cuthberti*, IV 5, 8, 9: Bede, *Vita Cuthberti*, 27.

175 Lowe, 'New Light on the Anglian Minster at Hoddom'; Wilson, 'Roman and Native in Dumfriesshire', pp. 136–137.

176 Jocelyn of Furness, *Vita Kentigerni*, 32–33. The problems with the evidence for Kentigern, and the probability that it reflects twelfth-century concerns, are spelt out in Jackson, 'The Sources for the Life of St. Kentigern', pp. 318–321.

177 Ralegh Radford, 'Hoddom'. The fate of the stones is set out by Maxwell-Irving, 'Hoddom Castle: A Reappraisal of Its Architecture and Place in History', p. 213 n. 1.

178 Collingwood, *Northumbrian Crosses of the Pre-Norman Age*, p. 119.

179 Keppie, 'Roman Inscriptions and Sculpture from Birrens. A Review', esp. pp. 39–40.

180 Lowe, 'New Light on the Anglian Minster at Hoddom', pp. 11–12.

181 Crowe, 'Early Medieval Parish Formation in Dumfries and Galloway', p. 203.

182 Meyvaert, 'A New Perspective on the Ruthwell Cross: *Ecclesia* and *Vita Monastica*'.

183 See Wilson, 'Roman and Native in Dumfriesshire', pp. 103–160.

184 For a map of the area in the Roman period, Wilson, 'Roman and Native in Dumfriesshire', p. 123.

185 Crowe, 'Early Medieval Parish Formation in Dumfries and Galloway', p. 202, with illustration, p. 203.

186 Bede, *Continuatio*, s.a. 750.

187 Bede, *HE*, II 5.

188 Bede, *HE*, IV 26.

189 McCarthy, 'Rheged: An Early Historic Kingdom near the Solway', p. 374.

190 Wood, 'Bede's Jarrow'.

191 Haywood, *Dark Age Naval Power: a reassessment of Frankish and Anglo-Saxon Seafaring Activity*, pp. 61, 75.

192 Bede, *HE*, III 4, trans. Colgrave, with changes.

193 Hill, *Whithorn and St Ninian. The Excavation of a Monastic Town 1984–91*.

194 Bede, *HE*, III 4.

195 Bede, *HE*, V 23.

196 Bede, *HE*, V 23: see also Plummer, *Baedae opera historica*, p. 343.

197 Ó Carragáin, *Ritual and the Rood*, p. 264. See also Meyvaert, 'A New Perspective on the Ruthwell Cross: *Ecclesia* and *Vita Monastica*', p. 148.

198 Cf. Plummer, *Baedae opera historica*, Vol. 2, p. 343.

199 Bede, *Continuatio*, s.a. 735.

200 *Anglo-Saxon Chronicle*, s.a. 805. The list is given by William of Malmesbury, *Gesta pontificum*, 115, p. 257: see Hill, *Whithorn and St Ninian*, p. 40.

201 Plummer, *Baedae opera historica*, Vol. 2, p. 343, gathers the evidence for Pecthelm.

202 Bede, *HE*, III 4.

203 Plummer, *Baedae opera historica*, Vol. 2, p. 343: William of Malmesbury, *Gesta pontificum*, 115: Henry of Huntingdon, *Historia Anglorum*, IV 22–23, pp. 125–126, where he appears as Witwine.

204 Bede, *HE*, V 18.

205 Boniface, *Epistolae* 32.

206 Bede, *HE*, V 13.

207 Bede, *HE*, V 18.

208 Levison, *England and the Continent in the Eighth Century*, p. 147: for the manuscript of the *Miracula Nynie*, Bullough, *Alcuin, Achievement and Reputation*, p. 177, n. 140.

209 Bede, *HE*, III 4. For the most recent views of Ninian, and whether there were one or two, Hill, *Whithorn and St Ninian*, p. 4.

210 Bede, *HE*, III 4.

211 Bede, *HE*, V 21: Duncan, 'Bede, Iona and the Picts'.

212 *Miracula Nynie Episcopi*, 2.

213 *Miracula Nynie Episcopi*, 3.

214 *Miracula Nynie Episcopi*, 4–5.

215 *Miracula Nynie Episcopi*, 6–8.

216 *Miracula Nynie Episcopi*, 10–13.

217 *Miracula Nynie Episcopi*, 13.

218 Paschasius Radbertus, *Liber de Corpore et Sanguine Domini*, 14, ll. 120–159.

219 See the suggestion of Constantinescu, 'Alcuin de les "Libelli Precum" de l'époque carolingienne', p. 56, with n. 183.

220 Meyvaert, 'A New Perspective on the Ruthwell Cross: *Ecclesia* and *Vita Monastica*', interprets the iconography of the monument largely through Bede's writings. The case for a link with Jarrow is presented on stylistic grounds by Cramp, *Early Northumbrian Sculpture*, pp. 10–11.

221 Bede, *HE*, V 13.

Chapter 6: Reckoning time

1 The points made in this chapter develop research first presented in Orton, 'The Bewcastle Monument, Rome, Bede, the Reckoning of Time, Sundials and the Renewal of Science'.

2 *Byrhtferth's Enchiridion*, II.3.

3 Webber, 'The Diffusion of Augustine's Confessions in England During the Eleventh and Twelfth Centuries', pp. 30–32 and ns 11–12.

4 Ó Carragáin, 'A Liturgical Interpretation of the Bewcastle Cross', pp. 34–36. Bailey and Cramp, *The British Academy Corpus of Anglo-Saxon Stone Sculpture*, Vol. II, *Cumberland, Westmorland and Lancashire North-of-the Sands*, p. 66.

5 Ó Carragáin, 'A Liturgical Interpretation of the Bewcastle Cross', pp. 34–35.

6 Ó Carragáin, 'A Liturgical Interpretation of the Bewcastle Cross', pp. 34–35.

7 *Corpus*, Vol. II, p. 66. On the Irish dials see Ann Hamlin, 'Some Northern Sundials and Time-Keeping in the Early Irish Church'. The single sundial so far recorded in Wales is

sited at Clynnog-fawr, Gwynedd. Hamlin records another fragmentary example of the same type at Kirk Maughold, Isle of Man.

8 *Corpus*, Vol. II, p. 66. See St J. H. Daniel, *Sundials*, p. 7.

9 *Corpus*, Vol. II, p. 66: the reference is to Waugh, *Sundials, Their Theory and Construction*, pp. 1–2.

10 Waugh, *Sundials: Their History and Construction*, p. 2, gives the table and, in a footnote, cites F. K. Ginzel, *Handbuch der mathematischen und technischen Chronolgie*, Vol. III (Leipzig, 1914), p. 88. Rohr, *Les cadrans solaires*, p. 15, points out that this table, often attributed to Bede, can be found in the fourth-century *Opus Agriculturae* of the agronomist Palladius.

11 The almost vertical line 3½ inches to the right of the dial's gnomon hole, which was first recorded in the engraving in Lysons and Lysons, *Magna Britannia*, pl. facing p. 28, is a weathered lamination in the stone. It is visible both above and below the dial.

12 The difference was first noted by Green, 'Anglo-Saxon Sundials', p. 495. Though the *Corpus*, Vol. II, p. 63, doesn't mention the difference in cutting, it does note that while 'the main lines seem to run to the edge of the semi-circular dial ... the lesser dividing lines end in small circular depressions short of the edge'.

13 On Anglo-Saxon use of the divider compass see Guillmain, 'The Composition of the First Cross Page of the Lindisfarne Gospels', pp. 535–536, n. 4. See also Guillmain, 'The Geometry of the Cross-Carpet Pages in the Lindisfarne Gospels', pp. 23–24, n. 9, 48.

14 For a practical introduction to sundials and dialling see Mayall, *Sundials: How to Know, Use, and Make Them*.

15 Mills, 'Seasonal-Hour Sundials', p. 152, citing Rohr, *Sundials: History, Theory, and Practice*. Schaldach, 'Vertical Dials of the 5–15th Centuries', p. 37, notes that the earliest example of an Islamic dial with a polar gnomon dates from 1371.

16 For useful discussions of natural time and social time see Adam, *Time and Social Theory*, pp. 9–47, 70–76, 91–93, 104–109. On the monastery's 'situatedness of action in time and place' see Giddens, *The Constitution of Society*, pp. 110–111, 123, 135–136, 144–147.

17 Asser, *De rebus gestis Ælfredi*, pp. 104, 108–119.

18 McCluskey, *Astronomies and Cultures in Early Medieval Europe*, p. 111, notes that 'as early as the tenth century the prosperous monastery of Fleury (St. Benoit-sur-Loire, founded 651) used a water-clock (or clepsydra) for time keeping' and, pp. 175–176, that Gerbert of Aurillac constructed a clepsydra at Ravenna where he was archbishop between 998 and 999. The *Dictionary of the Middle Ages*, Vol. III, p. 457, cites a reference to a 'water-clock alarm' in a tenth- or twelfth-century manuscript in the Benedictine monastery of Maria de Ripoll and gives what seems to be the first reference in published discourse to a water-clock in use in England: as reported in the *Chronica Jocelini de Brakelonda de rebus gestis Samsonis abbatis monasterii Sancti Edmundi* (London, 1840), in 1198 a clepsydra provided some of the water used to fight a fire at the abbey of Bury St Edmunds, Suffolk.

19 C. B. Drover, 'Sand-Glass Sand', *Antiquarian Horology* 3 (June 1960), pp. 62–66, cites what seem to be the first textual references to a sand glass, which date to 1345–1346 and 1380. D. W. Waters, 'Time, Ships and Civilisation', *Antiquarian Horology* 4 (June 1961), p. 82, thinks the sand clock was invented in the Mediterranean for maritime use. Balmer, 'The Operation of Sand Clocks And Their Medieval Development', p. 615 n. 3, directs us to Francesco da Barberino's 'Document d'Amore' (1306–1306), where a sand clock (*orologio*) is referred to as a navigational aid at sea. However, for the 'earliest known existence of sand clocks' he points to the 'well developed' hour glass that 'Temperance' holds in her right hand in Ambrogio Lorenzetti's fresco *Il Buon Governo*, in the Palazzo Pubblico, Sienna, 1338–1339. Balmer also points out that there is 'no currently accepted evidence' to support the belief that the Greeks used sand clocks or hourglasses in the third century BC, and that 'suggestions that the hourglass was invented by an 8th-century A.D. monk, Liutprand of Chartres, and that a twelve-hour sand clock was owned by Charlemagne A.D. 807' are likewise unsupported.

20 On monastic timekeeping during the hours of darkness see McCluskey, *Astronomies and Cultures in Early Medieval Europe*, Ch. 6, 'Observing the Celestial Order – Monastic

Timekeeping', pp. 101–110, which discusses the Regula Magistri of 520–530 and Gregory of Tours's *De cursu stellarum*, written some time after 573. Gregory, taking the seasonal changes of nighttime and daylight into account, gave several rules for singing a certain number of psalms each month. McCluskey also mentions Isidore of Seville's *Regula monachorum*, written between 650 and 700, which makes the sacristan responsible for nocturnal timekeeping.

21 On the church at Escomb see Taylor and Taylor, *Anglo-Saxon Architecture*, Vol. I, pp. 234–238. On the dial at Kirkdale see Wall, 'Anglo-Saxon Sundials in Ryedale', pp. 98–103.

22 *Corpus*, Vol. II, p. 66.

23 Turner, 'Anglo-Saxon Sundials and the "Tidal" or "Octaval" System', pp. 76–77. Haigh, 'Yorkshire Dials', pp. 134–222. Langenfelt, *The Historic Origins of the Eight Hours Day*, p. 28 n. 37a points out that the four (or eight) part division of the ancient Germanic day (and night) is unknown to him and has not been proved by experts in Old Norse.

24 Bede, *De temporum ratione*, 5.

25 *Byrhtferth's Enchiridion*, II.3.

26 *Byrhtferth's Enchiridion*, II.3.

27 McCluskey, *Astronomies and Cultures in Early Medieval Europe*, p. 24.

28 McCluskey, *Astronomies and Cultures in Early Medieval Europe*, pp. 24–25.

29 Vitruvius, *De architectura libri decem*, Bks VIII and VII.

30 On Ptolemy and Ptolemaic astronomy with regard to early medieval astronomy in the Latin West see McCluskey, *Astronomies and Cultures in Early Medieval Europe*, pp. 20–24.

31 Cassiodorus, *Institutiones divinarum et saecularium litterarum*, V.3, 'On Astronomy'.

32 Charles Homer Haskins, *Studies in the History of Medieval Science* 2nd ed. (Cambridge, MA, 1927), pp. 104–110, 157. Ptolemy's *Almagest* was first translated from Greek into Latin about 1160 and from Arabic about 1175.

33 Mills, 'Seasonal-Hour Sundials', pp. 147–71, esp. pp. 158–60.

34 Mills, 'Seasonal-Hour Sundials', p. 159.

35 Mills, 'Seasonal-Hour Sundials', p. 159.

36 See for examples Gibbs, *Greek and Roman Sundials*: 3066; 3091; 3103; etc.

37 Mills, 'Seasonal-Hour Sundials', p. 160.

38 Gibbs, *Greek and Roman Sundials*: 5012G; 5019G.

39 Gibbs, *Greek and Roman Sundials*, p. 73.

40 Gibbs, *Greek and Roman Sundials*, pp. 45–46, and Mills, 'Seasonal-Hour Sundials', pp. 159–160.

41 Mills, 'Seasonal-Hour Sundials', p. 160. The dial is exhibited upside-down on a shelf in the John Clayton Collection at Chesters Museum, inventory no. BH131 CH248. Wallis Budge, who catalogued and prepared Clayton's collection for exhibition, was uncertain as to what it was and labelled it 'Fragment from ?sundial'. Green, 'Anglo-Saxon Sundials', p. 145, who, because of the 'five deeply cut, wide lines radiating downwards, the extremities contained in a circular line', was convinced that what 'we have here rather less than half a dial which before it was broken consisted of a half-circle and thirteen lines'. However, we note the 'part of a style-hole' that Green saw is not clearly visible.

42 That the Romans or Romano-British in England were acquainted with sundials but were losing or had already lost knowledge of dialling is also shown by the dial represented on one of the fourth-century mosaic pavements in the Roman villa at Brading, Isle of Wight (Fig. 36). The image of the philosopher/astronomer seated in front of a sundial on a column and pointing to a globe has to be seen and understood in some contiguous relation of association with astronomer/philosopher scenes that survive from near Pompeii and Urbino. See for example, the so-called late second- or early first-century BC *Mosaico di Platone* found at Torre Annuziata, near Pompeii, now in the Museo Nationale di Napoli, inventory number 124545. It seems that the person who designed the Brading mosaic, perhaps as a visual memory of a stock theme, attempted to picture a conical dial but omitted its gnomon and misunderstood its network of lines – unfortunately, this dial, unlike the one represented in the *Mosaico di Platone*, could never cast a shadow and has only eleven hours.

43 For example see Jones, 'Bede's Use of Natural Science', pp. 125–129, espec. pp. 126–127; Harrison, 'Easter cycles and the equinox in the British Isles', p. 5; Stevens, *Bede's Scientific Achievement*, p. 30, n. 49; and Bede, *De temporum ratione*, 31, Wallis, 'Commentary', pp. 315–317.

44 Bede, *De temporum ratione*, 31, 33, re Pliny, *Natural History*, Vol. 1, Bk II, Chs LXXIV, XXXIX.

45 Bede, *De temporum ratione*, 31, 33.

46 (1) Ceolfrid's letter to Nechtan, king of the Picts, concerning the Roman observance of Easter, in *HE*, V 21; (2) *De temporum ratione*, 30.

47 See (1) *De temporum ratione*, 38–39; (2) *De temporum ratione*, appendix 3.3: 'Letter to Helmwald'.

48 Bede, *In Regum librum XXX quaestiones*, IV Reg. xx.

49 Jones, 'Bede's Use of Natural Science', p. 127, and Bede, *De temporum ratione*, Wallis, 'Commentary', p. 316.

50 See for example Bede, *De temporum ratione*, Wallis, 'Commentary', pp. 315–316, who thinks, incorrectly, that the equinoctial could be established on an 'ancient and medieval' sundial, 'mounted vertically on a wall, with a gnomon perpendicular' to its 'dial ... marked like a fan with eight or twelve divisions, representing the hours', empirically by incising a line half way between the gnomen and the edge of the dial corresponding 'to the sweep of the gnomon's shadow' on the summer and winter solstices. The solstice lines could be set this way, by observing the shortest and longest extensions of the shadow, but the equinoctial could be set only by calculating the half-angle of the sun's declination trigonometrically and inscribing it as a line on the dial plate. The equinoctial of a dial situated between 53 and 54° north would certainly not lie on the dial 'halfway between' the solstice lines. See also Harrison, 'Easter Cycles and the Equinox in the British Isles', p. 5, who would similarly establish the solstice lines empirically 'by observing noon shadows', but would then 'approximate' the equinoctial by the calendar.

51 Bede, *De temporum ratione*, 38.

52 We wonder if Anglo-Saxon visitors to Rome realised that the obelisk mentioned in the *Einsiedeln Itinterary*, Routes 2 and 4, was part of the monumental sundial, designed by Facundus Novius, which Augustus had erected in the Campus Martius to celebrate his victory over in Egypt in 30 BC. The obelisk, brought from Heliopolis in 10 BC, was the gnomon and the surrounding pavement, with a properly calibrated *pelecinum* network of lines set in bronze, served as the dial. This *pelecinum* dial was, in the early Middle Ages, very probably already obscured by the encroaching *disabitato*. On the dial of Augustus see Buchner, *Die Sonnenuhr des Augustus*.

53 Two semicircular duodecimal sundials are located at St Andrew, Bishopstone, Sussex, and St Andrew, Weaverthorpe, Yorkshire. On the Bishopstone and Weaverthorpe dials see Green, 'Anglo-Saxon Sundials', pp. 508–509, 512–513 and fig. 21. On the Weaverthorpe dial see Haigh, 'Yorkshire Dials', pp. 144–146, and Wall, 'Anglo-Saxon Sundials in Ryedale', pp. 108–112, ill. 9A. The circular dial at All Saints, Orpington, Kent, which is considered an Anglo-Saxon dial, should be noted also – see Taylor and Taylor, 'Architectural Sculpture in Pre-Norman England', pp. 23–25 and fig. 11. Part of the dial was cut away when it was recycled as a building stone. From the damaged hole in the centre radiate thirteen lines making twelve divisions, six on each side of the vertical, four of which – two each side above the horizontal sunrise–sunset line – would not, if it was intended function in the vertical plane, have received a shadow from the gnomon. For some German duodecimal semicircular vertical plane dials dating from the twelfth or fourteenth and fifteenth centuries, see Schaldach, 'Vertical Dials of the 5–15th Centuries', pp. 32–38.

54 See Cassiodorus, *Variae* I.45, 2 and I.46 – the sundial and clepsydra, 'inventions of the ancients', were dispatched accompanied by persons who could operate them – and Cassiodorus, *An Introduction to Divine and Human Readings, Divine Letters*, XXX.5, 5.

Chapter 7: The Ruthwell runes and *The Dream of The Rood*

1 For the facsimile of the Vercelli Book, see Sisam, ed., *The Vercelli Book*, with her description of the hand on p. 20. The standard edition of the poetry in the Vercelli book remains Krapp, ed., *The Vercelli Book*. For the prose works see Scragg, *The Vercelli Homilies and Related Texts*; see also Scragg's 'The Compilation of the Vercelli Book', pp. 189–207.

2 Another object, also unique, with which the Ruthwell monument is frequently compared because of its use of runic inscriptions is the Franks Casket. For a useful discussion of the relation between text and images see Webster, 'The Iconographic Programme of the Franks Casket', pp. 227–246.

3 See O'Brien O'Keeffe, *Visible Song: Transitional Literacy in Old English Verse*. The *locus classicus* for understanding the ways in which Anglo-Saxon culture represented the practice of textuality as embodied is Bede's account of Cædmon's 'ruminatio' – see *HE*, IV 24.

4 Here we follow the transcriptions made after computer-enhanced digital photographs given in McKinnell, 'Ruthwell Cross, § 2', pp. 626–629. Doubtful forms are in italics, and each present but illegible character is represented by a question mark. Three dots represent an uncertain number of lost characters. We have, however, kept editorial apparatus to a minimal: we do not add length marks and so forth. The translation is our own; here too punctuation, etc., is minimal.

5 For the visual elements of Anglo-Saxon texuality, see O'Brien O'Keeffe, *Visible Song*; see also the discussion of King Alfred's visual literacy in Lerer, *Literacy and Power in Anglo-Saxon Literature*, pp. 61–96.

6 The only half-line that does not alliterate is that beginning on the south side, top and right border, '[+] crist wæs on rodi'. The majority of the inscriptions, when arranged in metrical units, begin, strikingly, with the verb in initial position. For the important relationship between speech and silence, see, for example, Parkes, *Pause and Effect: An Introduction to the History of Punctuation in the West*.

7 We can think of *sententiae* as short moral, ethical or scriptural statements used for meditative reflection, a practice more common in the Latin tradition. Commonplace books from the later tenth century such as Wulfstan's offer a vernacular analogue, but see too the related practice of wisdom literature in Anglo-Saxon poetry in, for example, *Maxims I*. For Wulfstan's commonplace book see, for example, Cross and Tunberg, eds, *The Copenhagen Wulfstan Collection*. For *Maxims I*, see *The Exeter Book*, eds Krapp and van Kirk Dobbie.

8 For a related discussion of voice and its disappearing trace, see Lees and Overing, *Double Agents: Women and Clerical Culture in Anglo-Saxon England*, pp. 40–70.

9 The meanings of 'galga' (as in the Ruthwell runes) and 'gealga' (as in *The Dream of the Rood*), gallows, gibbet, cross, and 'rod', cross, rood, are fairly consistent (and often interchangeable) throughout the Anglo-Saxon period; see the relevant entries in the electronic *Old English Corpus, Dictionary of Old English*. The word choices on the two sides of the monument may signal differences between gallows and cross, rood or Cross, but since both sides encode fragments of inscriptions it is hard to be certain about this.

10 Although the subject of Rosemary Woolf's essay, 'The Ideal of Men Dying with Their Lord in *Germania* and *The Battle of Maldon*', pp. 63–81, is not the Ruthwell runes or *The Dream of the Rood*, Woolf does offer a useful way of thinking about the ties of obedience between the 'galga/rod' and the king. The 'rod' does not, of course, die with its lord, though it certainly is loyal even unto its lord's death and is, simultaneously, the means of that death even as its meanings are transformed by these events.

11 The classic essay on prosopopeia is that by Schlauch, 'The Dream of the Rood as Prosopopeia', pp. 23–34. The gendering of the apparent binarism of 'galga' (masculine) and 'rod' (feminine) has a lengthy history in interpretations of the Ruthwell monument and *The Dream of the Rood*; see, for example, Canuteson, 'The Crucifixion and the Second Coming in *The Dream of the Rood*', pp. 293–297 (which discusses a mystical marriage between Christ and the cross), and, from entirely different perspectives, Fountain, 'Ashes to Ashes: Kristeva's *Jouissance*, Altizer's Apocalypse, Byatt's *Possession* and *The Dream*

of the Rood', p. 200, and Mary Dockray Miller, 'The Feminized Cross of *The Dream of the Rood'*, *Philological Quarterly* 76 (1997), pp. 1–18. The issue has been most recently explored on Ruthwell by Karkov in 'Naming and Renaming: The Inscription of Gender in Anglo-Saxon England', pp. 43–50. The transgressive nature of the relationship between 'rod' and king comes into focus in part because of its Germanic reflexes, where the ties between lord and subordinate are more usually represented, implicitly or explicitly, as male.

12 Frank, '*Beowulf* and Sutton Hoo: The Odd Couple', pp. 47–64.

13 For the (casual) assumption that the Ruthwell runic inscriptions encode lines from *The Dream of the Rood*, see, for example, Brown, *The Lindisfarne Gospels*, p. 203; Rollason, *Northumbria, 500–1100*, pp. 158–159; Alexander, 'Old English Literature', p. 183; or Bennett, *Poetry of the Passion: Studies in Twelve Centuries of English Verse*, p. 1. The classic essay by Fleming, '"The Dream of the Rood" and Anglo-Saxon Monasticism', pp. 43–72, offers a good example of a long-lasting attempt by critics to argue that the runic inscriptions on Ruthwell are part of the same set of meanings (monastic, liturgical) as *The Dream of the Rood*. For a refreshing counter-argument, see Savage, 'Mystical and Evangelical in *The Dream of the Rood*: The Private and the Public', pp. 4–11.

14 This position is implied but not fully developed in Savage's 'Mystical and Evangelical'. Literary critics have by and large voted with their feet by restricting their analyses to *The Dream of the Rood*.

15 Ó Carragáin, 'Crucifixion as Annunciation: The Relation of "The Dream of the Rood" to the Liturgy Reconsidered', p. 488. For Ó Carragáin's most recent thinking on this matter see *Ritual and Rood*, pp. 316–317, 319, 327, 331.

16 Strictly, Cædmon's *Hymn* is not a dream-vision poem for according to Bede's account of its composition – it's the only account we have – the idea of the poem and the injunction to produce it – 'to sing' – was given to the poet in a dream. See Bede, *HE*, IV 24.

17 A useful introduction to this period of Anglo-Saxon literary culture may be found in Shippey, *Old English Verse*, pp. 81–84.

18 For the provenance of the Vercelli Book, see Sisam, *The Vercelli Book* and Scragg, *The Vercelli Homilies*, pp. xxiii–lxxix.

19 Laxness, *Under the Glacier*, p. 78.

20 The manuscript was in Vercelli in 1748 apparently, when a transcription of one of the homilies was made. Identified as an Anglo-Saxon manuscript in 1822 by Frederick Bluhme, the contents of the Vercelli Book were subsequently transcribed by C. Meier in 1833, prior to Thorpe's 1836 edition. For details, see Swanton, ed., *The Dream of the Rood*, p. 4.

21 Duncan, 'An Account of the Remarkable Monument in the shape of a Cross, inscribed with Roman and Runic Letters, preserved in the Garden of Ruthwell Manse, Dumfriesshire', pp. 313–326.

22 For Kemble, best known as the first editor of *Beowulf*, see Dickens, 'John Mitchell Kemble and Old English Scholarship', pp. 51–84; Wiley, 'Anglo-Saxon Kemble: The Life and Works of John Mitchell Kemble, Philologist, Historian, Archaeologist', pp. 165–273; see also the brief entry on Kemble in the *Blackwell Encyclopedia of Anglo-Saxon England*, p. 269.

23 Kemble, 'On Anglo-Saxon Runes', p. 352.

24 Kemble, 'Additional Observations on the Runic Obelisk at Ruthwell, the Poem of the Dream of the Holy Rood, and a Runic Copper Dish found at Chertsey', pp. 31–46. The inscription on the Chertsey dish that Kemble read as a mixture of runes and uncials was, in 1968, found by H. E. Pagan to be in modern Greek, see Page, *An Introduction to English Runes*, p. 7.

25 Kemble, 'Additional Observations', pp. 36–38.

26 For a brief account of Kemble and his role in the two opposed schools of Germanizing and anti-Germanizing scholarship, see Ackerman, 'J. M. Kemble and Sir Frederic Madden: "Conceit and Too Much Germanism"', pp. 167–181. See Frantzen's incisive comments on Kemble's scholarship, *Desire for Origins: New Language, Old English, and Teaching the Tradition*, pp. 34–35.

27 See 'On Anglo-Saxon Runes' and the related discussions by Page, *An Introduction to English Runes*, pp. 6–7, and Cassidy, 'The Later Life of the Ruthwell Cross: From the Seventeenth Century to the Present', pp. 12–15.

28 Cassidy, 'The Later Life of the Ruthwell Cross'.

29 Simpson, 'The Rule of Medieval Imagination', p. 11. This thesis is developed subsequently by Simpson in *Reform and Cultural Revolution*.

30 Iconoclasm has a different, though equally defining, role to play in the criticism of the early medieval period (to which Simpson is far less attentive), which some have seen as central to the visual dynamics of *The Dream of the Rood* in the first place; see Swanton, *The Dream of the Rood*, pp. 52–56. Swanton overstated the case; see now Brubaker and Haldon, *Byzantium in the Iconoclast Era (ca 680–750)*, who question the extent to which there really was an early iconoclastic phase (pre-760).

31 Benjamin, *The Origin of German Tragic Drama*, pp. 177–178.

32 Benjamin, *The Origin of German Tragic Drama*, p. 235.

33 Benjamin, *The Origin of German Tragic Drama*, p. 177. See also Beckwith, 'Preserving, Conserving, Deserving the Past: A Meditation on Ruin as Relic in Post-War Britain in Five Fragments'.

34 Cited in Cassidy, 'The Later Life of the Ruthwell Cross', p. 11.

35 For Page, see *An Introduction to English Runes*, pp. 150–151, and Howlett, 'Inscriptions and Design of the Ruthwell Cross', where a prior understanding of 'biblical style' explains the 'design' of the inscriptions though not their meaning(s).

36 Simpson, 'The Rule of the Medieval Imagination'.

37 Consider, for example, Kemble's remarks on Magnusen and Rep: 'Two learned Icelanders, however, with great valour, if not much discretion, have appeared in the field, to shame both England and Germany', in 'On Anglo-Saxon Runes', p. 350. Though Kemble's methods of study were very much based on the German school (as a friend and student of Jakob Grimm), his instincts were fiercely nationalistic.

38 Kemble, 'On Anglo-Saxon Runes', p. 350.

39 Kemble, 'Additional Observations', p. 38.

40 Kemble, 'Additional Observations', p. 37.

41 Kemble, 'Additional Observations', p. 33. For Cædmon, lay labourer turned poet, see notes 3 and 16 above.

42 Kemble, 'Additional Observations', p. 33.

43 Sisam, 'Dialect Orgins of the Earlier Old English Verse', p. 122.

44 See the discussion and bibliography in Backhouse, Turner and Webster, *The Golden Age of Anglo-Saxon Art 966–1066*, pp. 90–92. The inscriptions are taken from Webster (p. 91) but we have normalized the spelling and modified the translation slightly.

45 Sisam's work on this is part of a long critical debate about how to edit Anglo-Saxon poetry; for examples, see the essays collected in Scragg and Szarmach, eds, *Editing Old English*, and Keefer and O'Brien O'Keeffe, eds, *New Approaches to Editing Old English Verse* (Cambridge, 1999).

46 Sisam, 'The Authority of Old English Poetical Manuscripts', p. 35.

47 Sisam, 'Dialect Origins of the Earlier Old English Verse', p. x.

48 Sisam, 'Dialect Origins of the Earlier Old English Verse', p. 122.

49 Wilcox, 'Transmission of Literature and Learning: Anglo-Saxon Scribal Culture', pp. 55–60, offers a useful summary of this relationship as well as that of other Exeter Book riddles that survive in more than one copy.

50 As well as Schlauch, 'The Dream of the Rood as Prosopopeia', see, for example, Orton, 'The Technique of Object Personification in *The Dream of the Rood* and a Comparison with the Old English *Riddles*', pp. 1–18.

51 In addition to O'Brien O'Keeffe, *Visible Song*, pp. 23–46, see Kevin S. Kiernan, 'Reading Cædmon's "Hymn" with Someone Else's Glosses', *Representations* 32 (1990), pp. 157–174. Critical analysis and editorial theory is challenged by the manuscript traditions of Cædmon's *Hymn* in ways that offer useful analogues for thinking about the Ruthwell monument's runic inscriptions and *The Dream of the Rood*.

52 For *Beowulf*, see the bibliographical survey by Bjork and Obermeier, 'Date, Provenance, Author, Audiences', pp. 13–34. For Cædmon, see O'Brien O'Keeffe, *Visible Song*, pp. 23–46. Bede's *Death Song* has attracted less critical attention.

53 See, for example, Howlett, 'Inscriptions and Design of the Ruthwell Cross', pp. 86–87, and Wilcox, 'Transmission of Literature and Learning', p. 57.

54 Swanton, *The Dream of the Rood*, p. 38.

55 Wilcox, 'Transmission of Literature and Learning', pp. 56–57.

56 For those unfamiliar with Freud's *Beyond the Pleasure Principle* (1920), see the excellent brief article on the compulsion to repeat in Laplance and Pontalis, *The Language of Psychoanalysis*, pp. 78–80.

57 This is illustrated by the related case of the two related poems, *Soul and Body I and II* in the Vercelli and Exeter Books; see Orton, 'Disunity in the Vercelli Book *Soul and Body*', pp. 450–460, and 'The Old English "Soul and Body": A Further Examination', pp. 173–197.

58 In this table, and for the purpose of comparison, we adapt McKinnell's version of the runic inscriptions on the Ruthwell monument; we use Swanton's edition of *The Dream of the Rood*.

59 Goodman, 'Seven Strictures on Similarity', p. 87.

60 Goodman, 'Seven Strictures on Similarity', p. 88.

61 Goodman, 'Seven Strictures on Similarity', pp. 89–90.

62 Goodman, 'Seven Strictures on Similarity', pp. 90–91.

63 See, for example, Ó Carragáin, 'Liturgical Innovations Associated with Pope Sergius and the Iconography of the Ruthwell and Bewcastle Crosses', p. 140, and Ó Carragáin, *Ritual and Rood*, pp. 308–311.

64 See Clayton, *The Cult of the Virgin Mary in Anglo-Saxon England*, pp. 30, 38.

65 According to Æthelwulf's *De abbatibus*, XIV ll. 468–469, Abbot Sigbald (died 771) had to make insistent demands on his monks, 'gently with prayers', to get them 'to celebrate the solemn festivals honouring their pious mother'.

66 On the cult of the Virgin in the liturgy as it developed from the seventh and eighth centuries through the tenth and eleventh centuries see Clayton, *The Cult of the Virgin Mary*, pp. 52–89.

67 The classic studies are Zumthor, *Essai de poétique médiévale* and Cerquiglini, *Éloge de la variante*. See also Wilcox's introductory study, 'Transmission of Literature and Learning'.

68 See for example McKinwell, 'Ruthwell Cross', p. 628, and Ó Carragáin, *Ritual and Rood*, pp. xxvii, 181.

69 The Vercelli Book includes *Elene* and *The Fates of the Apostles*, two of the four poems (the others are *Juliana* and *Christ II*) in the Old English corpus that ends with a runic acrostic spelling out the name of Cynewulf. For an introductory discussion, see Greenfield and Calder, *A New Critical History of Old English Literature*, pp. 164–176.

70 And those texts are found in both poetry and prose and in a variety of religious genres such as saint's life and homily; see further the editions and articles on the Vercelli Book cited above, note 1. In this context, note that the Ruthwell monument inscriptions manifest no interest in English prose, a form that does not appear to have taken off until the reign of Alfred, for which see Bately, 'The Nature of Old English Prose', pp. 71–87.

71 For a related discussion, see Lees and Overing, *Double Agents*, pp. 98–100.

72 Isidore of Seville, *Etymologies*, I.iii.1–3; see the related discussion in O'Brien O'Keeffe, *Visible Song*, pp. 51–52.

73 Krapp and Dobbie, eds, *The Exeter Book*, following the numbering of the editors.

74 For analysis of the Alfredian scene of reading, see Lerer, *Literacy and Power*, pp. 61–96. For the celebrated problem of the 'aestel' and its meaning as some kind of a pointer or bookmark, see, for example, Brown, 'Old Irish *Astal*, Old English *Æstel*: The Common Etymology', pp. 75–92.

75 For discussion, see Howe, 'The Cultural Construction of Reading in Anglo-Saxon

England', pp. 58–79, and Parkes, '"Rædan, Areccan, Smeagan": How the Anglo-Saxons Read', pp. 1–22.

76 See the discussion and bibliography in Backhouse, Turner and Webster, *The Golden Age of Anglo-Saxon Art 966–1066*, pp. 30–31.

77 See the discussion and bibliography in Backhouse, Turner and Webster, *The Golden Age of Anglo-Saxon Art 966–1066*, pp. 33–34.

78 See Exeter Book Riddles 13 (ten chickens), 37 (bellows), 38 (bull), 42 (cock and hen), 52 (flail), 53 (battering ram), 59 (chalice), to name but a few.

79 *Vita Samsonis*, 48.

80 See Page, 'The Bewcastle Cross', pp. 57–64. They not only read the runes by sight but they also traced them with their fingers, made paper impressions of them, cleaned them, and sometimes scraped away at them with knives.

Chapter 8: The Northumbrian cross: evidence and silence

1 The classic overview is still that of Collingwood, *Northumbrian Crosses of the Pre-Norman Age*.

2 For Ireland, Harbison, *The Golden Age of Irish Art: Medieval Achievements, 600–1200*; Hamlin, 'Crosses in Early Ireland: The Evidence from Written Sources'.

3 The evidence is gathered in Wood, 'Anglo-Saxon Otley: An Archiepiscopal Estate and Its Crosses'.

4 Bailey, *England's Earliest Sculptors*, pp. 46–48.

5 Bede, *HE*, III 2. See Colgrave and Mynors, eds, *Bede's Ecclesiatical History of the English People*, p. 215 n. 2; Bailey, *England's Earliest Sculptors*, pp. 47–48.

6 Bede, *HE*, III 2, trans. Colgrave, p. 215.

7 Bede, *HE*, III 2, trans. Colgrave, p. 217.

8 Bede, *HE*, III 1, trans. Colgrave, pp. 213–215.

9 Bede, *HE*, III 2, trans. Colgrave, p. 217, with corrections.

10 See Colgrave and Mynors, eds, *Bede's Ecclesiatical History of the English People*, p. 217 n. 5.

11 Bailey, *England's Earliest Sculptors*, p. 50.

12 Alcuin, *Versus de patribus, regibus et sanctis Euboricensis ecclesiae*, ll. 234–264, trans. Godman.

13 Alcuin, *Versus de patribus, regibus et sanctis Euboricensis ecclesiae*, ll. 396–426: Bede, *HE*, III 11.

14 Alcuin, *Versus de patribus, regibus et sanctis Euboricensis ecclesiae*, ll. 427–441.

15 The earliest accounts call it a *signum crucis*: Nicholson, 'Constantine's Vision of the Cross'.

16 Bailey, *England's Earliest Sculptors*, p. 49.

17 Cramp, *Corpus of Anglo-Saxon Stone Sculpture*, Vol. I, Pt I, *County Durham and Northumberland*, pp. 112–113: Jarrow 16a–b; Bailey, *England's Earliest Sculptors*, p. 49.

18 Levison, 'The Inscription on the Jarrow Cross'.

19 Bailey and Cramp, *Corpus of Anglo-Saxon Stone Sculpture*, Vol. II, *Cumberland, Westmorland and Lancashire North-of-the-Sands*, p. 65.

20 Tony Abramson, 'Isaiah in Ryedale: Sceats and the Church', unpublished conference paper, Leeds, International Medieval Congress, 2005.

21 For Bede, Colgrave and Mynors, *Bede's Ecclesiastical History of the English People*, p. xxx: for Alcuin, Constantinescu, 'Alcuin de les "Libelli Precum" de l'époque carolingienne', p. 25.

22 Jerome, *Chronicon*, ed. Helm, pp. 228–234.

23 Wood, 'Gregory of Tours and Clovis', p. 251.

24 Bodden, *The Old English Finding of the True Cross*.

25 For what follows, Wood, 'Constantinian Crosses in Northumbria'.

26 In all probability this results from a conflation of the civil war with Maxentius with a campaign against the Sarmatians.

27 Cynewulf, *Elene*, I, ll. 88–94, ed. Gradon. The translation is that of Bradley, *Anglo-Saxon Poetry*, p. 167.

28 Cynewulf, *Elene*, II, ll. 99–104, trans. Bradley, p. 168.

29 Cynewulf, *Elene*, XIV, ll. 1177–1178, trans. Bradley, p. 193.

30 Henderson, *Vision and Image in Early Christian England*, p. 26.

31 See Borgehammar, *How the Holy Cross Was Found*.

32 Borgehammar, *How the Holy Cross Was Found*, p. 203.

33 See Bodden, *The Old English Finding of the True Cross*.

34 Bede, *HE*, V 16.

35 Adamnan, *De locis sanctis*, I 5, ed. Meehan: Bede, *De locis sanctis*, 2, ed. Fraipont.

36 Sebeos, *History*, Ch. 35, 117, trans. Thomson, Howard-Johnston and Greenwood, *The Armenian History Attributed to Sebeos*, See also Greatrex and Lieu, *The Roman Eastern Frontier and the Persian Wars, part 2, 363–630*, pp. 192–193.

37 Adomnan, *De locis sanctis*, I 5.

38 Bede, *De locis sanctis*, 2.

39 Hugeburg, *Vita Willibaldi* (= *Hodoeporicon*), ed. Bauch, pp. 58–59.

40 Theophanes, *Chronicon*, 86, 28, trans. Mango and Scott, *The Chronicle of Theophanes the Confessor*, p. 136. The account is rejected by Taylor, *Christians and the Holy Places: The Myth of Jewish-Christian Origins*, p. 123, with n. 16, referring to an unpublished paper by Christine Milner. It is accepted by Holum, *Theodosian Empresses: Women and Imperial Domination in Late Antiquity*, pp. 86–87, and 'Pulcheria's Crusade, AD 421–2, and the Ideology of Imperial Victory', pp. 162–167: and by Key Fowden, *The Barbarian Plain: Saint Sergius between Rome and Iran*, p. 47, where the gift is placed in the context of Theodosius's preparations of war against Iran.

41 Wood, 'Constantinian Crosses in Northumbria'.

42 *Chronicon Paschale*, Olympiad 348, trans. Whitby, p. 156.

43 Sebeos, *History*, Chs 41–2, 131, 136, with note on p. 226. See also Greatrex and Lieu, *The Roman Eastern Frontier and the Persian Wars*, p. 228.

44 Hunt, *Holy Land Pilgrimage in the Later Roman Empire AD 312–460*, pp. 116–117, 128; Wilkinson, *Egeria's Travels*, p. 80.

45 Egeria *Itineraria*, 37, 2, trans. Wilkinson, *Egeria's Travels*, p. 155.

46 Wood, 'Constantinian Crosses in Northumbria'.

47 This is discusssed by Drijvers, *Helena Augusta. The Mother of Constantine the Great and the Legend of Her Finding of the True Cross*; Borgehammar, *How the Holy Cross Was Found*.

48 *Liber Pontificalis*, 86, 10, trans. Davis, p. 85.

49 Bede, *Historia abbatum*, 15, 18: Bede, *De temporum ratione*, 47.

50 Bede, *De temporum ratione*, 66, s.a. 4652: trans. Wallis, p. 233. Bailey, *England's Earliest Sculptors*, pp. 48–49, says that the discovery was made in 701. Where he gets the date from is unclear. Bede (for no obvious reason) puts the event in the reign of Leo (695–698). The year is not given in the *Liber pontificalis*, which is Bede's source. Nor, despite Bailey's assertion, was Ceolfrith in Rome at the time of the discovery. Hwætbert was in Rome in 701, though probably not at the time that the reliquary was found: Bede, *De temporum ratione*, 47, trans. Wallis, p. 128, with n. 31. Despite Bailey's misrepresentation of the evidence, it is clear that Bede thought the discovery significant.

51 Ó Carragáin, 'Liturgical Innovations Associated with Pope Sergius and the Iconography of the Ruthwell and Bewcastle Crosses': Bailey, *England's Earliest Sculptors*, pp. 48–49.

52 Van Tongeren, *Exaltation of the Cross*, p. 54.

53 Dinwiddie, 'The Ruthwell Cross and the Story It Has to Tell', pp. 116–117.

54 Most of the evidence is gathered in Wood, 'Anglo-Saxon Otley: An Archiepiscopal Estate and Its Crosses', pp. 26–30.

55 Bede, *HE*, III 2.

56 Bede, *Vita Cuthberti*, 37, ed. Colgrave, *Two Lives of Saint Cuthbert*, pp. 272–273, with note, p. 354.

57 Stephanus, *Vita Wilfridi*, 66, ed. Colgrave.

58 Æthelwulf, *De abbatibus*, XXII, ll. 723–725, 737, ed. Campbell, pp. 56–59.

59 Æthelwulf, *De abbatibus*, XVII, ll. 537–539, pp. 42–43.

60 Hugeburg, *Hodoeporicon*, 1: translated by C. H. Talbot, *The Anglo-Saxon Missionaries in Germany*, pp. 154–155.

61 Symeon of Durham, *Libellus de exordio atque procursu istius boc est Dunhelmensis ecclesiae*, I 12, ed. and trans. Rollason, pp. 60–61.

62 *Historia regum*, 36, s.a. 740. The translation is by Collingwood, *Northumbrian Crosses of the pre-Norman Age*, p. 29.

63 Symeon of Durham, *Libellus de exordio*, I 12, trans. Rollason, pp. 60–61.

64 Brown, *The Lindisfarne Gospels*, p. 7.

65 *Vita Samsonis*, 48, ed. Flobert: 'In quo monte et ego fui signumque crucis quod sanctus Samson sua manu cum quodam ferro in lapide stante sculpsisset adoravi et mea manu palpavi': trans. Taylor, *The Life of St. Samson of Dol*, p. 49.

66 See Hamlin, 'Crosses in Early Ireland: The Evidence from Written Sources', pp. 138–140. The examples given in Wood, 'Anglo-Saxon Otley: An Archiepiscopal Estate and Its Crosses', pp. 28–29, are drawn from saint's lives regarded as early in Sharpe, *Medieval Irish Saints' Lives: An Introduction to the Vitae Sanctorum Hiberniae*.

67 *Vita sancti Finani abbatis de Cenn Etigh*, 34: *Vita prior sancti Fintani seu Munnu abbatis de Tech Munnu*, 19, ed. Heist. See also Hamlin, 'Crosses in Early Ireland', p. 139.

68 *Vita prior sancti Lugidi seu Molvae*, 37: Muirchu, *Vita Patricii*, II 2: Tirechan, *Vita Patricii*, 41. See also Hamlin, 'Crosses in Early Ireland', p. 138.

69 Adomnan, *Vita Columbae*, I 45; III, 23.

70 Muirchu, *Vita Patricii*, I, 12 (11). Hamlin, 'Crosses in Early Ireland', p. 139.

71 *Vita Leutfridi*, 10.

72 Constantius, *Vita Germani*, VI, 30.

73 *Vita Ansberti*, 34–35.

74 *Vita Boniti*, 38.

75 Sigebert, *Vita Landiberti*, 12.

76 *Vita Landiberti*, (1), 6.

77 Chrodegang, *Regula canonicorum*, 17: Krusch, Monumenta Germaniae Historica, Scriptores Rerum Merovingicarum 6, p. 358, n. 5.

78 Columbanus, *Regula coenobialis*, 3: 'Qui egrediens domum ad orationem poscendam ... crucem non adierit, xii percussionibus emendare statuitur'.

79 Jonas of Bobbio, *Vita Columbani*, II 6: trans. Wood, in Head, ed., *Medieval Hagiography: An Anthology*, p. 123.

80 Bede, *HE*, III 25. On the association of Rome and stone, see Hawkes, '*Iuxta Morem Romanorum*: Stone and Sculpture in Anglo-Saxon England'.

81 Walser, ed., *Die Einsiedler Inschriftsammlung und der Pilgerführer durch Rom (Codex Einsidlensis 326)*, pp. 168, 170, 172, 175, 176: for the inscription on the Vatican obelisk, p. 85. See also the entries on p. 227 for the columns of Marcus Aurelius, Antoninus Pius and Trajan.

82 Adamnan, *De locis sanctis*, I 5: Bede, *De locis sanctis*, 2.

83 Adamnan, *De locis sanctis*, II 16. But compare the different account in Hugeburg's *Hodoeporicon* of St Willibald (trans. Talbot, p. 165): 'On the very place where Christ was baptized and where they now baptize there stands a little wooden cross'. There is considerable variety in the descriptions of the Cross set up on the Jordan: according to Theodosius's *Topography of the Holy Land*, 20, there was a marble column with an iron cross on top, while the Piacenza Pilgrim, 11, talks of a wooden cross: Wilkinson, *Jerusalem Pilgrims before the Crusades*, pp. 112, 136. The changing course of the river and the liability of the region to earthquakes may have meant frequent changes to the monuments.

84 The observation is Celia Chazelle's.

85 Ó Carragáin, *Ritual and the Rood*, p. 109, suggests 'the late eighth or even the ninth century: perhaps two or more generations after the rest of the monument was sculpted'.

86 The latest transcription of the inscriptions is J. McKinnell, 'Ruthwell Cross, § 2', pp. 625–629. The following transcriptions are taken from McKinnell. For an attempt to fill in the missing letters, see Howlett, 'Inscriptions and Design of the Ruthwell Cross', pp. 71–93. Here we have simply followed McKinnell's readings.

87 Mathews, *The Clash of Gods: A Reinterpretation of Early Christian Art*, pp. 54–91.

88 Meyvaert, 'A New Perspective on the Ruthwell Cross: *Ecclesia* and *Vita Monastica*', pp. 129–130.

89 *Opus Caroli Regis contra Synodum*, IV 21, ed. Freeman and Meyvaert, p. 540.

90 Ó Carragáin, *Ritual and the Rood*, p. 156.

91 *Opus Caroli Regis contra Synodum*, IV 16, 21, ed. Freeman and Meyvaert, pp. 528–529, 540.

92 Howlett, 'Inscriptions and Design of the Ruthwell Cross', p. 75.

93 Hawkes, 'Symbols of Passion or Power? The Iconography of the Rothbury Cross Head'.

94 E.g. the ivory cover of Oxford, Bodleian Library, MS Douce 176: see Chazelle, *The Crucified God in the Carolingian Era. Theology and Art of Christ's Passion*, pp. 77–78.

95 See Connolly, *Bede on Tobit and the Canticle of Habbakuk*, pp. 68–69, n. 18. Meyvaert, 'A New Perspective on the Ruthwell Cross: *Ecclesia* and *Vita Monastica*', pp. 125–129, offers a further range of Biblical texts. One possible problem shared by all the texts suggested is that they do not use the verb *cognoverunt*.

96 Anon., *Vita Cuthberti*, II 3.

97 Bede, *Vita Cuthberti*, 10. See the comment in Schapiro, 'The Religious Meaning of the Ruthwell Cross', p. 163.

98 Examples are conveniently gathered in Kitzinger, *Byzantine Art in the Making: Main Lines of Stylistic Development in Mediterranean Art, 3rd–7th Century*, plates 5–8.

99 *Opus Caroli Regis contra Synodum*, IV 21, p. 540: 'Cum ergo depictam pulchram quandam feminam puerum in ulnis tenere cernimus, si superscriptio necdum facta sit aut quondam facta casu quodam demolita, qua industria discernere valemus, utrum Sara sit Isaac tenens aut Rebecca Iacob ferens aut Bertsabee Salomonem iactans aut Elisabeth Iohannem baiulans aut quedam mulier parvulum suum tenens? Et ut ad gentiles fabulas veniamus, quae plerumque depicte inveniuntur, unde scire valemus utrum Venus sit Aeneam tenens an Algmena Herculem portans an Andromacha Asthianacta gerens?'

100 *Opus Caroli Regis contra Synodum*, IV 16, pp. 528–529: 'Et si nomina superscripta haec, quae enumeravimus, ad eorum, quorum nomina sunt, honorem perducere minime queunt, nec illas quoque nominum inscriptiones ad sanctorum honorem quodam-modo perducunt. Et si istud prudenti consideratione abnuitur, et illud sollerti indaga-tione abicitur. Offeruntur cuilibet eorum, qui imagines adorant, verbi gratia duarum feminarum pulcrarum imagines superscriptione carentes, quas ille parvipendens abicit abiectasque quolibet in loco iacere permittit. Dicit illi quis: "Una illarum sanctae Mariae imago est, abici non debet; altera Veneris, quae omnino abicienda est."'

101 As Celia Chazelle has commented, a similar process of association might underlie the panel on the beasts: an iconographic image of Christ treading on the basilisk and asp may have been adapted to recall the beast's reverence in the wilderness.

102 The interpretation of the scene as a *Maiestas* is best set out by Meyvaert, 'The Apocalypse Panel on the Ruthwell Cross': also 'A New Perspective on the Ruthwell Cross: *Ecclesia* and *Vita Monastica*', pp. 112–125. The interpretation of the scene as John the Baptist with the *Agnus Dei* is reasserted by Ó Carragáin, *Ritual and the Rood*, pp. 160–164.

103 Howlett, 'Inscriptions and Design of the Ruthwell Cross', p. 76.

104 Gannon, *The Iconography of Early Anglo-Saxon Coinage. Sixth to Eighth Centuries*, pp. 105–106.

105 Meyvaert, 'A New Perspective on the Ruthwell Cross: *Ecclesia* and *Vita Monastica*', provides an important analysis of the monument scene by scene. Alternative readings are to be found in Ó Carragáin, *Ritual and the Rood*.

106 Already noted by Schapiro, 'The Religious Meaning of the Ruthwell Cross', p. 163.

107 Saxl, 'The Ruthwell Cross', p. 5: Schapiro, 'The Religious Meaning of the Ruthwell Cross', p. 166.

108 Here we do not follow the suggestion of Meyvaert, 'A New Perspective on the Ruthwell Cross: *Ecclesia* and *Vita Monastica*', pp. 102–104.

109 McKinnell, 'Ruthwell Cross', p. 627: +dominnæc|martha|mari?m?

110 Ó Carragáin, *Ritual and the Rood*, pp. 102, 138.

111 Sophisticated readings of Mary and Martha are, of course, perfectly possible: Farr, 'Worthy Women on the Ruthwell Cross: Women as a Sign in Early Anglo-Saxon Monasticism'; Karkov, 'Naming and Renaming: The Inscription of Gender in Anglo-Saxon Stone Sculpture', pp. 35–56.

112 Meyvaert, 'A New Perspective on the Ruthwell Cross: *Ecclesia* and *Vita Monastica*', pp. 138–140.

113 As is well known, Duncan reconstructed the top incorrectly, and the uppermost fragment currently faces the wrong direction.

114 There are excellent concise summaries in Meyvaert, 'A New Perspective on the Ruthwell Cross: *Ecclesia* and *Vita Monastica*', pp. 140–5, and Ó Carragáin, *Ritual and the Rood*, pp. 141–143.

115 Schapiro, 'The Bowman and the Bird on the Ruthwell Cross and Other Works: The Interpretation of Secular Themes in Early Mediaeval Religious Art'.

116 We owe this observation to Helena Edgren.

117 Wood, 'Ruthwell: Contextual Searches', pp. 112–113.

118 Wood, 'Bede's Jarrow': Bede, *Vita Cuthberti*, 3.

119 The most extended treatment of the iconography has been by Ó Carragáin, in a series of articles as well as his book, *Ritual and the Rood*. We have cited the book as being the most recent statement of his interpretation.

120 Meyvaert, 'A New Perspective on the Ruthwell Cross: *Ecclesia* and *Vita Monastica*', provides a useful survey of relevant passages in Bede.

121 *Liber pontificalis*, 86, 6–9.

122 Ó Carragáin, *Ritual and the Rood*, pp. 247–257. Kessler, *Spiritual Seeing*, pp. 109–110, appears to express some reservations about the redecoration of the façade of St Peter's.

123 *Liber pontificalis*, 86, 14: 'Hic statuit ut tempore confractionis dominici corporis Agnus Dei qui tollis peccata mundi miserere nobis a clero et populo decantetur.'

124 Meyvaert, 'A New Perspective on the Ruthwell Cross: *Ecclesia* and *Vita Monastica*', p. 163.

125 Ó Carragáin, *Ritual and the Rood*, pp. 225–228.

126 Bede, *HE*, IV 18.

127 Bede, *HE*, IV 18.

128 Ó Carragáin, *Ritual and the Rood*, pp. 80, 261–262.

129 Bede describes the ceremony in his commentaries on Ezra and Nehemiah: Cubitt, 'Unity and Diversity in the Early Anglo-Saxon Liturgy', pp. 49–50. Ó Carragáin, *Ritual and the Rood*, p. 128.

130 Ó Carragáin, *Ritual and the Rood*, pp. 128–137.

131 Ó Carragáin, *Ritual and the Rood*, pp. 153–160.

132 Van Tongeren, *Exaltation of the Cross*, p. 208.

133 Augustine's exegesis of the Tree of Life is conveniently discussed in Duclow, 'Denial or Promise of the Tree of Life? Eriugena, Augustine, and Genesis 3.22b', pp. 223–229.

134 Chazelle, *The Crucified God in the Carolingian Era: Theology and Art of Christ's Passion*, p. 153.

135 Bede, *HE*, IV 18.

136 Bede, *HE*, IV 18, trans. Colgrave and Mynors.

137 The Purifaction and Annunciation were not initially regarded as feasts of the Virgin, but feasts of Our Lord: Bullough, *Alcuin, Achievement and Reputation*, pp. 251–252.

138 *Liber pontificalis*, 86, 10, 14.

139 Brown, *The Lindisfarne Gospels: Society, Spirituality and the Scribe*, pp. 187–188.

140 Ó Carragáin, *Ritual and the Rood*, pp. 98–99: see also Bullough, *Alcuin, Achievement and Reputation*, pp. 251–252.

141 Evidence is gathered by Clayton, *The Cult of the Virgin Mary in Anglo-Saxon England*, pp. 38–40. To this one might add the contradictory evidence of Bede: all four feasts appear to have been included in the martyrology, H. Quentin, *Les martyrologes historiques du Moyen Âge*, pp. 49, 50, 54. This is what one might expect from Bede's interest in Sergius. By contrast only the Purification is to be found in the *Kalendarium* as edited by Jones,

Bedae opera didascalica 3, pp. 565–578, and there is a Bede homily (I 18) for the Feast. The Martyrology of Acca as reconstructed by Lapidge includes the Annunciation, Dormition and Nativity of the Virgin, 'Acca of Hexham and the Origin of the Old English Martyrology', pp. 53–57. The Calendar of Willibrord, ed. Wilson, pp. 4, 10, 11, includes three of the feasts: the Purification, Dormition and Nativity (but gives dates different from usual for the last two). The *Dei Laude Dei* of Alcuin seems to mention only the Purification, the Assumption or Dormition, Constantinescu, 'Alcuin de les "Libelli Precum" de l'époque carolingienne', pp. 45, 49–50, although there is an additional feast of the Virgin on 18 December.

142 Wilmart, 'Un témoin Anglo-Saxon du calendrier métrique d'York', pp. 65–68, ll. 9, 17, 47–48, 51–52.

143 Æthelwulf, *De abbatibus*, XIV, ll. 460–469. Clayton, *The Cult of the Virgin Mary in Anglo-Saxon England*, p. 39.

144 Ó Carragáin, *Ritual and the Rood*, p. 83.

145 For a full statement of these possibilities, Ó Carragáin, *Ritual and the Rood*, pp. 103, 138.

146 Pfaff, ed., *The Liturgical Books of Anglo-Saxon England*, pp. 9–10.

147 Hen, 'The Liturgy of St Willibrord', pp. 41–62.

148 Brown, *The Lindisfarne Gospels*, p. 54.

149 Ó Carragáin, *Ritual and the Rood*, p. 209.

150 Chapman, *Notes on the Early History of the Vulgate Gospels*, pp. 45–77. See also Brown, *The Lindisfarne Gospels*, pp. 184, 191.

151 Cubitt, 'Unity and Diversity in the Early Anglo-Saxon Liturgy', p. 50.

152 On Theodore's liturgical influence, Hohler, 'Theodore and the liturgy'.

153 Bede, *HE*, IV 1.

154 Bede, *Histora abbatum*, 3.

155 Cubitt, 'Unity and Diversity in the Early Anglo-Saxon Liturgy', p. 48: also pp. 49, 57. In general on the various influences involved in the development of the liturgy see Hen, 'Rome, Anglo-Saxon England, and the Formation of the Frankish Liturgy'.

156 Cubitt, 'Unity and Diversity in the Early Anglo-Saxon Liturgy'.

157 Bede, *HE*, IV 2.

158 Stephanus, *Vita Wilfridi*, 14.

159 Bede, *HE*, V 20. On Acca, see now Lapidge, 'Acca of Hexham and the Origin of the Old English Martyrology', pp. 29–78, esp. 65–69.

160 Baert, *A Heritage of Holy Wood: The Legend of the True Cross in Text and Image*, p. 70.

161 *Bobbio Missal*, 288–298, ed. Lowe, pp. 86–88.

162 We are indebted to Yitzhak Hen for guidance on this.

163 Cynewulf, *Elene*, ll. 1226–1228.

164 Chapman, *Notes on the Early History of the Vulgate Gospels*, p. 54.

165 *Calendar of St Willibrord*, p. 7: 'i nonas maii: inventio crucis'.

166 Lapidge, 'Acca of Hexham and the Origin of the Old English Martyrology', p. 56: the feast is also in the Old English Martyrology for 3 May, p. 35.

167 *Bedae opera didascalica*, Vol. 3, pp. 565–578.

168 Brown, *The Lindisfarne Gospels*, p. 184, notes that Bede was 'consulting a Neapolitan Gospel lectionary', and that this shows that 'such a system was in actual liturgical use at Wearmouth/Jarrow'.

169 Quentin, *Les martyrologes historiques*, p. 19.

170 Quentin, *Les martyrologes historiques*, p. 51. For a translation of one version of the martyrology, which also lacks any Feasts of the Cross, see that of Lifshitz in Head, ed., *Medieval Hagiography: An Anthology*, pp. 169–197.

171 Quentin, *Les martyrologes historiques*, pp. 53–54.

172 For the contents of the manuscript: see Ganz, 'Le *De Laude Dei* d'Alcuin': for Alcuin's antiphon for the *Hypapanti*, another feast championed by Sergius, see p. 389. Also Bullough, *Alcuin, Achievement and Reputation*, pp. 193–199: on the question of Alcuin and Marian feasts associated with Sergius, pp. 251–252.

173 Constantinescu, 'Alcuin et les "Libelli Precum" de l'époque carolingienne'.

174 Ed. Deshusses, *Le Sacramentaire Grégorien: ses principes formes d'après les plus anciens manuscrits*, Vol. 2, p. 44: the case for Alcuin's authorship is made on pp. 25–26.

175 Chazelle, *The Crucified God in the Carolingian Era*, pp. 34, 140.

176 Van Tongeren, *Exaltation of the Cross*, pp. 59–60.

177 Ó Carragáin, *Ritual and the Rood*, p. 91.

178 Wilmart, 'Un témoin anglo-saxon du calendrier métrique de York', p. 64.

179 For an account of eighth-century Gelasian sacramentaries, Hen, *The Royal Patronage of Liturgy in Frankish Gaul*, pp. 57–61.

180 For the date, Deshusses, *Liber Sacramentorum Gellonensis*: also 'Le sacramentaire de Gellone dans son contexte historique'. The text is edited by Dumas, Corpus Christianorum Series Latinorum 159. We are indebted to Celia Chazelle, David Ganz and Yitzhak Hen for guidance on the Sacramentary.

181 Chazelle, *The Crucified God in the Carolingian Era*, pp. 87, 91.

182 Baert, *A Heritage of Holy Wood*, pp. 55, 57.

183 Cubitt, 'Unity and Diversity in the Early Anglo-Saxon Liturgy'.

184 Cubitt, 'Unity and Diversity in the Early Anglo-Saxon Liturgy', p. 49.

185 Bede, *HE*, I 25.

186 Wood, 'Anglo-Saxon Otley: An Archiepiscopal Estate and Its Crosses', p. 37: Blair, *The Church in Anglo-Saxon Society*, p. 165, questions the conclusion. Despite the richness of evidence for Anglo-Saxon Otley, however, there is no indication in our sources that the estate was ever regarded as monastic. The issue is, of course, partly a semantic one.

187 Hugeburg, *Hodoeporicon*, 1.

188 Hugeburg, *Hodoeporicon*, 1.

189 Ó Carragáin, *Ritual and the Rood*, p. 261, talks of the images as 'food for joyful rumination'.

190 *Vita Landiberti*, (I), 6: Sigebert, *Vita Landiberti*, 12.

191 But see the suggestion by Ó Carragáin, 'A Liturgical Interpretation of the Bewcastle Cross', pp. 37–38.

192 Williams, 'An Architectural Fragment from Ruthwell, Dumfriesshire'. Rosemary Cramp remarked (personal communication), 'I think it is too big for the pillar of a box tomb, and could be a door jamb but the grooves need explanation'.

193 Meyvaert, 'A New Perspective on the Ruthwell Cross: *Ecclesia* and *Vita Monastica*', pp. 151–157, sees elements of an Anglian church in the present church at Ruthwell.

194 The building of a stone church may, however, have postdated the erection of the original monument. Commenting on the architectural fragment, Rosemary Cramp remarked (personal communication), 'It is clearly later than the cross, but good competent work'.

195 Meyvaert, 'A New Perspective on the Ruthwell Cross: *Ecclesia* and *Vita Monastica*', p. 157, n. 230, for the evidence of the Plan of St Gall, where there was an altar in front of a cross, *altare sancti Salvatoris ad crucem*, perhaps 'the place of worship for laymen'.

196 For an example from elsewhere, see Sawyer, *The Viking-Age Rune-Stones. Custom and Commemoration in Early Medieval Scandinavia*.

197 Ó Carragáin, *Ritual and the Rood*, pp. 41–43.

198 Wood, *The Merovingian Kingdoms, 450–751*, p. 135.

199 Gerchow, *Die Gedenküberlieferung der Angelsachsen: mit einem Katalog der libri vitae und Necrologien*.

Spiritual things/material things

1 Bede, *Epistola ad Ecgbertum*, 11 (hereafter Ep.).

2 Marx, 'Preface', *A Contribution to the Critique of Political Economy* (1859), pp. 173–174.

3 Bailey, *Viking Age Sculpture*, p. 81.

4 Bede, *Ep.* 10.

5 Bede, *Ep.* 11.

6 Bede, *Ep.* 13, 12.

7 Bede, *Ep.* 12.

8 Bede, *Ep.* 12.

9 Bede, *Ep.* 13.
10 Bede, *HE*, V 24.
11 Bede, *Ep.* 11.
12 Bede, *Ep.* 11.
13 See Wormald, 'Bede, "Beowulf" and the Conversion of the Anglo-Saxon Aristocracy', p. 34, citing Bede's *Ecclesiastical History*, Stephanus' *Life of Wilfrid* and Felix's *Life of Guthlac*. Wormald points out that this is how Beowulf, with fourteen others, arrived at the court of Hrothgar.
14 Bede, *HE*, V 23.
15 Stephanus, *Vita Wilfridi*, and Æthelwulf, *De abbatibus*, II–IV.
16 Ideology is one of those concepts that resist easy definition. The brief discussion here is based mainly on what Marx and Engels drafted between November 1845 and the summer of 1846 in *The German Ideology* and what Marx presented in summary form in the 1859 'Preface' to *A Contribution to the Critique of Political Economy*. It also takes from Roland Barthes's work on ideology in 'Myth Today', which draws on *The German Ideology*, T. J. Clark's 'Preliminary Arguments: Work of Art and Ideology', and O. K. Werckmeister's, 'The Political Ideology of the Bayeux Tapestry'.
17 See Althusser, 'Ideology and Ideological State Apparatuses (Notes Towards an Investigation)', pp. 165–170. While much of Althusser's essay was always bound not to withstand the criticism of Thompson, 'The Poverty of Theory: or an Orrery of Errors', pp. 193–397, this idea from its discussion of ideology's material existence and the way it interpellates individuals as subjects – Althusser's example is Christian religious ideology – has proved useful here. On gender as an effect performatively compelled by organising and controlling regulatory practices, see Butler, *Gender Trouble: Feminism and the Subversion of Identity*, espec. pp. 24–25, 33, 115, 134–141.
18 Benjamin, 'Theses on the Philosophy of History', IV, p. 256.

Bibliography

⌘

Abbreviations

Archaeologia = *Archaeologia; or, Miscellaneous Tracts Relating to Antiquity*

Archaeologia Aeliana = *Archaeologia Aeliana or Miscellaneous Tracts Relating to Antiquity*

BAR = British Archaeological Reports, British Series

CCSL = Corpus Christianorum Series Latinorum

Corpus = *The British Academy Corpus of Anglo-Saxon Stone Sculpture*

JW&CI = *Journal of the Warburg and Courtauld Institutes*

MGH = Monumenta Germaniae Historica

SLH = Scriptores Latini Hiberniae

SRM = Scriptores Rerum Merovingicarum

TC&WA&AS = *Transactions of the Cumberland and Westmorland Antiquarian and Archaeological Society*

T&JPD&GNH&AS = *Transactions and Journal of the Proceedings of the Dumfriesshire and Galloway Natural History and Antiquarian Society*

Primary sources

The Acts of the General Assemblies of the Church of Scotland, from the Year 1638 to the Year 1649. Inclusive. Printed in the year 1882. To which are now added the index of the unprinted Acts of these Assemblies; and the Acts of the General Assembly 1690 (Edinburgh, 1691).

Adamnan, *De locis sanctis*, ed. D. Meehan, SLH 3 (Dublin, 1958).

Adomnan, *Vita Columbae*, ed. and trans. A. O. and M. O. Anderson, *Adomnán's Life of Columba* (Oxford, 1991): trans. R. Sharpe, *Adomnán of Iona, Life of St Columba* (London, 1995).

Æthelwulf, *De abbatibus*, ed. A. Campbell (Oxford, 1967).

Alcuin, *Epistolae*, ed. E. Dümmler, MGH Epistolae 2, Karolini Aevi 2 (Berlin, 1985).

Alcuin, *Missa de Sancta Croce*, ed. Jean Deshusses, *Le Sacramentaire Grégorien: ses principes formes d'après les plus anciens manuscrits*, vol. 2 (Fribourg, 1979), p. 44.

Alcuin, *Versus de patribus, regibus et sanctis Euboricensis ecclesiae*, ed. and trans. P. Godman, *The Bishops, Kings and Saints of York* (Oxford, 1982),

Ammianus Marcellinus, ed. J. C. Rolfe (Cambridge, MA, 1935–1939).

Anglo-Saxon Chronicle, trans. Dorothy Whitelock (London, 1961).

Asser, *De rebus gestis Ælfredi*, ed. W. H. Stevenson, *Life of King Alfred: together with the Annals of St. Neots* (Oxford, 1904): trans. with intro. Simon Keynes and Michael Lapidge, *Asser's Life of King Alfred and Other Contemporary Sources* (Harmondsworth, 1983).

Augustine, *Confessiones*, ed. L. Verheigen, CCSL 27 (Turnhout, 1990): trans. and ed. Albert C. Outler, *Augustine: Confessions and Enchiridion* (London, 1955).

Augustine, *De civitate Dei*, ed. E. Hoffmann, Corpus Scriptorum Ecclesiasticorum Latinorum 40 (Bonn, 1899): trans. David S. Wiesen, *The City of God Against the Pagans* (Cambridge, MA, 1968).

Bede, *De locis sanctis*, ed. I. Fraipont, *Itineraria et alia geographica*, CCSL 175 (Turnhout, 1965).

Bede, *De temporum ratione*, ed. Charles W. Jones, *Bedae Venerabilis opera didascalica*, CCSL 123 B (Turnhout, 1977): trans. Faith Wallis, *Bede, The Reckoning of Time* (Liverpool, 1999).

Bede, *Epistola ad Ecgbertum Episcopum*, ed. Charles Plummer, *Baedae Venerabilis opera historica* (Oxford, 1896).

Bede, *Historia abbatum*, ed. Charles Plummer, *Baedae Venerabilis opera historica* (Oxford, 1896).

Bede, *Historia ecclesiastica*, Bertram Colgrave and R. A. B. Mynors, eds, *Bede's Ecclesiastical History of the English People* (Oxford, 1969): also ed. Charles Plummer, *Bedae Venerabilis opera historica* (Oxford, 1896).

Bede, *Homiliae evangelii*, ed. David Hurst, CCSL 122 (Turnhout, 1955).

Bede, *In Regum librum XXX quaestiones*, ed. David Hurst, CCSL 119 (Turnhout, 1962).

Bede, *Kalendarium*, ed. Charles W. Jones, *Bedae Venerabilis opera didascalica* 3, CCSL 123C (Turnhout, 1980), pp. 565–578.

Bede, *Vita Cuthberti*, ed. Bertram Colgrave, *Two Lives of Saint Cuthbert* (Cambridge, 1940).

The Bobbio Missal, a Gallican Mass-Book, ed. E. A. Lowe, Henry Bradshaw Society 58 (1920).

Boniface, *Epistolae*, ed. Michael Tangl, *S. Bonifatii et Lulli epistolae*, MGH, Epistolae Selectae in Usum Scholarum 1 (Berlin, 1916).

Byrhtferth's Enchiridion, eds Peter S. Baker and Michael Lapidge (Oxford, 1995).

Calendar of St Willibrord, ed. H. A. Wilson, Henry Bradshaw Society 55 (1918).

Cassiodorus, *Institutiones divinarum et saecularium litterarum*, ed. R. A. B. Mynors (Oxford, 1937): trans. Leslie Webber Jones, *An Introduction to Divine and Human Readings* (New York, 1966).

Cassiodorus, *Variae*, ed. A. J. Fridh, CCSL 96 (Turnhout, 1973): trans. notes and intro. S. J. B. Barnish, *The Variae of Magnus Aurelius Cassiodorus Senator* (Liverpool, 1992).

Chrodegang, *Regula canonicorum*, ed. Wilhelm Schmitz (Hanover, 1889).

Chronicon Paschale, trans. Michael and Mary Whitby, *Chronicon Paschale 284–628* (Liverpool, 1989).

Columbanus, *Regula coenobialis*, ed. G. W. S. Walker, *Sancti Columbani opera*, SLH 2 (Dublin, 1957).

Constantius, *Vita Germani*, ed. Réné Borius, *Constance de Lyon; Vie de Saint Germain d'Auxerre*, Sources Chrétiennes 112 (Paris, 1965).

Councils and Ecclesiastical Documents relating to Great Britain and Ireland, vol. III, *The English Church 595–1066*, eds A. W. Haddan and W. Stubbs (Oxford, 1871).

Cynewulf, *Elene*, ed. P. O. E. Gradon (London, 1958): trans. S. A. J. Bradley, *Anglo-Saxon Poetry* (London, 1982).

The Dream of the Rood, ed. Michael Swanton (Manchester, 1970).

Egeria, trans. John Wilkinson, *Egeria's Travels*, 3rd edn (Warminster, 1999).

Einsiedeln Itinerary, ed. G. Walser, *Die Einsiedler Inschriftsammlung und der Pilgerführer durch Rom (Codex Einsidlensis 326)*, Historia Einzelschriften 53 (Stuttgart, 1987).

Eugippius, *Vita Severini*, ed. Philippe Régerat, *Vie de saint Severin*, Sources Chrétiennes 374 (Paris, 1991).

The Exeter Book, ed. George Philip Krapp and Elliott van Kirk Dobbie, Anglo-Saxon Poetic Records 3 (New York, 1936).

Gildas, *De excidio Britonum*, ed. Michael Winterbottom, *Gildas, The Ruin of Britain and Other Documents* (London, 1978).

Gododdin, ed. Arthur O. H. Jarman, *Aneirin, Y Gododdin. Britain's Oldest Heroic Poem* (Llandyssul, 1988): also John T. Koch, *The Gododdin of Aneirin. Text and Context from Dark-Age North Britain* (Cardiff, 1997).

Henry of Huntingdon, *Historia Anglorum*, ed. Thomas Arnold, Rolls Series (London, 1879).

Historia Brittonum, ed. John Morris, *Nennius: British History and the Welsh Annals* (London, 1980).

Historia de Sancto Cuthberto, ed. Ted Johnson Smith (Woodbridge, 2002).

Historia regum, ed. T. Arnold, *Symeonis monachi opera omnia*, vol. 2, Rolls Series (London, 1885).

Hugeburg, *Vita Willibaldi* (= *Hodoeporicon*), ed. A. Bauch, *Quellen zur Geschichte der Diözese Eichstätt, Biographien der Gründungszeit* (Eichstätt, 1962): trans. C. H. Talbot, *The Anglo-Saxon Missionaries in Germany* (London, 1954).

Isidore of Seville, *Etymologies*, ed. W. M. Lindsay (Oxford, 1911).

Jerome, *Chronicon*, ed. R. Helm, Eusebius Werke 7 (Berlin, 1956).

Jocelyn of Furness, *Vita Kentigerni*, ed. A. P. Forbes, *The Lives of S. Ninian and S. Kentigern*, Historians of Scotland, vol. 5 (Edinburgh, 1874).

Jonas of Bobbio, *Vita Columbani*, ed. Bruno Krusch, MGH, SRM 4 (Hanover, 1902).

Liber pontificalis, ed. L. Duchesne, vol. 1 (Paris, 1955): trans. R. Davis, *The Book of Pontiffs* (Liverpool, 1989).

Liber sacramentorum Gellonensis, ed. A. Dumas, CCSL 159 (Turnhout, Brepols, 1981): introd. J. Deshusses, CCSL 159A (Turnhout, Brepols, 1981).

Liber vitae ecclesiae Dunelmensis, ed. J. B. Stevenson, *Publications of the Surtees Society* 13 (1841): see also the facsimile, ed. A. Hamilton Thompson, *Publications of the Surtees Society* 136 (1923).

Miracula Nynie Episcopi, ed. K. Strecker, MGH, Poetae IV 2 (Berlin, 1923), pp. 943–962: also ed. and trans. W. W. MacQueen, *T&JPD&GNH&AS* 38 (1959/60), pp. 21–57.

Muirchu, *Vita patricii*, ed. Ludwig Bieler, *The Patrician Texts in the Book of Armargh*, SLH 10 (Dublin, 1979).

Old English Corpus, Dictionary of Old English, ed. A. diPaolo Healey, accessed at http://ets/umdl.umich.edu/o/oec.

Paschasius Radbertus, *Liber de corpore et sanguine domini*, ed. B. Paulus, CCSL, Continuatio Medievalis 16 (Turhout, Brepols, 1969).

Pliny, *Natural History*, trans. H. Rackham, Vol. I, Bks 1 and 2 (Cambridge, MA, 1938); Vol. II, Bks 3–7 (Cambridge, MA, 1942).

Sebeos, *History*, eds R. W. Thomson, J. Howard-Johnston, T. Greenwood, *The Armenian History Attributed to Sebeos* (Liverpool, 1999).

Sigebert, *Vita Landiberti*, ed. Bruno Krusch, MGH, SRM 6 (Hanover, 1913).

Stephanus, *Vita Wilfridi*, ed. B. Colgrave, *The Life of Bishop Wilfrid by Eddius Stephanus* (Cambridge, 1927).

Symeon of Durham, *Libellus de exordio atque procursu istius boc est Dunhelmensis ecclesiae*, ed. and trans. David Rollason (Oxford, 2000).

Theodulf, *Opus Caroli Regis contra Synodum*, eds Ann Freeman and Paul Meyvaert, MGH, Leges 4, Con. 2, Suppl. 1 (Hanover, 1998).

Theophanes, *Chronicon*, ed. C. de Boor (Leipzig, 1883): trans. C. Mango and R. Scott, *The Chronicle of Theophanes the Confessor* (Oxford, 1997).

Tirechan, *Vita patricii*, ed. Ludwig Bieler, *The Patrician Texts in the Book of Armargh*, SLH 10 (Dublin, 1979).

Vita Ansberti, ed. Wilhelm Levison, MGH, SRM 5 (Hanover, 1910).

Vita Boniti, ed. B. Krusch, MGH, SRM 6 (Hanover, 1913).

Vita Cuthberti, ed. Bertram Colgrave, *Two Lives of Saint Cuthbert* (Cambridge, 1940).

Vita Sancti Finani abbatis de Cenn Etigh, ed. W. W. Heist, *Vitae sanctorum Hiberniae*, Subsidia Hagiographica 28 (Brussels, 1965).

Vita prior sancti Fintani seu Munnu abbatis de Tech Munnu, ed. W. W. Heist, *Vitae sanctorum Hiberniae*, Subsidia Hagiographica 28 (Brussels, 1965).

Vita Gregorii, ed. Bertram Colgrave, *The Earliest Life of Gregory the Great* (Lawrence, KS, 1968).

Vita Landiberti, ed. Bruno Krusch, MGH, SRM 6 (Hanover, 1913).

Vita Leutfridi, ed. Wilhelm Levison, MGH, SRM 7 (Hanover, 1910).

Vita prior sancti Lugidi seu Moluae, ed. W. W. Heist, *Vitae sanctorum Hiberniae*, Subsidia Hagiographica 28 (Brussels, 1965).

Vita Samsonis, ed. P. Flobert, *La Vie Ancienne de saint Samson de Dol* (Paris, CNRS, 1997): trans. Thomas Taylor, *The Life of St. Samson of Dol* (London, 1925).

Vitruvius, *De architectura libri decem*, trans. Morris Hicky Morgan, *The Ten Books on Architecture* (Cambridge, MA, 1926).

William of Malmesbury, *De antiquitate Glastonie ecclesie*, ed. and trans. John Scott (Woodbridge, 1981).

William of Malmesbury, *Gesta pontificum*, ed. N. E. S. A. Hamilton, Rolls Series (London, 1870).

William of Malmesbury, *De Gestis Regum*, ed. William Stubbs, Rolls Series (London, 1887).

Zosimus, *Historia Nova*, ed. François Paschoud, *Zosime, Histoire Nouvelle*, vol. 1 (Paris, 1971): trans. R.T. Ridley, *Zosimus, New History* (Sydney, 1982).

Secondary sources

Abels, Richard P., *Lordship and military obligation in Anglo-Saxon England* (London, 1988).

Ackerman, Gretchen P., 'J. M. Kemble and Sir Frederic Madden: "Conceit and Too Much Germanism"', in Carl T. Berkhout and Milton McC.Gatch, eds, *Anglo-Saxon Scholarship: The First Three Centuries* (Boston, 1982), pp. 167–181.

Adam, Barbara, *Time and Social Theory* (Oxford, 1990).

Alexander, J. J. G., 'Some Aesthetic Principles in the Use of Colour in Anglo-Saxon Art', *Anglo-Saxon England* 4 (1975), pp. 145–154.

Alexander, Michael, in Boris Ford, ed., 'Old English Literature', *The Cambridge Guide to the Arts in Britain: Volume 1 Prehistoric, Roman and Early Medieval* (Cambridge, 1988), pp. 178–193.

Althusser, Louis, 'Ideology and Ideological State Apparatuses (Notes Towards an Investigation)' (1970), in Ben Brewster, trans., *Lenin and Philosophy and Other Essays* (London, 1971), pp. 123–173.

Archibald, Dr, 'Account of the Curiosities at Dumfries by Doctour Archibald', in Arthur Mitchell and James Toshach Clark, eds, *Geographical Collections Relating to Scotland Made by Walter Macfarlane*, Vol. III (Edinburgh, 1908), pp. 185–194.

[Armstrong, G.], 'An Account of a curious OBELISK, of one Stone, standing in the Church Yard of Bewcastle, in the North East Part of Cumberland, about 16 Miles from Carlisle', *London Magazine* XLIV (August 1775), p. 388.

Austen, Paul S., *Bewcastle and Old Penrith: A Roman Outpost Fort and a Frontier Vicus*, 'Part I: Excavations in the Roman Fort at Bewcastle, 1977–78', Cumberland and Westmorland Antiquarian and Archaeological Society, Research Series No. 6 (1991), pp. 41–50.

Austen, Paul S., 'How Big was the Second Largest Fort on Hadrian's Wall at Bowness on Solway?' in V. A. Maxfield and M. J. Dobson, eds, *Roman Frontier Studies 1989: Proceedings of the XVth International Congress of Roman Frontier Studies, Exeter, 1989* (Exeter, 1991), pp. 6–8.

Backhouse, Janet, Turner, D. H., and Webster, Leslie, *The Golden Age of Anglo-Saxon Art 966–1066* (London, 1984).

Baert, Barbara, *A Heritage of Holy Wood: The Legend of the True Cross in Text and Image* (Leiden, 2004).

Bailey, Richard N., *Viking Age Sculpture in Northern England* (London, 1980).

Bailey, Richard N., 'The Ruthwell Cross: A Non-Problem', *The Antiquaries Journal* 73 (1993), pp. 141–148.

Bailey, Richard N., *England's Earliest Sculptors* (Toronto, 1996).

Bailey, Richard N., 'Innocent from the Great Offence', in Catherine E. Karkov and Fred Orton, eds, *Theorizing Anglo-Saxon Stone Sculpture* (Morgantown, WV, 2003) pp. 93–103.

Bailey, Richard N, 'Anglo-Saxon Sculptures at Deerhurst'. *Deerhurst Lecture 2002* (Deerhurst, 2005).

Bailey, Richard N., and Cramp, Rosemary, *The British Academy Corpus of Anglo-Saxon Stone Sculpture*, Vol. II, *Cumberland, Westmorland and Lancashire North-of-the-Sands* (Oxford, 1988).

Ball, Christopher, 'Inconsistencies in the Main Runic Inscriptions on the Ruthwell Cross', in A. Bammesburger, ed., *Old English Runes and their Continental Background*, Heidelberg, Anglistische Forschungen, Hft 217 (Winter 1991), pp. 107–123.

Balmer, R. T., 'The Operation of Sand Clocks and Their Medieval Development', *Technology and Culture* 19, No. 3 (1978), pp. 615–632.

Barbour, James, 'Regarding the Origin of the Ruthwell Cross', *T&JPD&GNH&AS* 26 (1899–1900), pp. 28–31.

Barnes, Barry, *Interests and the Growth of Knowledge* (London, 1977).

Barthes, Roland, selected and trans. Annette Lavers, *Mythologies* (1957) (St Albans, 1973).

Barthes, Roland, 'The Death of the Author', in *Image/Music/Text*, essays selected and trans. Stephen Heath (London, 1977).

Barthes, Roland, 'The Discourse of History', in *The Rustle of Language* (1984), trans. Richard Howard (Oxford, 1986), pp. 127–140.

Barthes, Roland, 'The Reality Effect', in *The Rustle of Language* (1984), trans. Richard Howard (Oxford, 1986), pp. 141–148.

Basso, Keith H., *Wisdom Sits in Places: Landscape and Language among the Western Apache* (Albuquerque, NM, 1996).

Bately, Jane, 'The Nature of Old English Prose', in Malcolm Godden and Michael Lapidge, eds, *The Cambridge Companion to Old English Literature* (Cambridge, 1991), pp. 71–87.

Beckwith, Sarah, 'Preserving, Conserving, Deserving the Past: A Meditation on Ruin as Relic in Postwar Britain in Five Fragments', in Clare A. Lees and Gillian R. Overing, eds, *A Place to Believe in: Medieval and Modern Landscapes* (University Park, PA, 2006), pp. 191–210.

Belting, Hans, *Likeness and Presence: A History of the Image before the Era of Art* (1990), trans. Edmund Jephcott (Chicago and London, 1994).

Benjamin, Walter, *Ursprung der deutschen Trauerspiels* (1924–1925) (first pub. Frankfurt am Main, 1963) trans. John Osborne, *The Origin of German Tragic Drama* (London, 1977).

Benjamin, Walter, 'Theses on the Philosophy of History' (1940), trans. Harry Zohn, in Hannah Arendt, ed., *Walter Benjamin: Illuminations* (Glasgow, 1973), pp. 255–266.

Bennett, J. A. W., *Poetry of the Passion: Studies in Twelve Centuries of English Verse* (Oxford, 2002).

Berkhout, Carl T., and McC. Gatch, Milton, eds, *Anglo-Saxon Scholarship: The First Three Centuries* (Boston, MA, 1982).

Bidwell, Paul, ed., *Hadrian's Wall 1989–1999: A Summary of Recent Excavations and Research Prepared for the Twelfth Pilgrimage of Hadrian's wall, 14–21 August 1999*, Carlisle and Newcastle upon Tyne, Cumberland and Westmorland Antiquarian and Archaeological Society and the Society of Antiquaries of Newcastle upon Tyne (1999).

Birley, Andrew, *Vindolanda's Military Bath Houses. The Excavations of 1970 and 2000* (Hexham, 2001).

Birley, Eric, 'The Roman Fort at Netherby', *TC&WA&AS*, n.s. 53 (1954), pp. 6–39.

Birley, Eric, *Research on Hadrian's Wall* (Kendal, 1961).

Bjork, Robert E., and Obermeier, Anita, 'Date, Provenance, Author, Audiences', in Robert E. Bjork and John d. Niles, eds, *A Beowulf Handbook* (Lincoln, NB, 1996), pp. 13–34.

Blackwell Encyclopedia of Anglo-Saxon England, ed. Michael Lapidge, John Blair, Simon Keynes and Donald Scragg (Oxford, 1999).

Blair, John, *The Church in Anglo-Saxon Society* (Oxford, 2005).

Bodden, M. C., *The Old English Finding of the True Cross* (Woodbridge, 1987).

Borgehammar, Stephan, *How the Holy Cross Was Found* (Uppsala, 1991).

Borges, Jorge Luis, trans. James E. Irby, 'Pierre Menard, Author of the *Quixote*', in Donald A. Yates and James E. Irby, eds, *Labyrinths, Selected Stories and Other Writings, by Jorge Luis Borges* (London, 1970), pp. 62–71.

Bowes, Kim, 'Ivory Lists: Consular Diptychs, Christian Appropriation and Polemics of Time in Late Antiquity', *Art History* 24, no. 3 (June 2001), pp. 338–357.

Boyarin, Jonathan, ed., *The Ethnography of Reading* (Berkeley, CA, 1993).

Breeze, Andrew, 'The British-Latin Place-names *Arbeia, Corstopitum, Dictim*, and *Morbium*', *Durham Archaeological Journal* 16 (2001), pp. 21–25.

Breeze, David J., and Dobson, Brian, *Hadrian's Wall*, 4th ed. (London, 2000).

Brown, Alan K., 'Old Irish *Astal*, Old English *Æstel*: The Common Etymology', *Cambridge Medieval Celtic Studies* 24 (1992), pp. 75–92.

Brown, G. Baldwin, 'Report on the Ruthwell Cross. With some references to that at Bewcastle in Cumberland', in the Royal Commission on the Ancient and Historical Monuments and Constructions of Scotland, *The Royal Commission on the Ancient and Historical Monuments and Constructions of Scotland, Seventh Report with Inventory of Monuments and Constructions in the County of Dumfries* (Edinburgh 1920), Appendix, pp. 219–286.

Brown, G. Baldwin, *The Arts in Early England*, Vol. V, *The Ruthwell and Bewcastle Crosses, the Gospels of Lindisfarne, and Other Christian Monuments of Northumbria* (London, 1921).

Brown, Michelle, P., *The Lindisfarne Gospels: Society, Spirituality and the Scribe* (London, 2003).

Brubaker, Leslie, and Haldon, John, *Byzantium in the Iconoclast Era (ca 680–750)* (Aldershot, 2001).

Bruce, John Collingwood, *Lapidarium Septentrionale: or, a description of the monuments of Roman rule in the north of England* (Newcastle-upon-Tyne, 1870–1875).

Buchner, Edmund, *Die Sonnenuhr des Augustus* (Mainz, 1982).

Budd, Paul, Millard, Andrew, Chenery, Carolyn, Lucy, Sam, and Roberts, Charlotte, 'Investigating Population Movement by Stable Isotope Analysis: A Report from Britain', *Antiquity* 299 (2004), pp. 127–41.

Bullough, Donald, *Alcuin, Achievement and Reputation* (Leiden, 2004).

Burgess, Colin, and Shennan, Stephan, 'The Beaker Phenomenon: Some Suggestions, Part I: General Comments on the British Evidence', in Colin Burgess and Roger Miket, eds, *Settlement and Economy in the Third Millennia B.C. Papers Delivered at a Conference Organised by the Department of Adult Education, University of Newcastle-upon-Tyne, January 1976*, BAR 33 (Oxford, 1976), pp. 309–323.

Burgers, Alfonso, *The Water Supplies and Related Structures of Roman Britain*, BAR 324 (Oxford, 2001).

Burns, Thomas S., *Barbarians within the Gates of Rome* (Bloomington, IN, 1994).

Bury, John B., *History of the Later Roman Empire*, Vol. 1 (London, 1923).

Butler, Judith, *Gender Trouble: Feminism and the Subversion of Identity* (London and New York, 1990).

Camden, William, *Britannia, sive Florentissimorum regnorum Angiae, Scotiae, Hiberniae, et insularum adiacentium ex intima antiquitate chorographica descriptio: nunc postremò recognita, plurimi locis magna accessione adaucta, & chartis chorographicis* (London, 1607).

Camden, William, *Camden's Britannia, Newly Translated into English with Large Additions and Improvements, by Edmund Gibson* (London, 1695).

Campbell, Ewan, 'The Archaeological Evidence from External Contacts: Imports, Trade and Economy in Celtic Britain A.D. 400–800', in Kenneth R. Dark, ed., *External Contacts and the Economy of Late Roman and Post-Roman Britain* (Woodbridge, 1996), pp. 83–96.

Campbell, James, ed., *The Anglo-Saxons* (Oxford, 1982).

Canuteson, John, 'The Crucifixion and the Second Coming in *The Dream of the Rood*', *Modern Philology* 66 (1969), pp. 293–297.

Cassidy, Brendan, 'The Later Life of the Ruthwell Cross: From the Seventeenth Century to the Present', in Brendan Cassidy, ed., *The Ruthwell Cross: Papers from a Colloquium Sponsored by the Index of Christian Art, Princeton University, 8 December 1989* (Princeton, NJ, 1992), pp. 3–34.

Cerquiglini, Bernard, *Éloge de la variante* (Paris, 1989).

Cervantes, Miguel de, *El Ingenioso Hidalgo Don Quijote De La Mancha* (Barcelona, 1915).

Chapman, John, *Notes on the Early History of the Vulgate Gospels* (Oxford, 1908).

Charles-Edwards, Thomas M., 'The Distinction between Land and Moveable Wealth in Anglo-Saxon England', in Peter H. Sawyer, ed., *Medieval Settlement* (London, 1976), pp. 180–187.

Chazelle, Celia, *The Crucified God in the Carolingian Era. Theology and Art of Christ's Passion* (Cambridge, 2001).

Chinnock, E. J., 'Etymology of the Word Ruthwell', *T&JPD&GNH&AS* 62 (1907), pp. 40–47.

Clapham, A. W., *English Romanesque Architecture before the Conquest* (Oxford, 1930).

Clark, T. J., *Image of the People: Gustave Courbet and the 1848 Revolution* (London, 1973).

Clark, T. J., 'Preliminary Arguments: Work of Art and Ideology', unpub. discussion paper for a College Art Association session on 'Marxism and Art History', Chicago, 1976.

Clayton, Mary, *The Cult of the Virgin Mary in Anglo-Saxon England* (Cambridge, 1990).

Clerk, John, transcribed and ed. W. A. Prevost, 'A Trip into England for a Few Days in 1741 by Sir John Clerk', *TC&WA&AS*, n.s. 62 (1962), pp. 246–264.

Cockayne, G. E., *Complete Baronetage*, Vol. II, 1625–1649 (Exeter, 1902).

Cockayne, G. E., *The Complete Peerage of England, Scotland, Ireland, Great Britain and the United Kingdom Extinct or Dormant*. Vol. I, *AB-Adam to Basing*. New revised and much enlarged by Vicary Gibbs (London, 1910).

Cockayne, G. E. *The Complete Peerage or A History of the House of Lords and All Its Members From The Earliest Times*, Vol. XXII, *Skelmersdale to Towton*. Revised and enlarged by Geoffry H. White (London: 1953).

Collingwood, R. G., 'The Roman Fort at Bewcastle', *TC&WA&AS*, n.s. 22 (1922), pp. 169–185.

Collingwood, R. G., 'The Bewcastle Cross', *TC&WA&AS*, n.s. 35 (1935), pp. 1–29.

Collingwood, R. G., and Wright, R. P., *The Roman Inscriptions of Britain*, Vol. 1, *Inscriptions on Stone* (Oxford, 1965).

Collingwood, W. G., 'The End of the Maiden Way', *TC&WA&AS*, n.s. 24 (1924), pp. 110–116.

Collingwood, W. G., 'Early Sculptured Stones at Hexham', *Archaeologia Aeliana*, 4th ser. 1 (1925), pp. 65–92.

Collingwood, W. G., *Northumbrian Crosses of the Pre-Norman Age* (London, 1927).

Collingwood, W. G., 'A Pedigree of Anglian Crosses', *Antiquity* 6 (1932), pp. 35–54.

Colvin, H., *The Architecture of the After-Life* (New Haven and London, 1991).

Connolly, Seán, *Bede on Tobit and the Canticle of Habbakuk* (Dublin, 1997).

Constantinescu, Radu, 'Alcuin de les "Libelli Precum" de l'époque carolingienne', *Revue d'Histoire de la Spiritualité* 50 (1974), pp. 17–56.

Cook, A. S., *Some Accounts of the Bewcastle Cross between the Years 1607 and 1861*, Yale Studies in English 50 (1914), reprinted with new preface by Robert T. Farrell, in *The Anglo-Saxon Cross* (Hamden, CT, 1967).

Cowan, Edward J., *Montrose: For Covenant and King* (London, 1977).

Cox, Thomas, ed., *Magna Britannia et Hibernia, antiqua & nova: or, A New Survey of Great Britain, wherein, to the topographical account given by Mr. Camden, and the late editors of his Britannia is added a more large history*, Vol. I (London, 1720).

Craig, John, 'Parish of Ruthwell', *The Statistical Account of Scotland 1791–1799*, Vol. IV, *Dumfriesshire*, ed. John Sinclair (reprint Wakefield, 1978), pp. 447–457.

Cramp, Rosemary J., 'Beowulf and Archaeology', *Medieval Archaeology* 1 (1957), pp. 57–77.

Cramp, Rosemary, 'The Anglian Sculptured Crosses of Dumfriesshire', *T&JPD&GNH&AS*, 3rd ser. 38 (1961), pp. 9–20.

Cramp, Rosemary, 'An Anglo-Saxon Pin from Birdoswald', *TC&WA&AS*, n.s. 64 (1964), pp. 90–93.

Cramp, Rosemary, *Early Northumbrian Sculpture*. Jarrow Lecture (Newcastle, 1965).

Cramp, Rosemary, 'The Evangelist Symbols and Their Parallels in Anglo-Saxon Sculpture', in R. T. Farrell, ed., *Bede and Anglo-Saxon England: Papers in Honour of the 1300th Anniversary of the Birth of Bede, Given at Cornell University in 1973 and 1974*, BAR 46 (Oxford, 1978), pp. 118–130.

Cramp, Rosemary, *Corpus of Anglo-Saxon Stone Sculpture*, Vol. I, Pt 1, *County Durham and Northumberland* (Oxford, 1984).

Cramp, Rosemary, *Whithorn and the Northumbrian Expansion Westwards*. Third Whithorn Lecture (Whithorn, 1995).

Cramp, Rosemary, 'The Pre-Conquest Sculptures of Glastonbury Monastery', in Paul Binski and William Noel, eds, *New Offerings, Ancient Treasures: Studies in Medieval Art for George Henderson* (Stroud, 2001), pp. 148–161.

Crawford, S. J., *Anglo-Saxon Influence on Western Christendom 600–800* (Oxford, 1933).

Cross, James E., and Tunberg, Jennifer Morrish, eds, *The Copenhagen Wulfstan Collection: Copenhagen Kongelige Bibliothek Gl. Kgl. Sam 1595*, Early English Manuscripts in Facsimile 25 (Copenhagen, 1993).

Crowe, Christopher, 'Excavations at Ruthwell, Dumfries, 1980 and 1984', T&JPD&GNH&AS, 3rd ser. 62 (1987), pp. 40–47.

Crowe, Christopher, 'Early Medieval Parish Formation in Dumfries and Galloway', in Martin Carver, ed., The Cross Goes North (Woodbridge, 2003), pp. 185–206.

Cubitt, Catherine, Anglo-Saxon Church Councils c.650–c.850 (London, 1995).

Cubitt, Catherine, 'Unity and Diversity in the Early Anglo-Saxon Liturgy', Studies in Church History 33, Unity and Diversity in the Church (Oxford, 1996), pp. 45–57.

Cummins, W. A., The Picts and Their Symbols (Stroud, 1999).

Curwen, John F., 'St Cuthbert's Church, Bewcastle', TC&WA&AS, n.s. 2 (1902), pp. 242–249.

Curwen, John F., 'Bewcastle', TC&WA&AS, n.s. 22 (1922), pp. 186–197.

Dark, Kenneth, R., 'A Sub-Roman Re-defence of Hadrian's Wall', Britannia 23 (1992), pp. 111–120.

Dark, Kenneth R., Civitas to Kingdom: British Political Continuity 300–800 (Leicester, 1994).

Dark, Kenneth R., 'The Late Roman Transition in the North: A Discussion', in Tony Wilmott and Pete Wilson, eds, The Late Roman Transition in the North. Papers from the Roman Archaeology Conference, Durham 1999, BAR 299 (Oxford, 2000), pp. 81–88.

Davenport, J., 'The Bewcastle Cauldron', TC&WA&AS, 96 (1996), pp. 228–230.

Day, J. B. W., with contributions by D. H. Land, D. H., Price, R. H., Mills, D. A. C. and others, Geology of the Country around Bewcastle (London, 1970).

Deanesly, Margaret, 'Roman Traditionalist Influence among the Anglo-Saxons', English Historical Review 58 (1943), pp. 129–146.

De la Bédoyère, Guy, Hadrian's Wall: History & Guide (Stroud, 1998).

Deshusses, Jean, 'Le sacramentaire de Gellone dans son contexte historique', Ephemerides Liturgicae 75 (1961), pp. 193–201.

Dickens, Bruce, 'John Mitchell Kemble and Old English Scholarship', Proceedings of the British Academy 25 (Oxford, 1939), pp. 51–84.

Dictionary of the Middle Ages, Vol. III, ed. Joseph R. Strayer (New York, 1989).

Dinwiddie, J. L., 'The Ruthwell Cross and the Story It Has to Tell', T&JD&GNH&AS, n.s. 22 (1909–1910), pp. 109–121.

Dinwiddie, J. L., The Ruthwell Cross and Its Story: A Handbook for Tourists and Students (Dumfries, 1927).

Dinwiddie, J. L., The Ruthwell Cross and the Ruthwell Savings Bank: A Handbook for Tourists and Students (Dumfries, 1933).

Dodwell, C. R., Anglo-Saxon Art: A New Perspective (Manchester, 1982).

'Donegal Studies-History of Donegal-Landlords of Donegal', http://www.donegallibrary.ie/memory/landlords.htm.

Dore, J. N., Corbridge Roman Site (London, 1989).

Drijvers, Jan W., Helena Augusta. The Mother of Constantine the Great and the Legend of Her Finding of the True Cross (Leiden, 1992).

Drinkwater, John F., 'The Usurpers Constantine III (407–11) and Jovinus (411–13)', Britannia 29 (1998), pp. 269–298.

Duclow, D. F., 'Denial or Promise of the Tree of Life? Eriugena, Augustine, and Genesis 3.22b', in G. Van Riel et al., Iohannes Scottus Eriugena: The Bible and Hermeneutics (Leuven, 1996), pp. 221–238.

Duncan, Archibald A. M., 'Bede, Iona and the Picts', in Ralph H. C. Davis and J. Michael Wallace-Hadrill, eds, The Writing of History in the Middle Ages: Essays presented to R. W. Southern (Oxford, 1981).

Duncan, Henry, 'An Account of the Remarkable Monument in the shape of a Cross, inscribed with Roman and Runic Letters, preserved in the Garden of Ruthwell Manse, Dumfriesshire', Archaeologia Scotica IV, pt 2 (1833), pp. 313–326.

Duncan, H., 'Parish of Ruthwell', The New Statistical Account of Scotland, Vol. 4, Dumfriesshire, Kirkcudbright, Wigton (Edinburgh and London, 1845), pp. 219–243.

Edwards, B. J. N., 'Reginald Bainbrigg, Westmorland Antiquary', TC&WA&AS, 3rd ser. 3 (2003), pp. 119–125.

Engels, Frederick, 'The Origin of the Family, Private Property and the State', in Karl Marx and Frederick Engels, *Selected Works* (London, 1968), pp. 430–558.

Esmonde Cleary, Simon, *The Ending of Roman Britain* (London, 1989).

Esmonde Cleary, Simon, 'Summing Up', in Tony Wilmott and Pete Wilson, eds, *The Late Roman Transition in the North. Papers from the Roman Archaeology Conference, Durham 1999*, BAR 299 (Oxford, 2000), pp. 89–94.

Evans, Frank, 'Bede's Time Keeping', *British Sundial Society Bulletin* (March 2001), p. 30.

Fairless, Kenneth J., 'Three Religious Cults from the Northern Frontier Region', in Roger Miket and Colin Burgess, eds, *Between and Beyond the Walls. Essays on the Prehistory and History of North Britain in Honour of George Jobey* (Edinburgh, 1984), pp. 224–242.

Farr, Carol, 'Worthy Women on the Ruthwell Cross: Women as a Sign in Early Anglo-Saxon Monasticism', in Catherine E. Karkov, Robert T. Farrell, and Michael Ryan, *The Insular Tradition* (Albany, NY, 1997), pp. 45–61.

Farrell, Robert T., ed., *Bede and Anglo-Saxon England. Papers in Honour of the 1300th Anniversary of the Birth of Bede, Given at Cornell University in 1973 and 1974*, BAR 46 (Oxford, 1978).

Farrell, Robert T., 'Reflections on the Iconography of the Ruthwell and Bewcastle Crosses', in P. E. Szarmach, ed., with the assistance of V. D. Oggins, *Sources of Anglo-Saxon Culture*, Studies in Medieval Culture 20 (Kalamazoo, MI, 1986), pp. 357–376.

Farrell, Robert T., with Catherine E. Karkov, 'The Construction, Deconstruction, and Reconstruction of the Ruthwell Cross: Some Caveats', in Brendan Cassidy, ed., *The Ruthwell Cross: Papers from a Colloquium Sponsored by the Index of Christian Art, Princeton University, 8 December 1989* (Princeton, 1992), pp. 34–47.

Faulkner, Neil, *The Decline and Fall of Roman Britain* (Stroud, 2000).

Faull, Margaret L., 'British Survival in Anglo-Saxon Northumbria', in Lloyd Laing, ed., *Studies in Celtic Survival*, BAR 57 (Oxford, 1977), pp. 1–57.

Faull, Margaret L., and Moorhouse, Stephen A., *West Yorkshire: An Archaeological Survey to A.D. 1500* (Wakefield, 1981).

Fentress, James, and Wickham, Chris, *Social Memory* (Oxford, 1992).

Ferguson, Richard S., 'The *Lapidarium Septentrionale*, &', *Proceedings of the Society of Antiquaries of Newcastle-Upon-Tyne*, n.s. 2, No. 17 (1885), pp. 142–144.

Ferguson, Richard S., 'Report on Injury to the Bewcastle Obelisk', *TC&WA&AS*, 12 (1893), pp. 51–56.

Ferris, Iain, and Jones, Rick, 'Transforming an Elite: Reinterpreting Late Roman Binchester', in Tony Wilmott and Pete Wilson, eds, *The Late Roman Transition in the North. Papers from the Roman Archaeology Conference, Durham 1999*, BAR 299 (Oxford, 2000), pp. 1–11.

Fish, Stanley, 'What Is Stylistics and Why Are They Saying Such Terrible Things About It?' in *Is There a Text in This Class? The Authority of Interpretive Communities* (Cambridge, MA, 1980), pp. 69–71.

Fleming, John, '"The Dream of the Rood" and Anglo-Saxon Monasticism', *Traditio* 22 (1960), pp. 43–72.

Foucault, Michel, trans. A. M. Sheridan Smith, *The Archaeology of Knowledge* (1969) (London, 1974).

Fountain, J. Stephen, 'Ashes to Ashes: Kristeva's *Jouissance*, Altizer's Apocalypse, Byatt's *Possession* and *The Dream of the Rood*', *Literature and Theology* 8 (1994), pp. 193–208.

Frank, Roberta, '*Beowulf* and Sutton Hoo: The Odd Couple', in Calvin B. Kendall and Peter S. Wells, eds, *Voyage to the Other World* (Minneapolis, MN, 1992), pp. 47–64.

Frantzen, Allen J., *Desire for Origins: New Language, Old English, and Teaching the Tradition* (New Brunswick, NJ, 1990), pp. 34–35.

Fustel de Coulanges, Numa Denis, *Histoire des institutions politiques de l'ancienne France*, Vol, 2, *L'invasion Germanique et la fin de l'empire* (Paris, 1891),

Fustel de Coulanges, Numa Denis, *Histoire des institutions politiques de l'ancienne France*, Vol. 5, *Le bénéfice et le patronat pendant l'époque mérovingienne*, 6th ed. (Paris, 1926).

Gannon, Anna, *The Iconography of Early Anglo-Saxon Coinage. Sixth to Eighth Centuries* (Oxford, 2003).

Ganz, David, 'Le *De Laude Dei* d'Alcuin', in Philippe Depreux and Bruno Judic, eds, *Alcuin de York à Tours, Écriture, Pouvoir et Réseaux dans l'Europe de l'Haut Moyen Âge, Annales de Bretagne et des Pays de L'Ouest* 111 (2004), pp. 387–391.

Gatty, Mrs Alfred, *The Book of Sundials; Collected by Mrs. Alfred Gatty* (London, 1872).

Gatty, A., *The Book of Sundials; Collected by Mrs. Alfred Gatty* (1872), new enlarged ed., ed. H. K. F. Gatty and Eleanor Lloyd (London, 1889).

Geary, Patrick J., *Phantoms of Remembrance: Memory and Oblivion at the End of the First Millennium* (Princeton, NJ, 1994).

Gerchow, Jan, *Die Gedenküberlieferung der Angelsachsen: mit einem Katalog der libri vitae und Necrologien* (Berlin, 1988).

Gibbs, Sharon L., *Greek and Roman Sundials* (New Haven and London, 1976).

Giddens, Anthony, *The Constitution of Society* (Cambridge, 1984).

Gilchrist, Roberta, *Gender and Material Culture: The Archaeology of Religious Women* (London, 1994).

Gillam, J. P., 'Recent Excavations at Bewcastle', *TCQWAQAS*, n.s. 50 (1950), pp. 63–69.

Gillam, J. P., 'The Roman Bath-house at Bewcastle', *TCQWAQAS*, n.s. 54 (1954), pp. 265–267.

Gillam, J. P., Jobey, I. M., Welsby, D. A., et al., *The Roman Bath-house at Bewcastle*, Cumberland and Westmorland Antiquarian and Archaeological Society, Research Series No. 7 (1993).

Gillespie, George, 'Parish of Cummertrees', *The New Statistical Account of Scotland*, Vol. 4, *Dumfriesshire, Kirkcudbright, Wigton* (Edinburgh and London, 1845), pp. 244–255.

Goodman, Nelson, *Problems and Projects* (Indianapolis and New York, 1972).

Goodman, Nelson, 'Seven Strictures on Similarity', in *Problems and Projects* (Indianapolis, IN, 1972); reprinted in Charles Harrison and Fred Orton, eds, *Modernism, Criticism, Realism* (London, 1984), pp. 85–92.

Gordon, Alexander, *Itinerarium Septentrionale: Or, a Journey thro' most of the Counties of Scotland and Those in the North of England* (London, 1726).

Gordon, Bruce, and Marshall, Peter, eds, *The Place of the Dead: 'Death and Remembrance in Late Medieval and Early Modern Europe'* (Cambridge, 2000).

Grabar, André, *Christian Iconography: A Study of Its Origins, the A. W. Mellon Lectures in the Fine Arts, 1961, The National Gallery of Art, Washington, D.C.*, Bollingen Series XXXV, 10 (Princeton, NJ, 1968).

Graham, T. H. B., 'Extinct Cumberland Castles (Part II)', *TCQWAQAS*, n.s. 11 (1911), pp. 233–258.

Greatrex, George, and Lieu, Samuel N. C., *The Roman Eastern Frontier and the Persian Wars, Part 2, 363–630* (London, 2002).

Green, Arthur Robert, 'Anglo-Saxon Sundials', *The Antiquaries Journal* 8, No. 4 (1928) pp. 489–516.

Greenfield, Stanley B., and Calder, D. G., *A New Critical History of Old English Literature* (New York, 1986), pp. 164–176.

Greig, D. C., with G. A. Goodlet, G. I. Lumsden and W. Tulloch. *British Regional Geology: The South of Scotland* (Edinburgh, 1971).

Grey, Iver, 'The Landscape of Bewcastle and Its Rocky Foundations', in Bewcastle Heritage Society, *A Bewcastle Miscellany* (Carlisle, 2000), pp. 9–14.

Guillmain, Jacques, 'The Composition of the First Cross Page of the Lindisfarne Gospels: "Square Schematicism" and the Hiberno-Saxon Aesthetic', *Art Bulletin* 67, No. 4 (1985), pp. 535–547.

Guillmain, Jacques, 'The Geometry of the Cross-Carpet Pages in the Lindisfarne Gospels', *Speculum. A Journal of Medieval Studies* 62 (January 1987), pp. 21–52.

Haigh, Daniel Henry, 'The Saxon Cross at Bewcastle', *Archaeologia Aeliana*, n.s. pt 3 (November 1856), pp. 149–195 = *Archaeologia Aeliana*, n.s. (or 2nd ser.) 1 (1857), pp. 149–195.

Haigh, Daniel Henry, 'Yorkshire Dials', *The Yorkshire Archaeological and Topographical Journal* 5 (1879), pp. 134–222.

Haldane, A. R. B., *The Drove Roads of Scotland* (London, 1952).

Hamlin, Ann, 'Crosses in Early Ireland: The Evidence from Written Sources', in M. Ryan, ed.,

Ireland and Insular Art, A.D. 500–1200: Proceedings of a Conference at University College Cork, 31 October–3 November 1985 (Dublin, 1987), pp. 138–140.

Hamlin, Ann, 'Some Northern Sundials and Time-Keeping in the Early Irish Church', in E. Rynne, ed., *Figures of the Past: Essays in Honour of A. M. Roe* (Dun Laoghaire, 1987), pp. 29–42.

Hanson, N. R., *Patterns of Discovery: An Inquiry into the Conceptual Foundations of Science* (Cambridge, 1958), excerpted as 'Observation', in Charles Harrison and Fred Orton, eds, *Modernism, Criticism, Realism* (London, 1984), pp. 69–83.

Harbison, Peter, *The Golden Age of Irish Art: Medieval Achievements, 600–1200* (London, 1999).

Harrison, Kenneth, 'Easter Cycles and the Equinox in the British Isles', *Anglo-Saxon England* 7 (1978), pp. 1–8.

Haverfield, F., 'Cotton Julius F.VI. Notes on Reginald Bainbrigg of Appleby, on William Camden and Some Roman Inscriptions', *TC&WA&AS*, n.s. 11 (1911), pp. 344–349.

Hawkes, Jane, 'Symbolic Lives: The Visual Evidence', in John Hines, ed., *The Anglo-Saxons From the Migration Period to the Eighth Century: An Ethnographic Survey* (Woodbridge, 1997), pp. 311–344.

Hawkes, Jane, 'Symbols of Passion or Power? The Iconography of the Rothbury Cross Head', in Catherine E. Karkov, Robert T. Farrell, and Michael Ryan, eds, *The Insular Tradition* (Albany, NY, 1997), pp. 27–44.

Hawkes, Jane, 'Anglo-Saxon Sculpture: Questions of Context', in Jane Hawkes and Susan Mills, eds, *Northumbria's Golden Age* (Stroud, 1999), pp. 204–215.

Hawkes, Jane, '*Iuxta Morem Romanorum*: Stone and Sculpture in Anglo-Saxon England', in Catherine E. Karkov and George Hardin Brown, eds, *Anglo-Saxon Styles* (Albany, NY, 2003), pp. 69–99.

Hawkes, Jane, and Ó Carragáin, Éamonn, with Ross Trench-Jellicoe, 'John the Baptist and the *Agnus Dei*: Ruthwell (and Bewcastle) Revisited', *The Antiquaries Journal* 81 (2001), pp. 131–153.

Hawkins, James Irving, *The Sandstone Heritage of Dumfriesshire* (Annan, 2001).

Haywood, John, *Dark Age Naval Power: A Reassessment of Frankish and Anglo-Saxon Seafaring Activity* (London, 1991),

Head, Thomas, ed., *Medieval Hagiography: An Anthology* (New York, 2000).

Heather, Peter, *The Fall of the Roman Empire. A New History* (London, 2005).

Heidegger, Martin, trans. John Macquarrie and Edward Robinson, *Being and Time* (1927) (Oxford, 1967).

Heidegger, Martin, 'The Origin of the Work of Art' (1935–1936), in David Farrell Krell, ed., *Martin Heidegger: Basic Writings*, revised and expanded ed. (London, 1993), pp. 143–203.

Heidegger, Martin, 'Building Dwelling Thinking' (1954), in David Farrell Krell, ed., *Martin Heidegger: Basic Writings*, revised and expanded ed. (London, 1993), pp. 347–363.

Heidegger, Martin, 'Letter on Humanism' (1946–1947), in David Farrell Krell, ed., *Martin Heidegger: Basic Writings*, revised and expanded ed. (London, 1993), pp. 213–265.

Hen, Yitzhak, 'The Liturgy of St Willibrord', *Anglo-Saxon England* 26 (1997), pp. 41–62.

Hen, Yitzhak, *The Royal Patronage of Liturgy in Frankish Gaul, to the death of Charles the Bald (877)*, Henry Bradshaw Society, Subsidia III (London, 2001).

Hen, Yitzhak, 'Rome, Anglo-Saxon England, and the Formation of the Frankish Liturgy', *Revue Bénédictine* 112 (2002), pp. 301–22.

Henderson, George, *From Durrow to Kells. The Insular Gospel Books 650–800* (London, 1987).

Henderson, George, *Vision and Image in Early Christian England* (Cambridge, 1999).

Henig, Martin. '*Murum civitatis, et fontem in ea a Romanis mire olim constructum*: The Arts of Rome in Carlisle and the Civitas of the Carvetii and Their Influence', in Mike McCarthy and David Weston, eds, *Carlisle and Cumbria: Roman and Medieval Architecture, Art and Archaeology, British Archaeological Association Conference Transactions* (Leeds, 2004), pp. 1–18.

Henshall, A. S., *The Chambered Tombs of Scotland*, Vol. 2 (Edinburgh, 1972).

Hepple, Leslie W., 'Sir Robert Cotton, Camden's *Britannia*, and the Early History of Roman Wall Studies', *Archaeologia Aeliana*, 5th ser. 27 (1999), pp. 1–19.

Hepple, Leslie W., 'Lord William Howard and the Naworth-Rokeby Collection of Inscribed Roman Stones', *TCᶜWAᶜAS*, 3rd ser. 2 (2002), pp. 87–101.

Hewison, J. K., *The Runic Roods of Ruthwell and Bewcastle with a Short History of the Cross and Crucifix in Scotland* (Glasgow, 1914).

Hickes, George, *Linguarum Veterum Septentrionalium Thesaurus Grammatico-Criticus et Archae-ologicus, Pars Tertia: seu Grammaticae Islandicae Rudimenta* (Oxford, 1703–1705).

Higgitt, John, 'The Stone-Cutter and the Scriptorium: Early Medieval Inscriptions in Britain and Ireland', in W. Koch, ed., *Epigraphik 1988. Factagung für mittelalterliche und neuzeitliche Epigraphik, Graz, 10–14 Mai 1988* (Vienna, 1990), pp. 149–162.

Higham, Nicholas J., *The Kingdom of Northumbria AD 350–1100* (Stroud, 1993).

Higham, Nicholas, J., *King Arthur: Myth-making and History* (London, 2002).

Hill, Peter, *Whithorn and St Ninian. The Excavation of a Monastic Town 1984–91* (Stroud, 1997).

Hoaen, A. W. and Loney, H. L., 'Bronze and Iron Age Connections: Memory and Persistence in Matterdale, Cumbria', *TCᶜWAᶜAS*, 3rd ser. 4 (2004), pp. 39–54.

Hodgson, K. S., 'Some Excavations in the Bewcastle District: I. A Bronze Age Tumulus on the Shield Knowe', *TCᶜWAᶜAS*, n.s. 40 (1940), pp. 154–162.

Hodgson, K. S., 'Some Excavations in the Bewcastle District: II. A Hut-Circle Near Woodhead', *TCᶜWAᶜAS*, n.s. 40 (1940), pp. 162–166.

Hodgson, K. S., 'Some Notes on the Prehistoric Remains of the Border District', *TCᶜWAᶜAS*, n.s. 43 (1943), pp. 167–174.

Hohler, Christopher, 'Theodore and the liturgy', in Michael Lapidge, ed., *Archbishop Theodore* (Cambridge, 1995), pp. 222–235.

Hollis, Stephanie, *Anglo-Saxon Women and the Church: Sharing a Common Fate* (Woodbridge, 1992).

Holum, Kenneth G., 'Pulcheria's Crusade, AD 421–2, and the Ideology of Imperial Victory', *Greek, Roman and Byzantine Studies* 18 (1977), pp. 153–172.

Holum, Kenneth G., *Theodosian Empresses: Women and Imperial Domination in Late Antiquity* (Berkeley, CA, 1982).

Howard, Henry, 'Observations on Bridekirk Font and on the Runic Column at Bewcastle in Cumberland', *Archaeologia* 14 (1803), pp. 113–118.

Howe, Nicholas, 'The Cultural Construction of Reading in Anglo-Saxon England', in Jonathan Boyarin, ed., *The Ethnography of Reading* (Berkeley, CA, 1993), pp. 58–79.

Howe, Nicholas, 'Rome: Capital of Anglo-Saxon England', *Journal of Medieval and Early Modern Studies* 34, No. 1 (Winter 2004), pp. 147–172.

Howlett, D. R., 'Two Panels on the Ruthwell Cross', *JWᶜCI* 37 (1974), pp. 333–336.

Howlett, David, 'Inscriptions and Design of the Ruthwell Cross', in Brendan Cassidy, ed., *The Ruthwell Cross: Papers from a Colloquium Sponsored by the Index of Christian Art, Princeton University, 8 December 1989* (Princeton, NJ, 1992), pp. 71–93.

Hume, David, *A Treatise of Human Nature* (Oxford, 1888).

Hunt, E. David, *Holy Land Pilgrimage in the Later Roman Empire AD 312–460* (Oxford, 1984).

Hunter Blair, Peter, 'The Boundary between Bernicia and Deira', *Archaeologia Aeliana*, 4th ser. 27 (1949), pp. 46–59, reprinted in *Anglo-Saxon Northumbria* (London, 1984).

Hutchinson, William, *The History of the County of Cumberland: and some places adjacent, from the earliest accounts to the present time: comprehending the local history of the county; its antiquities, the origin, genealogy, and present state of the principal families, with biographical notes; its mines, minerals, and plants, with other curiosities, either of nature or of art. Vols I and II* (Carlisle, 1794–1797, republished Wakefield, 1974).

Jackson, Kenneth H., *Language and History in Early Britain* (Edinburgh, 1953).

Jackson, Kenneth H., 'The Sources for the Life of St. Kentigern', in Nora K. Chadwick, ed., *Studies in the Early British Church* (Cambridge, 1958), pp. 273–357.

Jackson, M., 'Earliest Bewcastle', in Bewcastle Heritage Society, *A Bewcastle Miscellany* (Carlisle, 2000), pp. 15–16.

Jackson, M., 'The History of Bewcastle Castle', in Bewcastle Heritage Society, *A Bewcastle Miscellany* (Carlisle, 2000), pp. 32–35.

Jackson, M., 'Religious History of Bewcastle', in Bewcastle Heritage Society, *A Bewcastle Miscellany* (Carlisle, 2000), pp. 28–31.

James, Pamela, '*A pillar curiously engraven; with some inscription upon it': What Is the Ruthwell Cross?* Unpub. PhD Dissertation, Sydney, Centre for Celtic Studies, University of Sydney, 1999.

John, Eric, *Land Tenure in Early England* (Leicester, 1960).

Jones, A. H. M., *The Later Roman Empire (284–602)* (Oxford, 1964).

Jones, Charles W., *Bedae Pseudepigrapha: Scientific Writings Falsely Attributed to Bede* (Ithaca, NY, and Oxford, 1939).

Jones, Charles. W., 'Bede's Use of Natural Science', in Charles W. Jones, ed., *Bedae Opera De Temporibus* (Cambridge, MA, 1943), pp. 125–129.

Jones, G. B. D. and Wooliscroft, D. J., *Hadrian's Wall from the Air* (Stroud, 2001).

Karkov, Catherine E., 'The Bewcastle Cross: Some Iconographic Problems', in Catherine E. Karkov, Robert T. Farrell and Michael Ryan, eds, *The Insular Tradition* (Albany, NY, 1997), pp. 9–26.

Karkov, Catherine E., 'Naming and Renaming: The Inscription of Gender in Anglo-Saxon Stone Sculpture', in Catherine E. Karkov and Fred Orton, eds, *Theorizing Anglo-Saxon Stone Sculpture* (Morgantown, WV, 2003), pp. 31–64.

Kemble, John M., 'On Anglo-Saxon Runes', *Archaeologia* 26 (1840), pp. 327–372.

Kemble, John Mitchell, 'Additional Observations on the Runic Obelisk at Ruthwell, the Poem of the Dream of the Holy Rood, and a Runic Copper Dish found at Chertsey', *Archaeologia* 30 (1844), pp. 31–46.

Kendall, Calvin B. and Wells, Peter S., eds, *Voyage to the Other World* (Minneapolis, MN, 1992).

Keppie, Lawrence, 'Roman Inscriptions and Sculpture from Birrens. A Review', *T&JPD&GNH&AS* 69 (1994), pp. 35–51.

Kessler, Herbert, L., *Spiritual Seeing: Picturing God's Invisibility in Medieval Art* (Philadelphia, PA, 2000).

Key Fowden, Elizabeth, *The Barbarian Plain: Saint Sergius between Rome and Iran* (Berkeley, CA, 1999).

King, Anne, 'The Ruthwell Cross – A Linguistic Monument (Runes as evidence for Old English)', *Folia Linguistica Historica* VI/I (1986), pp. 43–79.

Kirby, David, P., 'Strathclyde and Cumbria: A Survey of Historical Development to 1092', *TC&WA&AS*, n.s. 62 (1962), pp. 77–94.

Kitzinger, Ernst, 'The Coffin Reliquary', in C. F. Battiscombe, ed., *The Relics of St Cuthbert* (Oxford, 1956).

Kitzinger, Ernst, *Byzantine Art in the Making: Main Lines of Stylistic Development in Mediterranean Art, 3rd–7th Century* (London, 1977).

Kitzinger, Ernst, 'Interlace and Icons: Form and Function in Early Insular Art', in Michael R. Spearman and John Higgitt, eds, *The Age of Migrating Ideas: Early Medieval Art in Northern Britain and Ireland. Proceedings of the Second International Conference on Insular Art Held in the National Museums of Scotland in Edinburgh, 3–6 January 1991* (Edinburgh and Stroud, 1993), pp. 3–15.

Kjølby-Biddle, B., 'Iron-bound Coffins and Coffin-fittings from the pre-Norman Cemetery', in Derek Phillips and Brenda Heywood, *Excavations at York Minster Volume I: From Roman Fortress to Norman Cathedral. Part 2: The Finds*, ed. M. O. H. Carver, Royal Commission on the Historical Monuments of England (London, 1995), pp. 489–521.

Koch, John T., *The Gododdin of Aneirin. Text and Context from Dark-Age North Britain* (Cardiff, 1997).

Krapp, George P., ed., *The Vercelli Book*, Anglo-Saxon Poetic Records 2 (New York, 1932).

Kuhn, Thomas S., *The Structure of Scientific Revolutions, Second Edition* (Chicago, IL, 1970).

Kulikowski, Michael, 'Barbarians in Gaul, Usurpers in Britain', *Britannia* 31 (2000), pp. 123–141.

LaCapra, Dominick, *Rethinking Intellectual History: Texts, Contexts, Language* (Ithaca, NY, 1983).

Lancaster, W. T., ed., *A General Selection of the Letters Addressed to Ralph Thoresby*, Thoresby Society, Vol. 21 (Leeds, 1921).

Lang, James, 'The Painting of Pre-Conquest Sculpture in Northumbria', in S. Cather, ed., *Early Medieval Wall Painting and Painted Sculpture in England Based on the Preocedings of a Symposium at the Courtauld Institute of Art, February 1985*, BAR 216 (Oxford, 1990), pp. 135–146.

Lang, James, *Corpus of Anglo-Saxon Stone Sculpture*, Vol. III, *York and Eastern Yorkshire* (Oxford, 1993).

Lang, James, *Corpus of Anglo-Saxon Stone Sculpture*, Vol. VI, *Northern Yorkshire* (Oxford, 2001).

Langenfelt, Gosta, *The Historic Origins of the Eight Hours Day: Studies in English Traditionalism* (Stockholm, 1954).

Lapidge, Michael, *The Cult of St Swithun, Winchester Studies 4.ii, The Anglo-Saxon Minsters of Winchester*, Winchester Excavations Committee (Oxford, 2003).

Lapidge, Michael, 'Acca of Hexham and the Origin of the Old English Martyrology', *Analecta Bollandiana* 123 (2005), pp. 29–78.

Lapidge, Michael, Blair, John, Keynes, Simon, and Don Scragg, eds, *The Blackwell Encyclopaedia of Anglo-Saxon England* (Oxford, 1999).

Laplanche, J., and Pontalis, J.-B., trans. Donald Nicolson-Smith, *The Language of Psychoanalysis* (London, 1973), pp. 78–80.

Laurie, James, 'Parish of Tinwald', *The Statistical Account of Scotland 1791–1799, Vol. IV, Dumfriesshire*, ed. John Sinclair (reprint Wakefield, 1978), pp. 485–492.

Laxness, Halldor, *Under the Glacier* (1968, reprinted New York, 2005).

Lees, Clare A., and Overing, Gillian R., *Double Agents: Women and Clerical Culture in Anglo-Saxon England* (Philadelphia, PA, 2001).

Lees, Clare A., and Gillian R. Overing, eds, *A Place to Believe in: Medieval and Modern Landscapes* (University Park, PA, 2006).

Le Goff, Jacques, 'Merchant's Time and Church's Time in the Middle Ages', in *Time, Work, and Culture in the Middle Ages*, trans. Arthur Goldhammer (Chicago, IL, 1980), pp. 29–42.

Leland, John, *De Rebus Britannicis Collectanea*, ed. altera, ed. Thomas Hearne, Vol. IV (London, 1774).

Leland, John, *The Itinerary of John Leland in or about the years 1535–1543*, ed. Lucy Toulmin Smith (London, 1910).

Lerer, Seth, *Literacy and Power in Anglo-Saxon Literature* (Lincoln, NB, 1991).

Levison, Wilhelm, 'The Inscription on the Jarrow Cross', *Archaeologia Aeliana*, 4th ser. 21 (1943), pp. 121–126.

Levison, Wilhelm, *England and the Continent in the Eighth Century* (Oxford, 1946).

Lewis, M. J. T., *Temples in Roman Britain* (Cambridge, 1965).

Lowe, Christopher E., 'New Light on the Anglian Minster at Hoddom', *T&JPD&GNH&AS*, 3rd ser. 66 (1991), pp. 11–35.

Lucy, Sam, *The Anglo-Saxon Way of Death* (Stroud, 2000).

Lysons, D. and Lysons, S., *Magna Britannia, being a concise topographical account of the several counties of Great Britain, Vol. IV, Cumberland* (London, 1816).

Lyttelton, Charles, 'An Account of a Remarkable Monument in Penrith Church Yard, Cumberland', *Archaeologia* 2 (1773), pp. 48–59.

MacDonald, George, 'The Bath-house at the Fort of Chesters (*Cilurnum*)', *Archaeologia Aelina*, 4th ser. 8 (1931), pp. 219–304.

MacDonald, J., 'Dr. Archibald's "Account of the Curiosities of Dumfries" and "Account Anent Galloway"', *T&JD&GNH&AS*, 2nd ser. 17, pt 1 (1901), pp. 50–64.

Macey, Samuel M., *The Dynamics of Progress: Time, Method, and Measure* (Athens, GA, and London, 1989).

Mac Lean, Douglas, 'The Date of the Ruthwell Cross', in Brendan Cassidy, ed., *The Ruthwell Cross: Papers from a Colloquium Sponsored by the Index of Christian Art, Princeton University, 8 December 1989* (Princeton, 1992), pp. 49–70.

Mac Lean, Doug, 'Technique and Contact: Carpentry-Constructed Insular Stone Crosses', in

Cormac Bourke, ed., *From the Isles of the North: Early Medieval Art in Ireland and Britain, Proceedings of the Third Conference on Insular Art held in the Ulster Museum, Belfast, 7–11 April 1994* (Belfast, 1995), pp. 167–168.

Maley, Gordon, 'George Smith the Geographer and His Ascent of Crossfell', *TC&WA&AS*, n.s. 48 (1949), pp. 135–144.

Marx, Karl, 'Preface' to *A Contribution to the Critique of Political Economy* (1859), in Karl Marx and Frederick Engels, *Selected Works* (London, 1968), pp. 172–176.

Marx, Karl, and Engels, Frederick, *The German Ideology Parts I and III* (1845–1846), ed. with intro. R. Pascal (London, 1938).

Mathews, Thomas F., *The Clash of Gods: A Reinterpretation of Early Christian Art* (Princeton, 1993), revised and expanded ed. (Princeton, NJ, 1999).

Maughan, John, 'The Maiden Way. Survey of the Maiden Way from Birdoswald, the Station of Amboglanna, on the Roman Wall, Northward into Scotland; with a Short Description of Some Remarkable Objects in the District. Section I – Survey of the Maiden Way through the Parish of Lanercost', *Archaeological Journal* 11 (1854), pp. 1–22.

Maughan, John, 'The Maiden Way, Section II – The Branch Way and Roman Station at Bewcastle', *Archaeological Journal* 11 (1854), pp. 124–135.

Maughan, John, 'The Maiden Way, Section III – Survey of the Maiden Way through the Parish of Bewcastle', *Archaeological Journal* 11 (1854), pp. 216–235.

Maughan, John, *A Memoir of the Roman Station and Runic Cross at Bewcastle with an Appendix on the Roman Inscription on Caeme Craig, and the Runic Inscription in Carlisle Cathedral* (London, 1857).

Maxwell-Irving, Alastair M. T., 'Hoddom Castle: A Reappraisal of Its Architecture and Place in History', *Proceedings of the Society of Antiquaries of Scotland* 117 (1987), pp. 183–217.

Mayall, R. N., and Mayall, M. L. , *Sundials: How to Know, Use, and Make Them* (Boston, MA, 1938).

McCarthy, Mike, 'Carlisle and St Cuthbert', *Durham Archaeological Journal* 14–15 (1999), pp. 59–67.

McCarthy, Mike, 'Rheged: An Early Historic Kingdom near the Solway', *Proceedings of the Society of Antiquaries of Scotland* 132 (2002), pp. 357–381.

McCarthy, Mike, *Roman Carlisle and the Lands of the Solway* (Stroud, 2002).

McCluskey, Stephen C., *Astronomies and Cultures in Early Medieval Europe* (Cambridge, 1998).

McFarlan, Helen, *James McFarlan* (Edinburgh, Privately Printed, 1892).

McIntire, W. T., 'The Fords of the Solway', *TC&WA&AS*, n.s. 39 (1939), pp. 152–170.

McKinnell, John, 'Ruthwell Cross, § 2', *Reallexikon der Germanischen Altertumskunde* 25 (Berlin, 2003), pp. 625–629.

McMillan, James, 'Parish of Torthorwald', *The Statistical Account of Scotland 1791–1799*, Vol. IV, *Dumfriesshire*, ed. John Sinclair (reprint Wakefield, 1978), pp. 497–509.

Mercer, Eric, 'The Ruthwell and Bewcastle Crosses', *Antiquity* 38 (1964), pp. 268–276.

Meyvaert, Paul, 'An Apocalypse Panel on the Ruthwell Cross', in F. Tirro, ed., *Medieval and Renaissance Studies (Proceedings of the Southeastern Institute of Medieval and Renaissance Studies), Summer 1978* (Durham, NC, 1982), pp. 3–32.

Meyvaert, Paul, 'A New Perspective on the Ruthwell Cross: *Ecclesia* and *Vita Monastica*', in Brendan Cassidy, ed., *The Ruthwell Cross: Papers from a Colloquium Sponsored by the Index of Christian Art, Princeton University, 8 December 1989* (Princeton, NJ, 1992), pp. 95–166.

Middleton, J. Henry, *The Remains of Ancient Rome*, Vol. II (London and Edinburgh, 1892).

Miller, Frank, *Annan and Its Neighbourhood: A lecture Delivered at the Annan Mechanics' Institute in 1880* (Annan, 1887).

Mills, Allan A., 'Seasonal-Hour Sundials', *Antiquarian Horology* (Winter 1990), pp. 147–170.

Mitchell, Arthur and Clark, James Toshach, eds, *Geographical Collections Relating to Scotland, Made by Walter Macfarlane*, Vol. III (Edinburgh, 1908).

Mitchell, John, 'The High Cross and Monastic Strategies in Eighth Century Northumbria', in Paul Binski and William Noel, eds, *New Offerings, Ancient Treasures: Studies in Medieval Art for George Henderson* (Stroud, 2001), pp. 88–114.

Murray, Andrew B., 'Parish of Mouswald', *The New Statistical Account of Scotland*, Vol. 4, *Dumfriesshire, Kirkcudbright, Wigton* (Edinburgh and London, 1845), pp. 442–449.

Nash, Ernest, *Pictorial Dictionary of Ancient Rome*, Vols I and II (London, 1962).

Nicolson, J., and Burn, R., *The History of the Antiquities of the Counties of Westmorland and Cumberland*, Vol. 2 (London, 1777).

Nicholson, Oliver P., 'Constantine's Vision of the Cross', *Vigiliae Christianae* 54 (2000), pp. 309–323.

Nicolson, William, 'A letter ... concerning a runic inscription at Beaucastle', *Philosophical Transactions of the Royal Society London* 15 (1685), pp. 1287–1291, in A. S. Cook, *Some Accounts of the Bewcastle Cross Between the Years 1607 and 1861*, Yale Studies in English 50 (1914), pp. 133–138.

Nicolson, William, *Letters on Various Subjects, Literary, Political, and Ecclesiastical, to and from W. Nicolson*, Vol. I, ed. J. Nichols (London, 1809).

Nicolson, William, 'Bishop Nicolson's Diaries: Part II', ed. H. Ware, *TC&WA&AS*, n.s. 2 (1902) pp. 155–230.

O'Brien O'Keeffe, Katherine, *Visible Song: Transitional Literacy in Old English Verse*, Cambridge Studies in Anglo-Saxon England 4 (Cambridge, 1990).

Ó Carragáin, Éamonn, 'Liturgical Innovations Associated with Pope Sergius and the Iconography of the Ruthwell and Bewcastle Crosses', in Robert T. Farrell, ed., *Bede and Anglo-Saxon England*, BAR 46 (Oxford, 1978), pp. 131–147.

Ó Carragáin, Éamonn, 'Crucifixion as Annunciation: The Relation of "The Dream of the Rood" to the Liturgy Reconsidered', *English Studies* 63 (1982) pp. 487–505.

Ó Carragáin, Éamonn, 'Christ over the Beasts and the Agnus Dei: Two Mulitivalent Panels of the Ruthwell and Bewcastle Crosses', in P. E. Szarmach and V. D. Oggins, eds, *Sources of Anglo-Saxon Culture* (Kalamazoo, MI, 1986), pp. 377–403.

Ó Carragáin, Éamonn, 'A Liturgical Interpretation of the Bewcastle Cross', in Myra Stoles and T. L. Burton, eds, *Medieval Literature and Antiquities: Studies in Honour of Basil Cottle* (Cambridge, 1987), pp. 15–42.

Ó Carragáin, Éamonn, 'The Ruthwell Crucifixion Poem in Its Iconographic Contexts', *Peritia* 6–7 (1987–1988), pp. 1–71.

Ó Carragáin, Éamonn, 'Seeing, Reading, Singing the Ruthwell Cross: Vernacular Poetry, Old Roman Liturgy, Implied Audience', *Medieval Europe, 1992, Prepublished Papers VII, Art and Symbolism, York, 1992*, pp. 91–96.

Ó Carragáin, Éamonn, *Ritual and the Rood: Liturgical Images and the Old English Poems of the Dream of the Rood Tradition* (London, 2005).

Okasha, Elisabeth, *Hand-List of Anglo-Saxon Non-Runic Inscriptions* (Cambridge, 1971).

Orton, Fred, 'Rethinking the Ruthwell Monument: Fragments and Critique; Tradition and History; Tongues and Sockets', *Art History* 21, No. 1 (March 1998), pp. 65–106.

Orton, Fred, 'The Bewcastle Monument, Rome, Bede, the Reckoning of Time, Sundials and the Renewal of Science', unpub. paper, *Cross and Culture in Anglo-Saxon England*, Interdisciplinary Seminar, University of Durham, August 2001.

Orton, Fred, 'Rethinking the Ruthwell and Bewcastle Monuments: Some Deprecation of Style: Some Consideration of Form and Ideology', in Catherine E. Karkov and George Hardin Brown, eds, *Anglo-Saxon Styles* (Albany, NY, 2003), pp. 31–67.

Orton, Fred, 'Rethinking the Ruthwell and Bewcastle Monuments: Some Strictures on Similarity: Some Questions of History', in Catherine E. Karkov and Fred Orton, eds, *Theorizing Anglo-Saxon Stone Sculpture* (Morgantown, WV, 2003), pp. 65–92.

Orton, Fred, 'Evidence the Terminal Feature: More or Less on the Bewcastle Monument', unpub. paper, *Theorizing the Visual*, Sources of Anglo-Saxon Art, 39th International Congress on Medieval Studies, Kalamazoo, MI, May 2004.

Orton, Fred, 'Northumbrian Identity in the Eighth Century: Style, Classification, Class and the Form of Ideology', *The Journal of Medieval and Early Modern Studies* 34, No. 1 (Winter 2004), pp. 95–145.

Orton, Peter, 'Disunity in the Vercelli Book *Soul and Body*', *Neophilologus* 63 (1979), 450–460.

Orton, Peter, 'The Old English "Soul and Body": A Further Examination', *Medium Ævum* 48 (1979), pp. 173–197.

Orton, Peter, 'The Technique of Object Personification in *The Dream of the Rood* and a Comparison with the Old English *Riddles*', *Leeds Studies in English*, n.s. 11 (1979), pp. 1–18.

Page, Ray I., 'An Early Drawing of the Ruthwell Cross', *Medieval Archaeology* 3 (1959), pp. 285–288.

Page, Ray I., 'Language and Dating in Old English Inscriptions' (1959), in *Runes and Runic Inscriptions: Collected Essays on Anglo-Saxon and Viking Runes* (Woodbridge, 1995), pp. 29–46.

Page, Ray I., 'The Bewcastle Cross' (1960), in *Runes and Runic Inscriptions: Collected Essays on Anglo-Saxon and Viking Runes* (Woodbridge, 1995), pp. 47–70.

Page, Ray I., 'The Use of Double Runes in Old English Inscriptions' (1968), in *Runes and Runic Inscriptions: Collected Essays on Anglo-Saxon and Viking Runes* (Woodbridge, 1995), pp. 95–104.

Page, Ray I., *An Introduction to English Runes* (London, 1973).

Panofsky, Erwin, 'Iconography and Iconology: An Introduction to the Study of Renaissance Art' (1939), in *Meaning in the Visual Arts* (Harmondsworth, 1970), pp. 51–81.

Parkes, Malcolm, *Pause and Effect: An Introduction to the History of Punctuation in the West* (Aldershot, 1992).

Parkes, Michael, '"Rædan, Areccan, Smeagan": How the Anglo-Saxons Read', *Anglo-Saxon England* 26 (1997), pp. 1–22.

Pennant, Thomas, *A Tour in Scotland and Voyage to the Hebrides 1772* (Chester and London, 1774).

Pennant, Thomas, *A Tour from Downing to Alston-Moor* (London, 1801).

Pfaff, Richard, ed., *The Liturgical Books of Anglo-Saxon England*, Old English Newsletter Subsidia 23 (Kalamazoo, 1995).

Phythian-Adams, Charles, *The Land of the Cumbrians: A Study in British Provincial Origins, AD 400–1200* (Aldershot, 1996).

Pococke, Richard, *Tours in Scotland 1747, 1750, 1760 by Richard Pococke, Bishop of Meath, From the Original Ms. and Drawings in the British Museum, edited with a Biographical Sketch of the Author, by Daniel William Kemp* (Edinburgh, 1887).

Postone, Moishe, *Time, Labour, and Social Determination: A Reinterpretation of Marx's Critical Theory* (Cambridge, 1993).

Pulsiano, Phillip, and Treharne, Elaine, eds, *A Companion to Anglo-Saxon Literature* (Cambridge, 2003).

Quentin, Henri, *Les martyrologes historiques du Moyen Âge* (Paris, 1908).

Radford, C. A. Ralegh, 'An Early Cross at Ruthwell', *T&JPD&GNH&AS*, 3rd ser. 28 (1949–50), pp. 158–160.

Radford, C. A. Ralegh, 'Hoddom', *T&JPD&GNH&AS*, 3rd ser. 31 (1952–1953), pp. 174–197.

Radford, C. A. Ralegh, 'Hoddom', *Antiquity* 27 (1953), pp. 153–160.

Raistrick, A., 'Report upon Earth-Samples from Bewcastle', in I. A. Richmond, K. S. Hodgson and K. St Joseph, 'The Roman Fort at Bewcastle', *TC&WA&AS*, n.s. 38 (1938), pp. 235–236.

Raistrick, A., 'Report upon Earth-Samples from Shield Knowe', in K. S. Hodgson, 'Some Excavations in the Bewcastle District: A Bronze Age Tumulus on the Shield Knowe', *TC&WA&AS*, n.s. 40 (1940), pp. 161–162.

Richmond, Ian A., 'The Tower at Gillalees Beacon, called Robin Hood's Butt', *TC&WA&AS*, n.s. 33 (1933), pp. 241–245.

Richmond, Ian A. and O. G. S. Crawford, 'The British Section of the Ravenna Cosmography', *Archaeolgia* 93 (1949), pp. 1–50.

Richmond, Ian A., Hodgson, K. S., and St Joseph, K., 'The Roman Fort at Bewcastle', *TC&WA&AS*, n.s. 38 (1938), pp. 195–237.

Ricoeur, Paul, trans. Kathleen Blamey and David Pellauer, *Time and Narrative*, Vol. 3 (Chicago, IL, 1988).

Riegl, Alois, 'The Main Characteristics of the Late Roman *Kunstwollen*' (1901), trans. Christopher S. Wood, in Christopher S. Wood, ed., *Vienna School Reader: Politics and Art Historical*

Method in the 1930s (New York, 2000), pp. 87–103.

Riegl, Alois, *Spätrömisch Kunstindustrie* (1901) (Vienna, 1927).

Rix, M., 'The Wolverhampton Cross-Shaft', *The Archaeological Journal* 117 (1960), pp. 71–81.

Rohr, R. R., *Les cadrans solaires* (Paris, Gautier-Villars, 1965), English edition as *Sundials: History, Theory, and Practice* (Toronto, 1970).

Rollason, David, *Northumbria 500–1100: Creation and Destruction of a Kingdom* (Cambridge, 2003).

Roscarrock, Nicolas, letter to William Camden, 1691, BL MS Cotton Julius C. V. fol. 77, extract, in A. S. Cook, *Some Accounts of the Bewcastle Cross Between the Years 1607 and 1861*, Yale Studies in English, 50 (New Haven, 1914), p. 131.

Rowland, Jenny, *Early Welsh Saga Poetry* (Cambridge, 1990).

Rowse, A. L., 'Nicholas Roscarrock and His Lives of the Saints', in J. H. Plumb, ed., *Studies in Social History. A Tribute to G. M. Trevelyan* (London, 1955), pp. 3–31.

Royal Commission on Historical Monuments (England), *Monuments Threatened or Destroyed. A Select List: 1956–1962* (London, 1963).

Royal Commission on the Ancient and Historical Moments of Scotland, *Eastern Dumfriesshire: An Archaeological Landscape* (Edinburgh, 1997).

Royal Commission on the Ancient Monuments of Scotland. *Roxburghshire*, Vol. I (Edinburgh, 1956).

Royal Commission on the Ancient and Historical Monuments and Constructions of Scotland, *The Royal Commission on the Ancient and Historical Monuments and Constructions of Scotland, Seventh Report with Inventory of Monuments and Constructions in the County of Dumfries* (Edinburgh, 1920).

Rushforth, G. McN., '*Magister Gregorius De Mirabilibus Urbis Romae*: A New Description of Rome in the Twelfth Century', *The Journal of Roman Studies* 9 (1919), pp. 14–58.

Said, Edward, *Beginnings: Intention and Method* (New York, 1985).

Sainsbury, I., and Welfare, H., 'The Roman Fort at Bewcastle: An Analytical Field Survey', *TCᴬWAᴬAS*, 90 (1990), pp. 139–146.

St J. H. Daniel, Christopher, *Sundials*, Shire Album, no. 176 (Princes Risborough, 1986).

Salway, Peter, *Roman Britain* (Oxford, 1981).

Savage, Anne, 'Mystical and Evangelical in *The Dream of the Rood*: The Private and the Public', in V. M. Lagorio, ed., *Mysticism: Medieval and Modern* (Salzburg, 1986), pp. 4–11.

Sawyer, Birgit, *The Viking-Age Rune-Stones. Custom and Commemoration in Early Medieval Scandinavia* (Oxford, 2000).

Sawyer, Peter, *From Roman Britain to Norman England*, 2nd ed. (London, 1998).

Saxl, Fritz, 'The Ruthwell Cross', *JWᴬCI* 6 (1943), pp. 1–19. Reprinted in Warburg Institute, *England and the Mediterranean Tradition: Studies in Art, History and Literature* (London, 1945), pp. 1–19.

Schaldach, Karlheinz, 'Vertical Dials of the 5–15th Centuries', *British Sundial Society Bulletin* (October 1996), pp. 32–38.

Schapiro, Meyer, 'The Religious Meaning of the Ruthwell Cross', *Art Bulletin* 26 (1944), pp. 232–245, reprinted in *Late Antique, Early Christian and Medieval Art. Selected Papers*, Vol. 3 (New York, 1979), pp. 150–176, 186–192.

Schapiro, Meyer, 'Style', in A. L. Kroeber, ed., *Anthropology Today. An Encyclopedic Inventory* (Chicago, IL, 1953), pp. 287–312.

Schapiro, Meyer, 'The Bowman and the Bird on the Ruthwell Cross and Other Works: The Interpretation of Secular Themes in Early Mediaeval Religious Art', *Art Bulletin* 45 (1963), pp. 351–355, reprinted in *Late Antique, Early Christian and Medieval Art. Selected Papers*, Vol. 3 (New York, 1979), pp. 177–186, 192–195.

Schlauch, Margaret, 'The Dream of the Rood as Prosopopeia', *Essays and Studies in Honor of Carleton Brown* (New York, 1940).

Scragg, D. G., 'The Compilation of the Vercelli Book', *Anglo-Saxon England* 2 (1973).

Scragg, D. G., *The Vercelli Homilies and Related Texts*, Early English Text Society, o.s. 300 (Oxford, 1990).

Scragg, D. G., and Szarmach, P. E., eds, *Editing Old English* (Woodbridge, 1994).

Sharpe, Richard, *Medieval Irish Saints' Lives: An Introduction to the Vitae Sanctorum Hiberniae* (Oxford, 1991).

Shippey, T. A., *Old English Verse* (London, 1972).

Simpson, F. G., Richmond, I. A., and St Joseph, K., 'The Turf-Wall Milecastle at High House', *TCᴨWAᴨAS*, n.s. 35 (1935), pp. 220–232.

Simpson, James, *Reform and Cultural Revolution, The Oxford English Literary History*, Vol. 2 1350–1547 (Oxford, 2002).

Simpson, James, 'The Rule of Medieval Imagination', in Jeremy Dimmick, James Simpson and Nicolette Zeeman, eds, *Images, Idolatry, and Iconoclasm in Late Medieval England* (Oxford, 2002), pp. 4–24.

Sisam, Celia, ed., *The Vercelli Book*, Early English Manuscripts in Facsimile 19 (Copenhagen, London and Baltimore, MD, 1976).

Sisam, Kenneth, 'The Authority of Old English Poetical Manuscripts', *Review of English Studies* 22 (1946); reprinted in Kenneth Sisam, ed., *Studies in the History of Old English Literature* (Oxford, 1953), pp. 29–44.

Sisam, Kenneth, 'Dialect Orgins of the Earlier Old English Verse', in Kenneth Sisam, ed., *Studies in the History of Old English Literature* (Oxford, 1953), pp. 119–139.

Smith, George, [Letter], *Gentleman's Magazine*, vol. 12 (June 1742), pp. 132, 318–319, 368–369, 529.

Smyth, Alfred P., *Warlords and Holy Men: Scotland AD 80–1000* (London, 1984).

Society of Antiquaries of London, *Vetusta Monumenta: Quae ad rerum Britannicarum memoriam conservandam Societas Antiquariorum Londini sumptu suo edenda curavit*, Vol. II. (London, 1789).

Spence, R. T., 'The Pacification of the Borders, 1593–1628', *Northern History* 13 (1977), pp. 59–160.

Spicer, Andrew, '"Defyle not Christ's kirk with your carrion": Burial and the Development of Burial Aisles in Post-Reformation Scotland', in Bruce Gordon and Peter Marshall, eds, *The Place of the Dead: Death and Rembrance in Late Medieval and Early Modern Europe*, pp. 149–169.

Spiegel, Gabrielle M., 'History, Historicism, and the Social Logic of the Text', *Speculum* 65 (1990), pp. 59–86.

Stancliffe, Clare, 'Oswald, "Most Holy and Most Victorious King of the Northumbrians"', in Clare Stancliffe and Eric Cambridge, eds, *Oswald, Northumbrian King to European Saint* (Stamford, 1995), pp. 33–83.

Stephen, W., *History of the Scottish Church*, Vol. II (Edinburgh, 1896).

Stephens, George, *The Old-Northern Runic Monuments of Scandinavia and England now first collected and deciphered by George Stephens, Esq., F.S.A.*, Vol. 1 (London, 1866–1867).

Stevens, Wesley, *Bede's Scientific Achievement*. Jarrow Lecture (Jarrow, 1985).

Stevenson, Robert K., 'Aspects of Ambiguity in Crosses and Interlace', *Ulster Journal of Archaeology* 44 & 45 (1981–1982), pp. 1–27.

Stevenson, Robert B. K., 'Further Thoughts on Some Well Known Problems', in Michael Spearman and John Higgitt, eds, *The Age of Migrating Ideas: Early Medieval Art in Northern Britain and Ireland, Proceedings of the Second International Conference on Insular Art, 1991* (Edinburgh and Stroud, 1993), pp. 16–26.

Story, Joanna, *Carolingian Connections. Anglo-Saxon England and Carolingian Francia, c.750–870* (Aldershot, 2003).

Stuart, J., *The Sculptured Stones of Scotland*, Vol. II (Aberdeen, 1867).

Swift, Graham, *Waterland* (London, William Heinemann, 1983).

Taylor, David J. A., *The Forts on Hadrian's Wall: A Comparative Analysis of the Form and Construction of Some Buildings*, BAR 305 (Oxford, 2000).

Taylor, David J. A., and Biggins, J. A., (TimeScape Research Surveys), 'Interim Statement of a Geophysical Survey of the Roman Fort and Vicus at Bewcastle, Cumbria', January 2003, unpublished.

Taylor, H. M., 'The Anglo-Saxon Church at Canterbury', *Archaeological Journal* 126 (1969), pp. 101–130.

Taylor, H. M., and Taylor, Joan, *Anglo-Saxon Architecture*, Vol. I (Cambridge, 1965).

Taylor, Joan, and Taylor, Harold M., 'Architectural Sculpture in Pre-Norman England', *The Journal of the British Archaeological Association*, 3rd ser. 29 (1966), pp. 3–51.

Taylor, Joan E., *Christians and the Holy Places: The Myth of Jewish-Christian Origins* (Oxford, 1993).

Thomas, Charles, 'Excavations at Trusty's Hill, Anworth, Kirkcudbrightshire, 1960', *T&JPD&GNH&AS*, n.s. 38 (1959–60), pp. 58–60.

Thomas, Charles, 'Ardwall Island: The Excavation of an Early Christian Site of Irish Type, 1964–5', *T&JPD&GNH&AS*, 3rd ser. 43 (1966), pp. 84–116.

Thomas, Charles, 'An Early Christian Cemetery and Chapel on Ardwall Isle, Kirkcudbright', *Medieval Archaeology* 11 (1967), pp. 127–188.

Thomas, Charles, *Christianity in Roman Britain to AD 500* (London, 1981).

Thompson, Edward A., *Romans and Barbarians. The Decline of the Western Empire* (Madison, WI, 1982).

Thompson, E. P., 'The Poverty of Theory: or an Orrery of Errors', in *The Poverty of Theory* (London, 1978), pp. 193–397.

Thomson, Thomas H., 'Parish of Dalton', *The New Statistical Account of Scotland*, Vol. 4, *Dumfriesshire, Kirkcudbright, Wigton* (Edinburgh and London, 1845), pp. 371–376.

Topping, F., 'A "New" Signal Station in Cumbria', *Britannia* 17 (1987), pp. 298–300.

Turner, A. J., 'Anglo-Saxon Sundials and the "Tidal" or "Octaval" System', *Antiquarian Horology* (September 1984), pp. 76–77.

Turner, A. J., 'Sun-Dials: History and Classification', *History of Science* 27, pt 3, no. 77 (September 1989), pp. 303–318.

Tweddle, D., Biddle, Martin, and Kjølbye-Biddle, Birthe, *Corpus of Anglo-Saxon Stone Sculpture*, Vol. IV, *South-East England* (Oxford, 1995).

Van Tongeren, Louis, *Exaltation of the Cross* (Leuven, 2000).

Wall, John, 'Anglo-Saxon Sundials in Ryedale', *Yorkshire Archaeological Journal* 69 (1997), pp. 93–117.

Wallace-Hadrill, J. Michael, *Early Germanic Kingship in England and on the Continent* (Oxford, 1971).

Wallace-Hadrill, J. Michael, *Bede's Ecclesiastical History of the English People. A Historical Commentary* (Oxford, 1988).

Ward, F. A. B., *Handbook of the Collection Illustrating Time-Measurement: Part I Historical Review* (London, 1936).

Waugh, Albert, *Sundials, Their Theory and Construction* (New York, 1973).

Webber, Teresa, 'The Diffusion of Augustine's Confessions in England During the Eleventh and Twelfth Centuries', in John Blair and Brian Golding, eds, *The Cloister and the World: Essays in Medieval History in Honour of Barbara Harvey* (Oxford, 1996), pp. 29–45.

Webster, Leslie, 'The Iconographic Programme of the Franks Casket', in Jane Hawkes and Susan Mills, eds, *Northumbria's Golden Age* (Stroud, 1999), pp. 227–246.

Werckmeister, O. K., 'The Political Ideology of the Bayeux Tapestry', *Studi Medievali*, 3rd ser. 17 (1976), pp. 353–395.

White, Roger, and Barker, Philip, *Wroxeter: Life and Death of a Roman City* (Stroud, 1998).

Wilcox, John, 'Transmission of Literature and Learning: Anglo-Saxon Scribal Culture', in Phillip Pulsiano and Elaine Treharne, eds, *A Companion to Anglo-Saxon Literature* (Oxford, 2001), pp. 50–70.

Wiley, R. A., 'Anglo-Saxon Kemble: The Life and Works of John Mitchell Kemble, Philologist, Historian, Archaeologist', *Anglo-Saxon Studies in Archaeology and History*, BAR 72 (Oxford, 1979), pp. 165–273.

Wilkinson, John, *Jerusalem Pilgrims before the Crusades* (Warminster, 1992).

Wilmart, André, 'Un témoin Anglo-Saxon du calendrier métrique d'York', *Revue Bénédictine* 46 (1934), pp. 41–69.

Wilmott, Tony, *Birdoswald. Excavations of a Roman Fort on Hadrian's Wall and Its Successor: 1987–92*, 'Appendix 1: The Maiden Way North of Birdoswald', English Heritage, Archaeological Report 14 (London, 1997).

Wilmott, Tony, 'The Late Roman Transition at Birdoswald and on Hadrian's Wall', in Tony

Wilmott and Pete Wilson, eds, *The Late Roman Transition in the North. Papers from the Roman Archaeology Conference, Durham 1999*, BAR 299 (Oxford, 2000), pp. 13–23.

Wilmott, Tony, *Birdoswald Roman Fort: 1800 Years on Hadrian's Wall* (Stroud, 2001).

Wilmott, Tony, 'A Possible Prehistoric Cist at Birdoswald, Cumbria', *TC&WA&AS*, 3rd ser. 4 (2004), pp. 29–38.

Wilson, Allan, 'Roman and Native in Dumfriesshire', *T&JPD&GNH&AS*, 3rd ser. 77 (2003), pp. 103–160.

Wishart, George, *The Memoirs of James Marquis of Montrose 1639–1650* (London and New York, 1893).

Wittgenstein, Ludwig, trans. G. E. Anscombe, *Philosophical Investigations* (Oxford, 1953).

Wood, Ian N., 'Gregory of Tours and Clovis', *Revue Belge de Philologie et d'Histoire* 63 (1985), pp. 249–272.

Wood, Ian N., 'Anglo-Saxon Otley: An Archiepiscopal Estate and Its Crosses', *Northern History* 23 (1987), pp. 20–38.

Wood, Ian N., *The Merovingian Kingdoms, 450–751* (London, 1994).

Wood, Ian N., 'Defining the Franks', in Simon Forde, Lesley Johnson and Alan Murray, eds, *Concepts of Nationality and National Identity in the Middle Ages* (Leeds, 1995), pp. 47–57.

Wood, Ian N., 'Ruthwell: Contextual Searches', in Catherine E. Karkov and Fred Orton, eds, *Theorizing Anglo-Saxon Stone Sculpture* (Morgantown, WV, 1997), pp. 104–130.

Wood, Ian N., *The Missionary Life. Saints and the Evangelisation of Europe 400–1050* (London, 2001).

Wood, Ian N., 'Genealogy Defined by Women: The Case of the Pippinids', in Leslie Brubaker and Julia M. H. Smith, eds, *Gender in the Early Medieval World: East and West, 300–900* (Cambridge, 2004), pp. 234–256.

Wood, Ian N., 'Land Tenure and Military Obligations in the Anglo-Saxon and Merovingian Kingdoms: The Evidence of Bede and Boniface in Context', *Bulletin of International Medieval Research* 9–10 for 2003–2004 (2005), pp. 3–22.

Wood, Ian N., 'York and the Anglo-Saxon Missions to the Continent' (forthcoming).

Wood, Ian N., 'Constantinian Crosses in Northumbria', in Catherine E. Karkov, Sarah Larratt Keefer and Karen Louise Jolly, eds, *The Place of the Cross in Anglo-Saxon England* (Woodbridge, 2006), pp. 3–13.

Wood, Ian N., 'Bede's Jarrow', in Clare A. Lees and Gilliam R. Overing, eds, *A Place to Believe In: Locating Medieval Landscapes* (University Park, PA, 2006), pp. 67–84.

Wood, Ian N. 'The Crocus Conundrum', in Elizabeth Hartley, Jane Hawkes, Martin Henig, Frances Mee, eds, *Constantine the Great: York's Roman Emperor* (Aldershot, 2006), pp. 77–82.

Woolf, Rosemary, 'The Ideal of Men Dying with Their Lord in *Germania* and *The Battle of Maldon*', *Anglo-Saxon England* 5 (1976), pp. 68–81.

Worm, Ole, *Danicorum monumentorum libri sex: e spissis antiquitatum tenebris et in Dania ac Norvegia extantibus ruderibus eruti* (Hafinae, 1643).

Wormald, C. Patrick, 'The Age of Offa and Alcuin', in James Campbell, ed., *The Anglo-Saxons* (Oxford, 1982), pp. 101–128.

Wormald, C. Patrick, 'Bede and Benedict Biscop', in Gerald Bonner, ed., *Famulus Christi* (London, 1976), pp. 141–169.

Wormald, Patrick, 'Bede, "Beowulf" and the Conversion of the Anglo-Saxon Aristocracy', in R. T. Farrell, ed., *Bede and Anglo-Saxon England. Papers in Honour of the 1300th Anniversary of the Birth of Bede, Given at Cornell University in 1973 and 1974*, BAR 46 (Oxford, 1978), pp. 32–90.

Wormald, C. Patrick, 'In Search of Offa's "Law-Code"', in Ian Wood and Niels Lund, eds, *People and Places in Northern Europe 500–1600* (Woodbridge, 1991), pp. 25–45.

Wright, Hannah Mary, *The Ruthwell Cross and Other Remains of the Late Hannah Mary Wright* (Edinburgh, 1873).

Zienkiewicz, J. David, *The Legionary Fortress Baths at Caerleon, I. The Buildings*, National Museum of Wales and Cadw (Stroud, 1986).

Zumthor, Paul, *Essai de poétique médiévale* (Paris, 1972).

Index

✠